Finishing Touches

A Guide to Being Poised, Polished, and Beautifully Prepared for Life

Anne Oliver

BANTAM BOOKS

New York • Toronto • London • Sydney • Auckland

FINISHING TOUCHES
A Bantam Book / June 1990

All rights reserved.
Copyright © 1990 by Anne Oliver.

Library of Congress Cataloging-in-Publication Data

Oliver, Anne.
Finishing touches : a guide to being poised, polished, and
beautifully prepared for life / Anne Oliver.
p.   cm.
ISBN 0-553-05279-9
1. Etiquette.   2. Beauty, Personal.   I. Title.
BJ1853.045   1990
646.7'0024042—dc20   89-18629
CIP

Published simultaneously in the United States and Canada

Bantam Books are published by Bantam Books, a division of
Bantam Doubleday Dell Publishing Group, Inc. Its trademark,
consisting of the words "Bantam Books" and the portrayal of a
rooster, is Registered in U.S. Patent and Trademark Office and in
other countries. Marca Registrada. Bantam Books, 666 Fifth Avenue, New York, New York 10103.

PRINTED IN THE UNITED STATES OF AMERICA

DH   0 9 8 7 6 5 4 3 2

To Perry,
my dear husband,
who is a perfect example
of the kind of supportive life partner
today's woman needs as she seeks to fulfill and enjoy
life's traditional and contemporary roles.

Acknowledgments

There are many persons to whom I shall be forever grateful for contributing *their* special touch to *Finishing Touches*. I particularly want to express my heartfelt appreciation to:

- Margaret Reynolds, my very special friend and mentor, who lent polish, grace, and literary voice to the book
- Maria Mack, my editor at Bantam, who attended my manuscript in a caring manner, and Barbara Alpert, our senior editor, for holding our hands along the way
- Corky Scarborough, my longtime friend, for his creative illustrations
- Jane Merrill for her élan and help in the budding stages
- Nancy Clark for her editorial assistance in smoothing the edges
- George Raymond of Cartier and my ingénues, who supplied the grand occasion invitations and announcements
- John Hansen of Crane & Co. for his assistance with the social paper illustrations
- Mother for telling me, "Pretty is as pretty does," and my father for his loving encouragement
- Staton and Jordan, my dear sons, for their many hugs as they passed my desk
- Diane Letheren, my patient secretary, for typing and retyping a thousand-and-one pages
- Each young woman who has attended L'Ecole des Ingénues in search of the finishing touches, as it is her quest for this knowledge that has inspired me throughout my writing
- Harvey Klinger, my energetic literary agent, for his frequent, enthusiastic calls and ever-present question "Have you finished yet?," to which I always replied, "Being 'finished' is just the beginning."

Contents

Starting to Be Finished

For young women today, much thinking and dreaming is centered upon growing up and claiming the independence and glamour of adulthood. Optimism is a normal, healthy, and attractive quality of youth, and it is exciting for you to know that your highest hopes and dreams can be realized. There are almost no restrictions on your prospects for doing and becoming what you want.

But you must prepare yourself to take advantage of the wonderful opportunities available, opportunities far beyond the life of domesticity and circumscribed social activity that the woman of only a generation or two ago could expect. Fortunately, today's society generally allows a generous maturation period during which a young woman may develop mentally, physically, culturally, and socially without the pressure of making her own way. And the span between the ages of twelve and twenty-five is the time in which you move through the school years to independent adult living and begin to establish your life.

As a young woman today, you have been born into a new era and you will want to take advantage of all it has in store. To ease your passage you can acquire an education and a knowledge of the arts and can travel and experience social interchange, so that you are an interesting conversationalist and an eager listener. You can also cultivate simple graciousness and consideration for others.

In addition to acquiring such knowledge and skills, you should also be using this precious time to become comfortable with the social amenities, so

2

that you will be at ease no matter where you find yourself, and should learn to dress with individuality and good taste, and to care for your body so that its vigor and beauty will endure.

I stress to you, however, these wonderful attributes will be at least partially wasted unless you can learn to get along comfortably with a diversity of people and to cope with a wide range of situations. The most intelligent, competent, talented, or beautiful women can fail to reach goals unless they are at ease with themselves and are able to make those around them comfortable also. Promising careers, social acceptance, marriages, relationships, and even parenthood can become casualties of an individual's inability to establish rapport with others.

A step in acquiring that essential rapport is to replace the self-absorption of childhood with a genuine concern for others. While this concern must come from the heart, it is more easily communicated by one who possesses the correct social tools. There is no place for rudeness, crudity, even for indifference or ignorance, in relationships between human beings. Reading this book is an indication that correct manners and proper actions are already important to you. You may have been motivated by finding yourself in situations in which you felt inadequate, or by observing behavior that you recognized as improper in others. Perhaps a party at which guests were boisterous or destructive disturbed you; or you visited the home of a friend where family members were rude and the quarreling made you uncomfortable. Whatever the cause, you have realized that the actions of the people you are with determine whether or not an occasion is enjoyable.

While elements of etiquette change with the times, the fundamental code is timeless, based as it is on kindness and consideration for others. The major difference in our era is that etiquette is no longer a code reserved for the privileged, but is a standard for society as a whole. It is just as important for the young woman at the supermarket check-out, or the teenaged babysitter, to know and observe correct social usage, as it is for the rising young executive or the debutante.

Just remember that you are a role model yourself, and you have many opportunities to raise the level of your social interactions. Consider the chances a teacher of young children has to develop good manners in coming generations by example and instruction. I often recall with pleasure the admonition of my first-grade teacher: "Like little ships go out to sea, I dip my soup away from me." That jingle certainly saved me discomfort in my growing-up years—and probably saved many a tablecloth, too.

The "Finishing Touches"

This book is intended to add the "Finishing Touches" to your education and to prepare you for your debut into a widening world. It will present you not only with the rules of etiquette, per se, but a discipline by which to live. It will enhance your social graces and, in addition, endow you with the knowledge necessary for experiencing the art of living at its best. It will guide you and make your coming-of-age the beautiful, pleasant, and meaningful experience it is meant to be.

The instructive material for *Finishing Touches* is based on the curriculum and philosophy of L'Ecole des Ingénues, the "finishing school" I began in 1976. I modeled L'Ecole des Ingénues along the designs of the Old World finishing school concept, refashioning it to meet the needs of the contemporary world and to be meaningful to the young woman of today. Throughout the year, our school presents a potpourri of international, in-residence finishing school programs: *Le Petit Programme,* our "well-mannered weekends" held throughout the academic year; *Le Grand Programme,* our famous finishing school summer camp; and during spring holidays, *La Pièce de Résistance,* when we are abroad on a socially sophisticated finishing tour.

The purpose of L'Ecole des Ingénues, as is the purpose of this book, is fivefold—I liken it to the five points of a star: personal beauty, visual poise, the social graces, aesthetic awareness, and a personal synthesis. Just as I challenge each girl who attends my school, so will I invite you, my reader, toward incorporating my "star" philosophy into your decisive decade.

I came to create L'Ecole des Ingénues from the world of fashion, where I was first a model and later director of fashion, protocol, and public relations at Atlanta's Saks Fifth Avenue. In both my private life and my professional life, I became utterly convinced of the importance of etiquette. Knowing what to do and how to do it in all situations frees a young woman from self-consciousness and enables her to concentrate on her studies, her work, and, most important, her relationships with other people.

Remember, also, that etiquette has its visual requirements and that your appearance is an important part of how you present yourself to others. In addition to fastidiousness and the correct choice of apparel for an occasion, a woman has the responsibility to make the most of her face and figure and to minimize flaws. The effort to look as lovely as possible is not only rewarding to yourself, but is also a subtle compliment to family members, friends, even strangers, and is, therefore, etiquette in its finest sense.

4

Visual impact is not restricted to your person but extends to your surroundings. Well-bred people do not tolerate uncleanliness or disorder in their environments; instead they expend much time and energy to bring beauty and charm into their lives.

In this book, I provide an easily assimilated program for the development not only of pleasant, correct behavior and attractive self-presentation, but also of the gracious inner philosophy that is a maturing woman's wellspring. The material is organized for enjoyable study and easy reference, and will become a valuable asset to the young woman who wishes to attain her full potential. It will make good manners—the most becoming garment she can wear—understandable and instinctive, and thereby help her to avoid the insecurity and embarrassment that ignorance can cause.

Etiquette

Rules of conduct in relationships were of necessity developed and refined through the ages. Each generation has sought to transmit these niceties of life to its successors and to inspire the young to even higher levels of culture and taste. Gradually the body of etiquette that is the standard for civilized people has come into being. As you wend your way through the decade that connects childhood to maturity, etiquette can serve as a road map, a set of directions to keep you from making the wrong turns, from choosing a dead end, socially or career-wise.

If the term etiquette seems stilted or has phony connotations, consider that etiquette is merely a name for a pattern of behavior that is based on consideration for others, appropriateness, and good taste, and which, once learned, helps you to do the right thing in almost any circumstance. The increasing appreciation of courtesy and proper personal conduct, especially among young people, is one of the most encouraging trends of our time.

Technically, the word *étiquette* comes from Old French, and means "ticket" or "label." The word etiquette originally meant the ticket of entrance to France's court ceremonies—upon this ticket were written the rules of court behavior. A similar "ticket" also listed the regulations to be followed within the walls of a feudal castle and was commonly found attached to a post inside the courtyard. Therefore, those invited into the castle were not at a loss as to how they should behave; all were put at ease, and business or social gatherings or ceremonies ran smoothly.

Consider your knowledge of etiquette as your "ticket" of admission into the conventions of a polite and caring society. Consider it a special pass that will enable you to relate to others with thoughtfulness and polished manners.

Some people, adults and teenagers alike, are uncomfortable with the "idea" of etiquette. Perhaps they remember the discomfort of being five years old, all dressed up for a party and constantly reminded by their mothers to "mind your manners." My husband, Perry, once attended a beautiful Sunday picnic in the garden of an Emory University professor. He was seated on the lawn with a group of faculty wives, one of whom inquired after me. "She could not be here today," he replied. "She is out West in the mountains with her finishing school." Almost in unison the women in the group straightened their bodies, and one of them quickly said, "Oh! I haven't a knife and fork for my chicken!" She then excused herself and went in search of utensils. She had been frightened by the concept of "finishing school" and, by extension, of etiquette, and she went overboard, requesting a knife and fork for fried chicken, which is quite properly eaten with one's fingers at a picnic.

If you have been "turned off" by the word *étiquette* or have felt that conventional manners were too rigid, let me assure you that the social forms and graces have been developed to make you, and everyone else, comfortable.

Being "Finished"

Finishing Touches is not about an extravagant finale or a *fait accompli*. It is, instead, the celebration of an ongoing process through which a woman can reach her highest potential. "Finish" in this connotation implies perfection, beauty, rightness in a human being (particularly in a young woman), which produce a glow akin to that emanating from expertly crafted furniture, elegant silver flatware, fine jewelry—a gloss so genuine that it only deepens with time and care.

Finishing Touches is not an end but an important and enjoyable segment of a journey. For some of you, it will be an awakening, a setting of goals and the satisfaction of achieving some basic ones. For older and more sophisticated ingénues, it will be a more structured experience for enhancing the level of polish and assurance to which you are already dedicated. And to the complete woman each reader can shortly become, it will be a lifelong resource of correct contemporary behavior and etiquette.

You will surely understand that your age, your present circumstances, and your experience will dictate that many of the formalities are not possible or

6

even appropriate for you at the moment. Remember, however, that your age, certainly, your situation, probably, and your experience, hopefully, will change. Large numbers of you will eventually find yourselves in high places with much expected of you, and it is well that you are, from an early age, at least aware of the highest standards while being completely comfortable in following the modifications which are acceptable in your present position.

Keep *Finishing Touches* on your bedside table. Read sections that interest you regularly and, especially, learn to turn to it for answers and support when faced with the more unfamiliar situations and settings life will constantly present.

Being "finished," you see, is actually just the beginning!

PART ONE

A Touch of Beauty

CHAPTER I

Inner and Outer Beauty

You have now reached the point in your life when, at last, you begin to take command. Until now, most of the guidelines have been drawn by others. Now, any changes for bettering yourself must be instigated by *you*. As an archer may shoot an arrow, your parents have "shot" you. They aimed you in the direction they considered most suitable for your growth. But although your parents may shoot the arrow, they cannot direct its course.

Let us play with that simile for a moment. Accept the fact that your parents, teachers, and all other role models in your life, have "shot" you—the "arrow." But also remember that you are no lifeless missile, helpless against the strength of the release or the currents through which you pass. You have within yourself the capacity to direct your own course—even through storms—and to choose your own destination. You will, of course, continue to receive and to seek advice and suggestions from many sources. However, it will be your right to accept or reject. Soon you will become more the archer than the arrow. In the end it will be *you* who sets the mark as to where you will fly.

One of your first marks, no doubt, is to be accepted by others. As you embark on a program to make yourself welcome wherever you may be, first consider your personal presentation—what others see before they have had the opportunity to know you as a person.

Your body is a wondrous creation, but it can be weakened by neglect or abuse. On the other hand, the glow of good health, good grooming, and a flattering use of cosmetics and clothing can insure that you fulfill your potential and make a positive impression on everyone you meet.

Taking Center Stage

Almost all of us have the secret desire to be "on stage"—to be a star. Fame is achieved by very few, but each of us is "on stage" in the social world we inhabit. Every time you communicate with someone, either face-to-face, via the telephone, or by letter, you are the center of attention as far as that person is concerned. By "on stage" I do not mean you should assume a false role. I mean that you should project to the world the best *you* have to offer.

Everyone is born with God-given looks and basic talents. In some aspects we are strong, in others weak. Some parts of yourself you can improve substantially, others you can do little about. You should not be concerned about the things that you cannot change—your height or the size of your feet, for example. Instead, you should concentrate on areas that you *can* change.

Defining Beauty

What is beauty? It is an innate quality, a way of being, a manner of acting. It is also a way of looking. When we think of beauty, we primarily think of physical beauty, knowing full well that sooner or later the personality and inner self must supersede the outer beauty of the face and figure. However, to achieve balanced beauty the inner and the outer must blend together and be joined by an ability to love and to be loved, by an awareness and curiosity about life, by intelligence, happiness, social grace, and by self-expression through all bodily movements—beauties are made, not born.

Beauty is also very much a state of mind. Beauty is a quality that should grow with each passing day and be developed to last a lifetime. A baby is beautiful in a way different from that in which an eighty-year-old woman is beautiful. Beauty must be nurtured in order to grow and be retained. A favorite quote of mine says it perfectly: "A beautiful girl is an accident of nature. A beautiful older woman is a work of art."

Beauty is enhanced by absorbing the beauty that surrounds you in your daily life. Your personal beauty will be enhanced as your awareness of beauty grows. As an exercise to help awaken your awareness of beauty, first open your eyes to the beauty of the elements of nature surrounding you—the stars, the moon, white clouds, blue skies, mountains, trees, flowers, and streams. This awareness can further be enhanced by strolling among the paintings in a museum, looking at the architecture as you walk in a city, observing the colors reflected in a prism, touching the fabrics of a couturier gown, listening to the melody of classical music, running your fingers along the stem of a crystal goblet, or even by admiring the sleekness of a new sports car!

An awareness of external beauty helps you establish your own standards for beauty and develop a philosophy by which you will wish to live. Throughout the pages to follow, I will introduce you to many aspects of beauty and instruct you in the art of becoming beautiful both inwardly and outwardly.

Facts and Facets

You surely have learned to distinguish qualities that characterize the girls you know. One of your friends may have great physical beauty, the kind that makes all the boys take notice. Another has a terrific personality—she is always bubbly and fun to be with. A third may not be so pretty or so contagiously happy, but is she smart!

No one is just physical appearance, personality, or intelligence alone. You are a combination of every facet. Think of yourself as a diamond, which must be cut with many facets in order to sparkle properly. Each facet should be proportioned in such a way that your complete beauty shines forth.

Inner Beauty

"To think beautiful is to be beautiful." Everything begins with your perception.

"I am beautiful." This is a statement you should feel comfortable making—if only to yourself.

Ready? With your eyes shut, think the words, "I am beautiful." With your eyes open, write, "I am beautiful." With a sincere smile, in the privacy of your room, say, "I am beautiful."

The seeds of beauty—an attitude by which to live and an image to project—are the most valuable seeds of thought you can plant and cultivate in your secret mental garden. Just now, by thinking, writing, and saying, "I am beautiful," you sowed the seeds.

Everything begins with thought. Thoughts rise from the level of the subconscious to the conscious and it is there that they become actions. At thirteen, I thought only about becoming a model. I planted that thought deep in my mind. Three years later, I walked down my first runway. By the age of eighteen, I had modeled in countless runway and television fashion presentations and appeared in many fashion photographs. A few years later, I appeared in advertisements in *Vogue* and *Harper's Bazaar* and national television commercials. The runway, accompanied by my college degree, led me to the doors of Saks Fifth Avenue and to the office of fashion, public relations, and protocol director. I became a successful model not because of natural glamour—though I had the luck to be lanky and tall in the mode of the times—but because I had focused on the object of my dream. Without fully realizing the power behind it, I first thought and said, "I am beautiful," and then worked toward developing my natural assets to become beautiful, both outwardly and inwardly. This is what I am asking you to do—not for a fashion runway, but for the runway of your life.

After sowing the seeds of beauty, cultivation must begin. Cultivation is comprised of the responsibility and the commitment on your part to make beauty become a reality in your life. This takes time and work. However, you will begin to feel beautiful as soon as you begin to work on your physical, emotional, mental, and aesthetic being.

Cultivating the thought "I am beautiful" requires self-analysis, goal-setting, commitment, discipline, and perseverance. You must learn to recognize your strengths and weaknesses, your good and bad qualities, and then decide what can be done about each of them—which will you play up and which will you play down, or ignore?

Liking Yourself

An essential to beauty is to like yourself, even to love yourself. Respect and love for your unique self and an understanding of your nature go hand in hand with respect, love, and understanding of others. Only when you begin to like yourself will you become a vital, interested, and interesting person. And only when you feel good about yourself and accept yourself will you begin to like yourself. The object is to develop a friendly relationship with yourself. If you would not want yourself as a friend, ask why. Your answer will reveal the small or large changes you need to make to become a person you can sincerely admire.

Making those changes is well worth the effort. The rewards of liking yourself are outward poise and inward confidence. And once you have discovered and developed self-confidence, you will have unearthed the single most important attribute of a great beauty. Confidence is magic! It brightens your eyes, straightens your posture, brings a smile to your lips, enables you to forget yourself, and draws others to you. It inspires the spark and the glow of genuine inner beauty, the luster of a finished person.

Beautiful Thoughts

If you think beautiful thoughts, you will automatically act in a beautiful manner. My mother told me again and again when I was a young girl, "Pretty is as pretty does." I found that following her motto never failed me, nor will it fail you. Everything you do should be something that helps, not hurts, another. All of us harbor some ugly, destructive attitudes and thoughts. We may think that because they are deep inside and we rarely, if ever, give voice to them, others do not know they exist. Yet negative thoughts, allowed to remain, will gradually affect our personalities and even become apparent—in unpleasant behavior and facial expressions, cutting remarks, and negative reactions.

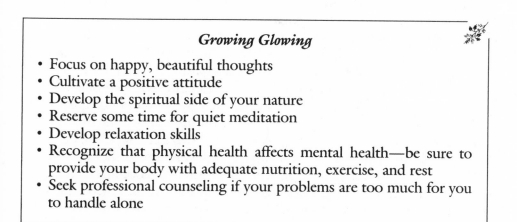

Growing Glowing

- Focus on happy, beautiful thoughts
- Cultivate a positive attitude
- Develop the spiritual side of your nature
- Reserve some time for quiet meditation
- Develop relaxation skills
- Recognize that physical health affects mental health—be sure to provide your body with adequate nutrition, exercise, and rest
- Seek professional counseling if your problems are too much for you to handle alone

I have discovered that I can control myself, my thoughts, attitudes, and emotions, much more easily than I can control other people or circumstances. I also know that what I believe is what tends to happen. My belief in positive things about myself and other people gives me an inner feeling of peace and a loving attitude. Inner beauty is calm, serene, optimistic, poised,

14

and self-confident, and once you have developed it, it will be reflected in your posture, your face, and your voice.

Failure to take care of your inner needs, to develop during youth the character and ideals with which you can live, can adversely affect your entire life. Eventually, any neglect of the inner person will begin to reflect negatively in the outer person.

No one knows as well as you the ugly, selfish, or overly competitive feelings that make you unhappy. To help you clear away those strangling thoughts, study Growing Glowing, which is guaranteed to help bring good things to your life.

Be Still and Know

Stress affects not only the actual functioning of body systems but also the more subtle process of aging. It is difficult for a worried, anxious person to look beautiful or to be efficient, no matter how well she may have developed her potential. We now know we can control the effects of stress through relaxation exercises—mental and physical—which help unwind the tension. A regular period of time spent alone and in quiet, or even a more formal time for meditation, can sustain health—and reduce wrinkles. Take the time to stop and be still, to relax, and grow beautiful within.

Although I realize that you are often frustrated at not being able to find time for all the things you want to do, it is important that you continually monitor your activities, relationships, and goals, and check them against your ideals and ethics. To do this in a meaningful way requires regular private times in a peaceful atmosphere. Even a small amount of quiet time will bring you self-knowledge and an inner beauty that will be reflected in your outward appearance. To help you cultivate this inner self, I suggest you follow my Four "R's"—an exercise I have used since my girlhood.

During these exercises your body and active mind will become completely relaxed, but your intuitive mind will be completely awake, alert, and in a state of readiness to communicate ideas, impressions, and intuitions. The more often your intuitive mind is in control, the more often positive, creative, and loving thoughts will flood your being—eliminating negative ones and thus increasing your patience, love, understanding, confidence, and inner serenity.

Faithful practice of the Four "R's", over time, will put you in touch with *la voix intérieure*—making you as beautiful and "finished" on the inside as you are on the outside.

The Four "R's"

Step I: Relaxation

Find a position in which you can be relaxed and alert at the same time. Close your eyes. Take three deep breaths and let them out slowly, breathing out all tightness and worry, breathing in peace and well-being. Take a few moments to experience your physical sensations, your feelings, and your thoughts.

As you move your attention to the thoughts entering your mind, do not dwell on any one. Look at the thought as if you were an uninterested spectator and then dismiss it. When the next thought enters, treat it in the same way. Continue to do this until you feel that you have gained some control at being able to push thoughts away. Imagine them carried off on the wings of a butterfly.

Step II: Receptivity

Now that your active mind is becoming still, you can contact your inner voice, that place within you that can suggest answers to your questions with honesty and wisdom. It may be found in many ways and in many different forms. Usually it speaks in images or impressions rather than in the language of normal speech. Because the image or impression may be fleeting, it is wise to note the answer as soon as you receive it, either by making a brief sketch or by jotting down a word or phrase that will later call it to mind.

As you speak to your inner voice, await receptively and patiently the response that will arise from the place of knowing within you. As you wait, visualize a rosebud slowly opening and developing into a full blossom, flowering in your mind. (It is this rose, from bud to blossom, around which I designed the crest for L'Ecole des Ingénues.) Trust whatever response comes and then let the image subside as you prepare to ask other questions. Questions can be answered generally, or applied specifically to a relation-ship, life decision, or any other challenging situation.

Step III: Reflection

During some relaxation periods, you will not have any questions. In these cases serenity and inspiration will be your goals. Follow steps one and two

16

for relaxation and insight and then focus on something of beauty. If nothing at hand satisfies, study a candle in your mind's eye. Imagine the changing size and color of the flame. Gradually, wonderful, loving, and serene thoughts will come to you—such an experience is an inner beauty treatment that will not long remain hidden inside.

Step IV: Responsibility

As you continue to increase your intuitive ability by practicing Relaxation, Receptivity, and Reflection, you will develop inner qualities that will help you achieve goals that, in the past, may have been difficult, or impossible, to attain. However, once the path to that goal opens up for you, it is your responsibility to commit yourself to following that path.

As the first step in this process, make a commitment to do something specific—something you know you can do—and commit yourself to it for a limited amount of time.

Once you have made the commitment, record it and pin it up as a reminder. Begin the statement with "I choose to" and then complete it with your commitment. You may wish to include a sketch of one of the images you have received on your "reminder card," to inspire you and strengthen your resolve as you accept the responsibility of fulfilling it.

As you practice your commitment, notice the effect it has on your life. When the time limit you have set is over, repeat the process again, using another commitment—perhaps an even larger one. In this way, you will always be actively accepting responsibility for your own growth.

Your Special Sparkle

Now that I have urged you to form the habit of "looking into yourself" regularly and have offered techniques for doing so, I must caution you that self-knowledge is not an end in itself, but rather a means to communicating with others. Knowing what you want and think and feel will give you a greater understanding of and compassion for others.

Nurturing beautiful thoughts and listening to your inner voice will bring great results if practiced regularly. Although you will probably be the last person to appreciate your inner change, those around you will know the progress you are making by your outward serenity, self-control, kindness, and helpfulness.

Outer Beauty

There are many ways to enhance outer beauty. Outer beauty is highlighted not only by personal attractiveness, but by outer behavior, poise, and education. Your speech, diction, grammar, and sensitivity in communication reflect your true nature. It is your total image that determines just how beautiful you really are. First you must survey your present habits of nutrition and exercise, and use of makeup and clothing. From there, you must embark upon a program of personal enhancement and development that brings out the positives and plays down the negatives.

Establishing the proper attitude has brought you to the exciting point when you are ready to cut an important facet of your diamond—the first impression. Although it is common knowledge that looks can deceive, there is no escaping the fact that physical appearance is the major criterion in making a first impression, and first impressions are of the utmost importance.

I counsel you not to minimize the importance of first impressions. Often they establish the quality of relationships. When you know you have made a good impression you tend to live up to it. While it is not impossible to supplant a poor impression, it is usually quite difficult to do so—like climbing a mountain, it is an uphill battle.

When preparing for a first impression, work to improve everything possible—even the most minute detail. What may appear insignificant when considered alone can combine with other imperfections to project carelessness. To each new person you encounter, the way you look and behave is a sample of your total self. Since you are at a time in your life when broadening your acquaintances is both fun and important, you must learn to use the tools needed to gain acceptance.

In presenting yourself to others, think in terms of your "packaging." You want the person you meet to think, "I want to know this girl better." Remember that it is natural in our society to rate those who come in pretty and proper packages more positively, to perceive them as more talented, more intelligent, more adept at the social skills.

Others meet the outer you before they are able to know the inner you. They respond to the "picture" you make and to the springy and energetic, or blah and uncommunicative, way you are feeling even before you exchange hellos. Therefore, it is necessary that you work to perfect your outer "packaging." This consists of your physical beauty and general personal appearance, which is enhanced through your clothing, accessories, makeup, and hairstyle, as well as the shape and condition of your body.

Personal packaging sends out messages to others. Does your self-presentation say that you have done your homework? Or does it camouflage the real you? Is your personal packaging a true picture of your inner beauty combined with your outer beauty? That is the goal.

Picture yourself as an exquisitely and brightly wrapped gift whose contents are unknown. Later, you will unveil the contents: the way you move—your visual poise; the manner in which you behave and speak—your social grace; the eclectic knowledge that you possess—your aesthetic awareness. To get beyond the first impressions made on others, you must package yourself attractively but never forget that there must be something of value inside the package.

Why cannot outsiders just take you as you are? Is not working on appearances false and pretentious? I believe you and I should, out of respect for ourselves and others, present the most attractive package possible. We know that we have something to offer that is very special beyond the outer wrappings, but the "gift wrap" shows that we are proud of ourselves. And it pleases others. It is, in fact, a compliment to them.

As you undertake the challenge to make the most of your outer image, consider it an adventure that is both joyous and rewarding. At the same time, quietly and with equal diligence, work to make the inner you nicer, happier, more considerate of others. In a short time your inner light will add sparkle to this facet of your diamond.

Facing Your World

Perhaps because it is the threshold for contact between the inner, private you and others, your face is the most conspicuous part of your physical being. "The eyes," wrote one poet, "are the windows of the soul," and facial expressions reveal thoughts and moods. Since your face is, essentially, your letter of introduction, it is the proper starting point for the beautiful you. The first step is to examine it face-to-face in the mirror.

Before you take your first peek, rid your mind of all idealized images of beauty placed before you by magazines, television, movies, and advertisers—movie stars, television personalities, rock singers, models, even classmates you think are especially pretty. Put aside all preconceptions. Just as important, discount everything you have ever been told about your own looks, good or bad. Jot all these thoughts on a mental blackboard and immediately erase the slate clean, or imagine yourself recording them on a mental tape and then press *erase*.

Now to get started! With mirror in hand, examine your reflection thoughtfully, as if you were looking at another person for the first time. Consider the face—first its general structure and features and then its expression—and try to imagine how you would react should you, astonishingly, meet up with your double.

Should your honest reaction lack enthusiasm, try a smile. Often a countenance that has little claim to beauty becomes dazzling when lit by a genuine, feature-rearranging smile. For other faces, the cultivation of eye-to-eye contact or a slight turn of the head to present a nice profile can do wonders. With practice, such refinements of expression and position become a natural and effective means of making the most of your looks. Even a brief smile, the evidence of genuine interest, or the ability to compose yourself and achieve an inner serenity can become instant beauty treatments.

Having assessed your own first-impression impact and experimented with facial expressions and head positions, concentrate on your individual features. While the total composite is probably quite pleasing, it is important to learn at a young age which components are the most striking and which are less attractive—not to alter any of them, but because there are ways to play up your best features and direct attention away from less appealing ones. The goal is to make your face as a whole as lovely and interesting as it can be.

And this is a goal that is possible for every girl. Surely you basically like what you see in the mirror. It is you. Every face, like every leaf and every snowflake, is different, individual, lovely. Accept the structural facts of your face—and your body—with the conviction that they are right for you. If you have wished that your pixie face could be exchanged for a glamorous visage, think again. Your face is right for your body and your personality. Your challenge is to make the most of what you have been given.

When I analyze my students during personal consultations, I find that the ratio of good points to bad is usually about ten-to-one, and I am certain you will come up with a similar appraisal of your face if you approach it with an open mind. To do a self-analysis, get a rather large sketch pad, 8 by 10 inches or 9 by 12 inches, and a charcoal pencil. Look into the mirror and sketch a picture of your face, features, hair, and neck. No great artistry is required. Sketch quickly. Pretend you are drawing a cartoon. (A caricature identifies outstanding features for better or for worse!)

Now, as you sketch your face, it will capture not only your prominent features, but also your personality, mood, and mental state. The quick sketch will appear happy if you feel happy, sad if you feel sad, perky if your mood is perky, droopy if you are down, and so on. It will even reflect whether or not you like yourself! Should you encounter an opportunity to have a friend or an artist sketch your caricature, take advantage of it as it will be revealing as well as fun.

Look at your sketch and think about the parts of your face that make it special. Now, on a separate page of your sketch pad, write the title "Star Qualities," and under that heading make two columns: star billing and second billing.

Enter notes about your face and hair in the columns you feel each deserves. For star billing, perhaps you have a fine straight nose that wins you many compliments, or big, deep-brown eyes that your blue-eyed friend says she envies, or high cheekbones, or even flat ears. Flat ears rate star billing? Yes! I have known models who were limited in hairstyles because of prominent ears.

Next, second billing is something you can correct quickly and enjoy immediate success. For example, eyes too close set. If you have this problem, you can simply begin your eye shadow color over the inner center of the pupil and extend it to the outer corner of the eye.

Never try to change an entire situation at once. This can be overwhelming and even depressing. I recall an ancient proverb that says "a journey of one thousand miles begins with a single step." Therefore, take "baby steps" before taking "giant steps" by numbering your list in order from the easiest to the most difficult to change. Over the coming days, weeks, and seasons, you will tackle them one at a time, beginning with the least difficult. Next to each item, enter target dates or "opening nights." Be certain to allow plenty of time to bring the change about; losing five pounds or finally being freed of your braces cannot happen overnight—these are "giant steps"! Success will breed success, and you will look forward to a series of spectacular Opening Nights.

Face Value

You have now taken the three essential steps to determine how your face appears to others. First, you have erased images of other people's ideas of beauty. Second, you have introduced yourself to yourself, feature by feature. Third, you have assessed your facial strengths and weaknesses. As a result, you now know your face and its features as you never have before. Remembering the importance of self-love—you also accept what you see.

Do not dwell on deficits. Everyone has a tendency to exaggerate weaknesses. Try, instead, to put them in proper perspective. Focus on the improvements you hope to make. Qualities that cannot be changed—the freckles that friends consider cute, for instance—you must acknowledge. Ask, "How do I work around them?" or "How do I work with them?"

Create another column entitled "Backstage," and list there those things that cannot be changed short of cosmetic surgery. Then just draw the curtain on these elements, concentrate on your star billings, and begin to make the needed changes on your second billings.

Sometimes a loss of weight, if called for, brings about surprising improvements not just in the body but in the face as well. By getting rid of heavy jowls and puffy fat from cheekbones, you frequently uncover elegant lines and handsome features.

Tricks with makeup, either developed on your own through private experimentation or with professional help, can do wonders to alter your facial image. Think of portraits and the way they capture the subtle beauty of the subject's being. With deft lights and shadings the artist's brush evokes an aura that is more than the physical structure. With eye shadow, blush, and lipstick, used with artistry and restraint, you can give the artist's touch to your own face.

Preparing the Palette

The basis for all facial attractiveness is beautiful skin. No tricks of makeup can hide a poorly cared for face, so determine to make good skin care a part of every day.

Scientists are continually discovering more causes and cures for various skin problems, and they are also finding success in their efforts to slow biological aging. No "breakthrough" cream, however, can produce a miracle unless you establish and follow a daily regime of skin care. Proper diet, exercise, rest, a positive outlook, and the avoidance of damaging chemical substances are all important components of proper skin care.

Facial tissues, unlike the underlying structure, are not "fixed." They change continually, for better or worse, depending on the care, nutrition, and protection you give them. But good results are worth the effort. A lovely complexion is not only an appealing asset but also the foundation for makeup magic that can direct attention toward—or away from—other features.

Although you probably did not realize it at the time, you were growing the skin you are wearing today several months ago. The surface of your face—indeed of your entire body—has risen through several layers. As the surface cells with their embedded grime flake off or are removed by cleansing, the next layer provides a new canvas. Over time, the bottom layer becomes your visible complexion.

For many women, dry skin is a problem. The first step in skin care should be to replenish moisture continuously. Water is constantly being taken from the skin through evaporation, especially in this technological world of central heating and air conditioning, which make for low indoor humidity and accelerated moisture loss. Washing in very hot water or long soaks in swimming pools or the sea all remove the water-retentive compounds of the skin. Both salty and artificially chlorinated water are moisture-robbers and should be rinsed completely from the skin after exposure.

Next to dryness, the most serious threat to lovely skin is dirt and other impurities collecting in the pores. Cleansing twice a day—upon rising and at bedtime—is recommended to remove old makeup, excess oil, bacteria, and dirt from the surface. The cleansing should be thorough but gentle, to avoid damaging the protective coating, and you must rinse completely to prevent drying. Salon facials every six to eight weeks are a great adjunct to diligent at-home care, and the products you use on your face should be reassessed seasonally with a skincare professional.

Excessive oiliness, common during puberty, can result in subsurface deposits, which finally push to the surface as blackheads. Acne, the plague of youth, can often linger into the twenties and leave permanent scars. Frequent cleansing with facial soap and water is usually prescribed by dermatologists, and for stubborn cases, medical treatment is necessary—and can be wonderfully effective.

Silkening Body Skin

Care of the body skin is as important as care of the face and requires much the same regime. Begin by brushing with a dry natural-bristle brush—to sluff off dead cells—prior to bathing. Using a loofa during your bath or shower further polishes the skin, and the combination will eliminate rough spots that might otherwise develop on the backs of forearms, thighs, feet, elbows, knees, and ankles. The occasional use of an exfoliating body soap or lotion or cream also helps in the sluffing process. The fresh, new skin provided by exfoliation accepts moisturizing creams and lotions more readily. Moisturizing cream or lotion and body oil should be applied to damp skin to trap or seal in the moisture and bring about long-lasting results.

Body skin, like facial skin, requires daily cleansing, conditioning, and protection from the elements and the sun. The use of a deodorant or antiperspirant after bathing will help to eliminate unpleasant body odors, and either a razor, chemical depilatory, or lightening agent will solve the problem of excessive body hair, completing your essential good-grooming routine.

Beauty Taboos

Just as there are many beauty dos, so are there many beauty taboos. One of these is junk food. No one is absolutely certain of the part diet plays in causing or curing acne, but most doctors agree that an excess of starches, sugars, and fats can be a contributing factor. No one can live on potato chips, pizza, hamburgers, soda pop, and candy and look and feel well. A balanced diet, including fresh fruits, vegetables, and whole grains, is the best prescription for a lifetime of health.

Another threat to beauty is permanent damage to the skin that results from careless suntanning. The UVA-UVB rays of the sun also cause dryness, wrinkles, premature aging, and skin cancer, if not properly filtered.

Although you may think of a tan as great makeup, it is obtained at tremendous sacrifice. The American Cancer Society tells us there is no such thing as a "safe tan." A tan is a warning—it is the body's response to damage from the ultraviolet (UV) rays of the sun. These rays are the major cause of skin cancer. It is now medically proven that the sun destroys the repair mechanism of the skin and weakens the collagen and elastin fibers supporting it. This causes a settling effect on the skin and eventually leads to wrinkles. Treat the sun with great respect and *never* consider using the indoor tanning machines!

Current medical advice is to sun in moderation, avoiding the peak hours from eleven to three o'clock, and only after the application of a sunscreen product. I recommend the daily use of facial and body creams and lotions that contain a sunscreen with a Sun Protection Factor (SPF) on any part of the body to be exposed. Select the SPF number according to your sensitivity to the sun and the length of your exposure. As serious sunburn can damage not only the skin but also the eyes, wear sunglasses whose lenses are treated to screen out UV rays.

Taboo, too, is smoking, which, like sunlight, damages the skin. It reduces the amount of oxygen that reaches the skin's cells and thus has a smothering effect, which results in a lifeless texture. In addition, the very act of inhaling purses the lips in such a way that tiny lines develop around them, and squinting through the smoke—a natural reaction—causes lines and crow's-feet around the eyes. The results? Premature wrinkles and accelerated aging. If you are not daunted by the damage smoking can do to your overall health, refrain for the sake of your beauty, your femininity, your fragrance, and your breath. To smoke is to "play with fire" as far as your health and beauty are concerned. "Never start smoking and you will never have to quit" has been my motto since my teens. It worked for me, and it will work for you.

Drugs destroy body, mind, and spirit, so any experimentation with drugs should be avoided. Young women possess one half of the genetic responsibility—something researchers declare to be enormously vulnerable to chemical abuse—as well as full responsibility for prenatal care. Alcohol should be avoided or taken in moderation. Recent research has revealed that young women are damaged much more quickly by the ingestion of alcohol than adults, and that women, at every stage of their lives, are doubly fragile in their ability to handle it.

In your endeavor to become inwardly and outwardly beautiful, never allow the roadblocks of the beauty taboos to come in the way of your path.

Oliver's Twists

Skincare rituals should be streamlined and simplified—in fact, they *must* be for today's young women with superactive lifestyles. Similarly, our makeup routine should be quick, easy, and natural.

Makeup, I believe, should serve as an enhancement of the natural beauty of healthy, well-cared-for skin. Color simply accents, sharpens, and defines facial features. Your goal is to appear real and natural—no line should appear on your face as evidence of the placement of blusher, accent to the lashes, shaping of the lips, or at the jawline where your foundation ends. The goal is, as we say at L'Ecole des Ingénues, *la beauté naturelle*. But, *before* you begin to apply makeup, look in the mirror and face up to a quick test. Do you see:

- A fresh, healthy complexion?
- An even skin tone?
- The absence of irritations, blemishes, clogged pores, and pigmentation spots?

Few faces pass this test with flying colors, which is why a quick and knowledgeable hand at skin care and cosmetics is essential. Following Ol-

1. The Cleansing

2. The Rinsing

3. The Preparation

Oliver's Twists

- A thorough cleansing with a facial cleansing bar, lotion, or cream followed by twenty-five or thirty rinses with very warm water. (See Faces 1 and 2.)
- Use of controlling lotion to balance the skin's pH (acid/alkaline) level. (See Face 3.)
- Moisturizer or day cream, as needed and only where needed, applied to warm, moist skin. (See Face 3.)
- A dab of eye cream gently patted around the delicate eye area with the ring or pinkie finger. (See Face 3.)
- If not contained in moisturizer and eye cream, application of lotion or cream designed to combat free radicals and a sun protection product of at least 6 or 8 SPF. (See Face 3.)
- All facial cleansing and treatment products should be from the same manufacturer as they are created to work together.
- A touch of under-eye concealer one shade paler than foundation or same shade as foundation. (See Face 3.)
- Foundation to even out the skin tone and protect it from the elements and pollution, in a color to match perfectly the complexion and carefully blended just over and slightly under the jaw. (See Face 3.) Foundation should be a thin, translucent one that lets a well-cared-for skin proudly show through when selected for daily and sports wear. For artificial or candlelight or photography a some-

4. The Powder

5. The Brow Shape

6. The Eye Accent

Oliver's Twists (*continued*)

what more opaque and creamy one is my choice. According to the skin and the season either of these can contain oil or be oil free.

- A light application of medicated tint for any minor mars to an otherwise perfect complexion to heal as it hides!
- A thorough dusting with loose translucent powder in a color to complement foundation and skin tone and to refine the skin and set the foundation, followed by a final circular buffing with a large cotton ball with the final strokes applied downward to place the facial hairs flat on the face. (See Face 4.)
- A *touch* of blush to accent the cheeks, remembering that cream blush goes before powder and powder blush goes after powder, otherwise they will not mix. (For proper placement, see Face 7.) In addition, an experienced hand can do wonders with contouring and highlighting powders. Placement of the magic powders for blush, contour, and highlights can visually alter the shape of the face.
- Eyes, highlighted, contoured, shadowed, and powdered beneath well-shaped and brushed brows, add the finishing touch to a glowing, lightly made-up complexion. Subtle, smoky eyelash colors are smudged at the base of the lashes so as to become a part of the lash base itself. Lashes are further accented, if need be, with the slightest

7. The Cheek Accent

8. The Lip Accent

9. The Finished Face

stroke of eyeliner placed at the base of the lashes only, never beyond, in a muted shade that whispers "accent." The eye's shape is contoured with soft shades of subtle color, never fearing a bare eyelid with just a hint of the palest pink for a wonderful daytime backdrop to eyelashes tipped with mascara. *Only* matte eye colors are suitable for day. Frosted colors *must* be saved for evenings. (See Faces 5 and 6.)

- Lip accent choices are as many as lip shapes themselves: transparent, translucent, and opaque lip color in shiny, wet, matte, or frosted finish. The tools of application range from fingertips to brushes to pencils to tubes to pots to applicators. The more naturally liplike the color and pencil accent line, the more believable the mouth. The more vivid the color, the more made-up lips appear. Artful changes can be made to the size of the lips with practice. I prefer the use of color to alter the lips rather than lines to redesign the lips. Unless applied by professionals, lines are easily detected. (See Face 8.)

- Finally, frame the finished face with the perfect hairstyle. (See Face 9.)

iver's Twists found on pages 25 to 27, you should be able, with practice, to go from cleansing through makeup in fifteen minutes or less.

Before enhancing your features with the subtle accents of makeup, look into a three-way mirror and run your hands over your face, pressing through to the bone structure with your fingers, feeling the facial muscles as you explore your face. Just as a sculptor is sensitive to lines, you must know the lines of your face. In order to know your face better, you may even want to consider taking sculpturing, portrait, or basic art class. Having absorbed the knowledge gained in these classes, think of your face as the canvas, your makeup as your palette of colors, your makeup brushes as your tools, and your hands as those of an artist. Enjoy painting the prettiest picture possible for those around you to enjoy and for your own personal satisfaction. Although beauty is in the eye of the beholder you must first capture the eyes of those around you and the artist's techniques are the key. In order to perfect your artistic abilities, practice Oliver's Twists on a daily basis.

A Tasteful Portrait

Before stepping away from your mirror, take one final peek as you ponder your finished portrait, remembering that makeup is not a facade behind which to hide. It is not to be worn as a mask, nor is it to be used to make a social statement. Makeup is solely to protect your facial skin and enhance your features. Masklike faces cannot reveal the real you any more than they can fool anyone. They can, however, send the wrong message. To appear "painted" has labeled a woman since the beginning of time and will certainly label you today. The label: poor taste! To be in good taste, makeup must be just as appropriate to the time, place, and event as clothing must be. Let your makeup play up your well-cared-for skin, accentuate the positive, and minimize the negative among your features. Let it be the invisible difference, a subtle enhancer between nature and natural beauty. And, always remember that makeup is at its most beautiful when worn with a sincere smile and a sparkle in your eye. It is also at its best and in the best of taste when applied in private, *never* in public.

Crowning Glory

Certainly for you, a young woman, beautiful hair has a major part to play in your personal attractiveness. The right hairstyle can create a flattering frame for the face and can also serve to focus attention on your more attractive features. Much as a frame for a handsome portrait gives the work background and form, lovely hair provides shape and identity to your features, skin, and facial expressions. And it also contributes to self-confidence.

But serious care is required every day, and there are some "do nots" to remember. The appearance of your hair is dependent on its natural characteristics, affected by:

- Cleanliness
- Cut
- Style
- Condition
- The elements
- Chemical processes
- Water type used
- Climate
- Diet and general health

Every healthy effort you make on behalf of your face and figure will also benefit your hair. During the teens, hair and skin are generally oily. Hormone changes are part of the normal development pattern of adolescence, and these stimulate the oil glands of the scalp. Special products teamed with daily shampooing can help control the oil flow.

As is the case with skin, the sun is one of your hair's worst enemies, robbing it of the moisture that is essential for flexibility and strength. A careful exploration of sun products for the hair is a must unless you wish to live with lifeless hair months after spring break or a summer of sun. Hair must be protected from the harm of the sun by hats and scarves even during the shortest convertible ride or outdoor activity. Special "leave-on" hair products containing sunscreen and conditioning agents should be used as added precautions during long exposures to sun and water—outdoor sports and exercise, boating, water-skiing, pool and ocean outings. Remember, too, when swimming for fun, fitness, competition, or gym class, that chlorinated water often gives blonde hair, whether natural or color-treated, a greenish tinge. This is the result of the blue dyes in chlorine compounds mixing with the blonde hair's yellow tones. Brown hair is often left with a "rusty" look as a result of the residue remaining after a swim in chlorinated water. Although special products are available to return the color to normal, precaution is the best prevention.

Salt water and chlorinated water are extremely drying and break down the hair's cuticle, or outer layer, leaving the hair damaged and brittle. The first preventive step against this damage is to wear a bathing cap. Second, and most important, rinse and preferably shampoo your hair immediately after swimming to remove all traces of chlorine or salt. The application of an instant conditioner should follow the after-swim shampoo. For the regular swimmer, deep-conditioning or hot-oil treatments are needed once a week to keep the hair in as healthy a condition as the swimmer herself.

Like skincare products, haircare products are relatively expensive and can take a big bite out of a young woman's budget. Survey the marketplace and select carefully. You might want to consider consulting a haircare specialist to have your hair and scalp examined and the best products recommended. Such a consultation should also include advice on improving your diet, increasing your exercise output, and learning some relaxation techniques, all of which contribute to the health and sheen of your hair.

The perfect hairstyle should suit and flatter your face, and it should be created by you and a hair stylist you trust. You two are joint collaborators. There are few hard and fast rules, but current fashion, your individuality, age, and lifestyle should not be ignored. To your initial ideas your stylist will add his or her professional evaluation of the suitability of the texture, condition, bulk, and growth pattern of your hair to any proposed styling.

In any collaboration about style, manageability should be a major consideration. You have an active lifestyle; you almost certainly do not have the time to sit around with curlers in your hair after every shampoo. And if you are not very adept with a blow-dryer and brush, you either need to be taught the technique—and practice till you are perfect—or you need a style that dries beautifully all by itself. To come up with the perfect combination, talk with your stylist about the amount of time you have to devote to haircare, the kinds of activities in which you participate, the image you want to project, and the harmony of your proposed hairstyle with your face and personality. Remember that your hairstyle must make the scene seven days a week, not just for one glamorous night. Never agree to a radical change at your first appointment with a new hairdresser, unless you are absolutely certain it is time to lop off those waist-length tresses.

Although it may be a great temptation to do so, altering the natural color of your hair during your teenage years is a mistake that falls into the category of poor taste as surely as too much makeup or inappropriate dress. Many mothers have come to me to ask my advice about their daughters who were students of L'Ecole des Ingénues, saying that when their daughter was a little girl she was a blonde, but now her hair is turning darker and she wants to recapture the shining blondness—so badly that she would consider chemical alterations. I counsel the mother to accept the natural darkening and to encourage her daughter to do so.

Blondes and light brunettes tend to darken with maturity and any attempt to fight this has its dangers. The natural highlights of summer add to the beauty of hair and are harmless to healthy tresses, but chemically created winter imitations damage hair and cause it to react badly to the sun, water, and wind, leaving the abused hair dull and lifeless. Attempting to correct the damage with yet another chemical continues what can become an endless cycle, each round of which is worse than its predecessor. When a father or brother tells a girl that "dyed" or streaked hair makes her look "cheap," he is, perhaps awkwardly, but honestly, telling her that she is not presenting herself in good taste. Men, even young ones, prefer women to be natural.

Once your hair is comfortably styled and in good condition, you should forget about it. Conversation about how difficult your hair is or about how unhappy you are with your present cut is not only boring but also may sound as if you are fishing for compliments. Along the same lines, you should never comb or touch your hair in public. Running your fingers through your curls or tossing your head to rearrange the style or constantly patting it into place are affectations. Trying to catch glimpses of yourself in restaurant mirrors or plate-glass windows is also unattractive and makes you appear self-centered. Once you leave the privacy of your room, try to forget your looks and concentrate all your interest on others. You will find by doing this that others will in turn pay more attention to you—a lovely circle.

Going to Extremities

Hands are among the most expressive parts of the body, and the hands of a fastidious young woman tell those she meets that she cares about herself and is sufficiently disciplined in her beauty routine to keep her nails and hands well groomed. Hands are frequently neglected and abused, which is serious since the skin on the top of the hand is extremely thin and delicate, requiring the same cautious care as facial skin. This means special protection from the elements—warm gloves for winter cold, rubber gloves for household chores, garden gloves for outside work, and white cotton gloves at night to hold in hand and nail creams. Also crucial are the invisible gloves of sunscreen whenever you are out of doors.

A manicure and nail polish are to the hands what skin care and makeup are to the face. Nails of an attractive length—neither chewed down to the quick nor grown to dragon-lady lengths—are a graceful finish to the hands. Nail color, like cosmetic color, should harmonize with skin tones and clothing colors. Save frosted and dramatic colors for festive evenings only. Most of the time, buffed, clear, or pale pastel polish is the right choice—chipped polish never!

Naturally, the feet should be as beautifully cared for and callus-free as the hands, an easy accomplishment if you incorporate daily pumicing and creaming and weekly pedicures into your beauty regime.

"The Bath"

The stage for many facets of your personal care is the bath, and throughout the ages "the bath" has meant more than simply washing up. It can be a glamorous ritual, and the properties of water are not only cleansing but relaxing and restorative to the body and mind as well. Be sure to add the soothing and healing qualities of aromatherapy—scented bath salts, soaps, oils, and herbal extracts. A warm bath dilates the blood vessels, stimulates circulation, and loosens muscle tension.

Just as your closet will set the stage for your daily dressing, so should your bathroom offer the background for the beauty benefits of bathing, caring for your skin, and adding the complements of cosmetics. Set in soft pale colors, designed with flattering artificial lighting and access to natural light, it may also offer soothing music, plant life, and candles emitting a delicious scent.

Soignée

During this, your decisive decade, you probably have more time to spend on yourself than you ever will again. Developing efficient routines now, at your leisure, will be doubly rewarding, since practice will help you streamline your regimens for later, more stressed periods; and because consistent early care of yourself will prevent the development of later problems.

You must work on your beauty routine just as you would academic studies, breaking it down into a daily, weekly, and monthly schedule, both at home and in terms of professional attention. Your regime should include regular medical and dental care in addition to haircuts and facials. You must care for yourself at all times, not just in anticipation of special occasions. Because impeccable grooming is to your body what correct manners are to your actions, both must be perfectly polished and so consistently followed that they become totally natural.

The French have a wonderfully descriptive word, *soignée,* which perfectly describes the fastidiously groomed woman—carefully done, highly finished, well-turned-out, neat, smart. Achieving this condition should be your goal, and to accomplish it takes discipline and perseverance, for only one neglected facet can spoil your beauty package.

CHAPTER 2

The Body Beautiful

The radiance that results from lovely thoughts, the zest of youth and health, good grooming, and the restrained use of makeup on well-cared-for skin will be all but lost if they are accompanied by a sloppy figure accentuated by poor posture.

The necessary basis of a beautiful woman is a body so fit and healthy that clothing seems to drape effortlessly upon it; a body so perfectly aligned that movements are as light and graceful as music or a bird in flight. One of the most important challenges facing a young woman is the development of correct posture, fluidity of motion, and a figure as lovely and as well-proportioned as possible. The training given models, young women attending finishing schools, dancers, equestriennes, and athletes leads to good habits, which should endure throughout life with enormous benefits to beauty and health.

No Body's Perfect

In order to present yourself in the most beautiful package attainable, you must take stock of your body. It is now time, as the director of your personal face-and-figure drama, to shift your eyes from your face to your figure, just as the onlooker invariably does when he or she meets you for the first time.

One of the most glamorous classes held at L'Ecole des Ingénues is entitled *Aplomb,* which is defined in the French dictionary as: "Perpendicularity to the horizon; equilibrium; assurance, self-command, self-possession, stead-fastness, coolness." This class concentrates on the visual poise of good posture, and the assurance it awards the body.

Just as my students do following the opening day class, take time now for The Quick Posture Quiz, which is designed to make you aware of your body and the good points and bad points of your posture. In the privacy of your

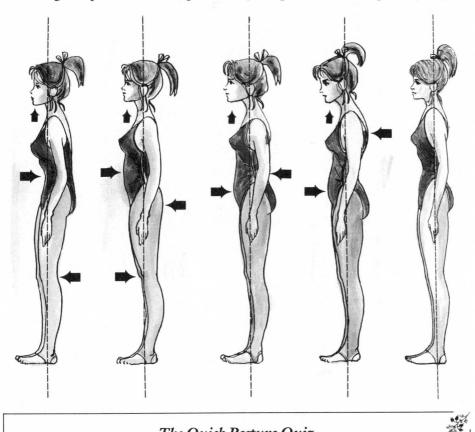

The Quick Posture Quiz

Side View

Does the head thrust forward or tilt downward?
Does the body tilt forward or lean backward?
Are the shoulders rounded?
Does the abdomen protrude?
Do the buttocks protrude?
Are the knees locked?
Are the heels raised?

bedroom, undress completely and stand in front of a full-length mirror. Judge yourself objectively, from the front and side, as you take the Quiz.

How do you stack up? To find out, mark a "plumb line" down the middle of your full-length mirror and stand sideways a foot away. The plumb line should fall vertically through the center of your earlobe, opposite your shoulder bone and hipbone, and slightly in front of your anklebone. Is any part of your body too far back or too far front of this line? You want to

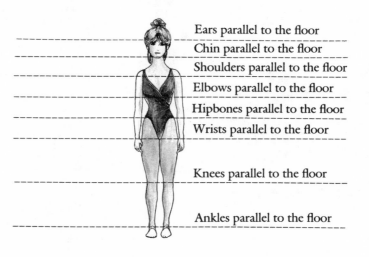

Ears parallel to the floor
Chin parallel to the floor
Shoulders parallel to the floor
Elbows parallel to the floor
Hipbones parallel to the floor
Wrists parallel to the floor

Knees parallel to the floor

Ankles parallel to the floor

The Quick Posture Quiz

Front View

Is one ear higher than the other?
Are the shoulders high and tense?
Is one shoulder higher than the other?
Is one hipbone higher than the other?
Is one wrist lower than the other?
Do the ankles roll inward or outward?
Do the toes turn inward or outward?

work on this section. Does the line fall in front of your hipbone? You are carrying your hips too far back. Does the line fall opposite the front part of your knee area? You are locking your knees, thrusting your body weight too far forward. If you find you do not stack up properly, take The Corrective Posture Measures outlined below.

The Corrective Posture Measures

Place feet parallel to one another, two inches apart
Balance weight evenly between feet; support it halfway between balls and heels of feet
Slightly flex knees
Place elbows slightly away from body and gently bent
Relax hands by sides with thumbs at sideseams
Let fingers fall gently curved
Contract buttocks by squeezing an imaginary coin between them
Tilt pelvis under
Tighten abdominal muscles by pulling up and in
Lift chest high by taking a deep breath and exhaling
Lengthen space between ribs and hips
Raise shoulders up, back, and finally down and relaxed
Straighten and lengthen spine and neck
Hold head high by imagining being lifted up from behind the ears
Hold chin at right angles to neck and parallel to the floor

The plumb line determines where one segment of the body should be carried over the other. You cannot correctly position one segment without properly aligning all the segments. Standing sideways before the mirror, think of the chief segments of your body balanced one over the other in this simple manner: head over chest; chest over pelvis; pelvis over balls of feet.

The perfect plumb line image of yourself that you now see in the mirror is the way you want to look in the future. *Hold this image in your mind.* Now relax. Naturally, you cannot maintain this newly acquired stance indefinitely. Fortunately, you do not have to. Old-fashioned theories of posture as rigid and static—as in the military—have given way to the idea that good posture can be a dynamic, flowing movement. If you coordinate conscious thought with body action, you can move easily and free of tension, maintaining a correct stance whether standing, walking, sitting, bending, or lying down.

"Pull Your String"

The head leads the body in all natural movements. One of the secrets of having the head control the body is to imagine a large, helium-filled balloon fastened on a string attached to the top of your head. Close your eyes and imagine this balloon pulling your head up and away from your body while drawing the back of your neck and spine up after it. Meanwhile, just imagine the rest of your body hanging loose and relaxed.

Pull Your String!

Enjoy the feeling of your spine lengthening, following the upward direction of your head. Everything else will drop into place and you will find yourself standing tall and erect, head held high, pelvis automatically tucked under, chest raised, the curve in your spine lengthened and your lumbar region straightened, tummy flattened, knees relaxed, and your weight balanced evenly upon parallel feet. Not only will you be breathing more deeply, but your whole being will feel balanced. Maintain this posture, keeping the back and neck straight, visualizing your head raised up and away from your body, as you sit, bend, or walk up and down stairs.

To achieve good posture you must first discover your bad habits and reprogram your brain to become alert to the body's correct positioning. In order to change poor posture you must exercise conscious control. You must be aware of your alignment and check positioning from time to time. With repeated practice of the correct posture, your body will learn new positions and old habits will be forgotten.

Anytime you wish, you can restore your perfect posture by visualizing the correct way and muscles will unconsciously assume the correct position. Or, as we say to one another at L'Ecole des Ingénues (in our secret code), "Pull your string." Decoded this means to remember the helium balloon, let it float upward, and feel the tug on the string where it attaches to the crown of the head. I say this to myself many times a day to insure that my head is held high and my posture erect. You too can "pull your string"!

Do not ruin your perfect posture by wearing high heels too often or for long periods of time. Why? High heels push the body weight forward onto the toes and shift the plumb line of good posture, thrusting out the chest and derrière and rotating the hips inward to compensate for the unnatural angle of the feet. Worn habitually, high heels result in foot problems, and these destroy good posture and interfere with many activities you enjoy.

The Body in the Round

As you continue to take stock of your body, peer at yourself closely in the mirror from all angles. Grasp a mental picture of how your body looks. Close your eyes briefly and recapture this picture. Open your eyes and look, then close them, and picture your body as you would prefer it to be. Return to reality with your tape measure—which serves as your calculator for totaling the attributes and shortcomings of the facts of your figure, your pluses and minuses—and measure the three major parts of your body described in The Body in the Round on page 40.

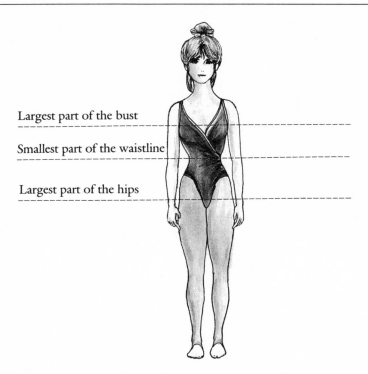

Largest part of the bust

Smallest part of the waistline

Largest part of the hips

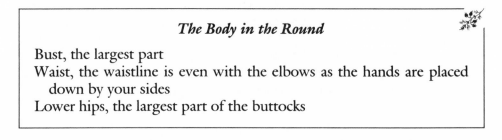

The Body in the Round

Bust, the largest part
Waist, the waistline is even with the elbows as the hands are placed
   down by your sides
Lower hips, the largest part of the buttocks

Now, as a quick assessment, remember that a figure is in its best proportion when the largest part of the bust and the largest part of the hips measure the same. That is to say, should your bust measure 34 inches, ideally your hips, too, would measure 34. Following this rule, your waistline should be ten inches smaller than hips and bust—24 inches. A two-inch variance one way or the other still results in a nice figure! However, if you vary more than two inches, you will want to work toward some long-range changes. An exercise program, restructured diet, and correct posture can help you to come nearer the ideal—or as close as is possible for your particular body.

The Body Segments

In addition to evaluating the circumference of your body, take stock of yourself vertically. When standing barefoot, from your head to the soles of your feet, the ideal vertical body is divided into four equal segments, as shown below.

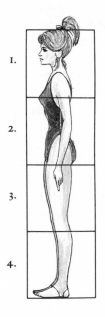

The Body Segments

1. The crown of the head to the largest part of the bust
2. The largest part of the bust to the coccyx bone
3. The coccyx bone to the bottom of the kneecap
4. The bottom of the kneecap to the bottom of the foot

Your body segments are comprised of God-given proportions as determined by your genes. There is nothing which can be done to change them, and the relation of these four parts, one to the other, constitutes your individual proportions. Become aware of these relationships and you can compensate for any shortcoming you may find.

The Fantastic Figure Formula

I would not ask you to so carefully critique your figure if I were not also going to help you attain the figure that is realistically yours to package! The Fantastic Figure Formula is my answer for making the most of the body.

First, on a piece of paper chart your body in the round, establishing your pluses or minuses with regard to the ten-inch differential between your bust and hip measurements and your waistline. Second, chart the lengths of the four vertical segments of your body, recording the number of inches in each and to what degree you are "off" as compared with the ideal vertical lineup.

With this information charted you can apply The Corrective Posture Measures (p. 37) you need and apply The Laws of Proportion described in Chapter 3 to assist you in your improvements. For example, if you find that your body segment—from bust to hips—is both shortest from a vertical standpoint and also out of proportion as far as waist circumference is concerned, then you will "pull your string," lengthening that segment to its maximum. In addition, you will look for outfits that are all one color or a vertical pinstripe from bust to hips, and you will avoid an accessory, such as a wide, brightly colored belt or a garment with shoulder pads, which gives a strong horizontal line—simply apply Laws number 1 and 10. In addition, you will want to set short-term and long-range goals to trim your waistline through diet and exercise.

Diet and Exercise

If you feel uncomfortable or threatened as you face the many numerical figures comprising your physical figure, please feel confident that your work toward understanding and correcting the pluses and minuses will reward you greatly. Believe me, the numbers involved in your body proportions are as important to the starring role you hope to play in your own orbit as Einstein's Theory of Relativity is to an understanding of the heavenly bodies. By allowing these ratios to dictate your choice of dress and accessories and by perfecting your posture, you streamline the vehicle that must carry the real you on its way. Then, knowing that you have made the most of what you were given, you acquire an assurance that will surely add a special glow.

Having made the most of your proportions through a combination of illusion (streamlining) and presentation (posture), you must think about the times when you cannot depend entirely on clothes to cover or divert interest from flaws. In summer, bathing suits tell all and shorts or sundresses provide little behind which to hide. Evening clothes are revealing in all seasons although they do offer camouflage for some body areas if carefully selected.

Beyond perfect posture and the use of illusion are figure flaws, and they must be addressed from within. Many young girls are, in varying degrees, overweight. In the early teens there may still be remnants of "baby fat," which is temporary. For the young woman who is pudgy, the problem usually lies with poor eating habits and/or inactivity. A proper diet and adequate exercise can normalize weight quite rapidly while you are young and will establish healthful patterns for the remainder of your life.

I had been hearing the ingénues refer to the "freshman fifteen" for some time before I received an explanation of the term: the fifteen additional pounds a freshman takes home from college with her at Christmas break. Away from the good nutrition at home, in a new environment with irregular hours of study and sleep, junk food, fast food, and dormitory food all add up to excess pounds and inches.

As a young woman enters her twenties, usually during her college years, some changes will take place. Health and vigor will have reached their peak, preparing her for the stresses of completing her education, beginning a career or family, and establishing independent living. With growth complete and physical activity reduced (no more required gym classes!), she may need to reduce caloric intake slightly and pay more attention to her diet.

By "diet," no physicians or beauty counselors recommend stringent, near-starvation programs. Drastic regimes for weight reduction are dangerous and their results usually temporary. To live fully in the active, exciting years ahead, a balanced diet is essential to supply your body with energy and resistance. You should eat three meals a day, including proteins, carbohydrates, and ample quantities of raw or cooked fruits and vegetables. Snacking, especially on rich, fatty, salty, or sweet items, should be kept to a minimum, and lavish desserts must be very rare treats.

The benefits of such a way of eating are surprisingly rewarding, especially for those in their teens and early twenties who can expect flab to disappear quickly from tummies, thighs, upper arms, and face. Any weight-loss diet, of course, should be pursued under the guidance of your doctor.

A small percentage of young women in their teens and twenties are too thin to fulfill their beauty potential, or even to fill out their clothes attractively. They usually need to eat only a little more—three, four, or five small meals a day made up of nutritionally balanced foods—and perhaps eat those meals more slowly and in a more relaxed atmosphere. An extra glass of milk or orange juice at bedtime can help. Tenseness, especially at mealtime, skipping meals altogether, and an obsession with thinness can contribute to eating disorders, which become psychologically serious and physically dangerous.

The Beauty of Exercise

Well-toned muscles are not only necessary for a beautiful body, but for supporting the skeletal bones in a correct posture. To achieve those goals, both strengthening and stretching exercises are necessary. The exercise regime taught to the ingénues is based on both hatha yoga (for developing flexibility and strength in the spine, back, neck, and abdomen) and yoga asanas (for correcting postural faults). For posture, body alignment, and figure control, it is also necessary to practice some tummy-tightening and spine-straightening exercises as part of your daily routine. You must also include special exercises to develop the upper and lower back muscles in order to maintain neck tone and align the head and neck with the spine.

Of course, very pleasant active sports like swimming, bicycling, dancing, tennis, golf, skiing, and skating, along with various team sports, and horseback riding, are also wonderful for figure and posture improvement and grace. Undoubtedly, one of the most perfect exercises of all is walking, be it a long-stride, fast-paced walk or a stroll in the country.

But, there is more to exercise than getting in shape to run or dance, and there is more to exercise than trimming flabby areas or toning underdeveloped muscles. Perhaps the word *exercise* itself has become misleading in our modern, fast-moving society. Ancient systems of exercise like hatha yoga were developed in order to turn a person's attention inward, to discover inner natural rhythms and ways of being. These descriptions may sound vague to you, but that only reveals how little importance has been placed on this type of experience in our society, as compared to the defined goal orientation of a running program that requires x amount of miles per week.

"Exercise," in an expanded concept, is the time in one's day to lavish on one's self, to reestablish one's sense of harmony and grace. There is no room here for punishment because we ate dessert last night or because our clothes are beginning to tighten around specific body parts. Self-punishment or penance for lapses are dangerous strategies to employ in our "exercise" time, for they are likely to be negatively motivating and can become reasons to abandon exercise completely.

Visual Poise

When I consider carriage, I think how hard a trainer must work a show horse; how it must be schooled in step and gait until it is visually poised and ready for the show ring. Young girls—*jeune filles,* if you will—must practice their gaits as well, and I am so happy and proud when each ingénue, on graduation day, glides with grace, pivots, and sits with ease before the cameras—many times the cameras of national and international television teams recording the event along with our own camera staff.

Each of the boxes and sketches that follow spells out for you, step by step, the way to walk, pivot, sit, and climb up and down stairs with grace. Practice these daily, just as though we were in the classroom together. If possible, have a friend or family member videotape you as you begin, and as you progress toward grace. Do not get depressed if at times you wonder whether you possess any coordination at all or feel you will never be anything but ungainly.

Each day, as you practice becoming more poised, take a few minutes to let your mind become the video camera. It is important to close your eyes and imagine your body in its newly defined posture and movement patterns. View your weak and strong points and identify them to yourself. Now, envision the way you want to stand, move, and sit. Let these new pictures register in your mind's eye. Picture yourself with the utmost physical self-confidence. Now, open your eyes and make the picture come to life. Each day you will become a little more at ease with the new picture of yourself. As you think of becoming poised, you will begin to be poised. By practicing the how-tos in the boxes, by picturing and by saying, "I possess poise," you will find that you do.

Grace

Grace is a quality every woman wants. It combines confidence with unself-consciousness. Although I have met a few young girls who have it, I find it a quality that appears more often as a girl matures into young womanhood. It can and should be learned, however, during your developing years.

The first lesson toward attaining grace begins with movement. The factors I have discussed that contribute to your aligned body also contribute to your grace: Proper exercise, improved posture, and correct body weight are the keys to grace and allow you to move more comfortably and with greater ease.

Sports and dance are wonderful teachers of grace. They impart a sure sense of balance, enhance flexibility, and increase muscle strength and coordination. They cause you to move with a purpose, developing movement patterns that are stored in your memory. Having instant recall or "replay" of these patterns enhances your self-confidence: You automatically do it right. My instructions for everyday walking, pivoting, standing, and sitting, when

Walking

From now on, your success with your walk will depend upon practice and application. Think of every block you walk as an additional opportunity to incorporate all of the techniques. Let me emphasize again the importance of checking and concentrating on one thing at a time. Usually, *three* months are required to master a beautiful walk. Simply follow these steps:

- *Prepare a practice floor.* Moving outward from the wall, place two rows of masking tape on the floor, perpendicular to the wall, making certain that they are straight and two inches apart.
- *Assume the proper plumb line position.* Stand against the wall with heels four inches from the wall; feet two inches apart and pointing straight ahead; buttocks, shoulders, and head touching the wall. Tighten the buttocks and slide them down the wall until each vertebra is as close to the wall as possible. Distribute the weight evenly on both feet. Finally, "pull your string."
- *Shift the weight onto one foot as you retain the proper plumb line position.* Nestle the heel of the front weightless foot close to the arch of the weight-bearing back foot, creating a small "V" between the balls of the feet.
- *Step out on the front, weightless foot.* As you do this, transfer the weight first onto the heel; then, onto the outside of the foot; and last, onto the ball of the foot. Repeat to yourself, "heel, outside, ball," as you take each step.
- *Allow the thigh to precede the torso.* As you step away from the wall, or take sequential steps, the torso should remain straight and the thigh should project forward. Remember to "pull your string."
- *Retain relaxed knees.* This assures a smooth glide to your walk, whereas locking the knees as the weight falls onto each foot causes the hips to sway. If the knees are too relaxed, the act of straightening them with each step causes you to bounce. If you can balance a book atop your head, you will have attained a graceful glide.

- *Keep the feet pointing straight ahead and two inches apart.* Use the lines on the practice floor as guides and make certain that you walk straight and that your toes do not point inward or outward.
- *Retain a tiny space between the knees.* Take care that the sides of the knees neither touch one another nor that there is a wide gap between them.
- *Establish your stride.* The length of your stride should be equal to the length of your foot. Measure this length. Place a strip of tape across the walking lines dividing them into six or seven sections, each the length of one of your feet. As you step, using the stride lines as guides, place one foot before the other, skipping every other section.
- *Control hip movement.* The hips should not swing from side to side. Keep the knees slightly relaxed, buttocks tight, and the pelvic bones parallel with the floor to assist in maintaining control of hip motion.
- *Raise the chest.* Breathe in deeply and then exhale. As you exhale, hold the chest in the same high position it assumed when you inhaled.
- *Hold the shoulders back and down.* Raise the shoulders up as though to meet the ears. Next, move them back; finally, place them down, keeping them parallel with the floor. As you walk, imagine a brick on each shoulder holding them down and even. Dare not to drop the bricks!
- *Hold the head and the chin parallel with the floor.* To hold the chin up causes you to appear "stuck-up," whereas to drop it makes you look as though you are lacking self-confidence. Imagine that you are tall and erect.
- *Swing the arms gently.* As they swing behind you, your arms should not extend beyond the largest portion of your buttocks. The arms swing in front of you the same distance as the width from your abdomen to the largest portion of your buttocks. Allow the arms to hang from the shoulders in a relaxed manner and bend the elbows slightly. Hold the fingers gently curved with the palms toward and parallel with your sides.
- *Step in rhythm.* To establish a rhythmic walk, repeat softly, "step, step, step, step," as you inhale for four steps. Then repeat, "step, step, step, step," as you exhale for the next four steps. Continue this until the rhythm becomes automatic.

added to the skills developed through sports, are certain also to contribute to your self-assurance and, hence, to your grace.

Grace encompasses a sense of calmness as well as a mental and physical center. These two factors lead to larger, freer movements, which add to grace, whereas a tense attitude causes energy to decline and movements to become very restricted, tight, and limited—with all grace lost.

Grace is beauty. Think of the grace and beauty in the ease with which peasants carry jars of water or baskets of fruit on their heads. Their move-

---

Pivoting

The pivot is simply a graceful, balanced turn. In order to develop balance and poise in walking, you must develop ease in pivoting by practicing the basic pivot:

- *Take five steps,* beginning with your right foot and ending with your right foot in front. (Right, left, right, left, right, stop.)
- *Turn* to the left by coming just slightly onto the balls of both feet and pivoting your body toward the left in the direction you wish to face. (Always turn in the opposite direction of the foot that is out front.)
- As you turn, *stop* your right or front foot as soon as it is at a 45-degree angle to the line pointing to the direction you are going. Allow the left or back foot to continue to pivot until its entire length is on the line. Be careful not to raise up on the ball of the foot and then drop sharply onto the heel. Just skim the floor with your heel as you pivot on the balls of the feet.
- *Transfer your weight* to the back foot and retain your "easy knees."
- Next, *close* your pivot by drawing the heel of the left foot back toward the instep of the right foot leaving about one inch between the heel and instep. The left toes face eleven on a clock and the right face one.
- *Pause and gather your balance and center.* Keep knees slightly flexed, hold your pelvic tilt, "pull your string," and let your helium balloon hold your head high.
- *Step out* on your forward "weightless" foot and repeat the above steps.
- Alternate the number of steps you take before pivoting and the foot on which you begin. Soon you will begin on either foot, take as many steps as you wish, and turn with ease and grace in any direction.

Climbing Stairs

Climbing stairs can lead to beautifully shaped thighs. The shape of your legs can be improved by this exercise, whether they are too chubby or too skinny. Develop shape and grace as follows:

- *Keep your knees flexed* ("easy knees") at all times. Do not bend and straighten them as you climb stairs. Let the large muscles in your thighs do the work and watch how your upper legs become trimmer and slimmer.
- *Keep your body upright* and in perfect alignment when you walk up steps, holding your "pelvic tilt."
- *Place your entire foot on each step,* ball of foot first. If stairs are too narrow, turn both feet in one direction when walking up or down stairs.
- *Look with your eyes, not your head.* Fashion models never bend their heads down to look at steps. As you go up or down stairs, hold your head in perfect alignment, with your plumb line running perfectly through your spine and your head held high by its helium balloon.
- When coming down stairs, your weight should go into the ball of the foot first, then heel; otherwise you thump. Do not turn your knees outward as if you were carrying a heavy bundle.

Sitting

Poise is associated with sitting; therefore, any time spent sitting should be a time for body composure. The very act of selecting a chair and of placing yourself into it should be made up of unhurried, graceful movements designed to make a dignified, ladylike impression. Practice each movement listed.

- *Do not be in a hurry to sit down.* In order to appear poised you must enter a room gracefully and take your time in seating yourself.
- *Select a chair in proportion to your body size* so that you will look attractive in it. Think of the chair as a nice frame for your body.
- *Approach the chair slowly and gracefully* once you have chosen it.
- *Pivot just as you reach the chair.* Make certain the heel of your back foot is under the chair (design of the chair permitting). Close your pivot and pause to regain your balance. Distribute your weight evenly on both feet.
- *Glance back briefly at the seat,* if you feel uncertain, before bending your knees. The calf of your back leg should actually come in contact with the chair. This assures you the chair is there! Be certain of your positioning and balance.
- *Relax your knees and lean forward slightly from the hips,* tucking your buttocks under and holding your plumb line and your head straight as you sit down gently into the chair. (Do not be guilty of making a "fanny first" approach or of accentuating it by slicking your skirt under you as you sit!)
- *Sit on the edge of the chair* and slowly ease back, placing your hands on the chair to assist if necessary as you assume one of these positions:

    The social sitting position is prettiest when the body is placed in the "basic S curve" by sitting in the center and placing the derrière sideways and to one side of the chair with the weight evenly distributed on both buttocks. Place the knees (held together) and the feet (in the heel-in-the-arch position) on the opposite side of the chair from the buttocks.

    The working sitting position finds the buttocks centered well into the back of the chair and the weight evenly distributed on both buttocks. The knees are slightly parted and the feet are facing straight ahead about four inches apart.

- *Never cross your knees* in either the social or working position. This cuts down on the circulation and may cause or aggravate varicose veins. In addition, it causes strain on the spine.
- *Place the calves at right angles to the thighs* in either position to evenly distribute your weight and to form an attractive line to your body.
- *"Pull your string!"* Hold your plumb line and your "pelvic tilt" so your torso will be straight, keeping a lengthened and extended spine and a flattened tummy. Remember your helium balloon pulling ever upward to hold your head straight.
- *Allow the arms to fall front and middle* and slide easily into your lap as you lower yourself into the chair.
- *Develop hand poise* by placing the hands on the top of the thigh of the leg whose foot is farthest back. Place the hands, palms down, one atop the other with the fingers gently curved. Position them about two thirds in from your knee.
- *Refrain from fidgeting* your body, your head, or your hands. Think in terms of their graceful movements as a means of accenting or accentuating your conversation.

Rising

When the time has come to get out of a chair, the same graceful and self-assured movements are as important as in the act of sitting. To be certain that you possess this poise, practice these simple steps:

- *Rock forward and back in your chair* from your hip joint. Rock forward and back smoothly, holding your body in alignment. Be careful not to lead with your head or break in the middle! (This is a private practice motion only!)
- *Allow your hands to fall naturally front and center* as you rock forward to begin your rising from the chair. Do not clasp them together or throw your arms out for balance or "push off" from your chair with your hands and arms.
- *Put the back foot slightly under the chair.* Lift onto the ball of that foot.
- *Distribute the weight between both legs and feet.* Be aware of the thighs taking on most of the action.
- *Rock forward slightly from your hip joint and rise.* Allow your thighs to do the work. Hold your "pelvic tilt," keeping the buttocks tucked under you, and allow your spinal column from your back to your head to form a gently rounded line.
- *Rise slowly* to an evenly paced count of "one, two, three," and resume your perfect plumb line and head position.
- *Shift your weight to your back foot and leg* and gather your balance.
- *Step away from the chair beginning with the front weightless foot* as you transfer your weight onto it.

ment is fluid and their balance so perfect that nothing falls off their head, spills from the jar, or falls from the basket. Graceful movement is free of tension, self-absorption, and pretension. Grace is also a state of mind—assuredness and balance—of knowing you have it all together, whether mentally in what you are about to say, or physically in your movements, or materially in your dress. For example, once you have prepared yourself to be in public, you are confident, you need not pull at your clothes, play with your jewelry, or touch your makeup or hair. As you develop grace you no longer fidget or fuss, you no longer move without direction or speak without thinking.

Achieving grace is an important step in becoming finished.

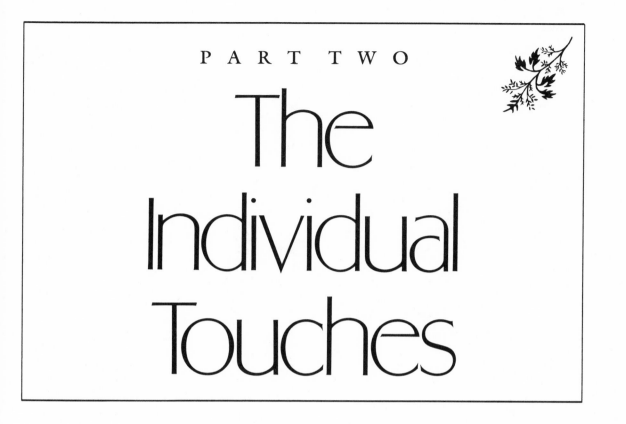

PART TWO

The Individual Touches

CHAPTER 3

Fashion Finesse

Clothing is for protection, comfort, modesty, and certainly for the enhancement of your beauty. To put on anything that is inappropriate, gaudy, vulgar, or otherwise offensive to others detracts from your appearance.

Now that you have learned how to be more beautiful by making certain improvements, adjustments, and refinements in your physical characteristics, consider what kinds of clothing will best set off that underlying structure, and at the same time express your unique spirit and style.

To dress correctly used to be a lot more difficult than it is now. *The Hours of the Day,* published in 1940, recommends different dress within one day for afternoon, visiting, dinner, ball, and the next morning for shopping, receiving, and leisure. Dressing for dinner is a pleasant reminder of a more formal era, and I require that the ingénues and staff wear dinner dresses each evening at L'Ecole des Ingénues. Afterward, everyone confides that they love the special feeling which dressing properly brings to the occasion.

In our current society clothes are an important and revealing part of life—beyond basic protection against the elements, they are a statement of individuality, status, creativity. How fortunate we are that contemporary attitudes allow for interesting dress. Everyone has a good deal of leeway to exercise innovation and flair. This freedom does, however, often bring about confusion because many women are in a quandary about what to buy and what to wear for certain occasions. I will, therefore, give you some guidelines to help you avoid expensive or embarrassing mistakes while teaching you to develop a personal style which celebrates your uniqueness.

Appropriateness Above All

Since what you wear can influence personal and professional relationships, the best rule is always to dress within the bounds of classic good taste. A sense of propriety, dictated by the occasion and the company, is necessary. Good materials and lines embellished with elegance—rather than flamboyance or modish extremes—are the unfailing guidelines that will insure you are comfortable and at ease. Appropriateness is determined by a number of factors, and it can change dramatically from situation to situation. Outside or indoors, mixed ages or peers, geography, building, event, and the weather can affect one's mode of dress.

Fashion is serious. What you wear reveals a significant message about you and your world. Even if you do not care about clothes per se, they communicate much about your attitudes toward the occasion, your company, and yourself. In the morning you make a decision about what to wear to which others respond all day long. Think of your clothes as the most communicative factor after your face and eyes—personal style is how you send nonverbal cues.

One dresses out of consideration for others as well as for one's own self-image. No one wants to fade into the woodwork—it is nice sometimes to lead the pack—and like most young people, you quite naturally want your clothing to communicate the feeling that you are "with-it" and "belong." But you certainly do not wish to look as if you were made from a mold because of a slavish acceptance of each passing fashion. Your goal is a wardrobe of clothes that are right for your body, your personality, your environment, and the specific occasion—they will help create your elusive aura.

Making Choices

In 1970, young fashion was blue jeans and a T-shirt. A generation later, the young dressed up again. There are not many constraints to fashion today and there are many alternatives. If you learn a bit about fashion history, by visiting museums and reading books, you might use your knowledge to bring to your dress some lovely touches and sensibilities—the way you wrap a shawl, say, or the boots you choose, not only because they look good on you and are comfortable and practical, but also because they remind you of fine old English riding boots.

When you received your first clothing allowance or were first permitted to shop for your own clothes, you probably learned the first lesson of fashion: You bought or considered a lot of junky, trendy clothes that did not last. You found neither their quality nor their style lasted. Then you moved up to fewer items of higher quality and a less extreme fashion statement and began assembling a timeless wardrobe.

Let us consider, for a moment, Second Empire France—an extravagant, incredibly feminine period for women's fashion—ladies wore their elaborate, crinoline-skirted dresses for many seasons, alternating what they had. It took a dressmaker many weeks to sew one of the fabulous creations worn by "The Queen of the Crinoline," and you can see the style in Winterhalter's painting, "The Empress Eugénie and Her Maids of Honor." The styling, workmanship, and materials were so beautiful and so timeless that such a gown would be magic if worn to a formal ball this evening.

Those of greatest means usually dress conservatively. Simplicity, expressed in the highest quality fabric and the most intelligent design, has a special elegance. "I've worn it ten years and I now feel comfortable in it," an elegant woman in her late twenties told me of her striking semimilitary jacket.

I share her sentiment. During my college years, I had the honor of being sponsored by fraternities as a contestant in several university beauty pageants. I never wore a new formal gown during competition, semifinals, or finals. I always wore old favorites, often my long white strapless evening dress of satin and tulle, in which I had enjoyed many college dances. I sincerely believe it was the comfort and self-confidence that the old favorites brought that afforded me the thrill of being the winner on so many occasions. I felt at home in what I chose to wear and was, therefore, more naturally myself—one criterion of any beauty pageant judge.

The most exciting thing about fashion is the artistic expression it permits. A strong sense of self can communicate a conservative or avant-garde personality—or anything in between. When society leader Muriel Newman of Chicago made the presentation of her art collection to the Metropolitan Museum of Art, she was more stunning than the paintings. As a young art student, Muriel searched for her own mode of expression. She discovered that she could express herself better by her dress than by drawing, sculpting, or painting, and she became known for her superb individualistic clothes sense. She shopped in out-of-the-way antique and clothing shops in Greenwich Village in the late sixties, and she learned to put together exotic and unusual combinations. She might wear an Egyptian chemise with pre-Columbian beads, or an Alexander Calder "shoulder sculpture," which she displayed on the simplest black dress. Muriel became a pacesetter, demonstrating that clothes are wearable art.

There is certainly self-discipline involved in fashion, but you can also, especially when you have a sense of fashion's past, indulge in appropriate whimsy—so long as you do not force yourself into a look cultivated by others in which you do not feel comfortable or at ease. The look must befit you and the occasion.

Fashion Forte

In order to discover your role as an "ingénue" in the drama of the ever-changing fashion scene, view the fashion of the present and, based upon your knowledge of its past, calculate its future as it relates to you and your lifestyle.

Many famous fashion designers go through fashion plates of past eras from many countries looking not for fashion per se, but for the quintessence of style. In fashioning your style, you, too, can develop an innate clothes sense by internalizing tradition and individualizing it.

I recall a marvelous experience I had as fashion director for Saks Fifth Avenue. The Peruvian and Guatemalan embassies in Washington sent an exquisite collection of native costumes, which I was to present in a fashion show and exhibit in the store. The models and I were overwhelmed by the beauty of these garments and particularly impressed by the *style* with which the embassy representatives taught us to wear them.

If you are privileged to travel—to Mexico, the Caribbean Islands, Europe, Russia, or the Orient—try to choose as souvenirs beautifully worked blouses and dresses, scarves and shawls, and native jewelry. Incorporate them into your wardrobe to provide flair, interest, and individuality. Take particular note of how these items are worn during your visit and add this worldly touch to your fashion forte.

"Je ne sais quoi"

What constitutes that "je ne sais quoi" (that indefinable something) that transforms a mere garment into a work of art and makes the person wearing it shine? Her ability to pull it together and carry it off well.

For example, there is a story about the clever Duchesse de Fontanges, who was one of the Sun King's favorites in seventeenth-century France. She was pretty and blonde, and one day when she was out stag hunting with the King, her elaborate hairdo caught on the overhanging branch of a tree. She tied it up quickly atop her head with one of her lace and jeweled garters. The next day, all the ladies of the Court appeared with their hair tied up in lace and ribbon with a bow in front, determined to please the King equally. Hence, *Fontanges* (named for the duchess) became the fashionable headdress for the women of Louis XIV's Court. The person who makes fashion work for her is not a peacock, but has the Duchesse de Fontanges's gift for the "je ne sais quoi."

Beyond personal qualities, a number of precise elements interact to create fashion: line, color, texture, mass, and movement. A good designer combines these qualities and so does the inspired clothes wearer. It was a mark of distinction in ancient Rome not only to have the finest silk, cotton, or linen tunic (wool was for the lower classes), but also to know how to hold and move in it. The same was true of shawls in the 1820s and fans in the 1830s. As essential parts of the evening toilette, a woman had to know how to handle the accessory with grace. Coco Chanel brought a long rope of fake pearls into fashion because it complemented the elongated silhouette and muted colors of her designs, and also because the image of Coco twirling her loose-hanging necklace with her elegant hands was a beguiling sight.

When you learn what clothes are right for you—for your face, your figure, your personality, your lifestyle—you become immune to the "rages" of commercial trend-makers. You can always give a nod to a fad you would not care to invest in heavily by using a dash of the prevailing color or other detail without risking serious after-effects for your wardrobe, or your budget.

To reject passing fancies, and recognize timeless quality when you see it, first learn about what is *au courant* by browsing through your city's chic stores and looking through fashion magazines. The Italian and French *Vogue* are more aesthetically focused, American *Vogue* more consumer-practical, and British *Vogue* most traditional. Peruse museum catalogues, too, for authentic copies of historic belts, scarves, and jewelry to add a touch of the past to today.

A first step in learning who you really are is to take a good look at yourself and what you do. Then decide in which general category—sporty, tailored, romantic, or sophisticated—you feel the most comfortable. Remember that the choice is not a "till death do us part" commitment and certainly does not forbid some crossing over for variety and experimentation. You are growing and changing, although many important traits of your character and personality are set, and you probably have matured physically to the point where you can determine what type of clothing suits you best. This is the right time to start planning an integrated wardrobe of pieces that will work well together—a valuable, enjoyable learning experience.

60

The art of wardrobing is much more than shopping—especially for a contemporary woman who, in all likelihood, will be juggling her time between career, marriage, motherhood, and social and community activities. It is also caring for, regrouping, often repairing or altering clothing one already has—and these tasks should be a consideration when choosing each new purchase. It takes time to master this art, and now is the time for you to begin.

Shop At Home

Having learned from fashion history and about current trends and styles, the next step is to go through everything you own. This survey should include year-round items and carryovers from the preceding spring/summer or fall/winter seasons. Remember to inventory accessories—belts, scarves, hosiery, jewelry—and such specialized wearables as uniforms and athletic outfits.

Consider your clothes objectively, with the same open-minded interest you give to fashion photographs and store displays. You may find that your things are as attractive and appropriate to your needs as new items—or could easily be made so. Keep as much as you can. The price is right! Then decide what in your wardrobe you should dispose of—outgrown and worn garments, those that are uncomfortable, and those in which you have never had a good time. Discard after careful thought and perhaps a consultation with your mother or friend. Get rid of the clutter, but only after reserving one passable outfit for grubby jobs. Also, look for those classic items that your fashion sense tells you are certain to be in style from one season to the next. These should be packed away carefully, as should seasonal items. Be sure that all are cleaned and stored, safe from dust and destructive insects, so that the old favorites can be welcomed back into your wardrobe when the season changes.

With the clutter and seasonally inappropriate pieces out of the way, turn your room into a private boutique. Try on everything that remains in your on-hand wardrobe before a full-length mirror. Create as many combinations as possible, assembling the right underclothing, shoes, and other accessories. Examine each piece carefully, noting any need for cleaning, repair, or alteration. If you are clever with a needle you will be able to do much of the work yourself, or maybe your mother can help. If not, find a good seamstress. Once put in order, most of your clothes will probably be stylish for the new season if you choose just one added touch—a new belt, sash, or sweater.

Keep in mind the activities—school, parties, dating, church, sports events, and possibly vacations, work, or job—in which you and your clothes participate. Balance the collection against what you expect your schedule to be, making certain that your wardrobe is weighted in the direction of those activities that will fill the greater part of your time. School or work, for instance, will be less boring if you have sufficient and attractive variety in your daily wardrobe, even if such an emphasis means fewer "femme fatale" dresses for occasional parties. (And there may be more party invitations if you look chic in geometry class or at the office.)

Taking Stock

As you go over your on-hand clothing, take stock of yourself, too, asking the following questions:

- Has my body size, weight, height, proportion changed?
- Has my lifestyle changed?
- Has my attitude changed?
- Have my friends, school, or workplace changed?
- What amount of time do I have to devote to the upkeep of my wardrobe?
- What are my monetary limitations this season?
- What impression do I want to make?
- Do I want to make any changes in my current style?
- How can I express my adaptation of the season's trends without sacrificing my fashion statement?
- Is there a role—or roles—I would enjoy acting out through dressing as I seek to discover varied facets of my nature?

It will be helpful to make a lifestyle chart with the months of the year across the top and the activities in which you expect to participate under each, with the hours each of these will require. Now write down an "ideal" list of clothing you would like to have to carry you through the period and an approximate cost for each. Balance the total cost of the "wish list" against your clothes budget. If there is a discrepancy, decide where you can cut and still be attractively dressed at all times in keeping with the pattern of your community and your social group.

62

The Basics

Basics need not be boring! They are the mainstays of your wardrobe, the treasures upon which to sprinkle the sugar and spice of the season's trends. A good basic wardrobe is money in the bank, a wonderful resource for unexpected invitations. Now is the time to experiment with the wardrobing principle that suits, skirts, sweaters, coats, tailored and softly feminine daytime dresses are lifelong items, which require only a dash of accent to keep up with fashion.

Fancy party clothes, which rarely wear out, may be considered almost as costumes and need not be expensive at this stage of your life: Two or three basic formals will provide excellent mileage.

Shopping Sense

With your carryover wardrobe in A-1 condition and assessed against the demands of your lifestyle, it is now time to consider additions.

Go shopping alone—or with your mother or a single friend whose taste you trust. Avoid a pack attack. Many serious mistakes are made through impulse buying under pressure of a vocal group. Be sure that you are attractively dressed and fastidiously groomed, wearing the proper undergarments for the kinds of clothes you will be trying on. Find a salesperson and tell her what you are looking for. Listen to her suggestions if she impresses you as knowledgeable and sincere. Be sure that you return garments to hangers if you decide against buying them and let the salesperson know your decision.

When searching for items to perk up the clothes you already have, consider versatility. Do not choose a costly sweater that goes with nothing in your closet, or that complements a skirt that may have only one more season left. If picking the season's trend, choose only what you feel has the staying power to become a tradition and what works well with your on-hand wardrobe inventory. Never pick a trend if you feel you could wear it for one season only. Treat yourself to a touch of today's trends but also invest in timeless traditions—select the best quality you can afford.

Do not overlook underclothing. Not only are the right undergarments important in achieving a finished look, but fresh and pretty ones make you feel lovely and feminine. "Have more than you show; tell less than you know" was my mother's motto, and she insisted that pretty "undies" were more important than fancy dresses. As for the second part of that saying, it, too, is applicable to wardrobing: To discuss the price of anything is never in good taste.

Once your basic wardrobe is ready to go, you can consider the fun, trendy things, the "dessert" that follows a well-balanced meal. But as with a chocolate sundae, a little goes a long way. Remember that you will soon tire of the splashy, especially if *everyone* is wearing it, and you will begin to feel that you have lost your identity and taken a step backward from a style of your own. And remember that establishing a personal style is your goal.

Accessories After the Fact

The addition of accents, known as accessorizing, is, first of all, a way to make an outfit yours, even if the clothes themselves came off a rack of similar or identical items. The careful, creative use of accessories is a young woman's first venture into dressing as an art.

And there are some very practical advantages to accessorizing. You can change a classic dress or suit from work, school, or street use to a dinner or party look just by substituting elegant earrings, necklaces, belts, lace collars, or flowers. This is a wonderful resource for the traveler, the weekend houseguest, or the school or working woman who must move from classroom or office directly to dinner date.

Accessory switching is also useful in making seasonal transitions. Black patent or kid pumps and bag, dark jewelry and belt or bow, provide a crisp fall look to a summer outfit when the calendar says the time has arrived to look autumn but the weatherman persists in predicting 90-degree days. You can reverse the procedure in April when spring is tardy and your spirits race ahead.

An accessory is almost anything you wear except the basic clothes—shoes, hats, gloves, belts, scarves, bows, and, of course, jewelry (costume or real)— and all accessories should be chosen in relation to your size. If you are small or short, choose scaled-down items that will not appear to be wearing you, and take satisfaction in the knowledge that exquisite and dainty can be memorable. If you are tall or have a larger frame, you can handle big and dramatic pieces magnificently.

Keep your accessories in good taste and the best of condition. Scuffed shoes, chipped jewelry, crushed bows, and spotted scarves can spoil a total effect.

Accessory Smart

- Moderation is the key. Never overdecorate your body.
- Your accessories should be appropriate to the occasion, your age, and to the company in which they are worn. Earrings in the shape of watermelons, for instance, which are fun for a group of your own friends, might be quite inappropriate when accompanying your parents or business associates to a gathering.
- Be certain that you do not rattle when you move because of an arm loaded with too many bracelets or a neck or chest armored with beads and trinkets.
- Day and night call for different accessories. So do city and country occasions. If you are in doubt about what is right, keep add-ons to a minimum.
- Avoid ostentation, especially the wearing of expensive jewelry in groups where others do not have or wear it. (Young women should not wear costly pieces in public as a safety, as well as a taste, consideration.) Even mature women today usually wear costume or imitation jewelry except for very special occasions and keep the real items in the safe deposit box.
- After you have it all together, take a final glance in the mirror. If you have doubts, take something off.

The Laws of Proportion

Throughout my years in fashion, both as a model and as a fashion director, I have come to rely on The Laws of Proportion—those fashion rules that camouflage the poor lines of your figure and accentuate the good. As a beginning, look at the following drawing of two vertical lines.

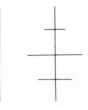

The Laws of Proportion

Although both are one inch in length, notice that the broken line looks shorter than the unbroken one. This is the first law of proportion. Among them you will find ways to counteract every possible figure flaw, and if you study them carefully and practice with the clothes already in your wardrobe, you will avoid costly errors when you go out shopping. The Laws of Proportion—practiced along with the perfect posture we discussed in Chapter 2—are my best method of attack against a figure's shortcomings.

The Laws of Proportion

1. *An unbroken line appears longer.* Contrasting colors, two-piece dresses, skirts and blouses, belts, horizontal stripes, large bands of color, or any horizontal lines make you appear shorter and add breadth to your figure.
2. *Height gives the illusion of slenderness.* Dress for height, breaking the vertical line only if your figure and height are correctly proportioned.
3. *Light colors add weight.* Whites and pastels will give the visual illusion of adding pounds to your body. Make it a point to place them only where this addition is needed.
4. *Dark colors diminish weight.* From the color palette place those colors in the dark to darkest range on areas of your body that require visual reduction of weight.
5. *Light-reflective and shiny fabrics add weight.* Satin, sequins, brocades, or metallic materials visually add pounds to your body. Place them only where this addition is needed or as very small fashion touches.
6. *Bulky or heavy fabrics add weight.* Angoras, tweeds, heavy knits, corduroy, or nubby fabrics add bulk and pounds to your figure.
7. *Large patterns add weight.* Large plaids, checks, florals, and geometrics each add the illusion of weight to the body. Large pastel or light-colored patterns add even more weight.
8. *Small patterns diminish weight.* Small plaids, checks, florals, and geometrics each give the illusion of less weight. Small dark patterns visually diminish the weight of your body even further.
9. *Transparent or clinging fabrics reveal figure faults and perfections.* Knitted fabrics, jerseys, laces, and chiffons should be placed on parts of your body that you want to emphasize rather than on problem areas.

The Laws of Proportion

10. *Scaled-to-size accessories are the secret to balance.* Small accessories should be assigned to the small and/or short figure. Large accessories should be assigned to the larger and/or tall figure.
11. *Every detail and every accessory must be coordinated with every other detail and accessory of the total ensemble.* This rule applies from head to toe, and from the front, sides, and back of your figure.
12. *Dramatize your good points.* Select clothing to "show off" your assets.
13. *Do not dramatize a weak point by dramatizing a good one.* Should a good point, when dramatized, accentuate or call attention to a weak point in return, the good has been undone by the bad!

Taking Care

The "sine qua non" (without which nothing) of good taste in dress is garments and accessories in perfect order. As a fashionable young woman, you will want to assume the full responsibility for the upkeep of your wardrobe.

A thoughtful young woman does not leave clothing she has worn lying around her bedroom or bath, even if the actual laundering is to be done by someone else. Clothing requires constant care. Every day, soiled items should be put aside for laundering or cleaning and necessary repairs. All clothing should be returned to proper hangers—rubber or foam-covered or lovely scented satin ones for sweaters and delicate blouses or dresses, hangers with rubber-coated clips for skirts. Use shaped jacket hangers for blazers. Clothing should hang outside the closet overnight before being returned to its place within a closed area. Shoes should be stuffed with tissue or with cedar (never metal) shoe trees to retain their shape and should be cleaned and polished when necessary.

No Skeletons in Your Closet

Think of your closet as a resource for your lifestyle. Your closet should be set up exactly like a fine specialty shop. It must be scrupulously clean and free of junk. Blouses, skirts, sweaters, dresses should be grouped together. Colors should be arranged to spark your imagination. Shoes should be stored in marked boxes at eye level for quick selection. Robes and longer dresses should be hung so that they do not touch the floor. One section of the closet might be double-racked to hang pants, skirts, blouses.

Your dresser drawers should also be cleaned frequently and lined—with scented paper if you choose—and should be partitioned to store panties, bras, slips, socks, and hosiery. The latter are best protected in ziplock plastic bags. Belts can be hung on a man's tie rack inside the closet door.

The time spent on keeping your clothes in order will be repaid when you do not have to hunt for things while dressing for an important party or when you have overslept on a school morning; as an added bonus, your clothes will last longer and look better.

Your Search for Style

To achieve true style your clothing and accessories must complement—and compliment—your body and be an expression of your individuality. This does not mean that you can ignore style and fashion, which, incidentally, are not synonymous. Style is timeless and fashion is changing, current, even trendy. Style is lasting and durable while fashion is fickle and commercial. Style is the best of all past fashions—the features that have proven to be the most flattering, the most comfortable, and the most practical.

Unlike fashion, you cannot buy style. With sufficient money you can go out and purchase a total seasonal "look," but style you must cultivate yourself through a knowledge of what is really beautiful and lasting. It takes honesty and discipline to evaluate yourself in relation to trends, but style is a priceless quality and one that animates the lifeless garments you wear. Style must be natural rather than affected, and it usually takes time to acquire—but one is never too young to start.

Dressing for the Occasion

Dressing for the occasion not only upgrades manners, it also enhances the poise and personality of the hostess and her guests and sparks their spirits. In order that you may unravel the many phrases that are used to describe the manner of dress appropriate to a given social occasion, I have provided The Terms of Dress.

Becoming Befitting

You must develop an eye for fashion, flair, and style just as you develop an ear for opera or a taste for caviar. However, fashion, flair, and style must be developed under the umbrella of good taste. Many times it is just as difficult to dress appropriately and in good taste for an occasion as it is to behave in a mannerly fashion once you arrive. There are as many temptations to misbehave in dress as there are in conduct. To avoid them, let good taste be your motto. In dressing to present yourself properly to others—and to pass the test of the first impression—try to:

- Dress properly to befit the occasion
- Interpret the season's fashion based upon the timeless qualities of past traditions
- Incorporate individual flair and style
- Keep a keen sense of appropriateness not only to the occasion but also to your figure, lifestyle and age

---

The Terms of Dress

Casual
Casual dress denotes sports or relaxed attire and is appropriate for barbecues, patio and pool parties, casual suppers, sporting events. If guests are to engage in the sport, the tennis dress or shorts, or swimsuit may be worn. Otherwise, trousers (long or short) and shirts without ties with a sweater or a sports jacket or blazer (depending upon the weather) are suitable for a man. A woman may choose slacks or skirts. Skirts may be mini, short, mid-calf, or long, but only of daytime fabrics.

Informal
Informal dress before six o'clock signifies an afternoon dress for the woman and for the man "coat and tie" (which before six in the evening may be a sports jacket or blazer worn with a tie) or a dark or light business suit (depending upon the season and geographical location). With the exception of the late-afternoon party that may extend beyond six o'clock or the informal supper, to which the afternoon dress is worn by the woman and the sports jacket or blazer optional for the man, after six o'clock the woman may wear a very dressy afternoon dress or a short or long cocktail, party, or dinner dress or suit of a dressy but conservative fabric; a dark or light business suit is worn by the man.

Semiformal
Semiformal dress connotes that the woman wears short or long cocktail, party, or dinner dress or suit of a dressy to very dressy fabric; evening dress with jacket. Before six o'clock, the man wears a dark suit and after six may wear a dark suit or a dinner jacket with a black silk bow tie (properly referred to as dinner jacket, "black tie," or *le smoking*, but commonly called "tuxedo" or "tux").

As the years pass and you have the opportunity to dress for a variety of events and occasions, your expertise will develop along with your instinct in knowing what clothing is appropriate and in good taste. With patience, study, exposure, expert guidance, and trial and error, your good taste will become refined and cultivated.

Until your expertise and good taste become fully developed—and even afterward—please remember that it is more important to adhere to the rules of appropriateness than to the dictates of fashion.

Formal

Formal dress means the woman wears a late afternoon dress and the man a dark suit before six o'clock in the evening. After six o'clock, formal dress falls into two categories: "Black tie" and "White tie."

"Black Tie"

"Black tie" denotes a double- or single-breasted dinner jacket with satin or grosgrain faille lapels; matching trousers without cuffs and with a narrow strip of faille or satin down the sides to match the lapels of the dinner jacket; starched white shirt with tucked front and wing or folded collar and French cuffs, worn with studs and cufflinks; black satin bow tie; black patent shoes and black silk stockings; and gray chamois or buckskin gloves. When the man wears "black tie," the woman wears a long or short dinner dress (or evening separates), which, if strapless or extremely bare, is worn with a matching or coordinated jacket.

"White Tie"

"White tie" denotes full-dress. The woman wears a ball gown and real jewelry if she has it. Long above-the-elbow, eighteen-button, white glacé kid gloves may be worn with sleeveless gowns. Gloves need not be removed when passing through the receiving line or dancing but are removed when one eats or drinks. The man wears a long black tailcoat with satin lapels and matching trousers with a narrow braid stripe; black patent pumps and black silk stockings; white piqué waistcoat; starched white shirt with bib front and French cuffs of piqué, worn with studs and cufflinks; white piqué bow tie; and white kid or bleached chamois gloves. When "White tie" or "*tenue de soirée*" (evening dress) is written on the invitation to any public event, full decorations—medals, orders, and miniatures—may automatically be worn by the man or the woman, or either may select the one decoration most appropriate to the particular occasion. Decorations are not worn to a private party unless the hostess's invitation reads "White Tie and Decorations."

CHAPTER 4

The Jewel Box

As your aesthetic senses are refined and your horizons widen, your appreciation of beauty will extend beyond your vision of yourself and include the natural wonders of the world around you. At the same time, you are certain to develop a desire to capture something of the environment's inimitable perfection and to incorporate it into your own image. Coincidentally, this leap in discrimination comes at the very moment you are maturing and moving from a social life of backyard barbecues and gymnasium hops to a more sophisticated scene, when it is appropriate for you to begin choosing quality rather than splash in your accessories. Real jewelry now appears, at proper moments, as an accent.

Perhaps you have always known instinctively the difference between real and imitation, and even as a child prized the birthstone ring your grandparents gave you more than the plastic one you found in a cereal box. There is nothing wrong with costume jewelry, but you are now at an age to start appreciating authenticity.

As you reach the maturity to love beautiful and valuable things and to assume the responsibility of caring for them, take a fresh look at the pieces your parents or other relatives have given you since birth: add-a-pearl necklaces, charm bracelets, dainty gold chains, class and other rings—all are an ideal beginning. Appropriate pieces from your mother's girlhood make wonderful additions, too. Treasure these things, which have sentimental as well as intrinsic value. Later will come the more expensive jewels to mark highlights of your life—engagement, marriage, the birth of children, anniversaries, professional achievements. They will be yours to wear, to appreciate, to enjoy. But remember, displaying jewelry for ostentatious, show-off purposes cheapens both the articles and the wearer.

Some women seem to have a talent for wearing gorgeous and expensive jewels without flaunting them, allowing a single piece to shine, never overdoing it. Certainly this is a talent well worth cultivating.

The Precious Past

Jewelry was once ceremonial, serious, conspicuous, and only for the high and mighty. From the dawn of history people have always loved, even worshipped, rare and colorful stones and fine metals. Possessors of such treasures have been murdered for them, wars have been fought, nations despoiled.

For a long time only elite members of society could wear jewels. In France, a law was established in 1283 forbidding anyone but the nobility to wear precious stones or pearls. In England, King Edward II decreed that only certain classes could wear specific ornaments—craftsmen and yeomen were forbidden gold or silver and only nobles and merchants of stated income could own precious stones.

Although such laws were mainly a means of establishing class distinction, the rulers also feared that the poor would sink into hopeless debt if they were allowed to acquire such expensive items. In France as late as 1720, the regent forbade the wearing of pearls, diamonds, and other gems by the common people.

In our society today, such laws are unthinkable, and beautiful pieces are widely affordable. Jewelry has, moreover, become an art form and an expression not only of the wearer's taste but her moods—it plays a significant role in image creation. For this reason, a young woman should be quite careful in the selection and wearing of jewelry, avoiding the faddish and seeking out the timeless.

This chapter will present some facts about precious stones and noble metals which will be of help to you as you start to acquire a collection of jewelry. I will also guide you to an understanding and appreciation of simple elegance in design, and dignity and restraint in the wearing. At the same time, I want to awaken you to an exciting trend, which is for fine craftsmen to explore jewelry-making as an art, often using stones that, because of small size or weight, were not considered acceptable for jewelry in previous eras. The results are often beautiful, dramatic pieces that are somewhat less costly, and youthful in spirit, yet of superb quality.

The Noble Metals

The distinguishing feature of fine jewelry as opposed to costume jewelry is that it is fashioned of quality metals and that any stones used are genuine—natural creations of nature. Platinum, gold, and silver are the metals used almost exclusively by jewelers because of their beauty, malleability, rarity, and resultant value.

Platinum. The rarest of these metals, platinum is silvery blond, very pale. It is usually alloyed with ten percent iridium to increase its hardness and is considered by many to be the most effective enhancer of colored gems and diamonds. Because it has commercial and dental use and is never in large supply, it is expensive. Platinum is more often the choice of older rather than younger wearers.

Gold. The gleaming aura of gold, together with other qualities, has made it the most prized of metals and the most suitable as a foil for gems. In its natural state, gold is extremely soft, not durable enough for use in jewelry. Therefore it is combined with appropriate alloys to give it strength and serviceability. The proportion of the gold content in any metalwork is measured in karats, with 14k being the minimum acceptable in fine jewelry. At 18k, the percentage of gold in a piece is three-fourths of its total weight, while 24k is considered fine gold.

Silver. Found in more generous quantities than either platinum or gold, silver has many industrial, electrical, and medical uses in addition to its role as material for the fashioning of fine tablewear, art objects, and jewelry. Although it is lustrous, beautiful, and malleable, silver has one disadvantage not shared by its noble sisters. At normal temperatures it unites with sulfur and forms sulfide (tarnish), making regular polishing necessary. Silver is less expensive than platinum or gold and makes a splendid foil for colorful gems. It always has value as a contrast for gold pieces and achieves additional status in seasons when certain colors dominate the fashion picture.

Marking Time

Often, the first piece of adult jewelry in a lifetime collection is a jeweled watch. A handsome timepiece is among the most appropriate of gifts for a young woman stepping into a time when her responsibilities, career, and social commitments demand precision. Graduation, social debut, and sixteenth, eighteenth, or twenty-first birthdays are among the traditional occasions for such a present.

The attractive and inexpensive electronic watches now available are good for sports, work, classes, and other informal activities, but for dress occasions a fine watch (or none at all) is in order. If you can, have two watches, one more delicate and dressy for night and the other more sporty for day. By strictest standards, no watch is proper for a woman to wear with formal evening attire; but that prohibition has been relaxed, and now if the watch is small and the bracelet beautiful and elegant, it is acceptable for evening. The watch face is customarily turned to the inside, or hidden beneath its cover, if one is wearing a formal gown. Do not, however, look at it too often and *never* wind or shake it during a gala evening.

The finest watches in the world are produced around Lake Geneva, and a highlight of the European finishing tour of L'Ecole des Ingénues is a visit to the little factory of Piaget in the Swiss mountain village of Côte-aux-Fées (Hillside of the Fairies). From this enchanting spot came the ultra-thin watch, the real gemstone dial, and the polished crystal face and back, which allow the interior workings to be seen.

"Jeweled" watches were introduced in the mid-eighteenth century to improve performance: Ruby chips were put in the spoked wheel of the workings so the axis's top and bottom turned against the jewels and lasted longer. Hence, a "jeweled" watch is not necessarily "be-jeweled."

When shopping for a watch, I always suggest that a young woman establish her budget, and then put the total amount into the watch case and the movement (workings). She can then buy a simple yet smart strap of black or brown suede, leather, or skin, or a band of a favorite color (you might have a set of them to interchange with the seasons). A band of silver, gold, or platinum can always be added later.

The Pearl

When society dresses up, the occasion is illuminated by the glow of pearls. Pearls are elegant, understated, and formal.

Pearls are singularly versatile, suitable for all formal gatherings, day or night, which makes them a *must* for a beginning or limited jewelry wardrobe. Today, moreover, they are comparatively reasonable in price, thanks to experimentation in Japan during the latter part of the last century, which led to the "farming" of oysters for pearls.

The Pearl Necklace

Styles

Dog Collar	A wide choker, usually of multiple strands with a jeweled clasp often worn in front.
Collar	A 12- to 14-inch-long necklace fitted and shaped gently to the lower portion of the neck.
Bib	A necklace with more than three strands of different lengths, which fits close to the base of the neck and extends over the upper part of the chest much as a child's bib.
Choker	A 15- to 16-inch-long necklace that drops just above the collarbone.
Princess	An 18- to 20-inch-long strand of pearls that falls midway between the collarbone and the bust.
Matinee	A 20- to 24-inch-long strand of pearls that reaches the center of the bust.
Opera	A 30- to 32-inch-long strand of pearls that falls midway between the bust and waist. May be wrapped around the neck twice to form a double-stranded choker.
Rope	A 45-inch or longer pearl necklace. May be knotted or wrapped several times. Also referred to as a "sautoir" or a lariat.

Terminology

Graduated	A pearl necklace that is strung with the smaller pearls placed on either side of the clasp graduating to the largest pearls in the center.
Uniform	A pearl necklace that is strung with all one size or nearly equal-sized pearls throughout.
Knotted	A term used to denote that the string running through the pearls has been tied in a tiny knot between each pearl and before the clasp. An important step for safety should the string break, this technique also helps the necklace to hang gracefully.

Prior to that pearls were, like diamonds, rubies, and emeralds, a gift of nature—inimitable, unique, created through a chance occurrence. When a foreign object gets inside an oyster shell, the creature's reaction is to coat it

Top to bottom: choker, princess, matinee, opera

The Pearl Necklace Styles

with the crystalline substance called nacre, which lines its shell, and the result is a beautiful, natural pearl. This is also the most valuable type of pearl, worth thirty times the value of "cultured" pearls.

The Japanese efforts led to the artificial implantation of "seeds" into oysters. The shellfish are then returned to "beds," and the pearls can be harvested in three or four years. This process enormously increased the supply of available pearls and served to keep the price down despite an increased demand. Even an expert has difficulty distinguishing a farmed, "cultured" pearl from natural specimens—either the saltwater variety or the natural freshwater type.

Pearls are assessed according to color, luster, roundness, and thickness of the nacre. Some people prefer irregularly shaped pearls (baroque), but the most perfectly round, finely lustered are the most prized.

Pearls come in a vast array of colors, tones, sizes, and shapes; and their settings—necklaces, earrings, bracelets, pins—are almost as limitless. For the first pearl necklace a young woman receives, I suggest a princess-length strand (5 to 7 mm in size depending on her height and frame) and the gems should be all the same size, not graduated. The princess length can be combined beautifully with a later gift or purchase of a matinee length composed of the same or a larger-size pearl, again, not graduated. Later, an opera-length string can be added. If you enjoy wearing one long strand—which you can also turn into a multiple-strand necklace—the pearl rope is the perfect finale to a gem trousseau. I personally feel that the choker is not flattering to many faces as it creates a horizontal line.

Pearl Care

Remember that pearls are produced by living things—they are not minerals like most gems. They need air and also warmth, and therefore become more beautiful with wear. But they are also sensitive and tender and damaged by perspiration—remove them during sporting activities. If you have very oily skin, that oil can penetrate the "skin" of the pearls and dim their glow. Thus it is necessary to have pearls cleaned at regular intervals by a professional—unless you learn and can carry out the special care yourself. They should be wiped with a damp cloth or washed gently with a mild soap and rinsed well, then dried and left out overnight on a dry towel. Avoid spraying hairspray and perfume directly on them, and store in a separate, velvet-lined box to prevent scratching by gold pieces or other, sharper stones. Never store pearls in plastic bags, as they need air.

The Gemstones

Certain stones—the sapphire, ruby, emerald, and diamond—are classified "precious" and are used in the finest jewelry. The opal, garnet, aquamarine, rubellite, topaz, turquoise, lapis, amethyst, and jade are considered "semiprecious." The somewhat arbitrary differentiation was made by German mineralogist K. E. Kluge in 1860, based on the stones' relative hardness. He allowed only the ruby, emerald, and sapphire into the "precious" category with the diamond, although none of them approaches the hardness of the diamond.

Today, all beautiful stones are highly prized, and the term "gemstone" has practically replaced the precious and semiprecious classifications. The line between "fine" and "costume" jewelry has blurred in recent years, as the design of certain types of jewelry has become more creative—although fine artists still insist on natural stones and fine metals. French designer Jean Schlumberger may have begun the trend in the 1930s with his plant- and animal-inspired pieces. From the Art Nouveau and Art Deco periods came other innovative designers like Vever, Foquet, and Lalique in Paris, and Tiffany in New York, who used gemstones and fine metals in exciting, interpretive ways. Important gemstone pieces today command prices in the thousands of dollars, and smaller, less perfect stones have a ready market for fashion jewelry. The very presence of either brings pleasure!

The Diamond

Although diamonds are probably what you think of first when you think of jewels—associated in your mind with romance, glamour, and sophistication—you are apt to possess other gems before you receive a diamond, most often an engagement gift from one's future husband. At that moment you will surely have a far greater appreciation of the beauty and value of this most glorious of stones, and also a deeper understanding of the enduring love for which diamonds have become the symbol.

The diamond engagement ring has an interesting history. Although the ancient Egyptians wore a bridal ring on the third finger, left hand, it was not until the fifteenth century that the diamond was recorded as a bridal jewel. Then in 1477 the Archduke Maximilian of Austria ordered two rings for his bride-to-be, Mary of Burgundy. One was a diamond engagement ring, the other a wedding band of gold.

For a long time, because of their rarity and cost, diamond engagement rings were limited to the wealthy aristocracy. But by 1870, when the great diamond mines of South Africa were discovered and the industrial revolution had created a prosperous middle class, diamonds became more widely available, with considerable variation, of course, in size and quality. It was to make the most of each stone that the Tiffany setting—in which platinum prongs hold the gem away from the metal to produce greater brilliance—became popular. White or yellow gold or platinum are the choice for a diamond's setting. In addition to their beauty and sentimental value, diamonds are an excellent investment. If purchased from reputable dealers, their monetary worth climbs steadily.

Made of pure or nearly pure carbon, diamonds are the hardest substance known. They are one hundred and twenty times harder than the next hardest material—rubies or sapphires. Steel cannot cut a diamond, only another diamond can.

The four factors that influence a diamond's price are called the four C's: cutting, color, clarity, and carat weight. The lower part of the diamond is the "pavilion," which acts like an automobile headlight, gathering the light and forcing it out the top in a concentrated beam. The upper part, called the crown, acts as a series of prisms on the light beam, dispersing it in a myriad of dazzling colored flashes. Even poor diamonds, when cut in proportion to the rays of light reflecting up through the top facets, can be spectacular.

Most diamonds, however, are not cut ideally, but rather to lose as little stone as possible, and they are less brilliant and flash less fire. Brilliance depends on the path of the beam of light traveling through the stone. There are fifty-eight tiny facets on the cut diamond. Think of them as mirrors. The cutter must place each of them in exact geometric relation to the others to achieve maximum fire and brilliance. The cutter who sacrifices brilliance for size is "padding" the diamond. When you choose a diamond, whatever its size, look for brilliance and fire. It is something you can see. Larger carat weight does not always mean a better gem. Study The Basic Gem Styles below as you select your favorite.

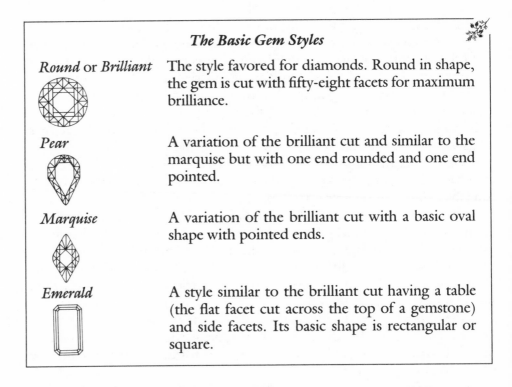

The Basic Gem Styles

Round or Brilliant
The style favored for diamonds. Round in shape, the gem is cut with fifty-eight facets for maximum brilliance.

Pear
A variation of the brilliant cut and similar to the marquise but with one end rounded and one end pointed.

Marquise
A variation of the brilliant cut with a basic oval shape with pointed ends.

Emerald
A style similar to the brilliant cut having a table (the flat facet cut across the top of a gemstone) and side facets. Its basic shape is rectangular or square.

The word *carat* comes from India's carob tree, the seeds of which were so uniform in weight that they became the standard for measuring gems, with one one-hundredth of a carat referred to as a "point." The smallest solitaire offered by leading jewelers is fifteen points or .15 carat. Size does increase the value of a good diamond for the simple reason that large stones are rarer than small ones, and so a two-carat diamond is worth more than twice as much as a one-carat stone of the same quality.

The traditional diamond color is white, but most stones contain slight pink, green, red, blue, yellow, or brown tints. The more colorless the diamond, the greater its rarity and value. Flawless diamonds are extremely rare. If one is magnified sufficiently, it is possible to find tiny carbon spots, feathers, or faint flaws in most. These are called "inclusions." A diamond is said to be flawless if no inclusions can be seen when the diamond is magnified ten times by the jeweler's loupe.

For most women, the price of a diamond is secondary and never discussed. The world was startled when the cost (28,500 English pounds, approximately $50,000) of the sapphire and diamond engagement ring that Prince Charles purchased for his princess-to-be, Lady Diana Spencer, was made public by the London papers. This "coup" was possible because the piece was listed in the catalogue of Garrard jewelers—Queen Elizabeth's only crown jeweler. As arbiters of good taste, neither the jeweler nor the royal family would have revealed the price.

Take Care

Because jewels are valuable, personally meaningful, and small, they require special, constant care. They should never be left thoughtlessly in dressing rooms, hotel rooms, or at home, especially in bathrooms and kitchens, which are the scenes of many down-the-drain tragedies.

Jewelry should, instead, be safely stored—in separate, lined containers for important pieces so that they will not scratch or otherwise damage each other. Plastic bags are not recommended.

Regular maintenance is necessary. Professional cleaning and checking for the security of the stones' settings should be done at least once a year. Silver jewelry should be cleaned like flat tableware with silver polish. Electronic cleaning works wonders on gold. (A small home unit for electronic cleaning is available.) Valuable necklaces should be restrung for beauty of hanging and for safety at five-year intervals.

If you have several good pieces, you will want to insure them. Do not flaunt costly jewelry in public, both for your own safety and for the safety of your treasures.

A young woman is not ready to begin accumulating a jewelry wardrobe until she has an appreciation of a jewel's creation. You must take knowledgeable care of pieces you own, and you must take care also to wear them only at appropriate times and with appropriate clothing. Just as a diamond, or other gem, must be polished so must its wearer.

CHAPTER 5

Fragrant Notes

If you happen to be starting this chapter at a time when the out-of-doors is fresh and sweet, before you read on, go to an open window. Close your eyes and take a deep breath, and in a moment your focus will change from things seen to an exquisite enjoyment of fragrance permeating your being.

Until now, we have been concerned with your "look"—creating a lovely picture that will not only bring pleasure to others but give you confidence as well. Now we turn to something you wear that will never be seen by anyone, but is a beautiful and important aspect of "finishing" your unique self—an enveloping, delicious scent.

As a maturing young woman, you probably have realized already that using fragrance involves more than soaking yourself with the atomizer on your dressing table. Perfume is a glorious, but complicated, form of self-expression, for which selection and restraint are as essential as they are in the choice of garments. It is no more appropriate to wear a heavy, sensual perfume with your tennis outfit than it would be to wear riding boots with an evening gown. And since the interaction of body chemistry and perfume compounds is unpredictable and highly individual, knowledge, fore-thought, and discrimination are necessary.

The very first thing to understand is that perfume is not to be used as a cover-up. The delicate combinations can release their messages only in an environment of cleanliness and health—despite the fact that the development of perfumery was probably an attempt to compensate for the absence of plumbing and accompanying lack of personal hygiene in premodern times.

Scented and spiced balms and liquid extracts have been used by the nobility from antiquity, but perfumery as an industry did not come into being until the Middle Ages. By 1190, France was established as the center for the creation of wonderful fragrances, which were used extravagantly in the increasingly lavish courts of Europe. During the French Renaissance, the Sun King was proclaimed "the sweetest smelling monarch." The Emperor Napoleon is recorded as having used sixty bottles of cologne a month. (One can only wonder how effective even these gallons of perfume were in combating the effects of limited soap and water washes!)

Today's enjoyment of adequate, often luxurious, bathing facilities throughout the Western world has changed the role of perfume from cover-up to subtle enhancer. Sophisticated women go to great trouble and no small expense to discover a scent or scents that complement not only their body chemistry but their personalities and lifestyles as well.

The use of scent as an important aspect of self-presentation became widespread in the more democratic world that emerged following the American and French Revolutions. Again, the French led the way. Partly due to the mild climate of southern France, where flowers grow profusely most of the year, and partly as a result of the French emphasis on luxury and sensuality, perfume was in great demand throughout the nineteenth century. Stylish women in other lands including America increasingly insisted upon French perfumes, which became something of a status symbol.

Beginning with this century, an array of glamour perfumes appeared as a part of the developing fashion industry. In 1921, designer Coco Chanel presented her incomparable Chanel No. 5, and became the first designer to offer an image label in France. Others followed, but it was not until 1969 that an American, Norman Norell, came out with a designer-label fragrance, simply called Norell. Now most of the leading fashion trend-setters have their own perfume lines.

Discovering Your Fragrance

For decades, women chose their personal fragrances on the basis of label. Although there is something exciting about wearing a signature scent, that is not the prime consideration today. Women no longer wear perfume for the symbol alone. They choose first to please themselves, to complete their own personal image. So much the better if it is individual and original.

Yet one does not ignore the classics. It is lovely to be able to recognize a scent as it wafts into a room. Classics endure because they convey an image. They are elegant and make one feel richly good about oneself. So as you begin trying perfumes, you will want to get to know a few of the more enduring classics. If you always wear the same fragrance, you may become so accustomed to it that your delight is diminished. As a changing young woman, it is important for you to diversify your perfume wardrobe. So let us study the makeup of fragrances as we search for the scents most suited to you.

The lily, signifying "innocence," is lovely as a first fragrance. Other scents, such as the Bulgarian rose, are heavier or more sophisticated. Some perfumes—honeysuckle, camellia, lily of the valley—whisper, while others like Oriental spices make a very bold statement and are better left until you are older. Tea olive is a floral perfume which is very feminine. So is jasmine. They both make me think of high-necked, frilly blouses and heart-shaped lockets. Florals set a party mood, but sometimes you want a fragrance that plays up your sporty or intellectual self. The gentle spice aroma of the carnation and lemon blossom seems to awaken the thought processes. Cedar and sandlewood are reminiscent of the woods and are out-of-doorsy.

If you like one fragrance in a line, try others. Most offer a range from sporty to romantic; fragrances for day, for night; for town, or country wear. A young woman who comes across as prim and sprightly may want to add mystery to an evening with an Oriental spice scent. If you want a sporty fragrance, you might even try one labeled "men's."

By sampling, you will learn what is right for your various moods, changing activities, and different associations. But remember, each scent sends a different message. You can even wear perfume in two levels using scents that are possible "twins." A soft, romantic perfume can enhance personality, but you must know yourself: You may not be able to carry off the sophistication of an enchanting fragrance any more than you can maintain the "cool" of the First Lady wearing a couture gown.

Shopping Scents

A "perfume bar" is an exciting place to shop seriously for a scent. Here, many brands can be tested and sampled. As the purchase of a fragrance is an investment, both of your personality and your budget, I suggest my four-part method for selecting a personal fragrance, using "touch papers," as outlined on page 83.

The "touch papers" are a favorite of mine, and the ingénues are introduced to them when we visit Parfums Caron on the Avenue Montaigne in Paris. Parfums Caron supplies long touch papers, which the expert dips, one at a time, into the large, antique, Baccarat crystal urns containing fragrances. She passes these to each ingénue, who fans them in the air to consider the bouquets. When we return the following day, each ingénue's choice is drawn into a tiny crystal bottle from one of the large urns, under the shimmer of an enormous crystal chandelier.

Reminiscent of the French Court *Parfumeur* is the tiny Hové Parfumeur which, in its eighteenth-century French Quarter home in New Orleans, has served as an inspiration to many wonderful shops devoted exclusively to fragrances. In such intimate shops as these, you can chat with the experts about your lifestyle and clothes and receive advice on the perfect scent for you.

Four-Part Method for Selecting A Personal Fragrance

1. *"Touch Papers"*
   Cut five or six strips from coffee filters that have no scent of their own. Take them with you to the perfumery and have them dipped into your favorite over-the-counter fragrances. Be certain to write the name of the fragrance on the strip. Take these strips home and sniff them at various times; when your favorites among your favorites evolve, return to the perfume counter for step #2.
2. *Perfume Samples*
   When you revisit the perfume counter, request samples of your three or four top favorites. Take these home with you.
3. *The Wrist Test*
   In the morning (with no other perfume worn) apply only one of the fragrance samples, a drop on each wrist. Wear this sample only for one day. Do the same until all samples have been experienced.
4. *The Purchase*
   Return to the perfume counter and purchase *the* favorite. Wear it now as your very own!

Personal Chemistry

One of the most important things you will learn in selecting a fragrance is that every perfume is a chameleon, altering with human contact. Thus the bouquet you receive, and impart, will depend on how the perfume "takes"— mixes with the chemistry of your skin. Dark complexions hold fragrances differently than fair skin, and fragrance experts point to the "dry-down" effect, the fact that it takes about ten minutes for the true scent to develop and for you to know its true identity.

When shopping for perfume, it helps to start with one you have already tried. If you are ready for a change and want a slightly different aroma, tell the salesperson what you have been wearing and ask to have one wrist sprayed with a more dramatic and mysterious scent. And if spring is in the air and you would like to try something flowery but a bit more subtle than you have had before, request that your other wrist be sprayed with a lighter floral fragrance.

The Basic Perfume Classes

There are eight basic classes of perfume as described below. As your knowledge increases and your senses are educated through experimentation, you will soon know which classes react best with your skin oils.

The Basic Perfume Classes

Single Floral
This captures the scent of a single flower such as a rose, carnation, violet, or lilac and has a dominant floral note. It is easy to wear and recognize. For the one who has a favorite flower it is easy to choose. The white and light-colored flowers make the most perfumy scents.

Floral Bouquet
A fragrance composition based on a combination of floral scents. The major components of this family are rose, jasmine, gardenia, carnation, as well as such favorites as lily of the valley and lilac. The blend is intricate, with the flowers given balance and body by a combination of bases like ambergris, musk, and vetiver.

Spicy
This word in perfume language means fragrances with strong ("pungent") scents from several sources. Spicy scents are made of actual spices like vanilla, cinnamon, cloves, ginger, and cardamon, and flowers that possess traces of spicy scents such as carnation and lavender. Spicy scents are both haunting and lingering.

Citrus
The oils of lemon, bergamot, lime, tangerine, and bitter orange blossom are known for their refreshingly tangy accent. Citrus imparts a

The Notes of Fragrance

Because of its intangible nature, fragrance has a close affinity with music. The scents of flowers are often compared to musical notes. When a perfumer wishes to design a bouquet, he or she first develops a theme and then uses the fragrance components to form a "chord," employing all the elements of harmony much as a musician would in writing a piece of music. Just as you like some tunes better than others, you are going to like some fragrances better than others.

As you begin to learn the language of fragrance, there are three important notes to know in order to describe the perfume you try: *top note, middle note,* and *base note*. Study The Notes of Fragrance on page 86.

---

sharp, clear scent. Usually citrus is detected as a "top note"—that which hits your nose first—rather than as a central character of the scent.

Oriental
These are a mixture of musk, civet, ambergris, and other exotic ingredients that smell sophisticated, mysterious, and sultry. The effect is achieved through a blending of brilliant exotic flowers, herbs, and fixatives.

Green
A fragrance with a top note that denotes the zest and energy of freshly cut grass and dewy leaves. Usually described as young and vigorous, "green" makes you practically smell the color!

Woodsy-mossy
Sandalwood, rosewood, cedar, and other aromatic woods are combined with earthy moss and fern notes to create fragrance types that are refreshingly foresty, clean, clear, and crisp.

Fruity
An impression of "fruity" in a fragrance blend means the fresh odor of citrus and the warm smooth tones rendered by peach, plum, and apricot.

The Notes of Fragrance

- *Top Notes*
  Have the first effect on your sense of smell.
- *Middle Notes*
  Give fragrance its character. The warmth of the skin mingles personal chemistry with the fragrance as it reaches its fullest effect.
- *Base Notes*
  Are the heaviest and most lasting. They are the woodsy scents and animal scents like civet and musk.

Originally, the animal scents came from nature. But today it is no longer necessary to kill musk deer or whales to get the makings of fine fragrances. The chemist can supply excellent substitutes, and most new perfumes combine natural ingredients with synthetic compounds called aldehydes.

The first use of synthetic notes occurred in the creation of Chanel No. 5. This glorious scent took its character from rose and jasmine, both set, like jewels, in aldehydes. That innovation revolutionized the making of perfume, permitting a wider range of fragrances and more lasting quality. Yet fine perfumes still contain mostly natural ingredients. The most expensive of these are jasmine, rose de mai, Bulgarian rose, tuberose, and mimosa. A legendary perfume such as Joy by Jean Patou, for example, has a high proportion of jasmine and Bulgarian rose and it smells as "dear" as it is.

From Blossom to Bottle

The world capital for perfume-making is Grasse, a rural area in the South of France, high in the hills above Nice on the Côte d'Azur. Here, in ever-flowering gardens, is a paradise where the seasons unfold in a riot of color and fragrance. In December and January there are carnations, tuberoses, violets, wild anemones, orange and lemon blossoms. At the end of January and through February come almond, apricot, and peach blossoms, mimosa in the woods, and eucalyptus. At the height of springtime rockrose, thyme, and rosemary burst forth. April and May bring jasmine and roses, and June offers bougainvillea and laurel rose. Throughout summer and fall there are late roses, mimosa, spicy grasses, and then red carnations again in December.

The flowers of Grasse are raised especially for their hauntingly beautiful afterlife. Beds of jasmine, roses, orange blossoms, and violets, and fields of other flowers are packed in straw matting at night to preserve their fragrant oils, then they are gently handpicked and rushed to the factory. There the leaves and stems are carefully removed and the fragrance is extracted from the petals. It takes so many blossoms to create an ounce of perfume that it is said the flowers used each year by Lanvin just to make My Sin and Arpège (the floral blend of *fifty* essences!) would fill a building the size of the *Arc de Triomphe*. A visit to the flower and perfume capital is a dream of almost every woman who loves fragrance and flowers.

The Aromatic Oils

When choosing your fragrances, you might consider the health- and mood-enhancing properties of aromatic oils. Also known as the raw essence, aromatic oils are unmixed and cost far less than perfume. It can be fun to "compose" your own fragrance once you are knowledgeable enough and have developed the "nose" to do so. Do take care, however, remembering that just as with brands of perfume, the oil of rose or any other blossom can vary from intoxicating to asphyxiating! Some aromatic oils from which to select a scent and a mood:

Rose is the essence of love, cool and clean. There are hundreds of kinds of roses used in perfume. The fragrant tea rose sends a scent that is said to relieve tension and lighten the spirits.

Ylang-ylang's heady, long-lasting scent gives its wearer the feeling of strength, power, and authority and is said to color dreams.

Orange blossom is calming, slows the mind, brightens the spirit.

Geranium uplifts and stimulates positive thoughts, yet it is also said to be a sedative.

Rosemary invigorates and awakens the mind with a cool, fresh feeling. According to the ancient Greeks and Romans, it was an aid to memory.

Jasmine (the most precious of the aromatic oils because it cannot be imitated) lifts the mood to euphoria, sedates the nerves, and instills optimism and confidence.

Perfumes create magic moods and we react to their scents physically and emotionally. According to my needs, I often return to my trio of cream concentrates from Parfums Caron. From each separate tiny pot, I blend just the right amount of jasmine, rose, and ylang-ylang to express or create a mood. Or I use just one of these mood-setters alone.

88

The Touch of Scent

The ultimate effect of scent is determined by the way you use it. Do not think of fragrance as the last thing you splash on before leaving the house. It should be for your benefit first, so apply it directly after a bath or shower. "Layering" is the most effective way to wear a fragrance: Begin by bathing with scented body soap or in a perfumed bath oil. After the bath, apply a scented body lotion to your damp skin and dust with a scented body powder when the skin is dry. Then splash on cologne or toilet water and finally follow with strokes of perfume, sparingly, on your pulse points. Because scent rises, do not fail to include pulse points at the ankles and backs of the knees. The bouquet of perfume unfolds best on thin skin over arteries. A final tip—do not use perfume behind the ears as the unique oils there interact badly with scent.

As with all "finishing touches," good taste is a must for the use of fragrance. Use a light touch as you layer, so that your scent will be shared subtly with others and you will never come on too strong! To further enhance your fragrant aura, study my Scent Secrets below.

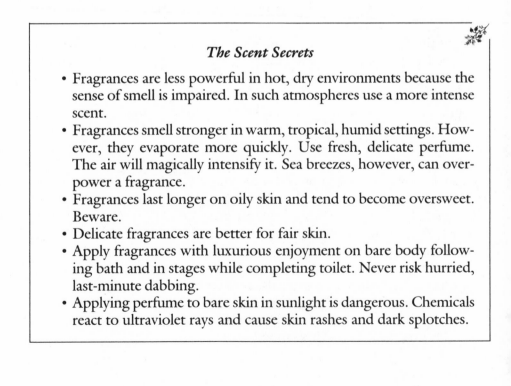

The Scent Secrets

- Fragrances are less powerful in hot, dry environments because the sense of smell is impaired. In such atmospheres use a more intense scent.
- Fragrances smell stronger in warm, tropical, humid settings. However, they evaporate more quickly. Use fresh, delicate perfume. The air will magically intensify it. Sea breezes, however, can overpower a fragrance.
- Fragrances last longer on oily skin and tend to become oversweet. Beware.
- Delicate fragrances are better for fair skin.
- Apply fragrances with luxurious enjoyment on bare body following bath and in stages while completing toilet. Never risk hurried, last-minute dabbing.
- Applying perfume to bare skin in sunlight is dangerous. Chemicals react to ultraviolet rays and cause skin rashes and dark splotches.

A Fragrance Vocabulary

In order to layer your fragrance with success, you need to acquire a fragrance vocabulary. Fragrance comes in many forms and the price is determined by the concentration. French is, of course, the language of perfume, and I have, therefore, included both the English and the French names in The Vocabulary of Fragrance Forms on p. 90.

Potpourri

A wonderful way to further indulge your sense of smell is with potpourri—a fragrant mixture of dry flower petals, spices, herbs, and aromatic oils. An open jar can give your room a fresh, pleasant fragrance, which almost makes you feel you are living in a garden boudoir. Potpourri also allows you to add another dimension to your personal fragrance: If you place sachets of potpourri among your clothing in your drawers, it will add a lovely depth and surprise to the scent of your perfume or cologne. It also adds the subtlety of scent to your dorm room or apartment.

A special advantage of potpourri is that it can become a cherished memory

- Realize that those who smoke never experience the full glory of perfume. The chemicals in cigarette smoke react badly with those in perfume, diminish fragrance, and also reduce one's capacity to enjoy the aroma.
- Medication or the Pill can change the skin's reaction to a fragrance, as can eating onions, garlic, and spicy foods.
- A scent may react differently with the skin during menstruation, and the sense of smell is often affected during that time.
- The warmer the body, the faster the fragrance fades. More frequent applications are needed in summer than in winter.
- Perfume evaporates even when not removed from the bottle. Store larger quantities in a cool, dark place. For current use pour some into small, lovely, and sealable bottles and position away from bright sunlight. Oxygen and light are perfume's enemies.
- Save your empty perfume bottles and place in dresser drawers and closet. They will impart their scent to garments for a long time.

The Vocabulary of Fragrance Forms

Parfum (Perfume)
The most concentrated form of fragrance oil—fifteen to twenty percent essential oil (scent concentrate or pure *extrait*)—with the remainder alcohol. The larger percentage of essential oil makes the scent stronger and more long-lasting than other fragrance forms. It has more lift and body, and may contain hundreds of ingredients. The ingredients are often of better quality substances than cologne, such as natural rose rather than synthetic. It is also the most expensive form and its scent lasts from four to eight hours depending upon the flowers used and the skin type.

Parfum de Toilette or *Eau de Parfum* (Perfume Water)
The next in concentration of the fragrance forms—it contains from twelve to fifteen percent essential oil, with the remainder comprised mostly of alcohol (spirit) and some water. It lasts from two to five hours and was developed in the United States to provide a form of fragrance with more longevity and strength than that afforded by "eau de toilette," yet not as strong or expensive as "parfum."

Eau de Toilette (Toilet Water)
The fragrance form third in strength to perfume is toilet water. It is created with five to twelve percent essential fragrance oil and a greater water content, diluted for a lighter concentration and more subtlety. It is the ideal all-over-the-body base for a fragrance application. It evaporates rapidly, lasting only two to four hours.

Eau de Cologne (Cologne)
The lightest form of fragrance—two to six percent essential oil with the remainder largely water with some alcohol. It was named and developed after the water of Cologne, Germany (Kolnischwasser). It is not merely diluted perfume; it can be composed of different, often synthetic, ingredients. It can be used lavishly after bathing, and lasts less than half the life of fine perfume, or about one to three hours. This is the most popular fragrance form in America, but in Europe "eau de toilette" is preferred because it is more lasting. It is good for those with oily skin, which holds fragrance longer and intensifies it.

Crème Parfumée Concentrête (Cream Perfumed Concentrate)
A solid-form scent in a cream base with a high level of perfume oil. It is appreciated for its mildness and practical, nonspilling form. It adheres well to the skin and is therefore best suited to dry skin.

bank when you add some petals from a corsage you wore on a wonderful evening or from a field flower someone picked for you on a summer picnic.

Rose-Colored Glasses

Perfume made from the attar of the most gloriously scented roses (and other flowers) is the olfactory equivalent of rose-colored glasses. Put it on and you alter your perception of life, tilting your mood toward enjoyment, optimism, and expectancy. Smell can deliver perhaps the most delicious experiences of the five senses, despite the fact that it is the most illusory, the most fragile. A beautiful piece of artwork is not diminished by ugly surroundings; a lilting melody can erase the effects of a harsh din; a sweet can dispel a bitter taste; and a gentle touch can bring comfort. But the sweetness of a flower cannot penetrate unpleasant air. It is essential first to have a wholesome atmosphere, so the lovely, if transitory, enjoyment of scent is not missed.

And as with all precious things, including jewels, to overdo is to offend. You must learn to use perfume excitingly but not rashly, perhaps to the verge of indiscretion but never beyond.

The use of perfume is an awakening and educating process for the senses. It is an art for painting your world "rose," for making the breath of life sweet indeed.

PART THREE

Keeping In Touch

CHAPTER 6

The Art of Conversation

Little girls love to dress up and look pretty—at least at one time or another. Sometimes I think it must be an inborn trait. And the desire to make an attractive impression does not fade, even as you grow up.

Certainly you have already been experimenting with techniques for making the most of your physical potential, discussed in the beginning chapters. Now I want you to understand that the auditory impressions you make are as important as the visual ones. The tones of a lilting voice are as appealing as dramatic coloring. An attractive, creative use of words is as interesting as smart accessories, and a lack of vulgarity and grammatical error in daily speech is as important as fastidiousness of body and clothing.

You must also accept the fact that what you say is as significant as the way in which it is said. Being pleasant and grammatically correct is not enough. Your conversation should be exciting, indicative of interesting thoughts and opinions, amusing and original. Do not delude yourself that members of the opposite sex are turned off by intelligence and thoughtfulness in their female friends. To the contrary. Bright, knowledgeable, articulate women are recognized as stimulating companions, wives, and business and civic leaders.

Through the ages (even when women had small public recognition), strong, smart women so influenced their husbands and sons that they actually exerted great power. In the Romantic period that followed the Renaissance, the most glamorous women of Europe presided over salons to which the powerful and the talented flocked. Without political power they swayed governments by impressing their ideas on leaders, and they influenced great works of art and literature by inspiring the genius of the poets and the artists.

It is to be regretted that now—when women are expected to provide sparkle and stimulating tone to conversation and to add sensitivity and authority to business and professional dealings—many young women are growing up with little or no preparation for these roles. For almost two generations the hectic lifestyle of the two-career family has all but eliminated good conversation from the family circle.

In past generations the dinner table was the source of mental as well as physical nourishment. Current events, literature, drama, and other cultural topics were discussed as well as the trivialities, which, when handled with grace and sophistication, are important to conversation as well. Today, incompatible individual schedules often lead to snatched, solitary meals hurriedly prepared in the microwave, and even when families gather, the television set often drowns out any attempts at important communication.

As you accept the responsibility to speak for yourself and to develop the art of conversation, you will become aware that age is not the only barrier that conversation can gracefully remove. Your life will be richer and more meaningful if you talk to many kinds of people from all walks of life. Sophisticated people respect the political, religious, cultural, and moral commitments of others and can listen to diverse opinions without anger or fear that their own beliefs are threatened. Almost everyone who is pleasant and sincere has something to offer that can widen your horizons.

The Art of Conversation

Sometimes people think polite conversation has to be boring and flat. Not at all. The most princely conversationalists have always been thinkers, people delicate in their respect for the feelings of others, but also, on occasion, sassy, funny, even uproarious, or politely dissenting. The best conversation has color, sincerity, and kindness. I have also noticed that people who believe it is worthwhile—and fun—to exchange ideas, whether in serious discourse or chitchat, are so much more adept at it than those who scorn conversation. And they enjoy it all the more.

Perhaps the first requisite for becoming a good conversationalist is to learn to be a good listener. Conversation, you see, consists not only of talk but of listening discreetly, with unfaltering and constant attention. By giving thoughtful consideration to what another is saying, you not only feed new facts and ideas into your busy mind, but you also win the appreciation of the speaker. It is rude to interrupt a speaker, even one who is rudely monopolizing the occasion with long-winded ramblings and repetitions. Never interrupt. By the same token, never be guilty of delivering a monologue rather than engaging in a two-way conversation. My personal motto is: "Monologues stifle; dialogues stimulate."

Let *Your* Speech Be Always With Grace

Just as every movement of a dancer reflects skill and grace, so your conversational poise reflects your outlook on the world. Your conversations should be a medley of three elements: talk about people, talk about things, and conversation in its highest form, talk about ideas.

Talk about people does not mean gossip. It means lively talk about persons of general interest. You do not have to restrict your conversation to "intellectual" topics—talking about the latest rock or movie star can be as interesting as the President's meeting with world leaders. As long as you are enthusiastic, the person or people you are talking to will be also. It is easy to think of people to talk about. Listen to programs on radio and television, see interesting movies, read a variety of books, magazines, and newspapers. And you can, of course, talk about people in your personal sphere, so long as you do not say anything *about* them that you would be embarrassed to say *to* them.

Things are the second subject area that feeds good conversation. Remember details of a trip, a building, artworks, your hobbies, and hobbies of others. Few can resist talking about their hobbies.

Talk about ideas can be perilous territory as well as glorious adventure. Politics can divide people quickly, as can religious beliefs. If you want to discuss current events, you must do so in a low-key, objective way that will not offend others. It is better to open with, "What do you think about our new mayor?" than "I think our new mayor is terrible (or wonderful)." And it is always more gracious to ask another's opinion before announcing or offering your own. In conversing with close friends, you may feel more freedom to express your innermost thoughts and opinions, of course, with consideration and respect for their beliefs.

Learn to talk about ideas without proselytizing, without ramming your point of view down someone else's throat. Imagine a sunny café on a European boulevard where you and traveling companions, close friends or new acquaintances, discuss the meaning of a revolution, or feminist issues. You will, perhaps, be there until the sun goes down, or continue the conversation as you walk along the river that winds through the city. Here you can trust yourself to discuss and explore ideas, but I advise you to give as well as take in these conversations. Ideas, of course, include much more than politics and religion. Weather, your surroundings, the arts, current or local happenings, what newspapers call "style"—food, fashion, entertainment, exercise, or health fads—sports, and travel are all good topics.

As lofty an ambition as fine conversation is, often your foremost aim is to make others feel at ease; the other elements become secondary. The sensitivity of your conversation in ice-breaking and other difficult situations will bring everyone a sense of comfort—feeling at home and having a good time.

Just as each of us upon occasion finds herself speechless, at times the students at L'Ecole des Ingénues "freeze up" just before the arrival of a guest and come to me asking, "What do I talk about?" I always remind them that she who says the least is many times the best hostess and most gifted conversationalist as she inspires her guest to talk. Seventeenth-century French moralist Jean de La Bruyère once said:

> "The wit of conversation consists more in finding it in others than in showing a great deal yourself. He who goes from your conversation pleased with himself and his own wit, is perfectly well pleased with you."

Selflessness

Selflessness is conversation's cardinal rule. Some people think that an exchange should be practiced in advance, but this is seldom called for and robs talk of its marvelous spontaneity. Rather, the point is to expand your horizons by extinguishing all thoughts of yourself.

Offer compliments—and always accept one graciously. An interesting person is someone who is interested in others. Ask questions about your partner—without, I caution, overdoing it so that flattering interest turns into interrogation and overcuriosity. When you give your opinion, it is always polite to follow with, "And what do you think?" Certainly do not disagree with everything the other person says in an effort at sincerity. One of the things about which I caution the students at L'Ecole des Ingénues is not to be a "door slammer." Perhaps someone asks you if you like the theater, and the honest answer is no. Just responding, "No, I don't," closes the door on the conversation. Instead, say, "No, but I love the movies," or whatever you do enjoy so a new conversational topic can be developed.

Conversational Dos and Taboos

Any topic can be unfriendly or friendly. Discuss a ski holiday in a sharing way, communicating your enthusiasm, and the topic is very friendly. But if you exhibit superiority, boredom, or impatience, the same topic becomes offensive. Body language—open posture, forward leaning, a light touch to an arm, eye contact, a nod—can enhance the friendliness of the topic greatly.

There are also topics that must be avoided. Never ask a question you would not want to answer yourself. The most obvious are very personal questions concerning marriage and divorce, death and disease, or questions concerning the cost of things, income, expenditures. Other inappropriate subjects are gossip and dirty or ethnic jokes. For the most part avoid obscure or difficult subjects, like wheat crops in southern Russia, which you might be inclined to bring up to impress others—unless, of course, your partner is an expert in Russian agriculture.

When you hear the voice of prejudice from one person or a group, let it be known that slurs, ethnic jokes, name-calling, and the like are not your style and you are made uncomfortable by such hurtful generalizations. Silence, unfortunately, might be taken as agreement. At least try to gracefully change the topic of conversation. It is far better to say, "I do not like jokes that belittle an ethnic group. Let's change the subject, please!"—than to be aligned with this type of conversation.

When in company, do not speak about a private matter or a mutual friend others in attendance know nothing about. If you wish to discuss such a subject, you must first give a bit of background information in order that the others are not "left in the dark." Likewise, when someone new joins your group, always draw him or her into the conversation by explaining the subject under discussion.

Do speak the truth. Never yield to the temptation to "color" or "pad" your conversation or to "top" another's story by saying things that are not true. Do not "toot your own horn," that is, brag or boast about yourself or your accomplishments.

When several people comprise a conversational group, make an effort to look at each person during the conversation. Direct some part of your talk, whether a statement or anecdote, to each one individually in turn. Never place your hand at the side of your mouth to shield something you are saying from the ears of another in the group—or in the room for that matter. Anything said in a group must be said to all present. Otherwise, it is a private matter and should be reserved for private discussion.

Share the conversational stage and even take a minor role, thereby making stars of the others—you should never try to "steal the show" by always being the most witty or by topping the stories told by others. Allow others a turn at gaining a laugh or two or adding their "two cents worth" or "bon mot."

Try to build upon the remarks of others. The slightest comment by the shy conversationalist might reveal his or her "hot button," a topic you, as a student of the art of conversation, know to "push," thereby opening up a stimulating conversational partner.

Be a good conversational "fisherman." If all else fails, "fish" for topics until your conversational partner "bites" and the topic is devoured "hook, line, and sinker." Keep a mental tackle box of baits from which to select at a moment's notice when no one is nibbling. Just as there is a bait for almost every fish, so there is a topic which cannot go unsampled by your conversational partner. Although the subject may not interest you, interesting your partner in it will ultimately interest him or her in you.

The Voice Behind the Word

A good speaking voice is essential to the enjoyment of conversation, and a perfect voice is rarely a natural asset; most must be developed. Though words are derived from thought, the tone of your voice expresses feeling and character. A loud, harsh, or strident voice appears bossy and arrogant; a monotone is boring and suggests a lack of enthusiasm; a whining voice discloses a selfish and demanding character. In addition to the fact that a good speaking voice is pleasant to hear, it is instantly recognized as a mark of culture.

In your effort to acquire a cultivated voice, do not, of course, strive to sound like an actress in London's Royal Shakespeare Company. Listen to women who speak with such softness and intelligence that everyone stops to listen. Naturally refined and disciplined, yet spontaneous, vocal expression is a charming and a necessary attribute of today's complete woman. A beautiful speaking voice is a part of a woman's feminine beauty, and it adds authority and strength to her words and opinions.

Voice Control

You can control your voice, beginning with mental control. A well-poised, flexible attitude of mind is reflected in your tone. Any habitual way of thought has a direct bearing on your speaking voice. Always consider the pace of your speech. Moderately slow speaking is best in ordinary conversation. Never talk fast. A measured pace gives you time to think, to choose your words, to form your sentences correctly, and to lay the emphasis in the right place.

The key to training your voice is proper breathing. The following exercise is one that can help you. Repeat it ten times daily, concentrating your mind fully on each action.

- Stand erect with your chest well forward, shoulders braced back, and arms by your sides.
- As you slowly raise your arms to a vertical position above your head, take in a slow, deep breath through your nose, until your lungs are full.
- Hold your breath for a few seconds, keeping your hands above your head, palms facing each other.
- Slowly lower your arms to your sides, releasing your breath little by little through your mouth.

A Well-Modulated Voice

The qualities that make a voice dynamic include modulation, inflection, melody, color, change in pitch, a good rate, and clarity. By practicing the points below, you can improve the sound of your voice.

- Breathe more evenly.
- Emphasize and heighten the words that convey more importance.
- Put energy into your voice.
- Vary your pitch.
- Slow down your speech.
- Because a young woman's voice tends to be high and thin, lower yours (at the same time lowering your shoulders), making this effort especially when you feel a little afraid, nervous, or overexcited.
- Enunciate clearly; never mumble.
- Watch your listener and those around you who are *not* a part of your conversation to check your voice volume: Should you be speaking too softly, you will see a leaning forward to catch your words, and maybe a frown; whereas speaking too loudly, for dramatic or bossy effect, can be "read" in the slightly disgruntled looks and the stares of others at greater distance.

Effortless Enunciation

A cultivated voice is of little value if the words are not understood. Not only is speaking clearly and distinctly of utmost importance, it is also a gesture of courtesy. The guidelines below, if practiced regularly, will improve your enunciation.

- Open your mouth adequately.
- Speak through the throat and not from it.
- Give full play to the lower jaw, and never speak through the teeth.
- Keep the tongue well forward in your mouth. Let it move freely; never tighten it.
- Let your lips move freely. (It may help to pretend you are speaking to a person who is deaf and a lip-reader. A deaf person's brothers and sisters often have very articulate speech!)
- Replenish your breath often, inhaling through the nose.
- Keep all the concerned muscles relaxed when you speak, especially those of the throat and mouth.

These exercises and rules will help to eliminate the most common faults of mumbling, gliding over syllables and single letters, and indistinct pronunciation of initial and final letters.

If your voice is weak or uncertain, do not be discouraged. Exercise of the muscles and continued practice will do an astonishing amount to strengthen and develop it.

Regional Accents

There are many schools and tutoring programs that offer public-speaking courses, which are a good way to begin learning to "perform" as a conversationalist in public. A tutor can also be of help in modifying a regional accent that is strong enough to distract a listener. To my mind, there are many interesting regional accents and I would not want us all to sound alike. Nevertheless, if yours embarrasses you within the social circle to which you want to belong, professional help can be effective.

Words—Winged, Whimsical, Wicked

Now that you have considered vocal intonations and have begun working on techniques for the improvement of your voice's quality, resonance, pace, and pitch, it is time that you give thought to the choice of words that your pleasant sounds will enunciate. Prepare yourself by beginning what should be a life-long passion for increasing and invigorating your vocabulary so that you can effectively express yourself. Think first of the marvel of word power—a gift available exclusively to the human race—which allows you to capture even your most intangible thoughts and dreams, and communicate them.

The ability to enter comfortably into a casual conversation, a more serious discussion, a sensitive exchange with a personal friend, or a sharing of dreams with a loved one is among the most satisfying of life's experiences. Words, in fact, are natural computer chips connecting you with other people in varying relationships. I knew a woman, long-admired for her conversational spark, who during her last long illness continued to search the dictionary for fresh and exciting words. Although physically weak, she remained mentally alert, and relatives and friends enjoyed visits as much as she did.

Words are not only the medium for thought-exchange; they allow you to orchestrate the beautiful, the mysterious, the tender, the amusing, the whimsical thoughts you wish to share with others. Collect words until you are word-wealthy. But never be ostentatious in the spending. Often, simple but less common words say it best.

Wonderful as they are, words can also be dangerous and damaging. Untrue or thoughtless comments and betrayals of confidences can hurt others. Misused words, extravagant overstatements, or obvious name-dropping place the speaker in a very unflattering light. Remember that words once said cannot be recalled.

Slang and Bad Language

The improvement of your speech must be preceded by a thorough cleansing of unattractive or distasteful patterns. Think of the delightful musical *My Fair Lady* and recall that Professor Higgins transformed the flower girl into a lady by removing all remnants of coarse language from her speech before introducing more polished words. (With the same relentlessness, he also had her coached in posture and carriage before attempting any adornment.) You should begin an immediate campaign to do the same for your own vocabulary.

First of all, no foul language. Four-letter words are absolutely unaccept-able. They shatter your image as a polished young woman and offend hearers. One disreputable word can destroy the importance of what you are saying. Such expressions come from the gutter and have only negative shock impact.

Less disastrous than vulgarity, but rarely attractive, is slang, which should have small place, if any, in a young woman's speech. Use it lightly only—as seasoning. Since some is certain to creep into your conversation, try weeding it out completely. Funk and Wagnall's *Standard College Dictionary* defines slang as "language, words, or phrases of a vigorous, colorful, facetious, or taboo nature invented for specific occasions or uses or derived from conven-tional use of standard vocabulary." Admittedly, slang has punch and is hard to resist, but remember that while not offensive, it tends to become tired and stale and is always short-lived in impact. Grizzled expressions such as "okay" and "yeah" do still surface in uninspired chatter, although more sophisti-cated speakers have graduated to the correct "yes" or "certainly." "Yeahs," "okays," "likes," "rights," and "alrights" overused in your talk can be as irritating as the drip-drip of a leaky faucet.

The Strength of Speech

Social scientists agree that speech, perhaps more than any other characteris-tic, "places" a person in a certain social class. The character of your speech not only identifies you, but actually tends to anchor you in a specific class, if unattractive characteristics are not overcome.

I know a young woman who moved to Atlanta and obtained a sales position in a city specialty shop. Quickly she achieved a "fashion-plate" appearance, but the image was destroyed when she spoke. Grammatical errors, crudities, clichés, and an obsession with brand names stymied her career progress.

I have watched promising relationships deteriorate and die because of the conversational inadequacies of one of the partners. Friendships, even court-ships, cannot grow when boredom or irritation at annoying verbal habits comes into play.

A Word Garden

Beyond the necessity of removing vulgarities, crudities, and worn-out slang from one's speech, positive action to enrich word power and background knowledge on a wide variety of subjects is required for good conversation. Repetitious use of even descriptive and expressive words—"fabulous," for instance—can be tiresome. The English language is so rich in words that describe minute shades of meaning that it becomes a challenge, a game, to make so many of them yours that you will never be at a loss for the right one. Nourishing your word garden is as important as weeding it. The tips below will help.

- Read widely, especially descriptive passages you may have skimmed formerly in your eagerness to follow the action.
- Turn to your dictionary whenever you are unsure of the particular word, and occasionally peruse its pages for a surprise treasure.
- Take care to pronounce each word—old or new to you— properly.
- If possible, study Latin for a command of root words and an understanding of basic grammar.
- Look at study books for college board examinations to check yourself on what is recognized as basic for an educated person. Learn the words gradually and use them over time until they become second nature.
- Play word games—Scrabble, crossword puzzles, television word-game shows.

A Foreign Flair

A good vocabulary consists of more than a purely English vocabulary. You should be aware that many foreign words have become an accepted part of our language, and you should be comfortable with them. Using foreign words and phrases, however, can sound pretentious, so be careful. Insert them sparingly into conversation, and only when you are certain of their correct meaning and pronunciation. Study my suggestions below to increase your "foreign flair" and familiarity with foreign phrases.

- Listen and look for foreign words. Look them up when you come upon them, and consider whether they have a natural place in your writing or speech.
- Brush up on English as it is spoken in England—you will find new meaning, humor, and wit in your native tongue.
- Read the menus in Italian, French, or Spanish restaurants.

- See foreign films and operas with English subtitles.
- Read magazines and newspapers written in another language.
- Start—and stick with—the study of a Romance language, never dropping it from your electives.

The Graveness of Grammar

Grammar and syntax are crucial to good speech, and these you develop continuously at home, at school, and at work. Make a determined effort to rectify any errors. Think of a grammatical error as a chip in your polish—a mar to your finish. For example, you would never say, "Me and my dad went to the beach," but rather, "Dad and I . . ." or "This secret is between you and I," but rather "you and me . . ."

Words in the Wrong

Choosing the correct word can be confusing sometimes. As the misuse of words mars good speech, care should be taken to choose the correct ones.

For example, consider the misuse of the words *pardon me* and *pardon*. "Pardon me!" is a rude and commanding exclamatory sentence, and the word *pardon* should never be used except in the complete sentence, "I *beg* your pardon." The correct phrase to use when you must pass in front of someone in order to get to or leave your theater seat is: "Excuse me, please!" or "I *beg* your pardon." Add, "I'm sorry" or "Thank you," if the person must rise for you to pass. The same expression is used should you bump into another person. When you have misunderstood someone or have failed to hear correctly, say, "What did you say?" or "I'm sorry—what did you say?" Never say, "Pardon?" or "Excuse me?"

Consider my tips below as you select words.

- Always choose the simple word rather than a flowery, evasive, complicated one.
- Use an English word rather than a foreign one (unless there is no English equivalent).
- Pronounce the word in full rather than using initials or abbreviations.
- Avoid any affectations or pretentiousness, such as saying "gown" instead of "dress."

Colloquialisms

Colloquialisms (speech idiosyncrasies that have grown up in isolated regional areas or in sections within large cities) are variations on standard words or phrases. These deviations have become accepted within the specific group and tend to identify the user with the culture or the locale. An example is the much discussed Southern "you-all"—which is redundant since "you" is plural as well as singular. Many residents of the area defend its use and hold that it expresses the expansive hospitality of the South and is a fitting way to include everybody. Similarly, New Yorkers say "you guys," and some Californians have developed the astonishing Valley Girl Talk, which cannot be interpreted by outsiders. Many ethnic and cultural groups who live in homogeneous areas combine foreign words with deviations of English into dialects that are comprehensible only to group members.

Much colloquialism and regionalism is gradually disappearing as education becomes better and the mobility of the population breaks down geographic barriers. Some regional and ethnic idioms are colorful, expressive, and charming and may find a place in the expanding language. Those that are ungrammatical should be avoided, however. Take care that conversations between you and your friends are not peppered with slang, special pet words, idioms, and phrases to a point that you are understood only within your immediate circle.

Names and Titles

A major consideration in conversation is the way those involved address others and are addressed. The use of names and titles should be, and usually is, determined by the relationships between the participants, and although customs in this area are continually changing, there are some guidelines that should be observed.

What one calls another person is determined by two major factors: intimacy and, for want of a better word, status. Young people are expected in most circles to show respect for their elders, teachers, older friends, and acquaintances, using the proper title preceding the surname unless they are invited to use the given name. Once out of school and in the business or professional arena, junior workers are expected to address their bosses and other superiors with the same proper formality. In the military service, this is mandatory. Fellow workers should also be addressed formally until sufficient intimacy is developed. In social situations, age and prestige are accorded the courtesy of appropriate social or professional titles. With peers, on the other hand, first names are used even with new friends. Young women of your age should address your friends' parents by title and surname unless specifically invited to adopt a more familiar form.

Within the family circle, the tone of address is more important than the term. While in most families Mother and Father, Mom and Dad, Mommy and Daddy are used, in many instances pet names or even the given names of parents are the choices, and so long as these are used with love and respect, the situation concerns no one beyond the family. Even more usual are pet names for grandparents. What one should call aunts, uncles, cousins depends on family tradition and differences in age, and needs to please no one except those involved.

There is a new and increasing problem that can be troublesome: how young people address a stepparent. Some boys and girls find it difficult to call the grafted parent Mother or Dad, and if a natural parent has been displaced, he or she may resent their doing so. With consideration and tact, a solution—perhaps the use of a given name or a pet name—can be worked out.

The name of a divorced woman can also be problematic. Is your mother's best friend still Mrs. Smith or has she chosen to revert to her former name? If a divorced woman has children, she rarely reassumes her maiden name but becomes Mrs. Alice Smith or Mrs. Alice March (her maiden name) Smith.

Whether single, married, or divorced, some woman choose Ms. rather than Mrs. or Miss as their title. The abbreviation Ms. has received some acceptance, especially in professional and business circles. Nonetheless, in *social* circles a woman is *traditionally* referred to as Miss until married and Mrs. thereafter. You are correct, therefore, to address a woman accordingly unless she asks that you address her as Ms.

Some women now choose to keep their maiden names after marriage and to adopt the title of Ms. In certain European countries, hyphenated names are sometimes used in marriages bringing together the sons and daughters of prestigious families. This practice is occasionally adopted in this country following the marriage of two equally well-known professionals, artists, writers, stage, or sports figures, or by a woman who wishes to retain her maiden name and, in addition, assume the last name of her husband. The presentation of one's name or title is a personal decision and should be respected by others!

The use of "ma'am" and "sir" as courtesy titles, although limited, continues today. If it is part of a family tradition, it has a place in that home.

Outside, however, caution should be exercised. Although the custom began as a sign of respect from a servant to the master and mistress of the house, it later developed as a gracious effort at politeness between children and adults of the same social status. Care should be taken to use these titles with a tone of sincere courtesy, as they can easily take on a sarcastic cast with the wrong inflection in the voice. They should be used only as a touch of respect reserved for those of the old school who expect or require it, or for a person of high position upon whom you wish to bestow honor. The use of "sir" or "ma'am" should be discontinued if the person to whom it is addressed reacts adversely.

The Importance of Introductions

Introductions are an integral part of good manners and you must accept the responsibility and perfect the skill of performing them with a natural ease. Surely you already have faced the need to introduce someone who was a stranger at large parties, social or scholastic meetings, church or civic gatherings. As you mature, and especially when you are attending college or beginning your career, this situation will occur often.

In formal social, business, or diplomatic situations, the rules for presentation are rather complex. They are, however, based on a few simple guidelines that will serve you in this phase of your life. The basic principles can be mastered through brief study and will form the foundation for more complicated protocol.

Act promptly to smooth the situation if someone you know (however slightly) joins a group in which you are a participant and is obviously uncomfortable. Even if you do not remember his or her name, turn to the newcomer and say brightly, "How nice to see you again. I'm Sue Carter. We met at Jane's party." The newcomer, grateful to be recognized, will then give his or her name, and the rest is easy. Introduce your friends round-robin, then say, "This is Steve Crowder," or whomever, and talk will continue, now including the stranger. To save others from the embarrassment of name "blackouts," start a conversation with, "Hello, I'm Nan Adams. I met you at Tom's New Year's Eve party." *Never* ask, "You don't remember me, do you?" Should you bring a friend—with the proper permission, of course— to a large party or meeting, it is your responsibility to introduce him or her at the door to the host or hostess, and to see that your guest is comfortably introduced throughout the event. When you are the hostess, you must welcome each arriving guest and introduce him or her—to everyone at a small party, to the next in the receiving line at a larger affair. If you have not met someone before and find yourself under the same roof at the party of a friend, it is polite simply to walk up and introduce yourself.

When making introductions, present the person of lesser prestige, status, or age *to* the elder or more celebrated. (For example, state the older person's name first, "Grandmother, I would like for you to meet my roommate, Nancy Butler.") With persons of comparable status the man is presented *to* the woman. (State the woman's name first, "Mrs. Oliver, may I present Mr. Grey.") A young girl, until she reaches sixteen, is presented *to* a mature man. Honor a guest or newcomer by introducing your friend *to* him or her. (State the newcomer's name first.) Introduce an individual *to* the group. ("Girls, meet John!") It is polite to address the more important person (the person you are honoring) first and to address the one who is being introduced second. To set the propriety of introducing others to one who is important or celebrated, remember what you have known from fairy-tale days: Subjects were presented *to* the king and queen. And with all introductions, say the names clearly.

The phrasing of the introduction is important as well. The words "present" and "introduce" are the most formal forms: "I have the honor to present . . . ," "May I present . . . ," "May I introduce . . ." Other forms, such as "This is . . ." (which indicates warmth) and "I would like for you to meet . . . ," are equally acceptable. Although you may properly introduce by saying the names of the two being introduced, "Mary Brown, Grace Smith," you need not repeat them in the reverse order.

"How do you do?" is the correct formal acknowledgment to an introduction and is said by both parties. If you wish to be more casual in your acknowledgment, you may say warmly, "It's so nice to meet you" or "I'm very glad to meet you." However, never say anything such as: "It's exciting to meet a famous person like you," or "Pleased to make your acquaintance," or the comical "Charmed!"

One hint to remember when making introductions is that it is helpful to tell something interesting about the person you are introducing. In this way, a topic of conversation will already have been established. Avoid, however, praising the person to the skies even if you are sincere, as it embarrasses him or her, and sounds phony.

From the time you enter a college or university or commence your career you will probably be in groups—scholastic, professional, military, diplomatic, or clerical—where more rigorous protocol is followed and the use of titles is obligatory. Protocol does not change to suit your whims—you must follow the rules if you expect to move with ease in all social circles.

Body Language

Body language can be as important as the words you say. Especially in first meetings, the impression you give should be one of friendliness and interest rather than indifference, boredom, or a blasé attitude. Smile when being introduced; make eye contact; do not appear hurried.

The handshake should be neither too weak nor too strong, but simply firm and sincere. Although a woman has the option of offering to shake hands, she must respond if the other party initiates it. For a warmer, more affectionate response, the left hand may be placed over the other's grasp and slight pressure exerted. Upon meeting a friend he knows but may not have seen for a time, a man may place his free hand on the other's arm or shoulder.

Legacies of the recent past are a slight curtsy or a bow (bending the head slightly from the neck). The full curtsy is a graceful movement made by placing the right toe slightly behind and to the left of the left foot, then bending the knees in a quick dip, then standing erect. As the curtsy begins, the right hand is extended and the older person accepts the hand as the dip (or curtsy) takes place. This gesture of respect is performed in full in many other countries as a sign of respect or reverence. In our country it remains a respectful gesture and is performed in full on the part of the young girl and the debutante, and in part (as a nod of the head) by women of all ages. The inclination of the head in a brief bow on the part of a man when introduced, combined with accepting the extended hand of a woman, or the touching or doffing of his hat, is a polite acknowledgment of another.

Family members naturally and spontaneously hug and sometimes kiss each other after absences. Socially, a light kiss on the cheek by a man meeting a woman friend or between two friends is proper if the situation is not a formal one. But greetings to strangers and public meetings of friends should not be effusive. Many object to being kissed, or "air kissed"—that is, a kiss in the air as the cheeks brush. In general, any overly dramatic, gushy show of affection is not in good taste and is pretentious.

The Receiving Line

Another social convention that introduces and involves guests in conversation of a formal nature is the receiving line. At a large reception given for a stranger, a bride-to-be, a celebrity, or a friend who has received an honor, the receiving line provides each guest with the opportunity to meet and speak briefly with the honoree. The hostess and/or host stands with the special guest and as each guest arrives presents him or her to the one being feted, usually with a brief identifying phrase—"my neighbor," "our school principal." If the host or hostess does not know the newly arriving guest, he or she will state his or her name after which the guest will immediately give his or her name and acknowledge the introduction. The host or hostess then presents the guest *to* the guest of honor. The guest of honor offers his or her hand, and the other guest accepts it, and says simply, "How do you do?" Always be prompt in supplying your name in this or any other situation when you see that the person attempting to introduce you does not know it or has momentarily forgotten it. The receiving line is not the place for conversation that would cause others to wait. Should you arrive at a party after the receiving line has dissolved, you must seek out the guest of honor and introduce yourself. It is rude to attend a party honoring someone and fail to meet or greet that person.

Rising to the Occasion

Many social situations call for the gracious ceremony of standing for someone. Certain situations call for both the man and woman, child or children, teen or young adult to rise or stand. Best remembered are very formal occasions or important persons for whom one rises: services of church, weddings, and upon meeting dignitaries. Familiarize yourself with the various other appropriate occasions for which you should rise, discussed below.

- *Rise when an older person enters the room.*
  A teen or young adult should rise when an older person enters the room and remain standing until the older person is seated.
- *Rise when introduced to an older person.*
  Any girl in her early teens or young adulthood should rise when introduced to any older man or woman. She extends her hand first when introduced to an older man, but waits for an older woman to initiate the handshake.
- *Rise when introduced to a newcomer.*
  At small gatherings, more and more women feel comfortable standing when the men stand to be introduced to a newcomer. This gesture simply shows consideration and special interest and undivided attention to someone new.

- *Rise when introduced to a hostess, host, or guest of honor.*
  A woman or man rises when introduced to the hostess, host, or to the guest of honor.
- *Rise or remain seated when women are introduced.*
  When women are introduced to each other and one is sitting and the other standing, the one who is seated need not rise unless the one standing is either her hostess, much older, very distinguished, or a friend she has not seen in a long time.
- *Rise when introduced to a prospective employer.*
  Any woman seeking employment rises when presented to her prospective employer, male or female. She waits for the interviewer to initiate the handshake.

Difficult Scenes

The grace to cover another's conversational blunder or embarrassment and to provide spoken relief in situations that are themselves sad, anxious, or difficult is a marvelous and rare talent. When cultivated, it can make you a welcome addition to any group. At times of loss or bereavement, a few words carefully chosen and sincerely spoken can bring great comfort. Clasping the bereaved one's hand with both your hands along with a gentle squeeze and a loving facial expression may eliminate the need for words. A cheery (usually brief) visit to a person in a hospital or confined at home is a precious gift. Amusing anecdotes or interesting newsy talk can cut through the feeling of isolation the bedridden often experience. Of course, do not attempt small talk with the doctor should he or she happen to be present. Professionals in the medical field prefer that their social conversations be restricted to their private lives.

The Traveler

When you travel, part of the excitement is the opportunity to meet new people as well as to see exotic sights. But liberated though you may be, you must take certain precautions with strangers, and you can do so in a way that causes them to respect you rather than to feel offended. Do not give your name or home address to a stranger you meet in a public place. If a conversation develops, keep to impersonal topics, and do not accept hospitality either in the form of an invitation for a beverage or to dinner. You may invite the stranger to your home base if you like, to meet your mother who is traveling with you, or the chaperone of your group, or even to accompany you to a cultural event. *You* call the shots!

On a plane, conversational gambits are usually made when the flight attendant passes the first refreshments. If you are in a talking mood, fine, but if you are not, there is no need to put up with a gregarious seatmate. Indicate that you would like to read, or rest, or whatever, and feel secure in the right to do so. For absolute privacy don a sleep mask.

When traveling in foreign countries, listen to the music of the different language and try your classroom French or Spanish on salespeople, waiters, guides. Although in many countries (including the Far East), English-speakers are common, you will find that in most places your attempt to use the native language is greatly appreciated—no matter how imperfect your command of the language is.

Tips That Talk

Here are some final tips to assist you toward your goal of knowing how to reach out pleasantly to others through stimulating and polished conversation.

- Think before you speak.
- Pauses and silence are allowed.
- No one should be left out; draw a reticent person into the conversation.
- Always look directly at the person with whom you are speaking.
- Make your meanings clear in a few words.
- Be genuine.
- Do not be afraid to speak articulately and with intelligence.

Conversation is an art and should be studied as such. The person who does his or her best to talk in a fashion that is worthwhile, both in subject matter and style, is doing a very real service to others. Even one member of a group can raise the general level of conversation and make it more gracious, stimulating, and amusing.

The Electronic Word—Beauty or Beast

The telephone provides a way to do all those things the ads remind us of—be in touch with a friend long absent, make a last-minute spontaneous plan, reach out to give and receive support, reserve a restaurant table or theater tickets, or double-check movie times. But a telephone can also, two times out of ten, be an intrusion on someone else's privacy. Some people have a tendency to remain on the telephone when the conversation is long over or to call compulsively whenever they are at loose ends. These are two patterns you must avoid.

Telephone Etiquette at Home and at Large

It is a good idea for your family to devise rules to avoid disagreements over the use of the telephone. Such rules protect as well as limit all family members reasonably and fairly.

The At-Home Rules

- Set hours when you may make and receive calls and hours when you may not (such as dinnertime or after ten o'clock in the evening).
- Decide on a reasonable upper limit of length for a call (perhaps fifteen minutes).
- Choose a style for answering the phone.
- Determine a procedure for message taking.
- Decide who will answer so that the telephone does not peal eternally on the one hand, nor do several persons dash to various extensions on the other.

The Rules at Large

- Be a considerate caller.
- Telephone at times you know will be convenient (take into account the time zones).

- If you dial a wrong number, check the number you were trying against the number of the wrong party and apologize for the error.
- Put a smile in your voice to compensate for the absence of body language.
- Speak up but do not shout.
- Do not create a three-way conversation by talking to someone in the room as well as to the person on the line.
- Do not eat or chew gum.
- Turn off the radio and television so these interferences do not distract from the conversation.
- If you must leave the phone to answer the door or take brownies out of the oven, do so quickly and give your party the choice of waiting or having you call back.

Etiquette for Outgoing Calls

- Dial carefully.
- When someone answers, say, "Hello, this is Jane Mitford. May I speak to Susan, please?"
- If Susan is out, do not just hang up or mumble "Ohh." Say, "Thank you," give your name again and ask to be called back, or say you will call again. Unless you are positive that the person you called knows your telephone number, leave it. If you are asking to be called back, you should not also expect the person to look up your number.
- When you have completed your business or conversation, the person who placed the call should be the first one to end the chat and say good-bye. If you did not initiate the call, you are the "guest" and cannot hang up until the caller has.
- When you reach a telephone answering machine, do not hang up. Leave your name and telephone number and a helpful message. Do not say, "This is Mary calling about dinner tonight." Instead, say, "This is Mary, calling to confirm dinner tonight at seven o'clock at (name of restaurant)." If you are calling to chat, say that, so the person can call you back at her convenience. If it is a family machine, announce whom you are calling: "This is Mary, with a message for Sarah . . ." And remember, if it *is* a

family machine, do not leave a message so personal that you—or the person you are calling—will be embarrassed if others hear it.

Etiquette for Incoming Calls

- Do not race for the phone when it rings or you will end up out of breath when you answer.
- Say, "Hello," or "Hello, this is Angie speaking." If you answer, "Berman's residence," you sound as though you might be the housekeeper. If you answer, "206-8501," you sound as though you are a secretary in an office. Of course, in a business or a sorority house or dormitory, you would answer with the name of the establishment.
- The caller should identify him- or herself before asking to speak with someone specifically. If he or she does not, however, do not say, "May I ask who's calling?" This question makes you sound curious and implies that other members in the family may wish to speak only to certain people.
- If the call is for you, say, "This is Priscilla," or "This is she," not, "This is me" or "Speaking."
- If the call is for someone other than you, say, "Just a moment please, Mary" (using the caller's name if it has been given you). Put the phone down quietly, move away from it, and call softly for the person requested, giving the name of the person calling (if it has been given).
- If the person for whom the call is intended is not at home, say, "Jane is not here. May I take a message?" Write the message carefully and post it where it will be found. Do not rely on memory or on seeing the person soon.
- If an answering machine is used on your personal or family telephone, use brief, precise information in the announcement. "Cutesy" recorded messages are boring the second time around, if not the first, and tend to breed nonsense replies.
- "Hold" or "call waiting," which interrupts a telephone call, are not appropriate for your personal or family telephone. It is rude to interrupt a conversation with one person in order to speak with another. The busy signal is sufficient to let a caller know your line is engaged and that he or she should try again. Only an

operator cutting in with an emergency is an acceptable interruption to a telephone call.

Ma Belle and Beaus

Should a young woman call a young man on the telephone? This is one of the most frequently asked questions by students at L'Ecole des Ingénues, and I am afraid my answer is not a very popular one. In my opinion, this can be a nice gesture *only if* there is a good reason for the call—not if you just want to chat and *never* to ask, "What are you doing?????" The reasons I consider good are: to return his call at his request; to issue or answer an invitation; to convey important news; or to notify him of a change in plans. I might even consider your calling to ask for the homework assignment, but *only* if you missed school that day.

When a young man calls you, let your voice show your pleasure, but do not gush. Remember that friends or family members might overhear you—and goodness knows who else in this era of computer technology and electronic eavesdropping.

"Small Change" Words

The small change of conversation—those indispensable little words that neatly get you into and out of discussions—cannot be overlooked. A proper greeting is an essential prelude to pleasant talk, even chitchat, and a sincere "good-bye" adds an enjoyable and lingering importance to what has been said, often holding a promise of future association. Between the start and the finish of an encounter there are often points at which the small words *please, thank you,* and *I'm sorry* are the only acceptable currency.

"Hello" recognizes and salutes the presence of a new person on the scene. Learn to really welcome additions to your group. On the other hand, "goodbyes" mark a change, sometimes regrettable or even painful. The conversational exit should be sincere but never emotional, especially if the separation is not completely private.

Please is another little word that says much more than its six letters would suggest. By not using "please," the person who has met a need, large or small, is deprived of the glorious pleasure of saying, "You are welcome," gracefully completing an important exchange.

Although these small words do a yeoman's duty, they are never overworked, never boring. Modifications are, of course, used and are appropriate in various social situations. To those you know well and see often, an enthusiastic "Hi!" or "Bye!" accompanied by a smile and a wave of the hand (if there is some distance between you) is, although the most casual greeting, no doubt the most popular one. "Hello" is less formal than "How do you do?" and is a nice middle-of-the-road acknowledgment in passing. The answer to "How do you do?" is more tact than fact. Simply, "Fine, thank you. And you?"

There are times, however, when differences in age or position and formality of setting call for salutations of a less casual nature. For these encounters, you should say politely, "Good morning," "Good afternoon," or "Good night," depending upon the time of day. Always accompany a greeting with a smile, and a slight nod of the head to someone much older or of respected position. Say the person's name after your greeting if the name is known. When time permits, you may correctly follow the greeting with, "How do you do?" The same greeting will be returned to you, completing the circle.

To your farewells, when time permits and you are leaving a friend or new acquaintance you hope to see again, add, "I'm looking forward to seeing you again" or "It was so good to see you again." Remember, anything said should be said sincerely. Trite expressions like, "Have a nice day" should be avoided. They do not sound sincere regardless of the expression you place behind the words.

The exchange of greetings and farewells must be reciprocal. To fail to return a greeting is a breach of etiquette. The same is true of failing to speak to someone in passing. You may even safely speak to a stranger in passing if you do so solely to be polite, maintaining reserve and the proper body language. To speak to another is not an invitation; it is a sign of courtesy, nothing more.

Take the "small change" words with you wherever you go; they are universally accepted in any language. Think of them as a magic code through which you can, without struggling for the right phrase, express the amenities and be certain that you will be understood. Call on them often, never reserving them as "company" words alone. "Small change" words are tokens of kindness. Bestow them freely and with sincerity.

CHAPTER 7

Letter Perfect

The personal letter is best defined as a conversation inscribed on paper. Despite the sophisticated electronic communication options now available—and the mounds of junk mail that often overload the mailbox—mail time can be a small-scale holiday in a young woman's day. A special missive is a gift, and few things are more enjoyable than regular correspondence with absent friends and loved ones. It is a matchless means of enriching established relationships and forming new ones, and I strongly recommend your initiation of a pen pal friendship with a young person in a distant land.

Sincere, old-fashioned letters are a better way to bring today's world closer together than the electronic miracles that have been shrinking it. The handwritten letter is, and always will be, the most personal and most satisfying substitute for being there. There is an aura of mystique about a letter. Think of the great ocean liners carrying world travelers and bulging mailbags. Think of the pony express. And in many ways, the written word is far more eloquent than the spoken word.

These pleasures, for both the writer and the recipient, are heightened today because good letters have too often given way to telephone calls. Convenient as it may be, the telephone has brought about a great loss—the neglect of the written word as a means of social communication. When you think about it, it is, in fact, more polite to write than call. Even the nicest telephone call intrudes upon the privacy of the other person. It may be received at an inopportune time and actually be an inconvenience. The letter, on the other hand, is a private matter. The recipient may choose to open and scan it first, then set it aside to enjoy at leisure. There are even some social occasions for which there is no correct substitute for a proper letter.

Writing helps you to organize your thoughts and explore your feelings, since you are free to express them without self-consciousness or interruption. In describing your emotions, you must first think them through and then in turn find the exact words to express them permanently on paper.

To receive a well-written letter is just as joyous as to send it. How many times have you held a letter for a moment or two in anticipation of its contents? Before opening it, have you ever refrained from turning it over to read the name of the sender? With a personal letter, I do not simply tear open the envelope and quickly scan the contents. Instead, I go to my writing table or a favorite chair, settle myself, and carefully lift the flap of the envelope. If I find it tightly sealed, I resort to my letter opener, but I prefer to seal my own letters fairly lightly so that my readers can open the flap with ease and enjoy the color of the envelope lining. Once the letter is opened, I relax in my favorite place and read with much pleasure, or sometimes sadness, words written especially to me.

I stress to you that letters have a permanent and tangible quality to them. A letter can be read and reread and preserved. It can be hidden away for inspiration at a later time. Letters bring with them friendship, caring, and the sharing of one's thoughts with another. Your letter is your personal envoy—make it your goodwill ambassador. Your letters distill and reflect the image of your personality, character, taste, and even your personal appearance—your letter tells all! Or, perhaps I should say that "you are the way you write."

Letter writing is an important form of communication, which should be taken seriously. Neatly written, it shows that you present yourself fastidiously; attractively placed upon the page, it shows you possess artistic judgment; correctly spelled and punctuated, the sentences depict your concern for accuracy. Just the right word denotes your pride in development of a distinctive vocabulary, and free of ink blots, strikeovers, erasures, or white-outs, your letter shows your pride in perfection. Words flowing as freely as you would speak them in person show your warmth, friendship, and sincerity.

The Art of Letter Writing

A wonderful way to learn to write personal letters is to study those you receive. When you were away at camp, at school, or on a trip, there may have been a special relative who wrote you letters you loved to open. What made them special? Think how they came to life, like a flow of conversation, so you could picture not only the writer, but yourself and that person together talking.

Many famous people throughout history have written unforgettable letters to their children, spouses, parents, and lovers. Some of this correspondence has been treasured and preserved, like that of Lord Chesterfield to his son in the eighteenth century. Below is an excerpt addressed "Dear Boy," and concluded simply "Adieu." Two centuries later, its good advice still rings true:

> When you write to me, suppose yourself conversing freely with me by the fireside. In that case, you would naturally mention the incidents of the day; as where you had been, whom you had seen, what you thought of them, and so forth. Do this in your letters! Acquaint me sometimes with your diversions; tell me of any new persons or characters that you meet in company; and add your own observations upon them. *In short, let me see more of you in your letters*.

It is, as Chesterfield points out, your spirit that will delight your correspondent in a personal letter. Using nice writing paper and writing with a good pen already says, "You count"—these constitute the shell, and putting yourself on paper fills it.

The art of letter writing has been almost changeless over the ages. You can experience the power of a letter to cast a spell or mood over another person when you read the old letters kept by your family, or between famous people of the past. In the library, look at the correspondence between Elizabeth Barrett and Robert Browning, who fell in love through the written word before they ever met, or from Scott Fitzgerald to his daughter and to his wife, Zelda, or Madame de Sévigné to her daughter when she moved far from Paris. These letters would have the same power and charm today; they are dated but are not out-of-date!

You, too, will write a well-turned letter if your thoughts to the other person are genuine, friendly, and appropriate to the relationship you have when face-to-face.

Putting Pen to Paper

At the writing table, prepare your mood and arrange your thoughts. Personally, I prefer a large writing table that I can fill and clutter with my social paper trousseau and personal business papers, pens, inkwells, letter openers, dictionaries, special-issue stamps, and a favorite plant and lamp.

You probably have your own favorite spot. It must be tranquil and should put you in a rather formal mood. You cannot write a proper letter lying on the couch in your recreation room or den with your sneakered feet up in the air and the television blaring. Instead, you should be quiet and composed, in a mood to write a letter where every word counts.

Think about the appearance of your writing on the page from the start. You want your handwriting, grammar, and punctuation to match the quality of your writing paper. Watch your fingers for ink, which might smudge the page as you write. Keep your other hand, elbow, arm, and hair off the page to avoid ugly smears. Consider putting a line guide under the page, so that the lines you write will be even and well spaced.

Sit Back and Close Your Eyes

Before you start your letter, close your eyes and picture the face of the person to whom you are writing. Allow their image to fill the blank page of writing paper before you. Relive the last time you were together in person. Now, open your eyes and write the very words you would say were you visiting face-to-face once again. Write your thoughts exactly as they appear in your mind. Do not embroider them or change them to words you do not normally use in your spoken conversation. This is the key to putting your spoken personality into your writing.

The Opening

Begin with your best. Begin on a high note of interest that brings the reader a sense of the tone and intent of the whole letter. Avoid opening with an apology for a delay in writing, with the words *I* or *thank you* (because they are trite), or with mention of the other's last letter (too businesslike). Begin graciously and with warmth. You might say, for instance, "Don't you wish we could have a nice long talk like the one we had at the beach last month? I have so much to say! First of all, my grades just arrived, and I am thrilled with them. Have you received yours yet? . . ." And so on, the letter continues—newsy and alive.

The Body

William Cobbett, an early-nineteenth-century writer, has given me inspiration of which I often think when I begin to write. Perhaps his words will also assist you in bringing life into your letters:

> Sit down to write what you have thought, and not to think what you shall write! Use the first words that occur to you and never attempt to alter a thought; for that which has come of itself into your mind is likely to pass into that of another readily and with more effect than anything which you can, by reflection, invent.

Think of yourself as a reporter on your life and tell the *news*. A sometime rule of letter writing is to speak only of the other person in the first paragraph, only of oneself in the second. I find this approach to be too cut-and-dried, but the lesson is there—do not write *only* about yourself; keep the receiver in mind. Although you are the one wielding the pen, make your correspondent feel involved, too.

The Close

The close of your letters is equally as important as the opening and the news in between. The close constitutes the last thought, the last embrace, so to speak, of a conversation between friends. If the conversation is businesslike in nature, the close is similar to a handshake; if between friends, it is a smile, a tight hug, and a wave good-bye; if between boyfriend and girlfriend sharing love letters, it is the final embrace before parting. The last sentence of a letter becomes the memory that lingers.

In closing your letter, never rely on "I am busy; my ride is coming; I have to run." You do not wish to give a person the impression you were writing merely to fill time. If you expect the receipt of your letter to be a special event, you must, in your closing, communicate that the writing was special.

The Complimentary Close

Bridging the closing sentence and your signature is the complimentary close, the short greeting written in a word or two. The words used are governed by the degree of formality or the closeness of friendship between the writer and recipient of the letter. Although you need not feel confined to the familiar and standard complimentary closes for informal social notes and friendly letters, you may find this list helpful: Yours very sincerely, Yours cordially, Faithfully yours, Sincerely yours, Most cordially yours, Always sincerely yours, Sincerely.

More intimate complimentary closings, suited to notes and letters between close friends and relatives, include: With love, Fondly, Yours affectionately, Your loving sister, Always affectionately yours, and "pet" closings of your own.

The Postscript . . . Never!

Avoid P.S.! Adding a postscript to a letter is messy form. Any thoughts worth expressing are worth being included in the body of the letter. Otherwise, they appear as afterthoughts, which indeed they are. Besides, they spoil the beauty of your closing, the harmonious tone of your letter, and look unsightly tagged onto a lovely piece of writing paper.

The Duty Letters

Just as I tell you today, so did *Young Lady's Own Book* tell its reader in 1838: "Various are the occasions on which you will be called upon to exercise your skill in the art of letter writing."

"Duty letters" are a test of your writing skill and your manners. They are also the very first letters you ever wrote when your parents insisted you write thank-you notes for your sixth or seventh birthday or holiday gifts. Was it such agony that you wished your great-aunt had not sent the lace handkerchiefs or ten-dollar bill? Duty letters can be much easier if you recognize them as that—a duty, and a pleasant one at that. They have a *point*. Determine what the point is in advance, filter it through your mind, and the duty letter will flow just like any other friendly letter.

All duty letters are structurally alike—the style is quite formal, the message brief. Whether thanking someone for a pleasant weekend or conveying condolence to a bereaved friend, each letter has the single purpose of conveying your feelings on a particular subject to another; and the formalized style is the most proper and effective way to do this.

Your choice of words and tempo, varying from élan to sobriety, will create the right mood within this proper framework. Letters prompted by loss, disappointment, or death need not be lacking in tenderness, especially when intimacy between the writer and the recipient exists. Above all, remember that your letters should not be stereotyped. They can and should reflect you and your relationship with your correspondent.

Appearance, choice of wording, and correctness of writing paper and ink are also important. Promptness in writing and posting this kind of letter is paramount. A tardy acknowledgment, except in the event of a major emergency, is little better than none at all.

Every young woman must develop the "art" of writing duty letters if she is to be in charge of her social situation. The types of basic duty letters are described and categorized below according to the circumstances in which they are used. My sample letters are certain to spark ideas as you pen your words.

The Letter of Thanks

Acknowledgments of gifts or other favors are the most frequent, the easiest, and the most pleasant forms of "duty" correspondence. Tips to make yours individual and special include: avoidance of starting off with a trite "thanks for"; mentioning the gift and your delight with it; replying promptly to let the giver know that the item arrived safely and to reinforce your pleasure in being remembered. Letters of congratulations, too, call for an immediate and gracious note of thanks. The notable exception to the requirement for an immediate acknowledgment is for wedding presents, especially when the wedding is large, an extended honeymoon is planned, and/or when the bride is continuing her career. In these circumstances printed cards (acknowledgment cards) informing the giver of the safe arrival of his or her gift and assuring that a "thank-you" letter will follow are now frequently dispatched and are appropriate. A limited delay is permitted, too, for sending thank-you letters for gifts or favors received when one has been ill, or similarly for flowers, letters of condolence, or courtesies bestowed upon one who has suffered bereavement. Letters of thanks are written on note paper. Hence the name "thank-you notes." Less formal, short notes to your peers can be dashed off on correspondence cards, longer more formal ones on folded letter sheets or half-sheets.

Dear Mrs. Atkins,

The lovely dinner plates in my china pattern that you and Mr. Atkins sent me are a wonderful and a generous gift. I was thrilled to receive them and will think gratefully of your kindness as I use and care for my service through the years. Because china is my special love, Dan and I chose an antique china cabinet that has spacious storage for my treasured Spode.

Thank you for your contribution to our new home.

Sincerely,

Marian Edwards Gregory

June the twentieth

The Bread-and-Butter Letter

Think of a bread-and-butter letter as an echo of a pleasant occasion, an opportunity to extend your appreciation for the warmth of the event to your hostess. Having been included at a seated dinner party, at a house party, on a trip, or for a family visit demands a written and an immediate expression of appreciation. The formality of the affair and the intimacy of your relationship with your hostess dictates the degree of formality in the wording. Visits or entertainments in a peer's home call for a bread-and-butter letter to the friend's mother (the senior, or formal, hostess) in addition to the friend (the junior hostess). The letter to the senior hostess is just as "bubbly" and enthusiastic—never stilted and stiff—as the one to the junior hostess. Printed "thank-you" cards are a social no-no for this or any duty letter. Correspondence cards are a bit too breezy for all but the most casual cookout. Use note paper for brief notes. Lengthy bread-and-butter letters are written on folded letter sheets or half-sheets.

Dear Kitty,

Having known me so long, you have to be aware that I am a summertime person. But after last weekend at your family's new lodge in the Adirondacks, my idea of Paradise has become a cozy cabin on a snowy mountain with a fire burning brightly inside and icicles gleaming on tall firs outside. My feeble attempts at skiing were fun despite the tumbles, and I am disgustingly proud of making one passable run. Food has never tasted so good nor company been more enjoyable. I have written to your mother to thank her for letting us have the house party. As I told her, I am studying harder and with better results since the invigorating break!

I will have to think hard to plan something for the crowd that will be even half as much fun. Be sure to keep in touch about the progress of your new romance.

Love,

Gwyn

February the eighth

Dear Mrs. Gray,

You and Mr. Gray were wonderful to plan the house party for us at your lodge in the mountains. The house is so attractive and so cozy and I, not always very adventurous, thought I'd be enjoying that magnificent snow from behind glass. I was, however, carried away, quite literally, by the enthusiasm of the others and never had so much fun nor felt more proud than when I actually skiied.

Everything was perfect—the food, the weather, the company—and being together, away from the school routine, got me out of the midwinter doldrums. I am studying more effectively and my grades are beginning to show it.

Thank you both for a fabulous time.

Sincerely,

Gwyn Alterman

February the eighth

The Letter of Congratulations

Letters of congratulations are short and to the point, sincere, spontaneous, and enthusiastic. The handwritten note is by far more personal and gracious and is always preferable to the message on a printed card. Be sure that no tinge of envy or jealousy creeps into your applause of another's good fortune. Congratulatory letters are called for when friends or relatives have birthdays, graduate, receive promotions, win awards, become engaged (letters of congratulations to the groom-elect, letters bearing good wishes for her happiness to the bride-to-be), and have babies. Your life will be richer if you enjoy these happy events with people you know. Depending upon the informality or formality of the congratulatory remarks, these happy letters can be penned on correspondence cards, notes, folded letter sheets, or half-sheets.

Dear Kevin,

It is so exciting to know someone smart enough to earn a fellowship for graduate study at a great institution like the University of Virginia! I have long suspected that you were extra intelligent for such a good dancer, and I know that you will do well and have a brilliant career.

I am returning to Sweet Briar for my junior year, but I get home often. Maybe we will meet at some of the parties during the holidays—I will be anxious to know that the dancing is not suffering from all the academics.

Sincerely,

Amanda Hutchings

August the fourth

The Letter of Introduction

The letter of introduction must strike a delicate balance between enthusiasm and discretion and should be written only for a person whom you can introduce with pleasure and confidence. Just as you must never ask for a letter of introduction, neither must you ask too much of the friend to whom you are presenting another. A stranger does not have to be asked to Thanksgiving dinner because you are calling his or her presence to the attention of another friend. Such an introduction should serve only to open the door to a meeting, leaving the course of any further exchange up to the parties involved. Although such a letter is more often mailed directly to the person to whom you are introducing someone, the letter of introduction is sometimes handed over (unsealed) to the friend for whom you are writing it, who in turn hands it over personally to the person to whom it is written. On many occasions, both letters are written. The folded letter sheet or half-sheet is best suited for the letter of introduction. The calling card may also be used, whereby the words *Introducing Fran Green* are penned above the engraved name on the card of the person making the introduction. The card is placed in an envelope and given directly to the friend for whom you are writing it; the private letter is sent to the other party.

Dear Eileen,

My college sorority sister Fran Green (now Mrs. Blake Andrews) and her new husband, who has accepted a position with the legal firm of Sellers and King in your city, have taken up residence at the Regency Apartments on Spring Drive, and I am hoping that you will meet and will become friends.

Fran is a wonderful person, fun to be with and always ready to participate in church, club, and civic activities. I do not know her husband well, but he is very attractive and, from his professional connection, I assume he is extremely competent. Perhaps he and Tom will be congenial as they are both avid tennis players.

I would appreciate any courtesy you could extend to them and would be pleased if two of my special friends should become friends themselves.

Affectionately,

Elizabeth Anne

August the eighteenth

Introducing Fran Green

Miss Elizabeth Anne Morgan

130

The Letter of Cheer and Encouragement

When someone you care for is "down," "blue," or in trouble of any kind—serious illness, accidents, disappointment, emotional upheavals, or important material loss—he or she needs you and you must respond. Even when the doctor permits visitors, a patient undergoing severe pain or one struggling with the handling of even a temporary disfigurement rarely wishes to be on display and should not be subjected to such stress. The emotional effect of substantial material loss or the pain and embarrassment of public rejection, such as a broken engagement, can be as devastating as physical illness and most people need privacy in order to cope.

It is during these times that a letter of support and caring is a sensitive and appropriate reaction. The heartfelt "encouraging word" is the essence of such a communication—it should not be a "doomsday" missive. It says, "I'm sorry," but its beat is "up" and it is focused on the recipient's interests rather than on the sender's exciting activities. While not minimizing the sufferer's pain or distress, it should communicate optimism. Do not risk becoming a "Job's comforter" by offering unsolicited advice. Avoid, especially, any "I told you so" inflection, or insinuate that the sufferer has brought the trouble on himself or herself. Come up with at least one newsy item that you think will interest the recipient of your letter but keep it short. Offers of help are important if they are sincere and appropriate to the situation. Mail the note promptly so that it will be there in your place when your friend feels like turning—and returning—to it. If the situation is an extended one, follow with a series of bright notes, perhaps interspersed with attractive and appropriate commercial greeting cards, until you are sure that a visit will be welcome. The note, half-sheet, or folded letter sheet offers the perfect backdrop for the letter of encouragement and a charming choice for your cheerful note. The colorful correspondence card adds a plus to the encouraging word for a peer or to a series of notes.

> *Dear Molly,*
>
> *Mary Brown told me about the automobile accident and your being in the hospital with two broken bones and some cuts. I am so sorry that it had to happen while you were visiting your aunt and uncle—I know how much you had looked forward to the trip.*
>
> *I'm sure you look beautiful piled up on your white eyelet pillows and suspect that you will tear through all the new best-sellers and be far ahead of the rest of us in the Contemporary Lit course next fall.*

The best thing about the entire situation is that none of your injuries will be permanent and that you will be all well and at home by the time school starts. If I can do anything for you here, please let me know.

Love,

Michelle

July the sixth

The Letter of Condolence

Delicacy, brevity, and caring are the keys to a proper condolence letter. Since it is written to a person at the time of grieving over the death of a loved one, think of this letter as a soothing and uplifting companion—ready to add comfort during a quiet, private moment. It is a tender letter, which will be read many times for the peaceful uplifting it bears. Make sure you read it before sending. Letters of condolence are written *only* on the perfectly plain (unmarked) ecru or pearl white folded letter sheet and in black or dark blue ink.

Dear Teresa,

It was a shock to hear of your grandmother's sudden death. I have seen her only rarely since you moved away, but when I did she seemed well and looked lovely. Our meeting always brought back memories of happy times she and your grandfather planned for us when we were small.

I hope that you are thinking of these and, of course, many other joys you have shared with her to help you through the first hard grief. Later, remembering her will help you—and some of your close friends like me who had the pleasure of knowing her—to be better mothers and someday better grandmothers than we otherwise might have been.

I continue to miss you and keep hoping that someday we will live near each other again. Please give my love to your mother and tell her how sad I am.

Love,

Luci

May the ninth

The Letter of Apology

A letter of apology is in order when perchance you may have been tardy to an appointment or social engagement, have had to cancel a commitment, have been remiss, negligent, or unkind, have embarrassed or offended or inconvenienced another. Do not belabor your apology even though this is distinctly a one-point letter. Regret and an explanation (if one is appropriate) meet the requirements of this special communication. No commercial greeting card fills the bill. Your own words should express your feelings. According to the length, letters of apology may be written on notes, half-sheets, or folded letter sheets.

> *Dear Sally,*
>
> *What can I say to make you understand how truly sorry I am to have been a part of the teasing session about you and Hal that made you cry. I had no idea that the two of you were quarreling and neither did Jane and Kate. That is no excuse for taking the chance of hurting someone you care about and you can be sure that I, for one, will never be guilty of such a thing again.*
>
> > *Your devoted friend,*
> >
> > *Carrie*
>
> *December the fourth*

The Letter of Complaint

The proper way to communicate complaints to others, including friends and neighbors, is through a written statement. It is not only more impressive and less embarrassing than a verbal complaint, but can be legally important as well. For instance, if one is to collect for damage to one's person or property from a neighbor's falling tree, one must, in some states, have warned the owner that the tree was dangerous.

A notification of complaint should be polite but direct. In critical situations it should be sent by registered mail. Date the letter correctly. Keep a carbon copy and the registration receipt when there is one. While it is important that a mature young woman be able to write a letter of complaint in protest of unsatisfactory business or other public situations, she is more apt to be facing unhappy personal relationships. In these, also, the written protest is less embarrassing to both parties. It also allows a statement of the misunderstanding or hurt feelings without interruption or argument, and provides a built-in cooling-off time, which should work toward a solution rather than an enlargement of the difference. As these are often businesslike, letters of complaint should be written on half-sheets or folded letter sheets, or they may be handwritten or typed on monarch or letter-size paper.

314 Park Circle
Orlando, Florida 32802
June 16, 1990

Mr. Marshall Q. Hill
298 Park Circle
Orlando, Florida 32802

Dear Mr. Hill:

    Twice last week your dog rushed at me when I was walking to the bus stop and jumped upon me. On one occasion he muddied my skirt and on the other he snagged my stockings. A third morning he was barking furiously at the Barnes' housekeeper who was just coming to work, and I tried to divert him since she was badly frightened.

    I am not really afraid of Rowdy, but it is inconvenient and expensive to have my clothing spoiled, and I sympathize with older people and small children who are afraid of him. You surely know that there is a leash law in our neighborhood, and I ask you to abide by it as other residents do.

Sincerely yours,

(Miss) Andrea Elder

The Letter of Recommendation

Letters of recommendation are written on behalf of a friend or acquaintance who is seeking or being considered for employment, appointment, a scholarship, membership in professional or social organizations, academic achievement, and other situations when qualifications, character, or personality are considerations. They are largely business communications and should be factual rather than flowery. Take care that you claim for the person only assets or attributes you know he or she possesses. Remember that you have an obligation to the individual you are addressing as well as to the one being recommended. Short letters of recommendation may be handwritten on half-sheets or folded letter sheets. However, many letters of recommendation are somewhat longer and more businesslike than other duty letters and should be written, preferably typewritten, on good quality letter-size paper.

Dear Dr. Kelsey,

   I have just found out that I have been accepted into a student program between State and the University of Mexico in which our group will study Spanish Lit and teach English to Mexican children in their demonstration school. As the program lasts from late June until early August, I will not be able to help you with the vacation reading program this summer.

   If you do not have someone in mind for my job (which I have so loved), I would like to suggest Elizabeth Harrison, who lives in my neighborhood and is a sophomore in the education school here. Beth loves books and children and we have worked together on a program for underprivileged youngsters here. I think she is good! You can reach her at the college, Box 384-G, or through her parents, Mr. and Mrs. Gray L. Harrison, 3749 Elm Street in Cleveland.

Affectionately,

Charlotte Miller

May the twenty-first

The Letter of Application

A letter of application has much in common with the letter of recommendation. Now, however, you are recommending yourself and you are on firmer ground when it comes to assembling facts, but on a very narrow path in the matter of extolling your intangible qualities. It is all right to report that you had a B plus or an A average, but not to say that you are smart. Up to this point, you have most likely had very little working experience, and it would be foolish to claim that you have. Yet you have probably accumulated a good deal of "know-how" through volunteer activities, summer programs, and part-time jobs. This is valuable and should not be ignored.

   The application letter is apt to play a significant part in the upcoming period of your life. You will be seeking part-time or summer jobs, special programs, college admission, scholarships, and then a career position, which could set the quality not only of your working but of your social life. It is, therefore, important to accumulate the academic record, the character reputation, the savoir faire, and the basic business skills that could make you an acceptable employee, and to acquire the skill of presenting them on paper as well as in person.

   A command of English grammar and a bit of flair in presenting your limited accomplishments and your unlimited aspirations will produce a very good letter of application. Give the essential facts in the body of the letter or in an attached résumé: age, education, work record, travel, special programs, hobbies, social and philanthropic organizations, and other pertinent facts.

Request an interview and provide information through which you may be reached by mail or telephone. Neatly type the letter on quality business letter-size paper. Go over your letter carefully for correctness and appearance and redo if necessary. Then fold it properly and insert it in a number ten business envelope. Mail it on the day it is dated. If the job is right for you and you are right for the job, a good letter can help get you together.

1204 Riverbend Drive
Columbia, Missouri 65201
February 19, 1990

Mr. Harold Parks
Director
The Design Connection
Hillside Square
Columbia, Missouri 65201

Dear Mr. Parks:

Please consider me for the training position your firm is currently advertising. I will graduate from Stephens College in June with an AB degree in Interior Design, and I hope to become associated with a design firm of the distinction of The Design Connection, where I can continue my education and, I hope, bring some of my ideas to reality.

My academic record for my four years at Stephens is approximately 3.7 with a solid 4.0 in courses in my major over the past two years. You may contact my counselor, Professor Louis Valle, for an estimate of my ability and my willingness to work hard on any project I undertake.

In January I received the first place award in a national collegiate contest for decorating a small urban apartment, sponsored by the Renaissance Furniture Crafters. During my junior year, I designed the sets for Stephens' Players presentation of *The Little Foxes,* and they received favorable mention in several reviews. I have had some sales experience working in gift and accessory shops during holidays.

I am twenty-two years of age and a native of Columbia, where my parents presently live at the above address. I am usually at home on weekends, and my parents will take messages when I am not. The telephone number is 871-9802. I can also be reached through the Design Department at Stephens and would appreciate your granting me an interview at your early convenience.

Sincerely yours,

(Miss) Mary Ellen Yates

The Letter

You are now ready for *the* letter that is never a duty, the love letter, known as the billet-doux.

Love letters have their own very special language understood only between the writer and the recipient. So fond am I of the love letter that I want to share with you my love letter "dos" and "do nots" and love letter "secrets."

LOVE LETTER DOS AND DO NOTS

Do be sincere. . . .
Do write as the heart dictates. . . .
Do let your romantic inclinations have sway. . . .
Do write in ink of a socially acceptable color. . . .
Do choose striking paper of the socially proper colors. . . .
Do wait for his reply before you shoot off another love letter. . . .

Do Not strain for effect. . . .
Do Not make any undying promises. . . .
Do Not say anything that can be misconstrued. . . .
Do Not say anything about which his little brother or sister could tease him. . . .
Do Not write anything that could be personally—or legally—embarrassing. . . .
Do Not write in flowery words that might confuse him. . . .
Do Not put perfume on letters to him. . . .
Do Not put lipstick prints on his letter. . . .
Do Not write coded messages on the outside of the envelope such as S.W.A.K. (Sealed With a Kiss)!
Do Not tuck in a handful of hearts to spill out all over his room. . . .
Do Not make him feel guilty for not writing; he probably hates the pen. . . .
Do Not send a formal studio photograph unless he asks for it. . . .

> LOVE LETTER SECRETS
>
> 1. Secret Number One— Tuck in a fortune from a fortune cookie. . . .
> 2. Secret Number Two— Tuck in a ticket stub from a concert that you attended with him. . . .
> 3. Secret Number Three—Tuck in a review of a play, movie, or concert that you attended with him or that you want to attend with him. . . .
> 4. Secret Number Four— Tuck in a photo of you, you and your kitty or dog, or you two together. . . .
> 5. Secret Number Five— Love lies between the lines. . . .

Packaging Your Letter

The letter, so beautifully and thoughtfully written, deserves the most perfect packaging. Packaging includes not only the envelope addressed in the proper fashion, but also the manner in which the writing paper is folded and slipped into the respective envelope.

The informal or note is folded once neatly and the name or monogram (or first page) faces up and toward the back of the envelope with the fold on top when the envelope is opened. The half-sheet folds forward in half, and the folded letter sheet (in addition to its original vertical left fold) folds forward in half a second time. Each is inserted into the envelope with the fold at the top and the left margin of the written message (or vertical left fold of the folded letter sheet) parallel with the left side of the envelope (when facing the back of the envelope). The correspondence card and the flat card informal are not folded, and the name or monogram and the message itself face the back of the envelope, reading the same direction as the address on the back flap of the envelope.

For personal business letters, the monarch sheet or letterhead sheet is folded twice (into three equal parts) and inserted into the envelope with the back of the top portion on top and facing the reader when the envelope is opened. The first fold should be on top.

Envelopes must be addressed in as careful a manner as the letter or note they contain. For social correspondence, I require of my students at L'Ecole des Ingénues that each word be spelled in full when addressing an envelope,

138

except for the state name, which the post office now requires be abbreviated. Full spelling is a must also for your return address.

If you have not yet invested in personalized writing papers, you need only write your address on the back flap of the envelope, without your name. As you await your personalized social paper trousseau, you may wish to purchase an inexpensive embosser with which you can blind emboss your address on the flap of the envelope.

Place the address of the person for whom your letter is intended attractively on the face of the envelope and affix the stamp in the upper right-hand corner with a small margin remaining on the top and right sides to frame it.

Now, the last remaining steps will be taken by the postman; and your personality—as you have properly expressed it, penned it, and enclosed it within the "puff" of your envelope—will soon be shared with the person to whom the letter was written.

A Point to Ponder

The computer and typewriter are no doubt a part of your everyday language. However, at L'Ecole des Ingénues, I do ask that my students "push the pen" for all social correspondence.

"Penned" social correspondence, even after the advent of the electronic age, has always been the mark of the socially correct throughout Europe and America. In the realm of pens, as with other luxuries, tradition continually reasserts itself. The more technically oriented our society becomes, the more emphasis we place on personal, handcrafted things. A return to the grace and distinction of the fountain pen throughout the world is part of this trend.

To those of you who have grown up in the ballpoint and felt-tip world, liquid ink (ballpoint ink is paste) is an exciting discovery. Ink from a fountain pen flows over a page more easily and with less exertion or pressure. Fine writing papers, with their rag content, are made to receive the ink beautifully. The ink also carries a lasting look, and adds the mark of good taste to your written words and signature.

The fountain pen you choose will be an expression of your personality as well as one of the most gracious personal accessories you own. Just like your first gold watch and strand of pearls, your fountain pen is certain to become a part of your personal statement.

Can you send a letter written on a computer? If your home computer or word processor has "cold print," no. But if you have a computer and like the idea of doing some of your correspondence on it, put a "letter quality" printer on your Christmas wish list and you can at least do your business correspondence on it. For business letters, set up a template with your address already at the top or right of the page as it might be engraved on stationery. This will save you time and prevent your typing in the address with an unnoticed error.

As you develop the art of letter writing, with the correct social writing papers and an elegant, precious pen, your success is nearly assured. As you grow letter-perfect, the flow of the ink becomes your "voice" and the letter your surprise "visit." Together they create your personality on paper. A corresponding point to ponder is that once sent, a letter can never be retrieved!

CHAPTER 8

The Social Paper Trousseau

Paper is so much a part of our everyday lives that we have come to take it for granted. Yet fine stationery can be a beautiful means of personal expression. And that is why the selection of your personal social papers is an important step in defining and refining *you*.

Your writing paper is as much a reflection of your good taste as your dress, makeup, and manners. The impression it makes begins even before the letter, note, or invitation is opened. As a subtle expression of your sense of quality, it should stand out from the rest of the day's mail.

When you receive a letter written upon beautiful paper, you sense a certain luxurious "touch" to the paper itself, a special "puff" to the envelope, which sets the communiqué—and its writer—apart, especially in this era of computer-generated junk mail. The correctness of this "touch" and "puff" is a compliment to you as well as to those with whom you correspond.

Now that you have been introduced to the somewhat complicated protocol of letter writing, you are ready to begin assembling the proper materials for your personal correspondence. In order to make the proper choices, you must first familiarize yourself with the terminology of social papers and acquaint yourself with the wide variety of available fine writing papers.

The Terminology of Social Papers

"Rag" Paper

Just as in the first century, cotton and linen rag fibers are still the most enduring materials from which paper can be made. For strength, durability, and "feel," the best writing paper is 100 percent cotton "rag," made from long, strong cotton fibers. Strength is advantageous if the paper is going to be folded or engraved in any way, and the cotton fibers are well-suited to the art of engraving. Legally, rag-content paper must contain from 25 to 100 percent cotton fibers and is usually watermarked to show that content.

Watermark

The watermark, which first appeared in Europe around 1280, is a translucent seal impressed or molded into the fibers of paper as it is being formed. When you hold a finished sheet of watermarked paper to the light, you may see not only the rag content but also the name of the paper and sometimes the private mark of the person or establishment who is going to use it.

Finish

The finish of writing paper is a physical property determined during the papermaking process. Laid finish is subtly patterned and bears a just perceptible texture of lines, giving it a ribbed effect. Wove finish is perfectly smooth, with no apparent pattern. Hold writing paper up to the light and you can see which of the two finishes it is. Beyond these two basic types, the word *finish* is often used to describe different surfaces of the paper such as vellum finish, parchment finish, and plate finish.

Engraving

Engraving is one of the oldest forms of the graphic arts, closely resembling illustrative etching. In this process, a design or lettering style is etched or hand-cut below the surface of the engraving die or plate. Engraving is considered the highest quality printing and is *de rigueur* for formal social papers when within one's budget.

Die or Plate

The engraving die is a copper or steel plate on which "copy"—the name, monogram, address—is carefully etched with a needle, by machine, by hand, or by lines from a computerized film etched in acid. The die is used to transfer ink to the surface of the paper. Once cut, the engraving die can be reused endlessly.

Die Stamping

Die stamping is the process that transfers ink to the paper from the die. The ink is applied to the die. It is then wiped clean, leaving some ink in the grooves formed by the engraving or etching process. Paper is then placed between the die and the "counter" in a printing press. The press puts pressure on the counter, the paper is forced into the cavities of the die, and the ink is transferred onto the paper.

For the most expensive engraved writing papers, the die is reinked and wiped clean for each sheet of paper. Thus each sheet is "one-of-a-kind"! Engraved or die-stamped lettering produces a clear, three-dimensional, finely detailed image that is raised above the surface of the paper and possesses a soft matte finish.

Blind Embossing

Blind embossing is also created with an engraving die or plate. The difference here is that no ink is applied. The letters are cut or etched deeper into the metal plate than for inked engraving, creating a monogram, name, or address that is raised. The result is a sophisticated, colorless relief in look and feel. This same plate cannot, however, be used for an inked design due to the depth of its cut.

Bruise

The bruise is the slight indentation or impression that the engraving die leaves on the back of the paper. It is caused by the pressure of the engraving plate or die on the paper during the engraving or die-stamping process, and is a means of identifying true engraving.

Thermography

Thermography, also known as raised printing, was invented to imitate engraving. It requires no engraving die or plate, and it leaves no impression on the reverse side of the paper.

In this style of printing, a dense ink is transferred to the surface of the paper. While still wet, it is dusted with a resinous powder. When the excess is vacuumed off, a residue adheres. The sheet of paper is next sent through a dryer, where the heat raises the letters and dries the ink. Certain fine lines and details cannot be reproduced with the thermography process, and the raised lettering has a shininess and can be scraped off the paper with a fingernail. Thermography is less expensive than engraving and offers a socially suitable alternate when one's budget is limited.

Weight

Writing paper comes in different weights: heavy, medium, and light. Poundage refers to the weight of a ream (500 sheets) of a certain standard size. Forty-pound and 32-pound paper are most often used for engraved, or otherwise printed, social writing papers. Naturally, airmail weight is much lighter—16-pound or less.

Card Stock

Card stock is thicker, heavier paper, two, three, or four times as thick as writing paper. Card stock is used for calling cards, card informals, correspondence cards, and flat invitations.

The Social Paper Trousseau

The word *trousseau* brings to my mind the image of a group of related items—a bundle—needed for a certain purpose. The social paper trousseau contains the varieties of proper social papers needed for three purposes that you, as a young woman, may encounter: identifying yourself socially, issuing and accepting invitations, and writing notes and letters. The social paper trousseau should be considered special and very personal. It represents your personality and also your knowledge of what is in good taste and proper at a given time and in a given social situation.

Assembling your social paper trousseau is as glamorous an adventure as coordinating a tasteful and fashionable wardrobe. It allows you to combine color, pattern, line, quality, fashion, and style into the statement you wish to make on paper.

It may well be that you already possess part of your social paper trousseau. You may have received calling cards as a gift or even have some left over from your childhood years. Did you ever receive monogrammed notes, or even letter sheets engraved with your name? Determine what your trousseau already includes, and then decide on your additional needs.

Your Paper Profile

First, list the kinds of written notes, messages, letters, and invitations you write and receive. Ask yourself:

Do I meet new people whose friendship I would like to develop?

Do I send gifts with a message or greeting on a card?

Do I receive or send invitations to informal parties or events?

Do I receive informal or formal written invitations to which I send written replies?

Do I write quick notes to friends?

Do I receive gifts for which I write thank-you notes?

Do I write congratulations to friends when something especially nice happens to them?

Do I write long friendship letters?

Do I write more formal or friendly letters to relatives?

Do I send notes to a host or hostess or to someone's mother after a lovely dinner or weekend at her home?

Do I write comforting letters to friends when something sad or unfortunate happens to them?

Do I write letters to my boyfriend?

Do I write a note of apology on occasion?

Do I write a friend in another city to introduce a friend from my hometown who is moving there?

Do I request brochures or order merchandise through the mail?

Do I write seeking a job or to ask a former employer for a recommendation?

In all these cases certain rules and regulations govern the type of paper upon which the message should be placed and the form it should take. This is the protocol and etiquette of social writing.

Trousseau Tips and Decisions

Before compiling a trousseau of writing papers, you must first consider the pieces that comprise it. I will introduce you to what I consider *Le Grand Trousseau* of proper papers for almost every social occasion a young woman might encounter, and the proper manner in which to personalize each. Then, from *Le Grand Trousseau*, I will take *Le Petit Trousseau,* a beginning collection of social papers, and you will learn the order in which to add social papers as you build toward *Le Grand Trousseau.*

Before choosing the different papers you will need, you should consider the following decisions:

- Name presentation style
- Engraving style
- Paper size
- Name placement
- Paper finish and weight
- Color choice
- Trousseau budget

Name Presentation Style

A name is a very personal possession. Yours involved a careful, loving, thoughtful process on the part of your parents. I remember how handsome I thought the names of my two sons were as they first appeared in formal print! My husband and I announced each birth on a miniature calling card engraved in sophisticated Shaded Roman lettering, and tied with a blue ribbon to the top of our larger "Mr. and Mrs." social card, which was engraved in the same style. You will experience a thrill, too, when you select the style in which you choose to present your name, formally engraved on your social papers!

For certain pieces of your social paper trousseau, your name must be presented in full; that is, your first name, middle, and surname (last name) spelled in full. After age thirteen, this is preceded by the social title "Miss." Not every piece of your stationery must be this formal. Sometimes the proper choice is your name in full without the "Miss" or just your personal monogram or initials. A nickname or the title "Ms.," however, is never used on proper social papers.

For a monogram style featuring a center initial larger than the two side initials, the center initial represents your surname. Your first name's initial will be on the left, and the initial of your middle name on the right.

If the monogram style features all initials in the same size, the initials of your first name should be on the left, your middle name in the center, and your last name on the right. I do not approve of the use of only one initial as it appears too general.

Engraving Style

The next decision to be made is the style of typeface in which your name will be engraved. Again, the selection is a very individual decision. You may prefer very flowing, rolling letters (script), or you may be attracted to the straighter, contemporary styles, or to the traditional Roman look.

While many styles of engraving remain traditional for many years, others are influenced by current fashion, as are designs of clothing and home furnishings. Because the expense of an engraving die is a one-time cost, I suggest you forgo trendiness when engraving. I favor a style that feels "young" but not too young, as it will probably represent your name throughout your developing years.

I suggest that you spend a few hours with your local stationer to study the styles of engraving illustrated in the sample books. You may experience "love at first sight" with a particular style or you may need to have several dates with the books to discover your "one and only."

Paper Size

Although there are certain rules governing the sizes of some of the pieces comprising the social paper trousseau, many of these decisions are yours to make. The first consideration is the size of your handwriting. Very small handwriting would look out of place on an oversize correspondence card, whereas large handwriting would simply run short of space on a smaller one. In the same way, the size of the monogram or full name should be attractively proportional both to your handwriting and to the paper. Thus, good proportion should be the governing rule in selecting the size of your writing papers.

Name Placement

The next choice you have is the placement of your full name, monogram, or initials upon the paper itself. Here again, proportion and an eye for design are necessary. You may place the engraving in the upper center, middle center, or upper left of note paper, or in the upper center or upper left of a correspondence card, half-sheet, or folded letter sheet.

Paper Finish and Weight

It is my firm opinion that 100 percent cotton fiber paper, milled by a paper manufacturer of indisputable reputation (whose watermark it bears), is the very best choice for social writing papers. To be most formal, you would select a 32- or 40-pound, perfectly smooth, wove vellum finish with its wonderful, velvety feel. Although the laid finish would be acceptable, it appears a bit businesslike and masculine for a young woman's social papers.

For overseas correspondence, you may wish to include in your trousseau letter sheets and envelopes of the lovely silk laid finish. "Silk laid" paper, which actually contains no silk, is 16-pound paper, which is considered airmail weight. Another choice for airmail is parchmentlike French tracing paper, which is most attractive when engraved. Though lining envelopes is an option in 32- or 40-pound paper, envelopes made of 16-pound must be lined for strength and opaqueness. Writing is permissible only on one side of this weight paper.

Color Choice

For many young women, choosing colors is the fun aspect of assembling a social paper trousseau! Ecru, often called ecru white or cream white, and white or pearl white are the most formal colors. You will find them correctly used for wedding, graduation, birth, anniversary, and debut invitations. Black ink is selected for these invitations and the formal papers of the trousseau. When I refer to your "formal" papers, I mean your calling cards and informals.

For your notes, correspondence cards, and letter sheets, you should certainly feel free to consider the beautiful array of soft pastels and gemstone colors as a means of creative and correct expression. However, once more I caution you against falling prey to trendy fashion-of-the-day colors or unusual combinations. Garish and electric mixes are not in good taste. You will tire of them easily, and so will those to whom you write—a luxury you cannot afford when investing in the paper, engraving die, and labor of die stamping. It is not proper to shock others with exotic color combinations any more than it is in good taste to dress in a manner that offends! Many beautiful and varied combinations of colors in paper and ink can say, "This is ME!" without shouting tastelessly.

Yet another lovely accent of color can be added as a border to those papers for which color is permissible. These handsome borders are hand-brushed on all four sides of notes, correspondence cards, and letter sheets, and you may select one, two, or three—one of which will match the ink color selected for your name, monogram, or initials, the others gently contrasting or complementing. As you can see, coordinating your social paper wardrobe can be as much fun as coordinating your clothing wardrobe!

Trousseau Budget

In order to stretch the trousseau dollar, as well as for the sake of convenience, select correspondence cards, notes, and letter sheets in the identical paper finish and color. Also select this trio in a size which fits the same envelope and select the same typeface for the return address. In this manner, only one envelope need be ordered, and, if you move, you can have your address changed with the purchase of only one engraving die.

It is much more economical also to select the same name or monogram format for use on your trio of correspondence cards, notes, and letter sheets.

As you can see, you have now narrowed your expenses to one engraving die for use on each piece of your trio, one die for the "one-size-fits-all" envelope, and one ink charge. Although a small savings may be realized if you choose blind embossing instead of engraving for your envelopes, if color is of prime importance in expressing your personality, budget for it!

You can, in time and as your budget allows, add a more vivid and contemporary correspondence card. Just as with the wardrobe, the basics are only the beginning and they need not be boring!

Le Grand Trousseau

To have access to a full wardrobe of personalized writing papers is a delight indeed, so much so that I have chosen to call such a wardrobe *Le Grand Trousseau:* calling cards, informals, notes, correspondence cards, letter sheets, and half-sheets.

Clockwise: Calling Card, Informal, Letter Sheet
Note, Correspondence Card, Half-Sheet

Le Grand Trousseau

Calling Cards

The calling, or visiting, card is believed to have originated in China. Its first known use in Europe occurred in Italy during the latter part of the sixteenth century, and the custom of "leaving a card" then spread to France and later to Great Britain. The calling card was originally intended for the nobility to hand to a footman when paying a call or to leave at the home of someone who was absent when called upon.

In the early nineteenth century the embellishments of borders, scrolls, flower designs, and other ornamentation on calling cards were abandoned—both in the United States, where the tradition had been adopted, and abroad—in favor of a fine card on which the person's name only was engraved.

The use of the calling card for its original purpose has diminished over the years. Outside the realms of military, governmental, and diplomatic circles, they are seldom used because formal calls are seldom made. In our jet age, the lovely old custom of paying a formal social call no longer seems practical. Also, many women are engaged in careers outside the home and are not at home to receive visitors—and few servants remain to collect cards in their employers' absence. Therefore, most of the silver salvers—small silver trays placed on the table in the foyer to receive calling cards—are but a memory or a decoration.

You will, however, find that the custom of exchanging calling cards remains in some areas of the United States, and certainly in many European and Eastern countries. Each member of a family paying a call may leave his or her separate card. You would leave your card for the lady of the house and her daughters who lived at home (although never more than three cards), but not for the gentleman, nor the sons, because ladies do not "call" upon gentlemen.

Aside from its original use, however, the card has a number of convenient, more modern uses, and I am sure you will grow fond of it. Think of the calling card as a "social" rather than a "visiting" card: to be used as gift enclosures; to accompany flowers; for issuing semiformal invitations; for replying to semiformal invitations; for reminders that follow up semiformal invitations; for abbreviated messages; for introducing mutual friends; and as a pew card for a wedding. But you must use your calling card correctly.

Social Introduction or Exchange. There are many times when you make a new acquaintance and want the person to remember your name. It is correct to give your card to this new friend. If you wish the person to telephone you, write (on the lower right corner) your number, and your address, too, if need be.

Use tact and discretion in giving your calling card to a new acquaintance. You should give it away as a meaningful compliment; your calling card is a *very* personal item. Do not pass it around a group of people like a pack of Life Savers! But when the occasion calls for it, it is a much nicer social gesture to take a handsome calling card case from your handbag, pull your card from it, and give it to your new acquaintance, than it is to tear a deposit slip from your checkbook or find an old shopping list on which to scribble.

You may also use your calling card as a means of introducing a friend, who will be moving to or visiting another city, to one of your friends who lives there. Details and an example of this use of the calling card are found on page 129 in Chapter 7.

Enclosure Card for Gifts and Flowers. The calling card is most often used as a gift enclosure card or tucked in with a bouquet of flowers. You may include your card with or without a brief message—either is correct. Should you wish to write a message, place it above your engraved name. Make it short: "Best wishes!," "Happy Birthday!," "Congratulations!," or any wish or thought you want as the personal messenger for your gift. But the message must be brief—the calling card is not the proper item of the social paper trousseau on which to write a letter!

If your present is going to a close friend or relative, you may feel that your name, as it is formally engraved, appears too stuffy and formal. In this event, "personalize" your calling card by drawing a fine line through your engraved name and simply signing above it, in pen, the name by which this person knows you best. In this case, you may even use your nickname.

For gift enclosures, your card goes into its matching envelope, sealed only if the message is personal. If you are sending the gift from a shop or store, write the name of the recipient (but not the address) on the front of the envelope. The card is placed inside the gift box prior to wrapping and posting. If you are sending the package from your home, you need not write the person's name on the envelope.

Strict social propriety disallows a handwritten message on a card enclosed with a wedding gift. Weddings are the most formal of all occasions, and a penned message detracts from the appearance of your handsome card. Other reasons for this rule include the fact that the giver's card is frequently displayed beside the wedding gift, and no personal message should ever be so displayed. Another reason is that, especially in the case of large weddings, members of the family, close friends, and even social secretaries sometimes open gifts, catalogue them, and dispatch printed cards assuring the giver that the item has been received and that a "thank-you" note will follow. (These may be sent by the mother or social secretary, never by the young woman who receives the gift.) Send your good wishes, love, and impish comments under separate cover.

When you send flowers from the florist, or present them personally to a friend on a special occasion, it adds a personal touch to enclose your calling card. You briefly express your wishes or a message apropos of the occasion. The card is enclosed in its matching envelope as with a gift. If the flowers are sent in a box, the card is placed inside the tissue among the flowers so that it will not be lost. In floral arrangements or living dish gardens, the florist slips your card into the holder designed for this purpose and then into the container. Sometimes you may wish to send flowers to a church or funeral home after the death of someone you knew well or admired. On the envelope, you write, "the funeral of Mary Smith," and no message is written on your calling card.

You may write, "With deepest sympathy," above your name if the flowers are being sent directly to the family of the deceased. In such a case, depending upon how well you know the person to whom you are sending the flowers, you may or may not wish to personalize your name on your calling card.

Semiformal Invitations and Replies. It is socially proper to use your calling card as a way of inviting someone "semiformally," a useful and intriguing way to issue a nice invitation. There is a certain essential style: Invitations written on calling cards must be worded in the third person. Why? Because the small card becomes an abbreviated, less formal version of the third-person engraved or handwritten invitation you receive for a wedding or formal dance. The invitation is written in longhand by pen. Full details and examples are given in Chapter 9, Invitations!

Reminders. Calling cards may be used as a "follow-up" or "confirmation" if invitations have been telephoned or issued personally to your friends. As a reminder, a card does just that—"reminds" your guest that you are expecting her. Just write in pen, "To remind you—Tea on Wednesday the 4th, 3 o'clock." In very informal situations, you may telephone your friend to confirm or to remind her of the lunch you told her about in person.

Pew Card for a Wedding. You may receive a wedding invitation within which you find the calling card of the bride's, or bridegroom's, mother depending upon with which family you are friends. Written on the left above her name will be "Pew No. 6" or "Within the ribbon," indicating that you are to sit in these specially reserved seats.

As the calling card is considered one of the formal pieces of your social paper trousseau, it must adhere to the strictest standards of formality and good taste. Can you imagine a calling card of bright blue with the name in raised silver lettering? Never!

As a young woman, your calling card must be engraved with your full name, no initials, prefaced by "Miss" after you have reached your teens. Prior to reaching the teens, the child's calling card, properly engraved without a title, may be used.

A variation of the calling card, the fold-over engraved gift enclosure card, made its appearance in the late 1980s. This fold-over card is marked—often in colored ink—with a monogram, initials, or name. As the calling card has been the socially accepted enclosure card for centuries, I suggest that you resist this trend in favor of tradition.

You should select from among the more traditional and formal of the engraving styles. The calling card is made of perfectly plain, two-ply card stock without a panel or raised border around the edges. The official size, once you have added "Miss" to your name, is 2⅞ by 2 inches.

Small matching envelopes should be ordered at the time you order your cards. These bear no return address on the flap, nor are they lined. Use them for enclosing your card in gifts or flowers, or for introductions. This small envelope cannot be sent through the mail, so if you plan to use your calling card for informal invitations and replies, you must also order matching envelopes 3½ by 5 inches or larger, which meet the U.S. Postal Service regulations. This larger envelope is the same one that is used for informals. You need not worry that the calling card is smaller than the mailing envelope, but it is most important that the finish, color, and engraving be identical. The matching small envelope may be used when the calling card is inserted in the larger postal regulation-size envelope for mailing, creating a nice double-envelope presentation.

Informals

Throughout the years, just as style and fashion cause change in dress, so do they cause change in writing papers. In the mid-1930s, what are now known as "informals" were introduced into the social paper trousseau to offer more space for writing than was found on the calling card. There are two styles of informals: the more traditional "fold-over" informal and the single flat "card" informal (often referred to as the message card).

You may wish to have informals prior to marriage; however, they are generally included with your new social paper trousseau at the time of your wedding: one bearing your full married name, "Mrs. Henry Michael McAlister," for your personal use, and another with "Mr. and Mrs. Henry Michael McAlister," for you and your husband's joint use for invitations and replies or gift and flower enclosures.

Although it is not a substitute for the calling card, the informal shares many of the same purposes, yet it possesses some all its own. It may be used to enclose with gifts and flowers (but only when a greeting or message is desired), for brief messages and short notes (but not for thank-you notes for wedding, shower, or other gifts or for a letter of condolence), and for informal invitations and replies. It may not be used instead of a calling card in social situations when cards are left or exchanged.

Enclosure With Gifts or Flowers. When an informal is enclosed with a gift or flowers, the message inscribed upon it may be written in the abbreviated form or in the longer, second-person form. As with the calling card, the informal has a matching envelope, sealed if the message is very personal, otherwise left unsealed. When gifts or flowers are sent from a commercial store or florist, the name of the recipient is written on the envelope; when the delivery is made in person, the envelope is left plain. Place the envelope with the gift or flowers just as the calling card is placed.

Brief Messages and Short Notes. The informal may be used to write a brief message or note to a friend. As when you send a semiformal invitation or reply, you may also use the abbreviated fashion without the full salutation and formal close or full date. Should you wish to be more traditional when using the informal, you may correctly do so. Your choice of form depends upon the nature of the message and relationship to the person for whom it is intended.

Semiformal Invitations and Replies. A semiformal invitation or reply may be written in the abbreviated third-person form, as is done on the calling card, or it may be written in the second person, which may not be done on the calling card.

Your name appears on the informal exactly as it appears on your calling card, in the same typeface, and in black ink upon the same color paper. Fold-over informals may be plain or paneled and are of 32- or 40-pound rag paper, whereas card informals are of two-ply card stock like the calling card. On the fold-over informal, your name is placed in the center of page one.

On the flat card informal, your name appears at the center top, and you may also choose to include your address. The positioning of the address depends on your personal preference. It is placed in smaller letters in the upper right corner of the card above your name. Alternatively, it may be placed in the lower right corner, although this position limits the amount of writing space remaining on the card. When the address is included on the card informal, all of the words are spelled in full. A smaller, simple, block-style lettering to complement the lettering style of your name, or one in the same style, may be used, according to your wishes.

As the card informal is flat and does not open, your brief message or greeting, short note, or semiformal invitation or reply is written on the face of the card beneath your name. On the fold-over informal, it is written on the inside (page three). You may write in the first, second, or third person, depending upon the formality of the occasion and the closeness of your friendship with the receiver. Details and examples are given in Chapter 9, (p. 168) Remember, brevity is the secret of success for either style informal—you must never write on the back! Each measures $3^7/_{16}$ by $4^7/_8$ inches and fits into its matching $3^1/_2$ by 5-inch envelope.

Notes

For a young woman's social writing needs, "notes" are a delight! When selecting this fold-over note paper, called notes, or semi-notes, only a few guidelines are imposed, leaving you to be as creative as you wish. All *but* the rules of good taste are lifted.

Notes may be used for all the same purposes as informals, except gift enclosures. You have the luxury of a more generous space upon which to pen a short note or even a very short letter. Unlike informals, the note is the proper social paper to use for writing a thank-you note. (Remember "thank-you *notes*.")

When purchasing notes for your social paper trousseau, you will enjoy selecting or designing the style that best suits you for the presentation of your name—be it monogram, initials, or written in full. Should you elect to present your name in full, it is written without the title "Miss" that was *de rigueur* on your calling cards and informals.

Your name is also written somewhat larger in proportion to the note paper, which is larger in size than the informal. It is socially proper to use your given name alone on your note paper, if you wish. I prefer, though, to see a young woman's name presented in full in one of the many rolling scripts or more tailored block styles, whichever suits her personality. Your full name is far more personal than simply Anne, Mary, Jane, or Jill! Just remember that the manner in which you present your name determines the personality of the notes. In other words, initials, monograms, or names presented in a bold graphic design will not be as formal or conventional as those in traditional engraving styles.

Always engraved on the first page of note paper, the placement of the monogram, initials, or name upon the page is a matter of personal taste and is influenced by the size of the style selected. The placement also determines where you begin writing on the note paper. Large monograms, initials, and names go in the center, and writing begins on page three beneath the inside fold. When the design is smaller, it is placed in the upper center or in the upper left portion of the note paper. In this case the writing begins on page one and continues on page three just as it would on perfectly plain note paper without marking.

The temptation to continue a note on the back (or page four) is one to which you must never yield! To avoid this dilemma, remember that a note is just that—a "note"—and do not try to squeeze a full letter onto your note paper! To have the proper paper for each writing need is the reason for the social paper trousseau. Is your handwriting large or do you tend to write lengthy notes? If so, consider one of the larger-size note papers, and have your monogram, initials, or name positioned in the upper left portion so you can begin writing your notes on page one.

Although the style may be informal and friendly, you write upon note and letter paper in the proper full social form, not in the abbreviated form permitted on the calling card or informal. That is, the greeting, the body, the complimentary close, the signature, and the date are each properly executed as described and as the examples show in Chapter 7, Letter Perfect.

On social notes and letters, the date is written in the formal style of social writing and engraving, although the year is omitted. The date is placed last, and it is spelled in full, "June the eleventh," "Monday the tenth." This is the informal version of the formally engraved date, "Tuesday, the eleventh of June." This gives a softer, more elegant and formal appearance than do figures. The date is placed after the signature and flush with the left margin of the body of the note. Remember that the complimentary close, the signature, and the date will take five lines because this looks more attractive when a space is left between the complimentary name close, and date. It is not correct to place all or any of these parts on a page by themselves. If this happens, you must add another line to the body in order to continue it on the next page. Think ahead, as you certainly do not want to squeeze a frivolous afterthought into an otherwise perfectly expressed note.

Paper for the writing of notes varies greatly in size. The most popular size is $3^{11}/_{16}$ by $5^{1}/_{9}$ inches, with varying sizes up to $4^{1}/_{4}$ by $6^{3}/_{8}$ inches. In addition to ecru white or pearl white, which are the most formal and always socially correct, lovely pastels, gentle gemstones, or even the most brilliant hues are acceptable for note paper. You can choose colored ink for the engraving of your monogram, initials, or name, and for the border, too.

Correspondence Cards

The correspondence card is the late-twentieth-century edition of the flat card informal. When lifestyles took on a more casual air in many parts of the country, there developed a need for a more casual item in the social paper trousseau. The correspondence card is larger than the older-style card informal. It serves many of the same purposes as the card informal, and many of those of the visiting card, the informal, and the note. Consider the correspondence card as fun as opposed to formal. Write upon it anything you may wish, from simply, "I am sorry," to "Congratulations," "Thank you," "Thinking of you," even informal invitations and replies. Whenever you have a message to mail and little time in which to do it, do not put it off, dash it off on a colorful correspondence card! Remember, it is the thought that counts. On the correspondence card a single thought can be presented in a casual, chatty way; by the same token, if your message is a serious thought, it can be presented very succinctly.

Officially, the correspondence card is used for: an informal brief thank-you (although not for an elaborate gift such as you might receive for a confirmation, Bat Mitzvah, coming-of-age celebration, shower, or wedding); a bread-and-butter note to a very close friend; a note of congratulations; a note of appreciation for something nice someone did or said; a reminder of an invitation issued over the telephone; a reply to an informal invitation; a note of apology to say you are sorry about something you may have said or done to another; a word of cheer or encouragement.

Accompanying the correspondence card are but two important rules: Be brief in expressing your thoughts, and write only on the front of the card.

The style of writing may be in the abbreviated version of the second or third person or in the full social form, depending upon the purpose of the message or the note.

The positioning of your monogram, initials, or name can be the same as on your notes and letter sheets, or it can be different, and you can include your address also if you wish. Once a young woman has created her personal marking through the design of her monogram, initials, or name, I prefer to see it used throughout. As some of your correspondence is to the same people, you will create a certain image by the repeated use of your chosen style. Soon your friends will know by color alone that they have received a note from you!

The more formal choice of colors is, as always, ecru white or pearl white card stock engraved with black ink. However, for a young woman's correspondence cards, color reigns as long as she adheres to good taste! The correspondence card is made of three-ply card stock and begins in size from 3⅝ to 5⅛ inches and extends to the very large and handsome 5½ by 7½-inch size. In European writing papers, often you will see the Continental, or monarch, size, 3¹³⁄₁₆ by 7½ inches, or smaller 4¼ by 6⅜ inches. While socially correct for women, these elongated sizes are most often selected for use by men.

Letter Sheets and Half-Sheets

The most traditional and formal of writing papers is the letter sheet (sometimes referred to as the "folded" letter sheet), which presents your letters in book form as it is folded along the left side just like a wedding invitation. Letters written upon letter sheets are certain to please friends and particularly your great-aunts and grandmothers, since when they were growing up it was considered the *only* correct paper upon which a woman with social knowledge and good taste wrote her letters!

Letter sheets were very much in vogue before the Second World War. However, during World War II, paper was in short supply and in England folded letter paper was forbidden by law by the British Crown because it was considered an extravagance for letters, which often terminated on one page. The letter sheet returned to favor shortly thereafter, though, and remains today the perfect paper upon which to inscribe your thoughts. There is not the shuffling of pages as there is with a letter written upon several half-sheets.

If you have not considered the folded letter sheet, I urge you to do so when coordinating your social paper trousseau and imagine your letters written in this timeless tradition. If some of your letters are generally longer than four pages, you may wish to also include the half-sheet (a single page one half the size of the folded letter sheet) in your social paper trousseau.

Whether you select the letter sheet or half-sheets, or both, for your letter writing, the choice of the engraved information is the same. It would be practical to use the same engraving die you selected for your notes and correspondence cards, but you may include your address on the letter sheet or half-sheet, placed beneath your name when presented in full. When combined with a monogram or initials, the address should complement or match the other engraving. I feel, however, that your monogram, initials, or full name, without the prefix "Miss" and without an address, is the most socially sophisticated selection for a young woman's half-sheet and that the monogram is best suited for the letter sheet. Without the address, should your family move, or when you go away to school or take an apartment of your own, you will not need a new engraving die.

The sequence of pages used in writing on the folded letter sheet varies with the length of the letter. When used for longer notes, which is socially correct, a wider margin will look best, and the note may be completed on the first page, leaving the remaining pages blank. If the note requires two pages, it continues from page one to page three, leaving page two blank. Lovely longer letters may be written by beginning on page one, then by opening the folded sheet and writing across pages two and three as though they were one long page. Or you may write first on page one, then on page two, and conclude on page three. The fourth page, or the back page, is left blank so that the writing does not show through when the letter is folded and placed in the envelope.

Letter sheets and half-sheets come in a variety of sizes and should complement the size of your handwriting and your engraving style. As they vary in size from 5 by 7 inches to 6³/₈ by 8¹/₂ inches, and range in color, they should be coordinated with your notes and correspondence cards so that, for economy's sake, the envelopes may be interchangeable and your color statement will be reinforced.

If you select half-sheets for your trousseau, it will be necessary to order "second sheets." These are sheets of the same size, finish, and color and are bordered (if the first sheets are bordered), or may remain plain, but bear no engraving. As you must never write on the back of a half-sheet, second sheets are used in combination with the personalized, engraved first sheet for letters of more than one page, whereas the one-page letter begins and ends on the personalized sheet.

Enveloping Your Writing Papers

Matching envelopes for each piece of your social paper trousseau are ordered at the same time as your papers. Although unlined envelopes are socially correct, coordinating, matching, or contrasting linings give follow-through to your personal color scheme and add a plus to your personality on paper.

You may choose to personalize the matching envelopes for your letter sheets by engraving or blind embossing your address on the flap. Blind embossing is done in a simple block letter style blending with, but not matching, the engraving style selected for the writing papers themselves.

Your name does not appear in a return address. Your address alone appears, providing a bit more privacy. The number of your house, apartment, or condominium may be presented in numerals if over twenty, but is always spelled in full when it is twenty or under. When engraved, the style of the lettering often determines which form is most attractive. Certainly the flowing lines of script spell out a shortly worded house number beautifully, whereas some of the more graphic and contemporary engraving styles have very dramatic figures! Shortly worded numbers of streets and avenues may be spelled in full. Street names are always spelled in full as are the words *avenue, lane, boulevard,* and *street.* The directions northwest, southeast, south, north, and such are also spelled in full. Although the words *post office box, post office drawer,* and *rural route* are spelled out, the numbers follow as numerals. Zip codes are always included in the return address and are presented in numerals.

Le Petit Trousseau

At this point you must be saying to yourself, "I will *never* need all of these writing papers!" And possibly you do not—not at this stage in your life. However, as you are now versed in the uses of all the pieces of a full social paper trousseau, you will find yourself "wishing" for certain elements. Grant yourself these wishes *slowly.* Just as you begin your clothing wardrobe with the basics, I encourage you to build your wardrobe of writing papers carefully. I have selected a trio of writing papers for this basic wardrobe, which I call *Le Petit Trousseau:* correspondence cards, notes, and letter sheets. Select them in the manner I outline, and you will have made an affordable investment in your written image.

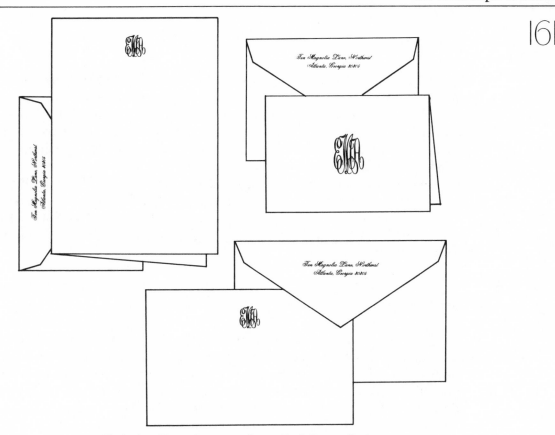

Clockwise: Note, Correspondence Card, Letter Sheet

Le Petit Trousseau

Correspondence Cards

The correspondence card is a must! You need it for your most basic writing trousseau. First, because its very presence and convenience encourages you to write, a habit I insist you develop! Second, the correspondence card makes writing fun. Although correspondence cards are still, for more formal uses, available in conservative sizes and ecru white or pearl white colors, today's version is brighter, bigger, and more frivolous. It may be your favorite piece of *Le Petit Trousseau*. With it you have at the tip of your pen a personal card for writing birthday wishes, holiday greetings, get-well cheer, party invitations, brief notes, and simply, "Just thinking of you!" In addition, it becomes a personalized invitation and reply card for the relaxed entertaining of your lifestyle.

Notes

Ready to take on a more serious note? This member of *Le Petit Trousseau* is socially correct for so many of your social correspondence needs that no writing paper trousseau is complete without it. Not only can you issue informal invitations on notes, but you can reply to the informal invitations of others. Notes are *the* writing paper of choice for thank-you notes, bread-and-butter letters, and mini-letters. They are young, fresh, and fashionable—and so appealing that yours will make you *want* to write all the "duty" letters that pertain to your social life. As a bride-elect, notes bearing your maiden name will be used to acknowledge shower and wedding gifts prior to the wedding. After your wedding, you will switch over to notes bearing your married name.

Letter Sheets

To create the proper mood for writing a wonderful letter, I show L'Ecole des Ingénues classes "La Lettre" by Mary Cassatt, a close friend of Claude Monet, and "The Letter" by French Impressionist Pierre Bonnard. Each is a tranquil, pleasant scene, one that is guaranteed to create the desire to write someone *the* letter! Somehow, the same emotion does not swell in me when I see a telephone, as when I see a young woman with a dreamy half-smile on her face sealing a letter to someone she holds dear.

Make your letter-writing paper your most personal and treasured corresponding touch. I recommend to you, as I do at L'Ecole des Ingénues, the advantages of the letter sheet rather than the half-sheet. It packages and frames your words more pleasingly for your reader and becomes a small booklet of the thoughts and news you want to share with another. It can be used also for any of the purposes claimed by "notes."

Recalling the Calling Card

Did you notice I omitted the calling card from *Le Petit Trousseau*? I wanted badly to include it, but I *was* budgeting for the basics! I do want to impress upon you, however, that calling cards are a charming part of your personal identity; they are not passé! They will always remain the most personal element of *Le Grand Trousseau* and are worth waiting for. They do, however, demand an engraving die of their very own and this may require too much of your trousseau dollar. So my advice is to defer them until you have completed *Le Petit Trousseau*.

At first, you probably will not be as eager as your grandmother might have been to issue invitations on your calling card. Most likely you find the telephone, colorful fill-in invitations, or note paper more suitable for your present style of entertaining. But does not the idea of writing "Best wishes" by hand on your very own engraved calling card, popping it into its tiny matching envelope, and placing it among the tissues of a gift or flowers sound like something special to you?

On holiday at a beach or mountain resort, you may find yourself wishing for calling cards to give to new summer friends. They can be like a handshake or light kiss on the cheek—only more lasting! Calling cards are tangible. With your address penned in the corner, they encourage letters in the long winter months to follow.

I can promise you, once calling cards become a part of your social paper trousseau, you will wonder how you ever did without them.

The "Plain Jane" Paper Trousseau

The "Plain Jane"—unmarked—Paper Trousseau is not as drab as my pet name may sound. In fact, one of the "Plain Jane" papers is really the most formal of all your trousseau pieces: the unmarked "formal," folded letter sheet.

This is the *only* paper on which you may write a letter of condolence, or a reply to a formal invitation engraved or handwritten in the third person. This formal, folded letter sheet *must* be selected in ecru white; or pearl white, in vellum finish, of 100 percent cotton fiber, and of 32- or 40-pound substance. Just think of the beauty of an ecru white or pearl white wedding invitation and the wonderful way it feels to your fingers. Black or dark blue ink should be used for the writing, and, of course, it should flow from a fountain pen! Black ink is the nicest for ecru white; either dark blue or black look pleasant on pearl white.

The second item of The "Plain Jane" Paper Trousseau is the proper one for letters devoted to personal business. You may select your business papers in one of two sizes: either traditional business letterhead, 8½ by 11 inches, with a matching 4⅛ by 9¼-inch envelope; or the monarch sheet, used by many business executives for their personal business letters. The monarch sheet is somewhat smaller, 7¼ by 10½ inches, with a matching envelope one third the size. Business letterhead is the most respected size to use for your résumé or for letters of application for jobs, schools, or colleges. It fits nicely into the standard file folder in offices. The monarch letter sheets can be used for letters of inquiry and other less businesslike purposes, or to write thank-you letters for a job or college interview.

Business letterhead and monarch sheets in ecru white or pearl white—never write a business letter on any other color—are very sophisticated. The 100 percent cotton fiber paper with a vellum finish takes the ink of the typewriter and your fountain pen beautifully, and your business image appears extremely professional and polished on this type of paper. These writing papers represent you with impeccably good taste without being expensive.

If you embark upon a professional career, you will add the monarch sheet to your personal business paper trousseau. All personal business letters are written on monarch paper. The full name is engraved on the top of the "first sheet" and "Miss" or "Mrs." is omitted. The address, only, is imprinted on the back flap of the envelope. All words are spelled in full for both the name and address.

The Family Paper Trousseau

For writing papers your whole family can enjoy, consider having The Family Paper Trousseau, writing papers personalized with the address of your home but without a name. This paper, so versatile and so much used, is really not a luxury at all. Because everyone can use it, it constitutes a savings for a family with several young adults. If your family already has family writing papers, by all means use them.

The Family Paper Trousseau may be coordinated for the house, cottage, or condominium where your family vacations as well as for your permanent home. Each dwelling can have its individual personality, address, *and* writing paper. A "stationery of the house" is also a special treat for houseguests. What a nice surprise it can add to the guest room desk!

As The Family Paper Trousseau will be used by all the family members and guests after they reach age thirteen, it must be suitable for all ages and for both men and women. Either the letter sheet or the half-sheet may be selected according to the family's preference. For your permanent home, conservative colors should be chosen for the paper and ink, and selections should be made democratically by a family ballot. Of course, ecru white or pearl white engraved with black ink are, as always, in good taste. You do not become bored with them as readily as with colors. For the address select a plain lettering or script to everyone's liking. This will be engraved at the top of the letter or half-sheet, and again on the flap of the envelope. Your telephone number may be placed on the opposite corner of the writing sheet, as your family prefers.

Matching correspondence cards in the size to fit the same envelopes as the letter or half-sheets are nice to have for quick messages from family members and guests. The engraving die will be the same for the letter or half-sheets, correspondence cards, and envelopes, saving the expense of another die. If the telephone number has been added, it is simple for the engraver to wax over that line and use this same die for the envelope.

The colors may be somewhat playful for your family's vacation home, where life and entertaining are casual. But if you have a more stately summer home, the same conservative forms should be observed as for your permanent dwelling. When a second home has been given a name, include this with the address. A small drawing depicting the house, called by engravers a "device," makes a nice addition to the house paper. The sketch can be drawn by a family member or a professional artist, or selected from what is referred to as "stock" art at the stationers. It will be a part of the engraving die and appear as a part of the engraved address, and it must be in perfect proportion to the lettering selected.

Place these family papers in baskets, along with pretty commemorative stamps, on the guest room writing table, or at the family desk with pens whose ink is coordinated. Naturally, a well-mannered houseguest would use these writing papers while staying with you, but would never take "spare sheets" along when she bids you adieu.

The Interim Paper Trousseau

The idea of The Family Paper Trousseau is so gracious that it can be implemented with a colorful selection of unmarked papers if your family does not yet have engraved varieties, and you can do the same for your personal papers! Even if your budget permits the immediate luxury of personally engraved social papers for you or your family, I suggest that you first try plain before investing in engraved papers. Try various size notes, letter sheets, and half-sheets. Try correspondence cards in different sizes with or without panels or hand-brushed borders. Experiment with color. Discover what suits your personality and matches your handwriting.

Each of the items that I have introduced in *Le Grand Trousseau, Le Petit Trousseau,* and The Family Paper Trousseau is available without engraving in quality 100 percent cotton fiber paper in socially correct colors and finishes. Even cards the size of the calling card, with their matching envelopes, can be purchased plain to use for enclosure with gifts and flowers.

Once you have assembled The Interim Paper Trousseau, you have taken an additional step toward good taste—you have purchased the same writing paper upon which your name will be engraved when your budget permits!

The Varietal Writing Papers

With the array of writing papers available today, you may have additional fun interspersing a potpourri of papers amid The Interim Trousseau, *Le Petit Trousseau,* or *Le Grand Trousseau.*

There are lovely fold-over commercial and museum art cards with artwork on the front, and the inside left blank for your note or greeting. There is colorful paper by the pound, which you can mix-and-match for mega-paged letters to peers. Travel lends the added corresponding touch of hotel writing papers and "picture postcards."

One writing paper I recall most fondly from my travels is train writing paper! The train is the Venice Simplon Orient-Express, and the occasion for travel was one of L'Ecole des Ingénues finishing tours. As the ingénues and I settled in our private cabins for the journey from Boulogne to Paris, the cabin porter presented each of us with a colorful writing paper portfolio filled with postcards of the train and dining car, and ecru white, handsomely textured single writing sheets and matching envelopes, each marked with the medallion-shaped logo and name of this historic train. Our four-and-one-half-hour journey to Paris passed only too rapidly with the writing of letters and a formal six-course dinner. Upon disembarking, we handed our letters and cards to the porter. Friends back home loved the postmark of the Orient-Express (Paris) and saved our cards and letters for our scrapbooks!!

Whilst One Waits

Each of us has a different amount of money to spend on the various necessities and luxuries of life. Whether you consider engraved social writing papers a necessity or a luxury or both, there is a way to express yourself that is affordable, elegant, and correct.

Proper writing papers are a necessity! Personalized writing papers are a luxury. If you are not prepared at the moment to invest in an engraving die, engraving, and ink, then wait. Or, perhaps you are awaiting this special gift for your Bat Mitzvah, Sweet Sixteen, graduation, or wedding. Do not, however, delay a single minute before investing in The Interim Paper Trousseau.

Certainly you need not apologize for unmarked quality writing papers. Writing papers do not have to be personalized to be socially correct. In addition, the difference in cost between quality writing papers of socially good taste and those of inferior taste and quality is so slight that you can easily choose quality and correctness and not "break the bank." Corresponding on less than acceptable paper is false economy.

There is simply no substitute for engraving. Have patience and wait a while longer, if need be. There is always the thrill of anticipation, as for many lovely things in life, and the pleasure of a substitute of quality whilst one waits.

CHAPTER 9

Invitations!

Oh, to be among those invited! "Invitation" has a charming definition: "The act of inviting; requesting one's company, an often formal request to be present or participate."

Just the thought of an invitation lifts my spirits. I love parties! I adore weddings (and I always cry). And I delight in lunching with friends. So an invitation to join others on a festive or ceremonial occasion, or just for soup on Sunday night, sparks excitement. All the world loves a party, and I am sure you do, too.

Many of the most memorable good times are impromptu or even serendipitous. If you like to gather with friends, however, you will encounter formal occasions, too. Socializing requires certain "formalities," not only in the form the entertainment or ceremony takes, but in the correspondence that heralds the upcoming event as well.

I use the word *herald* purposely. In fairy tales, the king's herald formally requests the presence of his subjects with the fanfare of a trumpet and the reading of a scroll—I am sure you can picture such an occasion in your mind!

To receive an invitation is to receive a compliment—someone wishes *my* presence, *my* company, *my* participation. Someone feels my being there would add to the event. Think of the phrase that appears engraved on the formal invitation: "request the pleasure of your company" or "request the honour of your presence." Before entering any social occasion, decide that you will add something by your presence, that you will fulfill your obligation as a guest, returning the compliment to the host or hostess.

Types of Invitations

Depending upon the nature of the event, invitations fall into three classes—formal, semiformal, or informal. A formal invitation implies a large or elaborate social function. It is sent out two to four weeks prior and follows a very definite and prescribed form. Among the occasions that call for formal invitations are the wedding, the ceremonial dinner, the dance or ball, the formal dinner, the important reception or tea, a special anniversary observance, and the official luncheon or reception. Your first formal invitation is likely to be to a graduation exercise, or to a reception or tea at the home of the school head or in the school's great hall.

The semiformal and informal invitations differ significantly from the formal one, although they, too, take a certain form—or several forms, to be exact. Social events with a lighter mood and little ceremony are many: a brunch, bridal or ladies' luncheon, small afternoon tea, intimate dinner party, house party, picnic, bridge party, musicale, and, of course, the birthday party.

The Formal Invitation

We shall face the formalities first! Once you have mastered The Formal Invitation Formula (p. 170), you need never fear a formal invitation again. The correct formula for a formal invitation has remained the same for over a century. Follow it carefully to create a beautifully handwritten, printed, or engraved invitation to your next special party.

The formal invitation follows a predetermined wording and word placement, line by line. Certain facts are presented on certain lines, and the lines are not placed flush to the left margin as in a letter, but are centered over each other. Formal invitations are always written in the third person. This style may seem stilted to you at first, but once you try it, you will see that the resulting message has an elegance that is in keeping with the occasion.

Formal invitations may be written by hand (the most dressy are handwritten). Realistically, the hostess can only hand write them when the guest list is small, as it always takes more time than you expect to pen each individually. Naturally, handwritten invitations require clearly legible and, better still, pretty penmanship. The color ink? Black or dark blue for all formal correspondence, flowing from a fine fountain pen.

Because formal invitations most often go to a large guest list, they are

---

The Formal Invitation Formula

- Name of hostess and/or host and joint host and/or hostess, if any
- a. Requests the honour of your presence (wedding in a church, synagogue, or other place of worship), or
- b. Requests the pleasure of your company (wedding outside a place of worship or any other social event), or
- c. Requests the pleasure of (name of guest handwritten in personalized form)
- The social or ceremonial event taking place
- The honoree, if any
- The day of the week and the date of the month
- The year
- The time
- The place
- The city and state
- The proper dress, if stated
- The R.s.v.p., if requested

---

usually engraved. The engraving should be in a classic script or handsome block-letter style. Formal invitations are *never* typewritten or issued from a computer.

Whether handwritten or engraved, the wording of the invitation appears on the first page of an ecru white or pearl white formal sheet of folded letter paper (fold on the left). The paper is the best 100 percent cotton fiber with a kid or suede finish. Engraved—but not handwritten—formal invitations may also be presented on a single card of heavier weight than the letter sheet. For either, there is a choice of plain or plate-marked (with or without a panel).

Notice that in each of the formal invitation samples "honour" is spelled in the British way? You will meet the "extra" vowel "u" again on invitations where "The favour of a reply is requested." These spellings are preferred for formal invitations.

With the exception of the abbreviations R.s.v.p. and Mr. and Mrs., *no* abbreviations are permitted in a formal invitation. The host's and/or hostess's names are spelled in full; so are the days of the week, the date, month, year, and time of the event.

When numbered streets are included, they are spelled in full. Words (if the words are short) are used for the house number if there is space. If not, figures may be used.

When writing the day and date, "Saturday, the thirty-first of January" is preferred over "Saturday, January the thirty-first." The hour has a special language, too. "Half after five o'clock" is socially preferred over "half past five o'clock." On a formal invitation, the time would never be written simply as "five-thirty."

Traditionally, social events beginning at eight o'clock were automatically black-tie affairs. Nowadays, with occasions such as charity benefits staged with differing degrees of formality, the desired attire may be stated on the right corner of the invitation (except for a wedding). The wording will read "casual," "informal," "semiformal," "formal" ("black tie" or "white tie") as described in "The Terms of Dress" box in Chapter 3.

Répondez s'il vous plaît

One of the gravest social faux pas is a failure to *répondre* or reply. Not to respond is an insult to whomever requested "the pleasure of your company." It does not matter whether the request is written in full, stating, "The favour of a reply is requested," "please reply," or "R.s.v.p."

Ideally, reply within twenty-four hours—and no later than three days after receipt of a formal invitation—and abide by my word of caution: Be sure to save the envelopes from your invitations. As the address to which the reply should be mailed is not placed under the R.s.v.p. (unless it is to be sent to a person other than the one from whom it was received), you can refer to the back of the envelope and find it (blind embossed or engraved for an engraved invitation, written by hand for a handwritten one).

When your reply is written to two or more hostesses, the envelope is addressed to the hostess at whose house the event will be held (unless otherwise noted on the invitation). As your formal papers for this purpose are not personalized, do not forget to handwrite your address on the flap of the envelope before mailing.

You will notice there is no telephone number given on formal invitations. Logically, therefore, your reply is never by telephone. Neither do you reply on your calling card, informal, correspondence card, note paper, or personalized letter sheets. The "formal" folded letter sheet, described in The "Plain Jane" Paper Trousseau in Chapter 8, is the only paper for this purpose.

Your reply is handwritten in black or dark blue ink, in the third person, on the first page of this formal letter sheet. It is addressed to the sender and states that you can accept, or must regret, the kind invitation. If for some reason you cannot attend, it is courteous to state your reason in a few words. Perhaps you will be out of town or have accepted another engagement for the same time. Tell your hostess just that. If, however, illness is the reason you cannot be present, it is the best taste and form not to explain that. Why shadow the happy event with sadness?

Interestingly, and unlike other invitations, an invitation to a luncheon or dinner at the White House is a command and automatically cancels any previous engagement the recipient might have had! The only acceptable excuse is an absence from the country, a death or wedding in the family, or personal illness.

Miss Elizabeth Anne Morgan
accepts with pleasure
the kind invitation of
Mr. and Mrs. James Edward Jones
for dinner
on Saturday, the tenth of October
at eight o'clock

THE HANDWRITTEN FORMAL ACCEPTANCE

Miss Elizabeth Anne Morgan
regrets exceedingly
that a previous engagement
prevents her accepting
the kind invitation of
Mr. and Mrs. James Edward Jones
for dinner
on Saturday, the tenth of October

THE HANDWRITTEN FORMAL REGRET

In responding, do not fear the protocol. The formula of the formal reply is exacting, dictated by the strictest of etiquette rules. But so much the better! Everything is beautifully spelled out, as you will see below in The Formal Reply Formula. As with the formal invitation, the rules pave the way.

The Formal Reply Formula

- Name in full prefaced by social title
- a. Accepts with pleasure, or
- b. Regrets exceedingly, or Sincerely regrets that (state reason for regretting) prevents her accepting
- The kind invitation of
- Full name or names of person or persons issuing invitation
- For (state the occasion, unless it is a wedding. Occasion need not be stated when regretting.)
- On (state the day and date, spelled in full)
- At (state the time, spelled in full, except when regretting)

Grand Occasions

You may be wondering why the rules of etiquette make such ado about the formal invitation and its reply. The reason is simple: Occasions grand enough to warrant a formal invitation or announcement usually concern life's momentous ceremonies.

The first is birth, a joyous occasion for a written announcement. Shortly after follows the religious ceremonies in Judaism devoted to the baby or the christening or baptism of the infant in other faiths. In just a few years, according to your faith, there may be a First Communion, and later a Confirmation or the Bat Mitzvah. Formal invitations are not sent for religious ceremonies held during childhood—with the exception of the Bar or Bat Mitzvah and occasionally the christening. Instead, family members and close friends are invited informally by handwritten note or telephone.

A charming tradition—and one that is befitting of the formal invitation—is the "Sweet Sixteen" party. Sixteen is considered to be the "advent of one's social age"—the sub-deb milestone.

Other important milestones in life include graduation from high school, and later from a college or university—each with its formal invitation to or announcement of the commencement exercises.

Some parents choose to present their college-age daughters to society at a small dance, a ball, or a cotillion. This high point in a young woman's social life—her "formal" bow as a debutante—is a moment when formal invitations abound.

Next among life's ceremonies that call for the formal invitation or announcement is the wedding, heralding perhaps the most serious decision in your life.

Interspersed with these grand occasions will be ceremonies or celebrations devoted to others. There may be your parents' silver (twenty-fifth) wedding anniversary or your grandparents' golden (fiftieth) wedding anniversary.

After noting the invitations and announcements that I have taken from my scrapbook of grand occasions (on pages 175 to 179), you may want to begin a scrapbook of ones revolving around you, your family, dear relatives, and close friends.

The Semiformal Invitation

It is socially proper to use your calling card, informal, or an engraved or printed fill-in invitation to invite someone "semiformally." But there is still an essential style. Invitations written on personally engraved writing papers must be worded in the third person. Preprinted fill-ins follow this style as well. Why? Because these more casual invitations are but a shortened version of the formal third-person form. Words may be abbreviated, figures may be used for the time and date, and all the "pretty" phrases are omitted and reduced to the bare facts to conserve space. As you study The Semiformal Formula found in the box below, think of semiformal invitations as formal invitations written in shorthand!

The Semiformal Formula

- Is written in the third person
- Is an abbreviated version of the formal invitation
- Words may be abbreviated
- Figures may be used for date and time
- Salutations and closings are not used
- Pretty phrases are omitted
- R.s.v.p. may include a telephone number
- "Regrets" and a telephone number may be used

Grand Occasions

Catherine Diana

Mr. and Mrs. Charles Lewis Hamilton

are happy to announce

the birth of their daughter

on the first of May

Nineteen hundred and ninety

The Birth

Mr. and Mrs. John Michael Ward

request the honour of your presence

at the christening of their daughter

Laura Alice

on Sunday, the twenty-seventh of January

at ten o'clock

First Methodist Church

and for luncheon following the service

3111 River Oaks Boulevard

Houston, Texas

R. s. v. p.

The Christening

Our daughter, Rebecca Elaine

will be called to the Torah as a Bat Mitzvah

on Saturday, the fifteenth of December

at ten o'clock

Temple Emmanu-El

We cordially invite you to worship with our family

on this happy occasion

and, following the services, to join us for luncheon

at our home

Mr. and Mrs. Samuel David Cohen

Ten Palm Way

Boca Raton

The favour of a reply is requested

The Bat Mitzvah

Doctor and Mrs. Nelson Grant Akers

request the pleasure of

Mr. Walter Moore's

company at a tea dance

in honour of their daughter

Miss Samantha Jordan Akers

on the occasion of her sixteenth birthday

Saturday, the seventh of April

at five o'clock

Windsor Court Hotel

New Orleans, Louisiana

R. s. v. p.
5512 Prytania Street
New Orleans, Louisiana 70015

The Sixteenth Birthday

The Faculties and Graduating Classes
of
Emory University
invite you to be present at the
Graduation Exercises
on Monday, the sixteenth of May
Nineteen hundred and eighty-eight
at half after eight o'clock in the morning
University Quadrangle
Atlanta, Georgia

The Trustees
Faculty and Senior Class
of
Miss Porter's School
request the honour of your presence
at the
Closing Exercises
on Monday, the eighth of June
Nineteen hundred and eighty-seven
at quarter after eleven o'clock
First Church of Christ, Congregational
Farmington, Connecticut

Rebecca Ellen Carroll

The College Graduation

Megan Anne McNealy

The High School Graduation

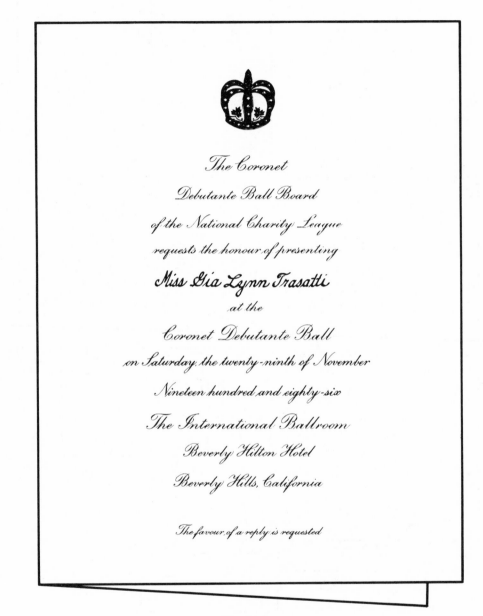

The Coronet

Debutante Ball Board

of the National Charity League

requests the honour of presenting

Miss Gia Lynn Trasatti

at the

Coronet Debutante Ball

on Saturday, the twenty-ninth of November

Nineteen hundred and eighty-six

The International Ballroom

Beverly Hilton Hotel

Beverly Hills, California

The favour of a reply is requested

The Debut

MR. AND MRS. JAMES PAUL SPENCE

REQUEST THE HONOUR OF YOUR PRESENCE

AT THE MARRIAGE OF THEIR DAUGHTER

ANNE-MARIE

TO

MR. LAWRENCE ALLAN RAINES, JUNIOR

ON SATURDAY, THE TWENTY-THIRD OF JUNE

AT FOUR O'CLOCK

THE LADY CHAPEL

SAINT PATRICK'S CATHEDRAL

NEW YORK

RECEPTION

IMMEDIATELY FOLLOWING THE CEREMONY

THE WALDORF-ASTORIA

NEW YORK

R. S. V. P.
TEN EAST SEVENTIETH STREET
NEW YORK, NEW YORK 10021

The Wedding

Invitations on Calling Cards and Informals

Let me go through the style with you point by point. First, the invitation is written in longhand with a pen. On the *front* of the calling card or informal—either above, below, or above *and* below your name—write the occasion for the gathering. Beneath give the day, date, and time. If you wish a reply, write R.s.v.p. in the bottom left corner. With so many facts in so small a space, you can see why I call it abbreviated!

R.s.v.p. is not your only choice when requesting a reply. Do you prefer that your guests let you know only if they cannot attend? Then write the word *Regrets* and your telephone number rather than R.s.v.p. In this case, the recipient is not required to send a written reply but may telephone you if he or she cannot attend.

Remember, when you are on the receiving end, you must R.s.v.p. or "regret" within a day or so. The reply follows the form of the invitation. That is to say, an invitation is accepted or "regretted" in the same manner as it was received. If you receive an abbreviated third-person version written on a calling card or informal, send your reply on your card or informal, with the same wording as the invitation. Compare the samples of invitations and replies below.

To meet
Miss René Blanche Trudeau

Miss Elizabeth Anne Morgan

Sat., Dec. 22
Brunch
11 o'ck.

The Semiformal Invitation on a Calling Card

Accepts with pleasure!

Miss Mary Ashley Rogers

The Semiformal Reply on a Calling Card

Luncheon

Miss Elizabeth Anne Morgan

Friday, July 20th
12:30 o'clock

R.s.v.p.
10 Magnolia Ln., n.w.

The Semiformal Invitation on a Fold-over Informal

Miss Mary Ashley Rogers

Sincere regrets
Friday, July 20 th

The Semiformal Reply on a Card Informal

Should you receive an invitation on a calling card and not yet have one of your own, what can you do? If you have assembled *Le Petit Trousseau* that I have described in Chapter 8, you can use your monogrammed note paper. Your reply should take the form of a very short note written in the first or second person, as illustrated in the samples of informal replies found on page 186. If you have only The Interim Paper Trousseau, reply to the invitation on an unmarked note just as you would on an engraved note.

Of course, if a telephone number is given with the R.s.v.p., you phone your hostess to tell her how happy you are to receive her invitation and whether or not you can attend. If the word *regrets* and a phone number appear, you need only call to decline. Do, however, be certain to mention the party if you see your hostess beforehand or speak with her on the telephone. Let her know you are looking forward to the event.

You may think of invitations issued in this manner as old-fashioned. However, once you have acquired *Le Grand Trousseau,* I think you, too, will find inviting and responding in writing not only convenient but fun as well. For instance, when your time is going to be limited on holiday break from boarding school, college, or career, how easy it is to mail personally hand-written invitations to your friends at home. The occasion? A luncheon, a tea, or a brunch. The guest of honor? Although there need not be one, it could be your roommate from school who is to be your houseguest. During the holidays, friends are often difficult to reach by telephone. A written invitation would be a pleasant surprise in their mailbox—a much more pleasant surprise than your phone call when they are sleeping late!

If you find this type of invitation too "stuffy" for your group, I advise you to develop the style gradually. The first time you issue this type of invitation you might strike a friendlier, more casual note by using the second-person imperative instead of the third person: On your calling card or the front of your informal, write, "Please join me for tea at the Ritz-Carlton, Wednesday, the 3rd, at 3 o'clock." Your friend would return her card or informal with a friendly, "Looking forward to tea on Wednesday at 3." Nothing could be simpler. Your invitation is mailed before you leave school for the holidays, and her reply awaits your arrival at home. The date is set with neither of you taking valuable time from term papers or exams for a long letter or an expensive telephone call.

As you become accustomed to this way of inviting friends, you will begin to be just as comfortable with the third-person style. It does take time and practice to acquire new social knowledge and to develop new social habits. By all means, do not let me or anyone else impose an awkward custom on you. Instead, wait until you are perfectly comfortable with its use and it has become a part of your thoughts and actions, for only then can it be a natural gesture on your part.

The abbreviated invitation on the calling card or the informal is perfectly proper for any semiformal event, but I sometimes find it a bit stiff for the kinds of festive social occasions young hostesses stage. Even with its many legitimate usages, this is not necessarily the form of invitation best suited to every situation.

With regard to formality versus semiformality or informality, I am aware that neither you nor my students at L'Ecole des Ingénues may find uses for *all* of the proper ways of issuing an invitation in your present social lifestyle. Then why bother to study them, you might ask? Because you must become familiar with the formalities in order to make wise decisions about the alternatives!

The Fill-in Invitation

Another socially accepted semiformal invitation—and one that I feel can be young and fun—is the "fill-in" (often referred to as a "blank" or "skeleton") invitation. As its name implies, it is partially engraved or printed with blank spaces left for the details. It is wonderfully handy for a hostess who does a great deal of entertaining. The fill-in is of the same quality card as the fully engraved invitation.

Fill-in invitations come in two forms: personal and impersonal. The impersonal form does not have the name of the hostess and/or host engraved at the top, nor does it include the address on the face of the card (as does the personalized form); therefore it can be purchased in small quantities, whereas the personalized form must be ordered.

The fill-in invitation may bear one of two traditional invitational phrases: either the impersonal, "requests the pleasure of your company" or the personal, "requests the pleasure of" above a blank to fill in the name of the invited guest. Or it may say, "cordially invites you to attend"—yet another invitational phrase. Although the fill-in can be quite properly imprinted or engraved in black ink upon the ecru white or pearl white card, it may also be colorful, bearing a decorative embellishment or bright borders with a matching ink for the printing. The envelope can be cheerfully lined with a matching color paper, and you, too, may feel free with color and use a matching ink to pen in the party plans.

If you decide you like the fill-in invitation, I suggest you invest in a thermoengraved (or engraved) fill-in, personalized with your name heading the third-person invitational phrase of your choice, followed by the customary fill-in blanks, and with your address beneath the R.s.v.p., or in the alternative style shown below. It will become your party signature. Just as you plan the papers of your trousseau to reflect your personality, by all means have the fill-in invitation do the same—so when the invitation arrives, your friends will rave, "Oh, Elizabeth Anne is having a party!" They will know by your colors, your festive attitude, your spirit and flair that the party is not to be missed. You will be on your way to becoming a successful hostess.

Elizabeth Anne Morgan
invites you to join her
for Dinner and Dancing
on Saturday, February Fourteenth
at seven *o'clock*
Ten Magnolia Lane, Northwest
Atlanta, Georgia 30305

Please reply
(404) 255-1000

The Semiformal Invitation on a Personalized Fill-in Invitation

The Informal Invitation

Informal, preprinted invitations manifest a different personality, starting with the invitational phrase: "It's a Party!" "Come Celebrate," "Join the Fun," "You Are Invited." These cards are colorful and have clever drawings depicting the theme of the party. As always with fill-ins, the blanks are for *your* party particulars. Although not of the same high quality as the semiformal, these invitations are on nice stock or on paper folded like a greeting card. If you are artistic or have a creative friend, why not make your own? A quick print shop can copy your original. This may cost more or less than preprinted, depending on the number, but the invitation will be one-of-a-kind.

In addition to the commercial possibilities, informal written invitations can be issued on your notes or correspondence cards. On your note paper write on page one or three, depending on the placement of your monogram. On the correspondence card, write on the front.

These invitations are called "informal" because they allow you greater freedom of expression than the "semiformal" form. Note the brief and simple rules in the box below.

The Informal Formula

- Is written in the second person (which can never be done on a calling card)
- Is written in two short paragraphs rather than in centered lines (as the formal)
- Begins with a salutation
- May or may not include a comma after the form of address, but never a colon. "Dear Anne" or "Dear Anne,"—never "Dear Anne:"
- Ends with a salutation and signature
- Need not give the year, but always the month and date, or day and date, or day, month, and date, in the lower left corner
- May use abbreviations for days, months, and dates

An informal invitation written in the second person might read as follows:

Dear Grace,

    Will you and your fiancé dine with us on Friday, the tenth of May, at eight o'clock?

    Looking forward to meeting him.

                          Affectionately,

                          Joan Taylor

Wednesday the first

The informal reply, written in the second person, would read as follows:

Dear Mrs. Taylor,

   It will give us much pleasure to dine with you on Friday the tenth at eight o'clock.
   Thank you for your kind invitation.

                                        Sincerely yours,

                                        Grace

Friday, May 3rd

To a very close friend, you may wish to be still more casual and adopt the first person, as follows:

Dearest Mary,

   Will you and your mother join Mother and me for lunch at the Capital City Club on Wednesday the tenth at twelve?
   I do hope you can come.

                                        Affectionately,

                                        Anne

Monday the 30th

The reply would be written as follows:

Dear Anne,

   Mother and I are looking forward to lunch on Wednesday.
   I am delighted to have the opportunity for our mothers finally to meet each other.

                                        Fondly,

                                        Mary

Dec. 2nd

Reply-in-Kind

You will notice that the reply to each of the samples is written to "match" the form of the invitation itself. There is a term for this that will always give you the socially correct manner in which to respond. That term is "reply-in-kind." In other words, write your response, whether you accept or regret, in the same person and on the same type writing paper as the invitation.

Although each of these examples is issued to two people—Grace and her fiancé and Mary and her mother—the note and envelope are addressed to only *one* person. Even though more than one person may be entertaining, only *one* signs the invitation. As a rule, the woman of the household still acts as the "social secretary" and invitations are issued and accepted by her. A bachelor, of course, will act on his own.

The Letter of Invitation

Written informal invitations, such as one asking you to spend a weekend at a friend's summer home, must often be longer than two paragraphs: They contain more details of travel, activities planned, clothing needed, and the like. Again, depending upon how close you are to the person you are inviting, you will write in the first or second person much like an invitation to lunch or dinner, adding details required by a guest who will spend the night.

When an informal invitation becomes too long to be written on informals or notes, it is socially correct to use your folded letter sheet or half-sheet, in which case your sentences can be expanded to more fully describe the excitement the visit holds in store. The reply may be written on your letter sheet, half sheet, or note paper.

A Letter of Invitation

Dear Diane,

Although I like working better than school, I am beginning to wonder about making it through the summer without that three-months vacation. Mom and Dad suggested that I take advantage of the long Memorial Day weekend to have a party at the lake. They will be there then and I hope you can come and bring Roy or whomever is your one and only of the moment. I am also asking Cathy and Corrine to come and bring dates. Mom says the fellows can bunk in the game room.

You'll need mostly slacks and shorts and your bathing suit. We were there this past weekend and the water is getting nice. You'll also want a dress as we are planning to go to the club for the teen disco/dinner dance one evening. Nothing fancy this time of year. Slacks and jackets will be okay for the guys.

I hope you are not busy for Memorial Day weekend and that you will come along and help me get "up" for my first summer as a "working girl."

Love,

Sherry

May the eighteenth

The Telephone Invitation

I certainly do not think all invitations must be handwritten, engraved, or printed to be socially correct. What about the informal telephone invitation? It is perfectly proper for the impromptu party with a short guest list, whether it be for a dinner, cookout, luncheon, or just getting together. Do "mind your manners" when issuing the telephone invitation, however, and adhere to The Telephone Invitation Formula below.

The Telephone Invitation Formula

- Telephone at times convenient for your guests.
- Never ask, "What are you doing Saturday night?" Say instead that you are having a party Saturday and give the details: time, date, location, type of party, appropriate attire.
- Invite the person to attend.
- Tell her or him the date by which you will need a reply.

The telephone reply "speaks for itself," and as with a written reply, be prompt in responding. If you cannot attend, you may tell your hostess why and that you hope she will invite you next time.

Now my one word of caution! Once you have turned down one invitation, whether it is issued formally, semiformally, or informally, you may *never* accept another for the same day and time. Do not decline one invitation because you are waiting for another.

Many hostesses send a written reminder after inviting a guest by telephone. On calling cards or informals, the words "to remind" are written above or below the name, and the day, date, time, and event are written below, following the form of the third-person semiformal. A reminder may also be written in the first or second person on informals or notes. With this combined approach, you can be certain to reach guests by telephone in plenty of time beforehand, and reinforce your invitation in writing. If you see prospective guests at school or work, or speak with them frequently over the telephone, your "reminder" will most often be spoken rather than written.

Your Inviting Touch

Now that you know the rules for inviting guests, be certain to obey them, but be creative. Make each of your invitations a pleasure to receive by taking the time to weigh the appropriate form, and to base your choice on these factors:

- The degree of formality or informality followed in your community
- How your friends will react to the invitation
- Whether you want to set a precedent or to abide by the established community code
- Whether you can carry off a little formality even if a detractor foolishly calls you a snob

Just remember, when the invitation's degree of formality matches the social occasion, it is appropriate. Your good taste would not allow you to send a casual note saying, "It's a ball" for a formal dance, any more than you would consider an engraved formal invitation "requesting the pleasure of your company" for a cookout. In the beginning of this book, I defined good taste as sensibility appropriate to a given time and place. An expensive invitation that you cannot afford is not in good taste any more than the casual summons to a formal dance.

It has been said that anticipation produces enjoyment equal to that of an actual experience. An invitation, then, can be thought of as anticipation in tangible form, a touchable promise of pleasure to come. Savor this enjoyment with every invitation you send or receive.

PART FOUR

The Gracious Touches

CHAPTER 10

The Dinner Party

One of the most accurate measures of civilization—be it a society's, a family's, or an individual's—is the way it feeds itself. How lucky we are to live in a time and a place in which food is plentiful and leisure is ample—breakfast, lunch, and dinner can provide pleasant and creative association with family and/or friends and can feed our aesthetic and emotional, as well as our physical, needs. A surprise cookie hidden under the bright napkin of a reluctant first-grader can change his or her whole day, and a boutonniere from the garden or window box beside the coffee cup of a hardworking husband or father can brighten his outlook. Think of love as the most effective seasoning in all seasons and "plate art" as the most stimulating of artistic experiences.

Having been born into a tradition of adequacy and some elegance places upon you a responsibility to maintain—and perhaps to elevate—the standard. First you must learn and unvaryingly use good table manners. Accept the fact that manners have come into being both for the comfort of the diner and to protect others from unattractive displays. For most foods, the proprieties are simple and quite natural. Neatness, noiselessness, sociability are the goals of dining etiquette.

For very formal dining situations, etiquette can be rigid and a bit complicated. Although a hostess can give a dinner party without help—and quite successfully—she cannot present a formally served one. Therefore, if she has no help, she chooses a method of service other than the one dictated for a formal dinner. At a formally served dinner, there must be two people to serve each six guests. Without a household staff, the hostess engages outside professional help in order to stage a formal dinner properly.

194

Consider facing a table for a formal dinner set with thirteen pieces of silver at each place. But there is actually a very simple regimen for choosing and using the correct piece.

Powerful corporations regularly engage me to teach grown men and women (some the age of your parents, but still ingénues—initiates—on the social scene of the business world) the proper ways to eat and to entertain, because they have found that these skills are as important to executives as any business or professional know-how. Recent studies reveal that when intelligent, capable people fail, it is often traceable to a lack of social skills.

In addition to being comfortable with how to eat, you need to be sophisticated in what you eat. Enjoyment of a variety of foods is a social grace in itself. Few things upset a hostess more than having a guest pick at something; and as a diner, your enjoyment is sharply curtailed if you limit yourself to just a few foods. Young people, so charming in most situations, can be the worst offenders by "turning up their noses" at new items. It is boring to insist on eating only familiar or fast-food-category favorites. The sophisticate is as adventurous in tempting the palate as in challenging the mind with new books or ideas. Early on you should acquire a taste for, the table skills to handle, and a proper vocabulary to discuss or to order a reasonable repertoire of interesting foods.

Creativity with food is an art that each of you should now be cultivating. Join your mom or your dad preparing food in the kitchen, and you will find that you are soon able, single-handed, to make attractive surprise birthday dinners. You may also find, a few years hence, that by sharing the cooking with your companion in a first apartment kitchen, your togetherness can help compensate for the stress of a two-career marriage. My ingénues love this part of their training, and many former students are now competent young matrons, gracefully sharing their talents with family and friends.

"Please Set the Table"

How many times in your growing-up years did your mother ask, "Will you please set the table?" And you no doubt replied, "What are we having?" Therein lies the simple formula for setting a table. Once the menu is determined, the silver required is placed beside each plate. Chaos would reign, however, were the flatware to be set out at random, since today's diner may be faced with much more than the solitary fork, spoon, and knife.

So let us, for fun *and* for practice, assume that you are to set the table, as do my ingénues, for *le grand dîner*—their gala graduation dinner at L'Ecole des Ingénues. **Study** the French menu below designed especially for the ingénues' last evening by Monsieur Herve Geze of Paris; who has served for several years as my *Premier Maître d'Hôtel*. His special menu is indeed a grand one, as it requires the maximum number of flatware pieces permissible to place before a diner at one time.

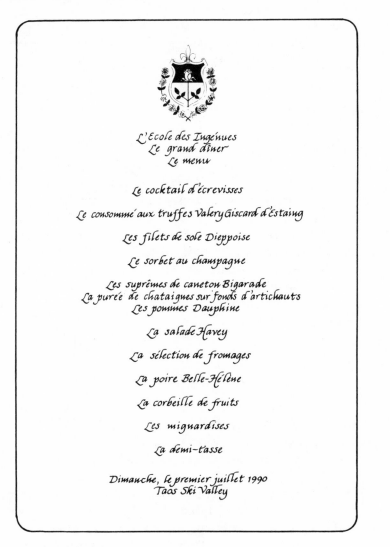

L'École des Ingénues
Le grand dîner
Le menu

Le cocktail d'écrevisses

Le consommé aux truffes Valery Giscard d'Estaing

Les filets de sole Dieppoise

Le sorbet au champagne

Les suprêmes de caneton Bigarade
La purée de chataignes sur fonds d'artichauts
Les pommes Dauphine

La salade Havey

La sélection de fromages

La poire Belle-Hélène

La corbeille de fruits

Les mignardises

La demi-tasse

Dimanche, le premier juillet 1990
Taos Ski Valley

The Formal Menu Card

Before any moves are made, the table must be sized properly to accommodate the number of guests who will be in attendance. As the hostess, you know how many can be seated at your main dining table and will make the decision, if needed, to include additional, smaller dining tables throughout the living areas. In order for guests to have ample room, twenty-four inches must be allowed for each diner.

Now comes the fun of arranging the pretty things. As though you were a photo stylist for a fashionable home magazine, gather the props that you will correctly place to please the aesthetic eye of your guests.

The Perfect Setting

A dinner such as the formal graduation dinner at L'Ecole des Ingénues calls for thirteen pieces of silver flatware in each guest's place setting. Thirteen pieces are the maximum number that can confront a diner at one time, and I like to remember this rule by thinking of them as the sterling thirteen.

Should a menu, as does our graduation menu, demand flatware in addition to the sterling thirteen, it will be brought in on a small tray by the server and placed on the table at the time of the course requiring it, with the exception of the fruit-course flatware. The dessert flatware may be in place as a part of the sterling thirteen in the Continental fashion or it may be presented separately. Prior to arranging the flatware, however, is the placing of plates as described below.

PLACING THE PLATES

1. The formal table demands the formal cloth. So, over the table silencer goes the pristine white linen or damask cloth.
2. Next, I suggest you put on a pair of soft, thin cotton gloves to prevent leaving fingerprints on the china, silver, and crystal. This is a true time-saver in the end!
3. What more festive occasion than this to use Grandmother's antique place plates? "Place plates" are special, often ornate plates set at each place, upon which other plates—from which to eat—are later placed. They should be positioned first on the cloth in order that you may play with the spacing and measuring of the table. First, put a place plate at each end of the table, then the proper number on either side.

4. Using a twenty-four-inch piece of ribbon or string or a twenty-four-inch dinner napkin as a measuring device, adjust the plates along either side of the table so that they are twenty-four inches apart from the center of one plate to the center of its neighbor. The plates on the far left and right sides should be no closer to the table edge than eighteen inches from the center of the plate. These measurements are critical to the proper positioning of the place setting, to entering and exiting the chair, to the service of the meal, to the dining comfort of the guest, and to conversation while dining.

5. Carefully position the place plates on each side of the table so they are directly across from one another. For an uneven number of guests, center the plates on one side across from the open spaces on the other.

6. Place the chairs directly in front of each place plate to make certain they all fit.

7. Position each plate one inch from the edge of the table with coat of arms, crest, monogram, designs, figures, or flowers facing the diner right side up and each exactly the same. Check this measurement by placing your thumb in a horizontal position at the table's edge and nestling the plate's edge against the opposite side of the thumb.

The Sterling Thirteen

Now, with the menu in hand, gather the necessary silver. One rule applies at this time: There can be no more than three knives on the right side of the plate and no more than three forks on the left. The exception is a fourth fork (the oyster, cocktail, escargot, lobster) which does not count as one of the three for it is placed on the right side, as is the soup spoon. The individual butter spreader is placed atop the diner's bread-and-butter plate, and the individual salt spoon rests in the small saltcellar. The dessert fork, dessert spoon, and dessert knife (if required) are placed above the plate.

With place plates properly positioned, the silver is now placed on either side, with the dessert silver above the place plate. The pieces for the first course are the farthest away from the plate, as they will be used first. Silver for subsequent courses progresses toward the plate; the silver for the last course is nearest the plate. The cutting edge of the knife blade faces the plate; the fork tines and the bowl of the soup spoon face upward. (This is the

198

American custom; in Europe the fork tines and bowl of the spoon are sometimes turned over.)

Follow my formula for the sterling thirteen until each piece has been properly placed for this gala menu in accordance with The Formal Place Setting illustrated below.

The Formal Place Setting

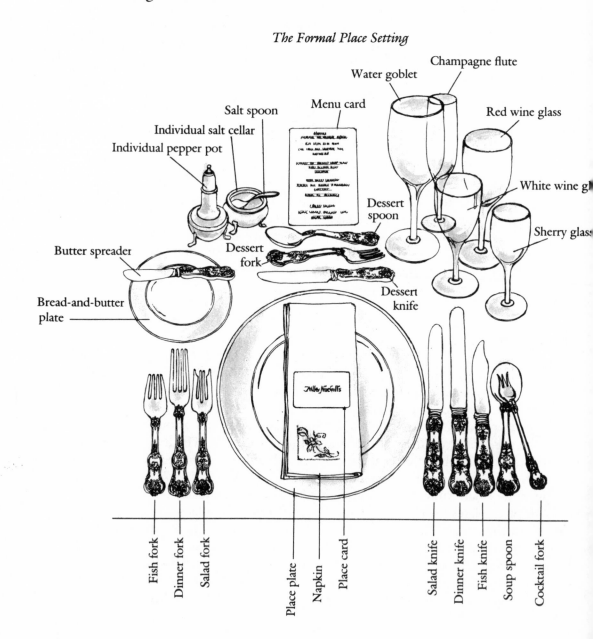

1. Place the cocktail fork on the far right of the place plate. (As an alternative, the tines of the fork may rest in the bowl of the spoon with the fork handle at an angle pointing to five o'clock.) The diner will use it first for the crayfish cocktail.

2. Place the consommé spoon or round-bowl soup spoon to the left of the cocktail fork. This will be used for the famous consommé with truffles.

3. The fish knife and fork are next in line for the *petite entrée* or *amuse-gueule* (a small appetizer to tease the palate) of poached sole. The fish knife goes on the right side of the plate and to the left of the consommé spoon. The fish fork is placed on the far left of the place plate allowing space for two additional forks.

4. As the teaspoon for the champagne sorbet looks a bit awkward between two knives (*and* since it will ultimately exceed our sterling thirteen), it should be brought in with the sorbet course. At that time it will be placed behind the stem of the sorbet glass, bowl up, with the bowl facing eleven and the handle facing five o'clock.

5. For the meat course, the *suprêmes* of duck, place the dinner knife to the right of the place plate and to the left of the fish knife. The dinner fork is positioned on the left of the plate and to the right of the fish fork.

6. The salad, served after the entrée in the Continental style, will require a salad knife on the right of the plate and to the left of the dinner knife. A salad fork will be placed on the left of the plate and to the right of the dinner fork. These will be the last pieces to be placed on the left and right of the place plate.

7. Stop! The limit has been reached, and there can be no more forks on the left and no more knives on the right of the plate. So, for the cheese course, additional flatware must be brought in. A fresh fork is placed to the diner's left and a new knife to the right.

8. Continuing with those pieces that can be placed before the diner is seated, add now the dessert flatware for the *poire Belle-Hélène*. This dessert requires three pieces. Place the dessert knife above and closest to the place plate and parallel to the edge of the table, with the handle to the right and the tip of the blade to the left, cutting edge parallel to the table's edge.

Above it position the dessert fork, tines up and facing the right of the plate with the handle to the left. The dessert spoon rests above the fork with the handle to the right and the bowl up and facing the left.

9. After all of the other silver has been placed, the bread-and-butter plate is set in position to the left of the place plate. It may be left of the outermost fork, with its top edge in line with the top edge of the place plate, or it may be just above the forks, depending on the eye of the hostess; she will determine that, once the butter spreader is placed across its upper third (with the handle facing right, tip facing left, and cutting edge parallel to the table's edge), it cannot be knocked off when the diner picks up any of the forks. All bread-and-butter plates and individual butter spreaders should be set in the same manner. And should the butter spreader be nearly in line with one of the pieces of dessert silver, adjust it slightly so that it is perfectly in line.

10. Center a pair of individual pepper pots and salt cellars above each place plate. Place the tiny salt spoon in the salt cellar and there you have it, the sterling thirteen! (If there are not enough pepper pots and salt cellars, a pair may be placed between two place settings for the guests to share.)

11. But, wait! Additional flatware is yet to come for the fruit course. Behind the scenes, before the basket of fruit is passed, the fruit fork will be placed on the left and the fruit knife on the right on top of the fruit plate (on either side of the finger bowl), the set brought out and placed before each guest. Have these sets "at hand" in the kitchen so that they may effortlessly be placed as your guests chat between courses.

12. Set the demitasse spoons, along with the demitasse cups, aside for safekeeping as they await adjournment to the living room for demitasse and *mignardises*.

13. Now that the flatware has been properly placed, the time has come for perfection. Be extremely militarylike in positioning the flatware, making certain that, as sterling soldiers, each is in line with the other, all are perfectly straight, and the ends of the handles are aligned one inch from the edge of the table. To check this accurately, insert a heavy card (a menu card or correspondence card works well), holding it perpendicular to the table, between the place plate and the salad knife. Allow its

width between the plate and the knife. Do the same between the rest of the knives, consommé spoon, and cocktail fork. Repeat with the remainder of the flatware. Now, step back from the table and admire your artistic endeavors!

The Crystal Companions

The fragile crystal stemware, gleaming companion to silver and china, is the final touch. Place it last, for it could easily be knocked over in your efforts to set the china and silver straight.

At L'Ecole des Ingénues, beautifully tinted herbal teas are served at formal meals. Each is chosen to add not only the proper flavor complement to the course that it accompanies, but for the eye appeal of its lovely color. The teas are slightly chilled and are served without sugar, lemon, or ice, for their flavors stand alone (and those condiments are a menace on the formal table).

For a sparkling table, I direct you now to The Sparkling Complements.

THE SPARKLING COMPLEMENTS

1. Center the water goblet just above the tip of the dinner knife. If more than three pieces of stemware are to be used, move it slightly to the left.
2. The remainder of the stemware stands to the right of the water goblet, moving ever closer downward to the diner's right (in reverse order of use). The first piece to be used is closest to the table's edge and within safe reach of the guest.
3. Factors to be taken into consideration in placing stemware are the order of use, the width of the table, the size of the crystal, the number of glasses, and the hostess's personal preference. Stemware may be placed in a straight line or a diagonal row toward the table's edge between the dinner knife along the plate. It may also be centered in a cluster or a row above the service plate. My favorite placement is to nestle it together in free-form fashion from the left of the salad knife tip across the other knife tips and above the bowl of the soup spoon, placing the pieces to be used last behind the others. A sixth piece of stemware, when called for, can be placed slightly to the right of the soup spoon.

The Formal Napkin

The napkin plays second fiddle to the silver, china, and crystal. The sophisticated flat napkin does this perfectly and is in the best of taste. Save high-standing, festive folds for casual, informal at-home tabletop adornment.

For the formal dinner, the napkin is folded flat in a manner that features the monogram or special decoration, and is placed in the center of the place plate. The three formal napkin folds are: the square fold, the rectangular fold, and the diagonal fold. Each name describes the manner of the fold.

The Placing of Place Cards

Completing the perfect formal table setting is the positioning of place cards—it is the final effort on the part of the hostess.

Place cards are a must at the formal table. The place card marks *the* spot special to each guest, who knows the hostess had a reason to assign just that seat. Place cards free the hostess from having to remember where she planned for everyone to sit and properly allow her to remain behind her guests and enter the dining room last. The place cards also enable a guest to "sneak a peek" at names. For the latter reason, I prefer a flat place card to the standing folded one or to the place card holder, so that the names can be more easily read. The flat place card is put on top of the napkin, taking care not to cover the monogram or decoration.

The name on the place card is hand-written in black ink for formal dinners. At official and public dinners, titles are written according to proper protocol. In the home, however, should notables be among those present, their courtesy titles are written on the place card along with their surname, just as it is for the other guests: Governor Green, Senator Smith, Dr. Downing, The Rev. Mr. Reynolds, Father Flanagan, Mr. Miller, Mrs. Moses, Miss Menlow. Of course, should there be two Mr. Millers, their cards would be written Mr. Frank Miller and Mr. Steven Miller.

When dinner guests are on a first-name basis, which is often the case with at-home entertaining, place cards are written without titles and include both the first name and surname: John Jones, Cathy Clark. The inclusion of the surname is quite helpful to those who are meeting for the first time. If all are old friends, first names may be used alone, taking care to add a last initial or name if duplicate names are a problem.

The Pleasures of Placement

1. To begin, the host and hostess are seated opposite one another at either end of a rectangular table or across from one another at a round table.

2. When a seated dinner is given in honor of someone, he or she becomes the guest of honor. A woman guest of honor is awarded a place of honor to the host's right, whereas an honored man is seated to the hostess's right.

3. Once the place cards have been placed for the host, hostess, and guest (or guests) of honor, the place card of the woman who is of next importance (or who is the wife of the male guest of honor) is placed on the host's left. Likewise, the man who is of next importance (or the husband of the female guest of honor) is seated to the left of the hostess.

4. Guests are then placed in descending order of importance, or "rank" (age, title, and such) as the seating moves toward the center of the table as follows: The lady ranking third in importance is placed to the gentleman of honor's right; the lady fourth in rank is seated to the left of the gentleman on the hostess's left.

5. The place of honor is awarded to the bride-to-be when a formal dinner is given in her honor. Even though she may be the youngest, she receives precedence.

6. If a seated dinner is given without a specified guest of honor, but instead for a group of friends of like standing, the positions of honor are awarded to those who are the newest acquaintances or who have traveled the farthest distance or are visitors from another country or who have not visited for the longest time. The friends of the longest standing are then placed in the middle.

7. The seating of family members is also governed by precedence. Were you to place the place cards for a festive holiday dinner given by your parents in their home for your family of four generations, positions of honor would be given to the oldest adults and so on down according to age. You would seat your mother and father

At-home entertaining—even the most formal dinner party—is, for most of us, unofficial, and therefore only a few basic rules serve as guidelines to seating.

opposite one another at either end of the table in the host and hostess positions. To your father's right would be your great-grandmother and grandfather, respectively. Alternating boy and girl grandchildren, when possible, are seated on either side between the great-grandparents and grandparents. The youngest grandchildren would be closest the center, and the older grandchildren seated next to the little ones would offer any assistance needed.

8. The alternate to "fixed" seating is to place only the lady and gentleman of honor according to the rules and to place the others according to personality. To do this, play "boy-girl, boy-girl" with the remaining dinner guests, which means seating the men and women alternately within the remaining spaces and separating girlfriends from boyfriends and husbands from wives. An exception to this rule is that an engaged couple may be seated together unless theirs is an extended engagement or all the guests are the same age and close friends. The number of guests, an uneven number of men and women, or the arrangement of the table sometimes prevent pure adherence to our "boy-girl, boy-girl" seating plan. If this happens, try moving the hostess clockwise one space to the left, but leave the host in his seat. Or, try positioning the host and hostess across from one another on the long sides of the table. Once you have done the best you can with the "boy-girl, boy-girl" arrangements, do not worry about it, even if you have a "boy-boy" or "girl-girl" situation.

9. Finally, match those seated side by side (who can be moved around as they are not guests of honor or second in importance) so that they will find one another enjoyable and stimulating conversation may be sparked.

The Playbill of Dining—The Menu Card

Just as the playbill guides the audience through a performance on stage, so does the menu card guide the diner through the pleasures of the table. At a formal dinner a menu card is placed before the host and hostess. One is also placed at each guest's place or for two or three guests to share.

Menu cards may be held upright in a special holder or may be placed flat on the table. Usually the space that remains after the place settings, the centerpiece, and the candelabra are positioned will determine where the menu cards will go. Ideally, they are placed above and to the left upper rim of the place plate.

The menu card must match the place card both in color (ecru or white) and in such decorative touches as gilded or silvered beveled edges. A bride may have the family coat of arms or crest engraved at the top and an unmarried woman or widow may use her lozenge. Although this is the only marking acceptable to staunch traditionalists, the new school allows the use of a monogram if the family does not possess the other. These markings are engraved and inked in gold or silver to match the beveled edges or may be embossed. Colors, however, are not appropriate. The markings are centered on the top of the menu card and may be centered in like manner on the place card or positioned in the left uppermost corner.

The formal menu is hand-written on the menu card in black ink. The word *Menu* is written at the top (or beneath the marking if there is one), and several spaces below; the courses are written in the order in which they are to be served. Each dish commands a line all its own, and if short in name, the sauce may be included on the same line (otherwise it is written beneath). As a part of the "roast" or main course, the potato and vegetable dishes are written beneath the roast. A space is left between courses to indicate a change of courses. When wines are served, they are listed to the left of the course that they accompany. The date (and sometimes the town or city) is written several spaces below the final course.

Many formal dinners are composed entirely of classic French dishes, and when this is the case, the menu is properly written in French. However, when native American dishes are served at a formal dinner, as they often are, they should be presented in English on the menu.

I suggest that you do as I do when you wish to write a menu in French: Seek a professional who is competent in menu French and engage him or her to assist you.

The Centerpiece

Something is missing from the table set simply with a perfect cover (or place setting) for each guest. The link is the centerpiece, a focal point that brings unity to the table and draws the eyes to the whole of the composition.

Although some hostesses like to create the centerpiece first and place it before anything else, I save it for last, for it is only then that I know how much room remains and what my mood is once the necessaries are in place.

The centerpiece can be the most exquisite porcelain or crystal bowl standing handsomely alone. Or it can be made of nature's bounty: flowers, fruits, vegetables, leaves, seed pods, sticks, and stones. The nature of the centerpiece must match the dinner presentation in formality or informality. Sticks, stones, and seed pods would perfectly complement a hearty black bean soup supper in the winter, whereas fresh, formally arranged, cut flowers would be most appropriate for the graduation dinner table with which you and I are practicing.

A centerpiece for the seated dinner must be below the eye level of the guests. A diner must be able to look into the eyes of another across the table. At the same time, the centerpiece should rise as high as the crystal stemware, lest it appear to have been sheared off. If it were a garland stretching the length of the table, it would have one center peak rising to this height and perhaps others a bit lower. No centerpiece can be so wide as to touch or threaten the individual covers, and the fragrance must be so delicate that a guest would have to lean into it to smell anything at all. For that reason, a magnolia or a gardenia from the garden should be relegated to a far corner of the living room.

The Dinner Party Table Favor

Certainly not a necessity, but a nicety, is the table favor. From childhood, we have all loved a little prize, a trinket, from a party. The hostess who retains a youthful spirit is the one who favors her guests with a surprise at their places.

So, be it a boutonniere for him and a single small flower for her waiting on top of the napkin, a tiny, gift-wrapped Cartier charm, or a fascinating fragrance sample tucked above each plate, a precious little gift package with a perky gift tag inscribed with each guest's name can serve in lieu of the place card, even at the most formal dinner.

Delighted dinner guests will wonder what their favor is, but a smart hostess will ask that they await their surprise until just before dessert. What better way to fill the lull as the table is cleared and crumbed before dessert and to spark new conversation?

The Music and Lighting

The background music and lighting for a dinner party serve as the backdrop against which the guests interact and should be as lovely as the formal table itself. As the guests arrive, the lights may be up and the music soft.

When it is time to progress to the dinner table, dim the overhead lights and light the candelabra or votives (ensuring the candles have no scent to distract from dining odors). Once the guests are seated, the service staff lowers the music to a faint whisper or turns it off completely. The music, not the lights, should brighten the after-dinner conversation areas.

"Dressing for Dinner"

At one time, an invitation to dinner automatically meant that the guests arrived at eight o'clock and the gentlemen wore dinner jackets. In keeping, the ladies wore dinner dresses, which were long but not of such dressy fabric or so bare a cut as the evening dresses they wore to balls or opening nights. The skirts were more slender, designed for sitting and standing without taking up a vast amount of room. In many large cities where strictly formal dinner parties are given, and at the graduation dinner at L'Ecole des Ingé-nues, this dress code remains *de rigueur*.

Whether fashion or local custom dictates long or short dinner dresses, the garment should not be strapless, have spaghetti straps, be cut revealingly low in front or back, or bare any skin via cutouts between the midriff and bikini line. Remember, you want your date or your dinner partner to remember the color of your eyes, not the position of your tan lines! A dinner dress may be strapless if worn with a carefully coordinated jacket, but in that case you do not remove the jacket. The top and sleeves (short or long) may be of see-through lace, organza, or tulle to the level where the opaque fabric ends well above the bosom, and it may also be sleeveless. Remember, you want to look your best from the waist up, as that is how you will be viewed by the other guests.

Today's hostess makes a point of telling her guests when she invites them what attire is expected. If you expect the gentlemen to appear in "black tie" and the ladies to wear long dinner dresses, indicate it by engraving "black tie" on the right lower corner of the invitation to a formal dinner or by writing it in by hand on any other form of invitation. If dress is not indicated on the invitation, male guests should assume that dark suits are in order and female guests should wear short dinner dresses. If the hostess wants her guests to forgo dinner clothes, she tells them so verbally: "We're not dressing tonight, just a dark suit," or "Please be casual, we're dining on the patio."

As you plan a seated dinner party, decide how you want your guests to dress and tell them so. You will find, however, that the evening takes on a very special glamour and your party will be remembered if the guests "dress" for dinner in the most formal manner your community accepts. Perhaps you will be a trend-setter!

The House Bell Rings!

Dressed appropriately, the guest rings the doorbell at the appointed hour, *never early* and never more than fifteen minutes late. The host and hostess are always dressed and ready to receive their guests at least a half hour before they are to arrive. Little mishaps do occur, last-minute details must be attended to, and if not, what better moment to sit down, stop, be still, gather your composure, and look forward to a successful evening.

Who answers the door to arriving guests? The answer varies greatly in today's changing domestic scene. Formerly (still, in the homes of the wealthy), the door was opened by the butler or his assistant. Today, in most households, a butler is not a fixture. His role, however, is frequently assumed by a caterer or a professional party planner (and staff), which is a prerequisite in staging a formal dinner party. Coats are accepted by the staff and placed in the designated areas.

As we rehearse this imaginary dinner party, I must caution you that as a guest you may not enter any room into which you are not specifically invited. The exception is the powder room. But do not go there immediately upon arrival. Remember, a hair out of place is of far less consequence than an escort awkwardly awaiting your return.

For the formal dinner the hostess has someone to answer her door, and she and the host remain standing in the living room near the door. In this position they may greet and welcome incoming guests. Their most important role at this time is to cordially and individually welcome each guest. In order to do so, the hostess must give them her undivided attention at that moment, look them in the eyes, grasp hands, smile, and say "I'm so happy you could come!" She then presents the new arrivals to the guest or guests of honor, who stand nearby. Little else need be said. The host steps up quickly to reinforce the hostess's welcome, then leads the guests into the living room and introduces or "injects" them (if everyone knows one another) into a group. And so on it goes until all the guests have arrived.

The Dinner Partner

Occasionally in a private home you may notice a little tray in the foyer upon which small envelopes are placed, each bearing the name of a male dinner guest. Your escort will pick up his, open it, and remove the card within, which bears the name of the lady he is to escort into the dining room, to seat at the table, and to enjoy as his dinner partner.

Alternatively, the hostess may present each gentleman with a small fold-over card with his name on the front and the name of his dinner partner and table number inside, along with a diagram of the table on which are marked the doorway and his position at the table. She may have a small drawing, known as *les plans de table*, on the foyer table numbering the tables.

At times, a man will not know his dinner partner. It is his responsibility to locate her and be introduced prior to the announcement of dinner. The tiny envelopes and cards certainly add charm to a large dinner party and create a lovely predinner game as each gentleman seeks his partner.

Understanding this private ceremony may save you from embarrassment. When a young man you have not met seeks you out, is introduced to you, and later offers his arm to escort you in to dinner, you now know to accept it rather than say, "I'd planned to sit with my date, Bill." The choice is not yours but your hostess's. Neither are you jealous when Bill is "seen with another brunette" as his dinner partner! These are the rules of fair play at the seated formal dinner.

The Prelude to Dinner

As the prelude to dinner, the staff passes hors d'oeuvre to appease the appetite and a beverage to encourage it, whetting the palate for the first seated course. The hostess sees that this prelude is neither too short nor too long. A hostess is wise to tell the guests, "Please come at eight for hors d'oeuvre. Dinner is at eight-thirty."

The Late Guest

The late guest is a rude guest unless the delay is unavoidable. Should you be late, telephone the hostess and tell her whatever the *truthful* story may be. Insist that she go on with dinner without you and tell her when to expect you. If it is to be just twenty or thirty minutes, she may wish to await your arrival, but if longer, she will more than likely begin.

A late guest is ushered into the dining room by the butler, the housekeeper, the caterer, or party planner. The guest speaks quickly to the hostess and takes his or her seat at the table (easily found for it is the empty one!). Gentlemen need not rise for the newcomer. A woman guest may be seated by her escort who then takes his place, or if she has come alone, the servant may seat her, or the gentleman to whom she has been assigned as a dinner partner may do so.

"Dinner Is Served"

Once all the guests have arrived and the prelude to dinner is drawing to an end, the hostess circulates to ask if anyone wishes to refresh before dinner. She has already coordinated with her kitchen help (or with her checklist if she is entertaining "solo" and informally), to make certain all is in order and that the candles are lighted.

Then the magic words "Dinner is served!" announce that the dining is about to begin. Quite formally, a butler may say them softly to the hostess or even give her a knowing nod. She then seeks out the gentleman of honor, and the host seeks out the lady of honor. The hostess will then invite her guests into the dining room. (The "solo" hostess announces softly to several of her guests after she and the host have first told their respective guests of honor.)

When dinner partner envelopes and cards are used, the announcement is the cue for each man to locate his dinner partner so that he may offer his right arm and lead her into the dining room. When this formality is not observed, conversational groups merely break up into pairs of men and women who go in together.

Entering the dining room is a game of follow the leader. Arm in arm, the host and lady of honor lead the way. In no particular order, other gentlemen and their dinner partners follow the host. The hostess enters last, accepting the arm of the gentleman of honor.

Each gentleman unhurriedly guides his companion to seat her, making certain that she will enter her chair from the left, thus avoiding a traffic jam. Without waiting for the hostess to enter, he immediately pulls back the chair of his dinner partner, comfortably repositioning it once she is seated. With the women guests seated, the men stand until the hostess (aided by the male guest of honor) is in her place—fulfilling the etiquette requirement that the hostess awards precedence to her women guests and the men award it to all women.

Sitting Pretty

It has been said that "no lady leans back in her chair." This is certainly true in formal settings, which is not to say that a lady does not sit well back into her chair and touch her back to it slightly. It is with her spine that she supports herself; the back of her chair only offers encouragement.

Time would be well spent reviewing the directions for sitting properly found in the box in Chapter 2 (p. 50). Once your dinner partner has pulled the chair out for you, follow the steps in that description. After he has repositioned your chair, assume the "working sitting position." Those who ride horseback will know what I mean when I say to assume the "easy seat." The feet-apart position may be alternated with the feet in the "heel-in-the-arch" position. The feet are never to be entwined around the legs of the chair, and never are the shoes to be slipped off! Now, remember steps eight through thirteen throughout the meal. When the meal is over, rise in accordance with the steps found in the box on rising, also in Chapter 2 (p. 52).

When engaging in any food-related activities at the table, the arms move freely from the arm sockets and swing comfortably close to the sides. The elbows move to and fro but never swing out toward a neighboring diner. As food or liquid is conveyed, think of transporting it to the mouth rather than collapsing the spine and drooping the head in an effort to meet the food. As food or beverage is brought to the mouth, the upper body rocks forward *slightly* from the hip points. (Place your hands on the hip points to feel this rotation while at the same time forever "pulling the string" of your spinal column.) At no time must the spine curve so that you appear to fall into your food!

At any time during the meal when the hands are not in use, they may rest in the lap. An alternative position is to place one hand in the lap and rest the wrist of the other hand on the table's edge with the hand extending over the tabletop. Again, assume a graceful raised position with the fingers gently curved. This takes considerable strain off the back and enables a diner to "sit straight" throughout a long formal dinner. Resting both wrists on the table can appear rather "regimented," although this position is proper and is done throughout Continental Europe. In any case, remember "wrists only," never more!

Neither the elbows nor the forearms are placed on the table while anyone among those seated is eating. However, during the interim between courses or after the meal is finished, it is permissible *occasionally* to rest the elbows on the table. If both are on the table, the fingers of one hand may rest, gently curved, in the palm of the other.

If a diner must "lean" into a conversation across the table between courses, it is much more graceful to do so by lightly supporting the head between the tip of the thumb and the second joint of the forefinger (again, with the fingers gently curved) than to prop it on a fist. To "hold up the head" on one or two fists looks lazy and sloppy at the table.

The Graceful Pause

For even very formal dinners, many hostesses adhere to the custom of having grace before the meal. Grace is usually quite brief and is ordinarily offered by the host, but a guest may be asked to do the honor, assuming prior acquiescence. Grace is said before anything on the table is touched, including the water goblets and the napkins. As a guest, you should watch the hostess pick up her place card, position it above the dessert silver, and unfold her napkin for a signal as to whether or not a blessing is to be said.

The Niceties of the Napkin

In order to unfold your napkin gracefully, pick it up from the place plate by the upper corner opposite the fold. If the fold is placed on the right, as it should be, you will pick up the upper left corner. The large dinner napkin is left folded in half (the smaller luncheon napkin is opened fully) and is placed across the lap with the fold facing the waistline. Should it be necessary for you to leave the table for any reason, the napkin is placed on the seat of the chair. The napkin is returned to the lap when you return.

Just as the hostess is the first to lift her napkin to signal the beginning of dinner, so is she the first to place it on the table to signal the close of the meal. The hostess makes certain that all her guests have finished before she makes this move. Once she has done so, the guests follow suit. The napkin is not refolded, but is picked up by the center and placed loosely at your place.

The Formal Dinner Service

While your first role in the formal dinner party will no doubt be that of a guest, to be completely comfortable you must understand the details of the formal service from the perspective of the hostess and the server as well as of the guest. At L'Ecole des Ingénues the students enact each of these roles so that each may not only be a better guest and hostess, but also be better prepared to instruct those assisting her in the proper manner of formal service. I suggest that you help your parents with their next dinner party. Along with several friends, rehearse all of the points outlined in this chapter, and, as do the ingénues, even go so far as to serve the dinner. Could there be a nicer gift for your parents' or grandparents' anniversary?

Little has changed in the service of the formal dinner since the worldwide adoption of *service à la russe* in the late nineteenth century. No food, other than ornamental fruit or after-dinner candies, is put on the table. Instead, the meats are precut and portioned in the kitchen, then artistically arranged and garnished on serving platters. Vegetables are placed in service dishes; sauces are in sauceboats. These service pieces may be of either silver or china, with one choice made for all pieces.

The platters and dishes are taken around the table and presented to each diner by whomever is serving. A diner's portion of food is transferred from the container to the diner's plate by the server, or the diner may serve him- or herself. At private formal dinners served in the home, the diner generally serves him- or herself, whereas at public dinners, the server may serve the portion.

The Silver Rule calls for the presentation of the untouched tray to the lady guest of honor, making her the first person served from it. After the lady of honor, all guests are served in turn, regardless of their age, sex, or importance.

The Puzzle of Plates

At a formal dinner, you will be faced with an ever-changing array of plates. At no time, other than the interim when the table is cleared for dessert, will you be without a plate before you, nor will a plate from which food was eaten ever be exchanged for a plate with food on it.

Some hostesses exchange plates as soon as guests have removed their napkins. The server takes away the initial place plate and puts an exchange plate in its place upon which to serve the first course. The hostess might choose to do this for several reasons: Her place plates are extremely valuable, sometimes irreplaceable; they contain heavy gilding, which might be harmed by certain foods or scratched by flatware or other china; they may not go well with the plate to be placed upon them for the next course; or the next course may require a hot or a cold plate.

For example, if a first course of caviar and toast points were eaten directly from the initial place plate—or from the new exchange plate—the server would remove it and replace it immediately with a clean plate. The soup plate without an additional plate beneath it would then be placed directly upon the new plate, or the soup plate with another plate beneath it may be exchanged for the clean plate. These are removed together when the diner finishes this course and a fresh plate is set down for the next course.

On the other hand, a first course of seafood cocktail, served in a stemmed glass resting on a small plate, is set directly on the place plate. The small plate and stemmed glass are removed together and the place plate remains. The soup plate (with its underlining plate) is then placed upon the place plate. The soup plate and underlining plate are removed together. The place plate remains throughout the fish and sorbet courses (the plates for each are placed upon the place plate). The place plate is then removed with the sorbet course and replaced with a warm plate for the entrée.

First Things First

Once the guests are seated, the hostess positions her place card above her place plate and puts her napkin in her lap. The guests follow suit, after which the service begins with the pouring of water. All beverages are poured from the guest's right. A guest may take a sip of water at once, if desired, and need not wait for the hostess to do so.

After the water is poured, the butter is served. Standing at the guest's left, using a butter pick or a cocktail fork, the server places an individual butter ball or curl or pat on the bread-and-butter plate. The bread is presented on the guest's left as well, from the bread basket, which rests on a small tray, and the guest takes a piece with his or her fingers. A hostess has the server place the bread so that her guests are not disturbed, in which case the server does so with a small serving fork and spoon held in the right hand. You may refuse bread and butter if you wish, but generally you will prefer to take it, for the pieces are small and each especially selected to complement the course with which it is served. A guest should not ask for butter if it is not served, and need not wait for the hostess to begin before taking a bite of bread.

The Serving Secrets

So, liquids are poured from the right, food is served from the left, and plates exchanged from the right. In addition, serving trays, serving dishes, and preplated foods will be served from the left. Be aware of the service so you may lean to the right a bit, if necessary, in order for the server to present the tray. You will seldom need to lean for the exchange of plates, but you should keep your left arm out of the server's way and your right one, too, between courses, so that he or she may exchange not only your plate but your neighbor's, too. What better reason to keep elbows off the table between courses?

Positioned side by side on the service tray, with the handles facing the guests, will be a large serving spoon (bowl up) and a large serving fork (tines down), fork on the left and parallel with the spoon on the right. The guest takes the fork in the left hand, tines down, and holds it in a "spearing" position. The serving spoon is held in a "filling" position with the bowl up in the right hand. The food is steadied with the fork as the spoon is slipped beneath the *entire* serving. For instance, to lift a quail from the toast point on which it is served would leave the sauce-soaked bread on the tray for the next guest to see. Should a soft food need to be cut from the ring or mold before taking a portion, it is cut with the side of the serving spoon held in a "cutting" position. After cutting, the spoon is switched to a "filling" position.

Once served, the courteous—and socially savvy—guest returns the serving pieces in the correct positions, making certain that the handles extend over the tray an inch or two so that they will not slip into it. Thus, the server need not reposition the serving pieces.

Painting a Pretty Plate

Does it matter where you place the portions on the dinner plate? Yes. For one thing, some foods are more difficult to cut than others and positioning will affect the ease and grace of cutting. Second, a space must remain free on the plate in order to place the knife and fork in their "rest" positions.

As you serve yourself, visualize the hood emblem of the Mercedes-Benz— a circle around a three-pointed star whose points touch twelve, four, and eight on the face of a clock. The twelve o'clock position is reserved for the most difficult to cut, for example, a chop or bone-in meat. (And if there is a slip of the knife, nothing is pushed off the plate.) The second most-difficult-to-cut food is placed in the eight o'clock position. The easiest to eat is, therefore, placed at the number four position. The space between four and eight o'clock is reserved for the "rest" position of the knife and fork.

"Try It, You'll Like It!"

As a mannerly guest, you should never refuse a dish that has been portioned and preplated, such as a seafood cocktail, oysters on the half shell, soup, *petits pots de crème,* or soufflés. It would call undue attention to you to sit before an empty place plate as others were eating. To do this in a fine home or restaurant in Continental Europe or England would bring a direct question: "Is something wrong?" Of course, if you have a food allergy or religious belief that prevents you from eating certain foods, you would have told your hostess when you accepted the invitation to dinner. She would have prepared a substitute dish for you, which would have been served without comment.

When serving yourself, take a portion of every item that is presented. A "token" portion of a food with which you are not familiar is acceptable. In fact, I have grown to like a number of the "token" servings I have sampled over the years and now find them to be among my favorites. I always wonder, "What if I had never tried them?"

To Speak or Not to Speak

A perplexing question to the uninitiated is whether or not to speak to those serving. First of all, accept the fact that this situation is very different from an informal American dining establishment with chatty waiters and waitresses. The server at the formal table does not speak to a guest except to ask if he or she wishes to have wine poured in the glass, and the guest respects that silence. During the many courses of a formal dinner, the server stands attendance several times, and you may feel the urge to express gratitude. But an eye-to-eye glance to the server, accompanied by a grateful nod once or twice, is sufficient acknowledgment. A server feels he or she has done the best job when it was done without interrupting polite conversation.

"Shall We Begin?"

To signal that guests should start eating, the hostess will do one of three things. She will *insist* that those who have been served begin by saying, "Please don't wait! Do start eating so your food doesn't get cold." Or she will wait until each guest has been served and then pick up her fork and knife or spoon (whichever the course requires) indicating that everyone may begin. She may even say, formally, "Shall we begin!"

In the formal service, so beautifully orchestrated and perfectly timed, a hostess waits until all her guests are served before she lifts her cutlery. Incidentally, waiting will give you the opportunity to see exactly which piece, or pieces, of silver the host and hostess pick up and how they use them. To perfect your dining style, with a knife, fork, and spoon at hand, study Flatware Finesse in the Glossary.

"Wine, Mademoiselle?"

Beginning with the first course and after each additional course has been served, wine is poured by the server, or servers, if it is being offered with that course. A small sip is first poured into the host's (or hostess's) glass for approval and then served to the guests in the order of service. The server asks each guest if he or she wants wine by saying, "Wine, Mademoiselle?" (or the title of whomever is being addressed). You either accept or refuse. It is most certainly proper to refuse, indicated by a slight pass of the right hand (palm down) above the top of the glass. A glass should not be turned upside down to denote refusal. Whether or not a guest drinks wine is a personal matter based upon personal preference and often upon health or religious reasons. Therefore it is never in good taste to comment to another about the fact that someone does not accept wine.

Although a guest may refuse wine and drink only water throughout the formal dinner, he or she must never ask to be served another beverage (if it is not on the table). The exception is when water is not served (some wine connoisseurs believe that water is not compatible with wine), in which instance the guest may request it at a time convenient to the server or hostess.

Clearing the Stage

As the drama of dining progresses, additional silver appears at each diner's place when required. In the case of our graduation dinner menu, a spoon is slipped in for the sorbet, properly positioned on the lining plate that holds the sorbet glass or dish. Just in time for the cheese course, when all the knives and forks on either side of the plate have been used, the server places a clean knife on the right and a clean fork on the left of the clean plate that was previously placed for the cheese course.

At last, the time arrives for the grand finale—the dessert! As the plate for the last course is removed, you find yourself for the first time without a plate before you—the serving staff is preparing to clear and crumb the table. Salt-cellars, pepper shakers, used glasses, and unused silver are cleared. The place cards may be taken up at this time also. I, however, prefer to leave them for one last glance lest a guest still be trying to "catch" another's name. The menu cards may be removed, too, though I prefer to leave them, for they give clues as to what is yet to come. Also left are the water goblets, the stemmed glasses for the dessert wine, the centerpiece, the candelabra or candlesticks, any decorative accents, and the festive dishes of candy.

After it is cleared, the table is "crumbed." Any crumbs, salt and pepper, and particles of food are brushed off the table by the server. Standing on the left of the guest, the server holds a small china plate or silver tray just beneath the table's edge and, with a tightly folded napkin, brushes the crumbs onto it.

At no time should a dinner guest apologize about crumbs. Simply lean slightly, if need be, as your place is crumbed and continue with spirited dinner table conversation.

The Finale: Sweet Treats

The dessert course serves as a festive finale to any dinner, but its presentation is ceremonious at a formally served meal. It can also be a tricky course.

There are two correct ways to present the dessert silver at a formal meal. One is to place it above the place plate in the initial place setting, where it remains until needed. A second method is to rest it on the dessert plate and present it with the plate (fork on the left, tines up, and spoon on the right, bowl up, with the handles of each perpendicular to the table's edge and facing the diner).

For our graduation dinner, I elect to place the dessert silver as a part of the initial place setting for I feel it adds beauty, sparkle, *and* anticipation throughout the dinner. Once the table is cleared and crumbed, I have the servers slip the dessert silver from its original position to the sides of the empty space where the dessert plate is to be placed: fork to the left, and knife, then spoon to the right. (The diner may do this, instead, at an informally served meal.)

Another intricate part of the dessert service is the presentation of the finger bowl. The finger bowl, doily, and matching glass underplate may be placed atop the dessert plate upon which also rests the dessert silver, in which case the diner picks up the finger bowl set (using both hands to avoid spills), places it in the now empty bread-and-butter plate position, and proceeds to position the dessert silver. Ideally, and more formally, the finger bowl set is brought out after the dessert course has been completed and the dessert plate and silver have been removed, and it is centered before the diner for immediate use.

When the finger bowl set, the dessert silver, and dessert plate are brought out together in a single service, it signals the diner that there will be no fruit course and that the meal will end with dessert. The same message is conveyed when the finger bowl set is presented alone after the dessert course.

If *mignardises* are listed on the formal dinner menu card, they are presented by the server, and each guest picks up one or two with the fingers and places them on the dessert plate to eat from the fingers along with the dessert. If *mignardises* do not accompany dessert, the little sweet treats may be served after dessert at the table or saved and passed in the living room with the after-dinner demitasse.

The Fruitful Finish

If the finger bowl set, fruit knife, fruit fork, and fruit plate are presented in a single service following the dessert course, you know that a fruit course is to be served. As the eating of fruit often necessitates frequent cleansing of fingertips, the finger bowl set accompanies the fruit course in the single-service method, so that the guest may use his or her finger bowl at any time and avoid staining the napkin with fruit juices.

Once the fruit and finger bowl paraphernalia have been properly positioned and you have made your selection from the platter presented at your left by the server, the challenge of the fruit itself faces you!

Although never listed on the menu card, attractive candies or candied fruits are eaten after the fruit course. These candies are placed on the table as a part of the initial setting and may be passed among the guests. And these sweet treats, too, may be reserved for savoring with the demitasse.

Finger Bowls, Flowers, Fingertips

At a formal dinner, when the finger bowl follows the dessert course or accompanies the fruit course, it is filled one-third to one-half full with cool water. (To fill it any fuller might cause splashes.) It is quite proper, and pretty, too, to float a small flower in the water. Violets, individual geranium blooms, a baby orchid, or rose petals are lovely.

If the finger bowl set is presented alone, after the completion of the dessert, a highly fragrant flower such as a miniature gardenia may be used, for there are no foods remaining to compete with its aroma.

Part of the daintiness of the finger bowl presentation is the doily that accompanies it. This doily is made of lovely lace, or of linen or organdy, and is often monogrammed or initialed. Paper doilies are not acceptable for the formal meal. Sometimes the finger bowl and doily rest directly on the dessert plate in the single service presentation and an underplate is not used. In this case, the diner simply lifts the doily along with the finger bowl (or the doily in one hand and finger bowl in the other) and places them to the upper left of the dessert plate. The dainty doily does *not* serve as a tiny towel with which to dry the fingertips.

When using the finger bowl, gently dip the fingertips of one hand into the water, return the hand to the lap, and dab the fingers dry on the napkin. Repeat the action with the other hand. The hands and the napkin must remain beneath the tabletop as the fingers are dried. Do not raise the pinkie finger in an affected manner, and do not appear either too dainty or too zealous. If your fingers are not soiled, you need not use the finger bowl, although you may feel more a part of the formal scene to do so, if only for ceremony. Once the fingers are clean and dry, if absolutely necessary, dampen the forefinger (not the napkin) in the finger bowl, touch it to the corners of the mouth, then lift the napkin to each corner and dab dry.

"Sorry, No Seconds!"

Quite different from the informal or family table, no seconds are offered at the formal table, and none should be requested. A courteous hostess would never embarrass a guest by refusing, but she may find herself embarrassed if there is no second serving available! By the same token, a guest should not take more than one share of a favorite when serving him or herself. The formal dinner, with its many courses, will never leave a diner hungry.

Proposing the Toast

The custom of toasting was among those ceremonies of Old World dining that settlers brought with them to the New World. It was with hope and anticipation that they toasted their new-found liberty and their kin who had remained behind. Today, throughout the world, the toast remains a social, diplomatic, and patriotic ceremony at table.

So whether the toast is tête-à-tête, when the gentleman looks into the eyes of his lady, raises his glass, and whispers *à vos beaux yeux* (to your beautiful eyes)—my favorite toast from my husband—or whether it is a child raising a milk mug with the other family members at holiday time as Father proposes a toast "to health, happiness, prosperity, *and* to our being together on many Christmases to come," the goodwill and sentiments expressed through the ceremonious act of toasting add drama to the dining scene.

At a private formal dinner, or at any gathering of friends or family at table, the proposing of toasts adds warmth and gaiety to the party. In a home, or at a private dinner staged in a restaurant, it is by tradition the host who raises the first toast, generally proposed at the beginning of the dinner once the first wine has been poured. It is equally proper to present a toast at the time of dessert, or at both times. At public dinners or banquets and at official White House dinners, protocol demands the toast be given by the official toastmaster at the close of the meal, either before or after dessert, and before the after-dinner speech.

In anticipation of a toast, a guest does not take a sip of wine once it is poured until the host or hostess does so. Likewise, a guest properly waits for the host (or hostess) to propose an opening toast to welcome all the guests or to acknowledge a guest of honor. Following the host's toast and the recipient's return toast, any guest is free to propose one.

More than one toast may be drunk from the same glass of wine, as glasses are no longer drained to "capture the toast" (except toasts to rulers or the President or to the bride and groom at their wedding reception), and for each of these occasions but a small amount of champagne is poured into the guests' glasses.

In respect to abstinence, it is no longer mandatory today that toasts be drunk with wine, nor is it thought to bring bad luck to toast with water. So just as the child may raise a milk mug, so may the abstaining teenager or young adult—or grown-up—raise a glass of water and drink it to the toast, accept a small amount of wine for the purpose of pretending to drink it when toasting, or, if you have neither water nor a token amount of wine, raise an empty glass and go through the pretense of drinking from it. To fail to participate in a toast is an insult to the toastmaker, recipient, and other participants.

It is traditional that the toastmaster stands to propose a toast and the guests follow suit, but the person to whom the toast is raised remains seated. Should the toastmaster choose to remain seated because the party is small or for another reason, the guests remain seated also.

In a private home, however, although the one proposing the toast may stand (and the guests may also), the guests generally remain seated, for space is limited and the shuffling about is awkward. Of course, for a very distinguished recipient, guests do stand out of respect.

The person to whom the toast is proposed remains seated and may hold the glass, but does not raise it or touch it to the lips until the others have done so. To toast along with the others would be raising the toast to oneself and is a social faux pas. A woman merely accepts a toast with a soft "Thank you" and remains seated. She may, if she wishes, return it in the form of a compliment to her host. A man may stand, if he wishes, to return the toast with yet another.

Once the dessert wine is poured at the end of a beautiful meal, one of the nicest compliments a guest may pay is to propose a toast, on behalf of him or herself and fellow guests, in praise of the host and hostess for a delightful dinner. Toasts should be "short and sweet," never drawn out, cynical, sarcastic, or off-color.

When welcomed as a group by the host in an opening toast at a private dinner party, each guest acknowledges not only the toastmaster, but his or her dinner partners seated on either side. Neighboring guests may touch glasses. However, to touch each glass is best saved for the intimate dinner when the gesture can be accomplished with grace and ease.

A vôtre santé!—To your health!

Exiting the Stage

With most formal dinners, the drama of dining ends with the fruit course. Just as she does with each preceding course, the hostess waits until all her guests complete their fruit before placing her silver in the "finished" position—that being the signal to the servants to clear. In order not to appear to be waiting for a guest to finish, she manages with each course to leave a little food on her plate in order to keep even the most methodical diner company.

A word of caution to guests: Avoid being tagged the turtle or the hare at table. Mind your manners and your speed and do remember to place your silver in the "finished" position (see Flatware Finesse in Glossary) so that your hostess knows your intentions.

Once everyone has finished the final course, the hostess may signal her guests to leave the table in one of several ways: She may glance at another lady at the end of the table, preferably the lady guest of honor, and give a little nod; or she may simply say to her guests, if the party is small and all can hear her, "Shall we move to the living room for coffee?" Once she gives her guests such a signal, the gentlemen assist the ladies with pulling back chairs and repositioning them. The guests depart the dining room, ladies first, the senior woman leading the other women, and then the hostess. The men follow, and award precedence to one another just as have the ladies, with the host leaving last.

After-Dinner Delights: Coffee and Conversation

At the formal dinner, or at casual gatherings for that matter, nothing is more delightful than the welcome that the living room or library extends to guests once they leave the table.

Although the partaking of coffee is optional, participating in conversation is compulsory. The clever hostess shuffles her guests as they settle in the new setting so that they may talk with those other than their dinner partners. As a mannerly guest, you compliment your partner on his companionship throughout dinner, thus releasing both of you to mingle with the rest of the party.

The clever hostess's secret of success in combining guests is to plant at least one adept conversationalist within each of her after-dinner groups. (Your secret to becoming that highly prized guest lies in preparation—refer to Chapter 6, The Art of Conversation!)

Once the guests are settled into their conversational groups, the server appears with the silver tray set with the niceties for the service of demitasses: a silver coffee pot filled with richly flavored, very strong, piping hot coffee; a small silver sugar bowl filled partway with brown or white crystals or small lumps of sugar (never granulated or powdered) and, according to the type of sugar, a sugar shell or sugar tongs; and a few doll-size demitasses on whose saucers rest the demitasse spoons with a mere sliver of lemon zest in the bowl. As a doily is only placed on a tray that contains food (a breakfast tray, a bread tray, a tray of *petits fours*), the coffee tray has no doily, nor does it contain a cream pitcher as cream is not served with demitasses (your clue not to ask for it).

Alternatively, the server may place the coffee service on the coffee table and the hostess may serve. In either case, the guest is offered coffee. The hostess or server places the sugar in the cup before pouring the coffee.

A guest may feel free to reply "No, thank you" when offered coffee, but you may never add, "but I'd like a cup of tea, please." If the hostess provides tea as an alternate, then you may select it.

The beauty, and practicality, of a demitasse (the French word means literally "half cup" or small cup of coffee) is that it can be balanced easily in the palm of the hand. This is exactly what a graceful guest does while dropping the zest of lemon into the cup and stirring it with the dainty demitasse spoon.

A hostess's collection of demitasses can, in themselves, spark after-dinner conversation. I have never failed to create a stir with my collection from

Vienna, each enhanced with a silhouette of a famous composer beneath which is a copy of his signature. Guests are quick to recognize that they have been given the demitasse of Hayden, Mozart, Beethoven, Schubert, Chopin, Bach, or Verdi, and conversational openers come naturally.

Demitasses and *digestifs* are generally served as after-dinner partners at formal dinner parties, and a small variety of *digestifs* from which to select is passed on a tray by the server or offered by the host. These after-dinner drinks may most certainly be refused, as may the *apéritif* and the wines served with the meal itself. As a part of the after-dinner service, once the demitasses and *digestifs* have been offered, a tray of freshly filled water goblets is passed among the guests, and, if not, a guest may properly ask for a glass of ice water at this time.

After-Dinner Entertainments

Were a hostess to consider any activity other than conversation after dinner, she might consider musical entertainment. A classical ensemble or a solo pianist make a lovely addition to any evening.

When L'Ecole des Ingénues summered in Aspen, I often engaged a college-aged string quartet from The Aspen Music Festival. The formally dressed performers and their light chamber music added greatly to the ceremony and festivity of our graduation dinner and served as a backdrop for farewell conversations afterward. Perhaps you have a friend or relative with a particular musical talent, whose services you could employ.

The hostess who plans after-dinner games or indoor sports, who turns on the television, shows home videos, or insists that her guests dance or play cards destroys much of the elegance of a formal evening. Such activities are appropriate only at those informal gatherings that are centered around them—when the plans are noted on the invitation; that way a guest who does not wish to participate may decline the invitation.

Bidding Adieu

Approximately an hour is the customary time for the enjoyment of conversation after dinner. Unlike a stage director, a hostess cannot drop the curtain on the drama of dining, raise the house lights, and usher her guests out of the house. This final act falls upon the shoulders of the guests.

A proper guest of honor is the first to depart. If the party has no "real" guest of honor, this responsibility is assumed by the guests who were seated to the right of the host and hostess at the dinner table. The hostess rises to acknowledge their good-bye (as she does when the remaining guests leave), but it is the host who walks them to the door of the living room, where, in a formal setting, the butler or maid takes over securing coats and escorting the guests to the front door. The host, however, does walk an unescorted woman to the door and to her car if need be. After the departure of the honored guests or their "stand-ins," the other guests may leave or remain for a little while.

If you are not a close friend, but instead a new acquaintance of the host and hostess, you should never be the last to leave. The prerogative of lingering belongs only to the closest of friends and then only at the insistence of the host and hostess and for a half hour at the most.

Someone who, for some important reason, must leave a private formal dinner party before the departure of the guest of honor should tell the hostess, if possible, upon accepting the invitation. If not, the guest explains to her privately during the prelude to dinner. Then, at an opportune moment, he or she speaks to the guest of honor and expresses regrets for having to leave prematurely. At the appointed time, the guest bids the host and hostess a quiet farewell and takes his or her leave as unobtrusively as possible to minimize the possibility of breaking up the party prematurely.

Accidents, Not Incidents

Having enjoyed the drama of a dinner party in its most formal form, you are now also well-rehearsed not only for *le grand dîner,* but also for the many less formal variations that are the mainstay of our daily lives.

As you have certainly observed while following the ritual of our graduation dinner, the rules of dining etiquette have come into being to assure the pleasure and comfort of each member of the company. Dining dos and do nots are a way of keeping everyone in step, developing an appropriate rhythm. Interruptions of this rhythm can destroy the harmony, a faux pas of which no socially aware person wishes to be guilty.

But no matter how socially aware and careful you and your fellow diners are, mishaps, mistakes, minor mix-ups, and occasionally major problems are going to happen on even the most elegant of occasions. How you react is probably the true measure of your social skills. You need to develop a special graciousness to see you through uncomfortable moments.

Fortunately for all of us, the modern Western attitude is that the best response to an awkward situation is the least response possible. An over-turned goblet, a spilled sauce, a misstep, an unfortunate remark, an ungraceful sneeze are accorded only the quick attention they require and are not allowed to threaten the perfection of the occasion.

In my philosophy of modern manners, I contend that although socially active people should know and follow the proprieties, I stress that they should never allow trivial mishaps to spoil a lovely event. So while it is important that you know the rules for formal dining, it is equally important that you learn to act with instinctive grace when something threatens the event. My philosophy makes it possible for you to keep your poise when things get out of sync, whether it is you or another guest who upsets the goblet. Should you find a bone, a pit, an unchewable piece of gristle, you must detach and swallow any food from the offensive item before you remove it with a fork or spoon (whichever was used for the course) and place it on the edge of your plate. Small fish bones or pits or seeds of foods eaten with the fingers are removed with the thumb and fingers. Of course, if the problem is of a serious physical nature, expediency overrules etiquette: Those who know what to do should act quickly and those who do not should get out of the way.

Most chills and spills are, fortunately, trivial and are accorded only brief attention. If you have upset the goblet, right it, apologize (once) to your hostess and move slightly to allow the server to attend the spill. Then let the affair proceed beyond the missed beat without the inharmonious effects of recurrent regrets.

A Formal Affair

As I reach the end of this long and detailed chapter, I urge you not to be overwhelmed by the complexity of the information. You will need all of it, but if you look through it again, you will see how neatly it falls into place, how natural and fitting are the rules, and how much easier and enjoyable the partaking and the presentation of food are when one knows and uses the proper etiquette—which is, actually, a codification of what is comfortable and courteous.

If formal dining and entertaining are not on your immediate horizon, for reasons of youth or circumstance, take some time to familiarize yourself with the scope of the material, select and learn the correct usage for the kinds of activities in which you participate, and make a mental note to come back to the remainder as your needs change.

It has always been my philosophy to study and become familiar with every detail of the social graces as they apply to the *most* formal event, because with this complete knowledge at my fingertips, I can apply the rules to a similar situation in a semiformal, informal, or casual setting.

Proper social graces are as important in your own home as they are in restaurants and clubs. By inviting others into your home and entertaining them properly, you are bestowing a compliment. You are also creating a comfortable and tasteful setting in which your chosen company will be able to converse with one another without interruption. You can plan the menu with your own unique flair and use your exquisite china, crystal, and silver, choosing creative accents and effects to make a personal statement. And you are accepting an important responsibility. As Brillat-Savarin put it, "To invite someone is to take charge of his happiness for the time he spends under your roof."

Children who grow up in a home where the graces of life are celebrated, even though they may see the actual party through the upstairs banisters, will have a natural inclination to carry on in the same traditions. I am sure that some of you have had such a head start, and now the time has come for you to prepare yourself to participate.

CHAPTER II

The Art of Entertaining

Glamorous though it may be, dining would become quite tedious were each meal as lengthy and as formally served as *Le Grand Dîner,* which you and I experienced in The Dinner Party chapter. And were each party a gala ball, soon the festivity of formality would be gone. Today's social code embraces both the simplest and the grandest entertainments, and these, as well as those that fall in between, are acceptable *and* pleasurable to hostess and guest alike.

A hostess should entertain in a manner with which she is comfortable, can afford, and can execute with apparent ease and effortlessness. Your entertainments should be a highly polished version of your normal lifestyle. To stage a pretentious entertainment beyond your means or social know-how would be "putting on airs," which is in very poor taste.

A Party Personality

What is your party personality? Just as you have a certain style of dressing, so you will discover that you have a party personality. Perhaps you feel at home at old-time theme parties or are romantically inclined and want soft music and soft lights. You could be an advocate of the avant-garde and have the party no one else would ever think of. The traditionalist is a born natural for holiday entertaining. And if you are an easygoing, laid-back person, choose the casual and relaxed atmosphere. The beautiful part about parties is that a tea, a luncheon, a dance, even a wedding, can be presented to fit almost any party personality you possess.

Party Perfect

Good parties do not *just* happen. Ultimate pleasure and success lie in pre-party planning. Gala fund-raisers and balls, for instance, are planned for a year or more in advance by several committees comprised of many members. The social stages surrounding a wedding can consume from days to months. The party you pick will determine the time that will be needed for its successful production.

Large or small, most entertainments command the same systematic strategy. You will be steps ahead if you have worked with others in planning school or club-related social events, and will find that planning on your own follows much the same course. As the hostess, however, you will be in charge of all twelve categories listed in the box below, rather than just the one assigned to you as a committee member.

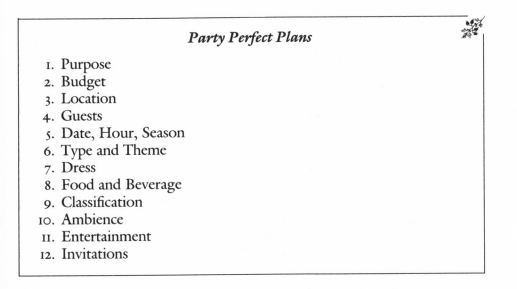

Party Perfect Plans

 1. Purpose
 2. Budget
 3. Location
 4. Guests
 5. Date, Hour, Season
 6. Type and Theme
 7. Dress
 8. Food and Beverage
 9. Classification
 10. Ambience
 11. Entertainment
 12. Invitations

PARTY PERFECT PLANS

1. *Purpose.* Why are you having a party? What is its purpose? The purpose may be the celebration of one of life's landmarks, such as a birthday party for a friend's sixteenth, eighteenth, or twenty-first birthday. The oncoming of a new season can spur a swimming party on the twenty-first of June. A concert in the park can call for a poetic sunset picnic. And a special out-of-town houseguest can be the perfect reason for a formal dinner party. Perhaps you simply want to gather together a few friends.

Once the question "Why the party?" is answered, your head will spin with ideas. Proceed now to the remaining of my dozen Party Perfect Plans, remembering that adherence to budget and good taste is the first step.

2. *Budget.* A good time does not bear a price tag, and the amount of money spent on a celebration does not determine success. Nonetheless, it is an inescapable fact that it does take money, whether the amount is large or small, to entertain.

In budgeting, consider both your time and money. Do not be more ambitious than either will allow, lest you find yourself and your guests shortchanged.

The entertaining budget has many headings. Depending upon the type of party, the following categories may be applicable: invitations, postage, place cards, menu cards, food, beverages, decorations, flowers, party or place favors, entertainment, paid party helpers, security.

The wise hostess puts pen to paper the moment she proposes her party. While a limited budget need not alter the purpose of the party in any way, it influences the degree of extravagance. Be careful not to expend the budget on costly invitations and decorations, then fall short on funds for food and beverages.

3. *Location.* Where will you stage your party? The available space will determine its size, while the style of the space will serve to set the scene. The site should confine your guests cozily so that there is an immediate and intimate party atmosphere.

Indoor stages include the living room, dining room, or dining area; library, den, playroom, great room, solarium, or enclosed porch. Nontraditional areas such as the foyer, beneath the stairs, or the stairs themselves; in hallways and on balconies; anywhere is possible.

If your guest list swells to overflow, plan to have your guests spill into the great outdoors. Outside settings are limited only by your creativity and weather: the patio, pool, or garden; the deck, balcony, rooftop terrace, porch, gazebo, or garage; the barn, pasture, or lawn. Remember, though, that uncovered outdoor spaces should have an alternate rain site, lest your party spirit be dampened!

The best of both environments can be enjoyed if you choose a party staged "under the big top," and heated and cooled tents have extended the season of tent parties tremendously.

Although the most personal settings are your own at-home sites—for these can never be duplicated by another hostess—you may decide to "go public." The possibilities are endless, but with one determining factor, the cost, which is indeed important. Budget permitting, you may consider a floating party on a yacht, houseboat, or riverboat; a historical mansion, village inn, or a quaint bed-and-breakfast parlor and porch. More natural settings such as a beach, woods, lake, mountain meadow, or sand dunes all have their appeal too.

4. *Guests.* Selecting the guests for your informal or semiformal entertainment is very much the same as casting the formal dinner party. The goal, however, need not be an even number of guests, for seating and service are less structured.

Although I have known hostesses to agonize over a guest list, choosing the guests for your party should be a treat, not a torture. As you compile the list, the purpose of the occasion will provide a starting point. If the party is in honor of a bride, for instance, she will supply you with the guest list according to the number you can accommodate, and most of the guests will be more closely acquainted with her: members of the bride's and groom's families and wedding party, friends of the parents of the bride and groom. If you choose to honor an out-of-town houseguest, on the other hand, she may know only you, so the purpose of a social gathering is to introduce her to your friends.

A first-time hostess often makes the mistake of inviting everyone she knows. Casting a party is similar to selecting the wardrobe for a trip. It is easier to simply throw everything into the suitcase, but much more successful to select especially for the occasion instead. So it is with guests. They must be carefully coordinated.

While a cleverly calculated mix-and-match of guests can create a spirited and stimulating, yet harmonious, party, there is a rule of thumb: Each guest should know at least one guest other than the hostess and the person with whom she attends the party. I have been at parties where I knew no one other than the hostess, and I went home feeling as though I had "partied" with a group of strangers in a shopping mall. As lovely as the party may have been, it was not warm and personal for me.

To be placed upon a guest list is an honor, and, as a hostess, you will want to bestow this honor with care. To eliminate a hodgepodge, think instead of mixing old friends with new— each complementing the other. As your circle of friends grows throughout your college and career years, make an effort to be the catalyst who pulls people together and makes exciting, well-thought-out social introductions.

5. *Date, Hour, and Season*. Celebrations motivated by the calendar—Christmas or a milestone birthday, for example— leave little leeway for picking the date and season. On the other hand, impromptu parties know no datelines other than openings in the social calendars of the hostess and her guests.

Festive, lengthy parties require the relaxed schedule of a weekend date, whereas an all-girl bridal shower might best be held on a week night or during a lunch hour. A casual cookout can be called for late afternoon on Sunday, thereby allowing early good-byes to ensure timeliness for early Monday morning classes or job commitments.

Parties saluting a guest, or guests, of honor are, of course, scheduled on a date that is compatible with the honoree's calendar. A hostess selects several dates during which she is free to entertain the guest of honor, and then suggests them to the honoree for her choice.

6. *Type and Theme*. While it is not necessary that a party have a theme, it is important to decide upon the style of your party. Do you want a small intimate gathering? Is your preference a stand-up, a sit-down, or a combination? Will it be held indoors or out? Will the party center around food, beautifully and bountifully presented, or will dancing, entertainment, or sports take precedence? Will your party be a preface or a follow-up to another entertainment?

A theme can center around a foreign land, capsule a past or future time, or highlight a holiday, a season, even a color. Using a theme properly and knowing when to stop are important; overkill is a bore.

7. *Dress*. Partytime poses a favorite, frustrating question: "What to wear?" As hostess, you set the dress code and alert your guests to appropriate attire when you invite them.

Many factors influence the choice of dress, including the purpose, location, date, hour, season, type, and theme of the occasion. Some occasions have rigid dress codes while others are more flexible. Still others are completely at the discretion of the hostess.

I contend that dress definitely influences manners! If you condone sloppy attire, you can expect sloppy manners. Established and accepted dress requirements encourage proper manners.

8. *Food and Beverage*. When deciding upon these important elements, appeal to the senses: sight, smell, touch, taste.

Whether it is to be eaten from forks or fingers, party food needs to be creative, the best you can provide. Needless to say, the best need not be the most costly, and all need not be homemade.

Theme parties make party food and drink ideas come easily. Certain social occasions that feature food call for prescribed items—a wedding cake at the wedding reception, thin tea sandwiches for afternoon teatime, hotdogs at a wiener roast, clams for a clambake.

Whether simple snacks or elaborate spreads, food and beverages need to be presented handsomely. The presentation is as important as the food and drink themselves.

Resist the urge to experiment with food for the party. Test your menu before the date, making certain every item is foolproof. If time does not allow for testing, file new ideas for your next social event and fall back on tried-and-true favorites.

9. *Classification*. Once you have established the purpose, budget, location, date, hour, and season for your event, decide which social classification you wish to adopt: casual, informal, semiformal, formal.

This decision determines many things: the way the invitations are issued, the manner in which the guests will dress, the style of food and beverage, the number of courses, the table setting, how the food will be presented and served, whether or not help will be required and, if so, how many.

For an informal event, you would invite guests by telephone or in person, and, depending on the hour and purpose of the party, you would ask that they wear party dress or daytime

234

clothes, or dress in a special fashion to match your theme. The food would be simple, as would the table setting and presentation, and you would serve but a few courses. You and your guests would participate in the service of food and beverages, buffet style, for example.

To entertain in a semiformal manner, you might invite guests in person or by telephone or with a fill-in engraved invitation and would ask that they wear the appropriate daytime clothes, or for an evening affair, evening or dressy clothes. Your choice of food would include multiple courses—three to five—and the table would be set much as it was for the formal table I discussed in the chapter devoted to the dinner party. You may also add place cards and menu cards if you wish. You and your guests might have the luxury of being served by others, freeing you of this responsibility.

As you will remember from the dinner party description, complete formality is exacting: handwritten or engraved-in-full invitations written in the third person, evening dress, assigned dinner partners (and the dinner cards and envelopes), the announcing of guests, the entrance, arm-in-arm, of dinner partners into the dining room, a strictly laid table with place cards written in full and menu cards written in French describing the five to seven courses (traditionally French food), and the strictest of formal service. Dramatic, yes! A daily happening, no!

I find it refreshing—and my guests love the idea—when I intertwine the classifications. You, too, may wish to experiment with this style. For example, you may decide to use partially engraved, fill-in invitations (semiformal), have the gentlemen guests wear casual and colorful sport coats, ties, and slacks while the ladies choose long summer patio attire (informal), have beverages passed on a silver tray by a server (formal), and have guests serve themselves from a buffet, then join one another at preset tables on the lawn (informal), and finally have the tables crumbed and cleared and the dessert course served by the server (formal). The guidelines on social occasions such as this are bound only by good taste, the party personality of the hostess, and the traditions and trends of the community in which she lives.

10. *Ambience*. This French word best describes that final feeling only you can bestow upon the event you choose to hostess.

Ambience is the catalyst that brings together all of the other components. Just as you sprinkle the right spices into a sauce to heighten its flavor and blend the various tastes into one, so will you want to sprinkle just the right spices over all the parts of a party to create "a distinctive atmosphere." Ambience is created by final touches.

So add those touches. Enter your entertaining space and do a walk-through as though you were an arriving guest. Think of every element: the sidewalk aglow with twinkling lights, the front door graced by a beribboned bough of dried flowers, the parlor alive with sophisticated jazz and soft pink lighting, the powder room accented by jasmine-scented soaps and candles, the buffet table focused on a cornucopia of fresh fruits. Be careful, though, not to overdo the effects.

11. *Entertainment.* Parties are always fun. All parties are not, however, always fun *and* games. As you determine the program, consider how you wish to entertain your guests. Will the plot revolve solely around food and fellowship? Will its story line be food, fun, and games, perhaps snacks and charades? Will it be supper and sports, such as a cookout and croquet? How about dining and dancing?

Many social events feature as entertainment the opening of gifts: birthdays, bridal and baby showers. Guests find pleasure—and at the same time are entertained—as they share the enthusiasm of the recipient. Other occasions revolve around a guest of honor. A cotillion may feature anything from a presentation to dining and dancing to live music from not one band, but two.

If planned entertainment seems in order, possibilities are endless. To decide whether or not your idea is valid, ask yourself these questions: Will the party stand on its own and be a success without special entertainment? If so, why add anything? Does my idea blend smoothly into the overall party theme? Will it be fun and interesting to those in attendance? Is it suitable to the ages of the guests? Does it befit the occasion, purpose, and location of the party?

As the entertainment begins, realize that some guests will not participate. Some will prefer to chat. Therefore, if you wish to add lawn sports to the agenda of an outdoor ice cream social, choose horseshoes, badminton, croquet—activities in which several or all the guests could choose to participate. Do not try to organize a volleyball game that requires all of the guests to join a team.

The informality of the family's game room or den may provide the perfect backdrop for indoor sports such as billiards, darts, or pinball. Weather permitting, guests can be treated to indoor and outdoor sports on the same occasion. Also, the advent of the family screening room, à la old-time Hollywood moguls, has made the movie at home into prime-time entertainment suited to a duo or a dozen guests.

As an entertainment, live music cannot be topped—if your budget can accommodate it. Realize, though, that the purpose of music falls into two categories: first, as background against which guests can talk or dance, and second, music to which guests must listen without talking. The distinction needs to be clear to both the guests and entertainers at the time of inviting and booking. Needless to say, attentive music cannot hold the stage for too long before guests become edgy and want to return to conversation. With due respect for entertainers booked for solo performances, invite guests who will appreciate this type of music and award the entertainer proper attention.

Whether it be strolling musicians, mimes, dancers, movies, sports, whatever, added entertainment is often the icing on the cake. The secret of success is to blend it into the action effortlessly so that it never breaks up the party. One of my secrets for keeping a party going after the entertainment is finished is to have the artists join the guests.

12. *Invitations*. As you can see, every detail of the planning must be done before you send invitations.

The invitation is the first glimpse for the guests of what lies in store. So every effort should be taken to make yours tempting, for it is your access to your guest's social calendar. It also reflects your social know-how and creativity—for greater detail refer to Chapter 9, Invitations!

Invitations may be issued in many ways. The more formal occasions call for handwritten or engraved invitations in the third person. Others, however, may be issued informally, and these can be especially festive. The methods of issuing them are as varied as the hostesses who entertain. Verbally, you may invite guests face-to-face or by telephone. As a change of pace, consider video, tape cassette, telegram, even having invitations personally delivered by a professional courier service. (That option would almost certainly be too costly for a young hostess, but you might persuade your little brother to do it for a modest price. And college sorority hostesses need only commandeer the pledges!)

Most important, an invitation should bear all of the pertinent details: type of party, purpose, date, time, place, dress, honoree (if any), method of reply, special entertainment (if any), a separate map (when necessary). Having done this, the next move is the guest's!

The Seated Meal

It will not take long to reach your goal as a party-perfect hostess for the social stages of "everyday" casual, stand-up parties. Your next goal—and a much more difficult one to reach—will be to become the sophisticated hostess of lovely seated entertainments such as a brunch, luncheon, informal afternoon tea, dinner, or supper party. This may take a long time, and you may look forward to its development over several years as your social horizons expand.

As the art of entertaining for the seated meal may be overwhelming to you, the budding hostess, I want to explore the variety of styles of entertaining for these festive and fun-filled events which you, at one point or another, may wish to hostess *and* which you will certainly attend many times as a guest.

Over the years, as I have designed and staged the many seated meals for L'Ecole des Ingénues, I have found one of the most important aspects—and one with which the beginning hostess has the most difficulty—to be the manner in which the food is presented and served. Just as it will for you, this aspect of the art of entertaining holds both fascination and challenge for my ingénues in their classes devoted to *La Présentation de la Cuisine et le Service de la Table*.

Quite simply, food may be presented beautifully on platters or in bowls, and may be served by servers or a caterer's waitstaff, the host and/or hostess, or by the guests themselves; or the food may be attractively arranged on the individual diner's plate prior to serving. Simple though the presentation and the service of food at the seated meal may sound, it is somewhat more complex, as each style of food presentation and service bears definite guidelines.

Before exploring the many types of seated meals, consider the fact that there are four styles of entertaining: formal, semiformal, informal, and casual.

Of the seated meals, the three B's—the breakfast, the brunch, and the banquet—are rather straightforward. However, the words *luncheon, dinner,* and *supper* bear further explanation.

The words *dinner* and *supper* are not to be used interchangeably. The word *dinner* is reserved for the main meal of the day, which in America is usually the evening meal since most American adults and children do not come home for their midday meal as do many Europeans. However, on weekends and holidays, some American families adopt the European custom of serving dinner in midday, followed by a light "supper" in the evening. Suppers may also follow dances, afternoon weddings, theater, opera, or ballet evenings.

Dinner may also be distinguished from supper by the fact that soup must be served in a flat soup plate at dinner, whereas it may be served in a bowl or cup at supper. The dinner menu showcases the roast, the whole fish, or a freshly designed casserole, whereas supper may feature creative "leftovers" from these dinner items.

The words *lunch* and *luncheon* have certain usages, too, with which you should be familiar and to which you should adhere. The word *luncheon,* when used as a noun in speech, is reserved for formal and ceremonial instances, and, when written, is limited to a third-person invitation. In your personal conversation, you may use "luncheon" as an adjective, but you must say "lunch" rather than "luncheon" as the noun, and "to lunch" as the form of the verb. For example, say, ". . . join me for lunch . . ." rather than "luncheon."

The Formal Style of Entertaining

The Formal Dinner

At a formal seated meal, the food presentation and service are handled entirely by the servers. Formal service requires a prescribed servant-to-guest ratio and the menu is comprised of four to seven courses. This service is described in Chapter 10, The Dinner Party.

When you are the hostess to an all-girl affair, you must assume the duties of both host and hostess. If assistance is needed, ask a guest to assume the duties of the host. In a male-female function, request the assistance of a male guest to act as host.

The Formal Luncheon

The formal luncheon offers a lovely social stage upon which to celebrate many of life's landmarks that I describe in Chapter 12. Or, it may be given in honor of a special guest or a noted person.

As the length of the formal social luncheon exceeds the normal hour designated for lunch during the fast-paced weekday schedule, you may wish to reserve it for weekends or holidays. Although the cherished all-girl luncheon is a favorite, it may include both men and women.

The formal luncheon follows the same format as the formal dinner with the following exceptions:

- The invitation may be issued on your calling card, informal, or note paper, on a fill-in engraved card, or by telephone. It may be extended seven to fourteen days in advance. The engraved invitation is reserved for luncheons in honor of a noted person or a milestone occasion, with the maximum of lead time allotted to it.
- The guests may be all women or men and women. Men and women guests need not be equal in number; however, they usually are at weekend, holiday, and official luncheons.
- Formal luncheons begin at twelve-thirty, one o'clock, or one-thirty and last from one and a half to two and a half hours.
- Guests arrive punctually, as the prelude to the luncheon service is but fifteen to thirty minutes.
- There is no receiving line. Guests are received at the door, directed as to where to place their coats, ushered into the living room by the servant and announced to the hostess.
- If the person who answers the door for the hostess cannot handle the announcement of a guest with ease, the guest simply makes his or her way to the hostess, who rises to speak and makes any necessary introductions.
- Alcoholic beverages need not be served during the prelude to lunch. However, if served, *apéritifs* are preferable to cocktails and nonalcoholic *apéritifs* and juices must always be offered. Light hors d'oeuvre may accompany either.
- The hostess enters the dining room first, alongside the guest of honor (if one is present) and the other guests follow.
- There are no official luncheon partners. A man does not offer his arm to a woman upon entering the dining room, unless she is elderly.

- A man walks in with whichever woman guest he is chatting with, or, if alone, follows last.
- A younger guest—man or woman—allows an older guest to enter the dining room first.
- Placemats—with a matching runner, if desired for an opaque tabletop and necessary for a transparent tabletop (lest laps, napkins, and knees show through!)—of damask, linen, lace, organdy, cutwork, or a needlework or a pastel damask tablecloth take the place of the white damask formal dinner cloth. The more delicate fabrics are reserved for the all-girl luncheon.
- Matching smaller luncheon napkins are used. Dinner napkins (folded as for the formal dinner) may be used instead, particularly when men are present. Either must match the placemats or tablecloth. Luncheon napkins are folded in the traditional luncheon fold: the diagonal or rectangular.
- The dinner or luncheon-size plate, and dinner, luncheon, or place-size knife and fork may be used for the main course.
- There are no candles on the table, as candles are not lighted during daylight hours.
- Place cards and menu cards are used at luncheons marking the landmarks of life and at official luncheons. Otherwise, they are a matter of choice, though place cards—on which titles and last names are used—do facilitate ease in seating when guests number more than eight.
- The menu is comprised of no more than four courses. The food is lighter and somewhat more delicate in nature when selected for women guests, but is more substantial when men are present.
- Bouillon or clear soup is served in a two-handled bouillon cup with its matching plate and is eaten with a teaspoon or bouillon spoon until it has cooled sufficiently to sip directly from the cup which is then lifted by the handles with both hands. Cold or jellied soup may also be served and is eaten with a teaspoon or a bouillon spoon.
- Herbal or regular iced tea or iced coffee (caffeinated or decaffeinated) or iced chocolate is often offered instead of wine, particularly in warm weather or when guests are not of age.
- If wine is offered, rarely are there more than two: a sherry with the soup, followed with a second wine of a light variety with the main course; or, champagne alone may be served from the soup through the dessert or from the main course through the dessert; or, if one wine, it may accompany the main course. Chilled tea

punch or iced coffee is poured from a pitcher into the diner's glass by the server, at the right of the guest. The condiments are offered separately to the guest at his left from a tray containing a superfine sugar or artificial sweetener (removed from the wrapper and placed in a salt cellar together with a salt spoon), a pitcher of cold milk, and one of heavy cream.

- The iced-beverage spoon is positioned at the right of the piece of silver designated for the first course. Alternatively, it may be placed (handle facing right, bowl facing up and left) atop the place plate, if the dessert flatware is to be brought out on the dessert plate.
- Coffee may be offered after dessert, in which case it is served in the living room, in the same manner as outlined for the formal dinner. If iced tea or iced coffee is served with the meal, hot tea or coffee is not served with or after dessert.

The Semiformal Style of Entertaining

The semiformal style of entertaining, by eliminating some of the strict regimentation of the formal style, becomes a much more comfortable, as well as practical, manner of entertaining. No doubt it is the style you and I most often associate with a "fancy" seated luncheon or dinner, and it is one that you might like to try for a very special occasion if you are limited to one or two servers.

The Semiformal Dinner

The semiformal dinner follows the same format as the formal dinner with the following exceptions:

- The fully engraved or handwritten third-person invitation is not used. Invitations may be issued in any of the invitational forms used for the formal luncheon and within the same time frame.
- The hostess has great flexibility in the choice of foods she serves, insofar as she serves her courses in the classic progression, such as:

Three courses
Soup, main course, dessert
Fish, main course, dessert

Four courses
Soup, main course, salad, dessert
Fish, main course, salad, dessert
Soup, fish, main course, dessert
Shellfish, soup, main course, dessert
Five courses
Soup, fish, main course, salad, dessert
Shellfish, soup, fish, main course, dessert
Shellfish, soup, main course, salad, dessert
- Dinner partners are not assigned.
- Place cards and menu cards are optional. If used, place cards are written without full title (first and last names only) and menu cards may be written in English or French.
- One server can serve a party of two to eight guests if the courses are not complicated to serve and are limited to three. Two servers provide more expedient service, more complex service, and/or the option of additional courses.
- The guests remain for forty-five minutes to an hour afterward, but never depart before the guest of honor.
- The guests write a thank-you note to the hostess.

The Semiformal Luncheon

The semiformal luncheon follows the same format as the formal luncheon and semiformal dinner with the following exceptions:

- After dessert, hot coffee (or tea) may be served at the table or in the living room.
- Guests remain no longer than thirty minutes after the dessert and coffee courses have been completed or until after the speech or presentation at an official luncheon.
- Guests write a thank-you note to the hostess. Close friends may write a note or telephone.

The Informal Style of Entertaining

When the host and/or hostess—and often the guests—take part in the overall service, the entertaining style becomes informal. To present a seated meal in the informal entertaining style should be one of your immediate goals as hostess, as it can be staged in so many ways and is adaptable to so many settings. You may give it with only one server to assist you or you may handle it alone. You may choose to serve the food at the table with or without the participation of the guests. Or, you may elect to present it from a buffet and have the guests serve themselves and either stand or be seated to eat.

Should you choose to hostess an informal luncheon or dinner with one server or without help, you must never attempt to serve your guests in the same manner as a server would. This not only makes your guests feel uncomfortable but causes them to feel concerned that you must go to so much trouble on their behalf. Therefore, when you serve, you must always do so while you are seated at your place as hostess of the dining table.

Just as the options are many, so are the details ensuring success, but once you master the format of the informal style of entertaining, you will find it to be quite an intimate, friendly, and leisurely manner in which to entertain.

The Informal Dinner

The informal dinner follows the same format as the semiformal dinner with the following exceptions:

- The invitations may be extended and accepted face-to-face or over the telephone or on note paper and as close as five to seven days beforehand.
- Men and women guests need not be equal in number.
- The informal dinner may begin at an earlier hour: six-thirty, seven, or seven-thirty.
- The guests may wear either cocktail or daytime clothes, as the hostess chooses and advises, but men and women must dress "in kind," that is with the same degree of formality or informality.
- China, sterling, crystal, and fine linens may be replaced with more casual tabletop amenities provided they are compatible with the food: heavier and coarser for hearty food; lighter and refined for a delicate menu.
- A white or pale damask cloth may be used as may place mats. Linens and candles may be colored.
- Menu cards are not used. A china menu stand, upon which the menu is written in English, may be used and adds a nice touch.
- Colored inks may be used on the place cards and china menu stand.

- Place cards, if used, may be written with first names only. If there are no place cards, the hostess enters the dining room first with the women guests, followed by the men (the host last). The hostess indicates to each guest where he or she is to sit.
- When the women guests outnumber the men (whereby there may not be a man seated at the right of the hostess to seat her), the hostess may seat herself. Alternatively, the gentleman guest of honor (if there is one) may seat her after he seats the lady on his right.
- A hostess has an infinite variety in the food she chooses to serve, so long as she limits the menu to be served at the table to two or three courses and adheres to the fact that dishes should be as complete as possible within themselves with additions scaled down to appropriate side dishes and one sauce.
- Iced tea, coffee, or chocolate may be served instead of wine or, if wine is served, may be offered as an alternative when a guest declines wine.
- Prior to the guests entering the dining room, the beverage glasses may be filled. The bread and butter may be preset on the bread-and-butter plate or placed on the table in a bread tray to be passed from one guest to another, or passed by a server.
- The first course, including a soup served in a bouillon cup, may be served in the living room from a tray passed among the guests (who may be seated or standing), by the server, or the hostess. Or, a first course of soup or any other food may be preset at each place at the dining table prior to the seating of the guests. If the first course is preset, the folded napkin is placed to the left of the fork.
- Soup may be served in a flat soup plate, cream soup bowl, bouillon cup, or round-sided bowl. When in place prior to the guests entering the dining room, hot soup is served in small covered bowls.
- Individual saltcellars and pepper pots to be shared or a master salt and pepper shaker may be placed on the table to be passed round by the guests.
- If wine is offered, it may be in place on the table before the guests are seated. The wine bottle, a carafe, or decanter (placed in a coaster or on a small tray) may be used and is passed round by the guests.
- A host does not sample wine that is served in a carafe. If the wine is served from the bottle, the host pours a little in his glass to taste, and, if he approves, he then pours the wine for the lady to his

right, next he passes the bottle to the closest gentleman on his left, who pours for the lady on his right, and then pours his own, and so on round the table. The host serves himself last. A different wine need not be offered with every course, and both a red and a white wine (from which the guest may choose) may be offered throughout. Wine glasses are not removed during the meal.

When the hostess has help . . .
- The servant or server may answer the door.
- Place plates may be used.
- The server may seat the hostess if the women outnumber the men.
- The server may serve the courses in the same fashion as is done for the formal and semiformal dinner. Alternatively, the hostess (or the host and hostess) may serve the guests' plates at the table from tureens, serving dishes, or platters which are placed before them by the server.
- The gravy, sauce, or condiments may be served by the server, the host or hostess, or passed among the guests.
- The ladle is placed in the sauceboat or gravy boat or bowl, which rests on a small serving plate. The spoons for condiments or jellies, which are served in small bowls (each placed on a small serving plate), are laid on the serving plates to which they are returned after a guest serves him- or herself.
- The host serves meat which requires carving. He also serves fish which requires deboning. Either the host or the hostess may serve fish which needs portioning only. When the host serves, he may also complete the plate by adding the accompanying potatoes, vegetables, and gravy or sauce, after which the plate may be passed from guest to guest or taken by the server from the host's left and placed before the guest.
- The plate may be completed in several ways. One, it may be taken to the hostess (by the server or passed round to her by the guests) and the hostess will add the side dishes, after which it is handed round from guest to guest, first to the lady at the right of the host. Second, the plates may be passed round from the host to the guests by the guests or the server, after which the server may serve the side dishes.
- The hostess serves soup from a tureen, the main dish from a casserole (or one which requires portioning only), the salad (for which she may also mix the dressing at her place), the dessert, and the coffee. The filled plates may be given to each guest in any

246

of the ways described for the host's service. In any event, the host and hostess are served last.

- Salad may be served on a plate or in a bowl as a separate course. Or, it may accompany the main course, in which case it is placed to the left of the forks.

- Second helpings may be offered; therefore, the serving dishes and platters remain on the table throughout the course. A guest places the knife and fork at the top of the plate (knife tip and fork tines within the plate at eleven o'clock and handles at three, extending an inch beyond the plate) and passes the plate to the host or hostess for seconds.

- Salad and cheese may be served together after the main course either before or instead of a dessert course.

- The server removes the serving dishes or platters after each course and then the used plates. After the final course, he or she additionally clears the bread-and-butter plates, the bread tray, the salt and pepper, and any unused silver, and crumbs the table in preparation for the dessert course. The wine decanter, carafe, or bottle remains on the table.

- The dessert silver may be brought out on the dessert plate if it is not in place on the table in the initial place setting. Or, it may be taken from the serving cart and placed on the dessert plate by the hostess. She then serves the dessert from her place. The guest does not remove the dessert silver and place it on the table if it is positioned on a plate upon which the dessert has been placed.

- The finger bowl may be omitted.

- After-dinner coffee may be served at the table either with or after the dessert by the servant. Alternatively, the hostess may serve from a tray set before her. The server takes the cup round to the guest, or it is passed round by the guests. Finally, coffee may be served in the living room by the server or, more personally, coffee may be served by the hostess as described in The Dinner Party chapter.

- Many polished hostesses prefer the final touch of the after-dinner tea ceremony as described in The Informal Afternoon Tea section on page 258. As a lovely closing to an evening, the after-dinner tea ceremony may be delayed for an hour or so after dinner, in which event very small, thin cookies or tiny cakes may be passed round from guest to guest and are taken with the fingers from the tray and placed on the saucer. A tea napkin is provided.

- Liqueurs are not often served.
- Guests remain for approximately one hour after the completion of the meal, unless a special activity has been planned which requires a longer length of time.
- Guests write a thank-you note or telephone the hostess within a few days.

When a hostess does not have help . . .
- She answers the door herself. Later, a guest may answer the door and direct them to the hostess.
- Place plates are not used, and the folded napkin is placed between the knives and forks.
- A carafe of water and pitchers containing the chilled beverages are placed on the table and passed.
- The hostess must design her menu so the foods for each course may be in place (in the manner of the English service) on the dining table, or on a service or tea cart positioned at the hostess's right. If the host is to participate, the food he is to serve is before him or on a cart at his right. Plates and serving pieces are on the carts.
- If the dining table will not accommodate the platter from which the host is to carve, the roast may be carved in the kitchen or on the sideboard and the platter placed before the hostess, who remains seated, and initiates the passing of the platter from guest to guest, as each serves him or herself. The vegetable and other courses, which have been placed before the hostess or on her serving cart, are passed in the same manner. After serving herself, the hostess places the returned dishes and platter on her serving cart in a manner whereby she can serve seconds.
- When a course has been completed, the guests pass their plates round to the hostess, who places them on the second shelf of the cart, where she quietly scrapes the plates, stacks the used plates, and places the silver on the top plate.
- If salad has not been served with the main course (for which salad plate or bowl would have been in place in the initial place setting), it is served in the same manner as the main course. Each guest holds the bowl for the next guest. Before passing the salad bowl, the hostess passes a salad plate or bowl to each guest.
- After the last course, the guests pass all condiments and such to the hostess, who places them on a lower shelf of her cart.
- The table is not crumbed, but instead each guest unobtrusively

places any small pieces of bread or large crumbs on his or her plate before passing it to the hostess.

- The hostess then serves the dessert from the top shelf of her cart or, nicer yet, moves it in front of her so that her guests can admire it. The dessert plates are passed round in the same fashion as the other plates; however, they may remain throughout the service of after-dinner coffee (if it is to be served at the table) or may be passed back to the hostess before she serves the coffee or tea at the table.

The Informal Luncheon

The informal luncheon follows the same format as the semiformal luncheon and the informal dinner with the following exceptions:

- The menu is comprised of no more than three courses and the food may be "everyday" favorites given a "company" flair.
- If there is no first course (or if it has been served in the living room), the main course, if cold, may be preset before the guests enter the dining room. The main course, if a hot "all-in-one" dish, may be preset and, in order that it remain hot, it is served in individual casserole dishes or ramekins, which are placed on the plate. A hot main course that cannot be served in this manner is served from a serving dish by the hostess or server.
- Soup, if presented as a hearty, "all-in-one" main course, is served in a flat soup plate.
- Salad, unless it is designed as a main course, is not often served as a separate course.
- The after-dinner tea ceremony is a favored ending at the informal luncheon. Or, coffee may be served in any of the ways set forth for the informal dinner.

When the hostess has help . . .
- Salad, prearranged in the kitchen on the diner's plate, may be placed at the diner's left by the server immediately following the serving of the main course.
- Dessert may be portioned and plated in the kitchen. If the dessert spoon and fork have not been placed in the initial place setting, they are placed on the dessert plate with the dessert (fork left, spoon right). The server places the dessert before the guest.

Alternatively, the server may take round the plates after the hostess serves from her place.

When the hostess does not have help . . .
- Salad, prearranged on individual plates, may be preset before the guests are seated and, at the invitation of the hostess, may be eaten with the first course (if there is one) and/or with the main course. Salad may also be served at the table by the hostess.
- The hostess serves the dessert at her place and passes it round among the guests. It is best that she preposition the dessert silver in the initial place setting to prevent its falling off as the plate is passed round.

The Buffet

The word *buffet* conjures up thoughts of a bountiful array of food in a "serve-yourself" fashion. I imagine that you will choose the buffet as the stage upon which you debut as a hostess when you want to have friends in for a meal. Whether your guest list is comprised of six or sixteen, your budget is penny-pinching or limitless, your surroundings large or small, with careful planning you can be assured of success.

For the sake of clarity, I shall use the word *buffet* for the manner in which the meal is presented and the words, *sideboard* or *buffet table* for the pieces of furniture upon which the food is placed.

A buffet supper or dinner follows the same format as the informal luncheon and dinner with the following exceptions:

- In order that guests may plan their arrival and departure times accordingly, the hostess must be explicit in the wording of her invitation. She does not use the word *buffet* when it is to be a normal *seated* affair, or an unserved "fork" or "lap" buffet for a *small* group. Instead she invites her guest to brunch, luncheon, dinner, or supper, as the case may be, at a given hour. For a come-and-go unserved "fork" or "lap" buffet for a large group, she uses the word *buffet* before the name of the meal that is to be served and states a beginning and ending time, with an allowance of two to three hours between the two.
- Guests must arrive punctually for a buffet preceding a special occasion (theater, ball game, or such) and depart in ample time to reach the event.
- Guests may arrive punctually at the stated time or no more than

ten or fifteen minutes afterward for a seated buffet or an unserved "fork" or "lap" buffet given for a small number of guests. Guests remain for forty-five minutes to an hour after dessert and coffee have been served.

- Guests may arrive on the hour or up to thirty or forty-five minutes after the stated hour for an unserved "fork" or "lap" buffet for a large number of guests (for which the buffet is ongoing for one or two hours). Guests remain for thirty minutes to an hour after they have eaten.

- A hostess may choose from a variety of foods for a buffet menu, as long as they are pretty together colorwise, attractively presented, easily served, and easily eaten.

- Naturally, a beautiful buffet table or sideboard is the starring attraction of a buffet party, and a hostess is free to express her personal style and artistic creativity in its presentation. She need adhere to no rules other than those of common sense and appropriateness. Depending upon her dining room or dining area, she may serve the buffet in the round from a round table; from a rectangular or square table placed against the wall (in which case the presentation faces only one direction); in the center of the room when a two-sided duplicate presentation allows for two guest lines, or an all-the-way-round-the-table presentation allows for one guest line.

- A buffet table or sideboard is arranged to allow a logical progression according to the order of the courses, with plates first and appropriate serving pieces on the table beside each dish, bowl, or platter. A food which is to be served beneath another, such as rice topped with curried shrimp, is placed first; sauces or gravies are in position after the food they are to top. To eliminate the need of another plate, salad and bread and butter may be placed on the buffet plate. Condiments are in position toward the end of the buffet table. Forks and napkins (when not in place at preset tables) may be at the beginning or end of the table. Most importantly, a space must remain free next to any dish that requires two serving utensils (serving pieces should be limited to one whenever possible) in order that guests may put down their plates while serving themselves.

- Beverages and desserts may be placed at the end of the main buffet table; but, for convenience sake and to keep guests moving along the buffet line, a separate table for each is preferable. Glasses (stemmed ones for ease of handling), chilled beverages in pitchers, wine and water in carafes or decanters (all placed on trays) may comprise one small table. Desserts are handsomely displayed on yet another table or on the sideboard and are surrounded by the dishes and forks to accompany them.

- The after-dinner coffee and tea and condiments (placed on the tea tray) and the cups, saucers, and spoons may be placed on the table with the dessert, or on a separate table.

- Floral or fruit centerpieces may be a part of the buffet table as may candles after dark. When space is at a premium, either may be eliminated, whereby the food itself becomes the focal point.

- A buffet should be a fork-*only* affair—with foods selected accordingly—when guests are expected to eat while standing, perched on sofas and chairs, or even sitting on the floor, as they balance their plates on their knees!

- For the "lap" or "fork" buffet, to offer more seating, the dining chairs may be interspersed among the other chairs and sofa, and small, attractive, individual tables may be placed about upon which guests may place their plates or glasses.

- At the other extreme—known as the "seated" buffet—a hostess may choose to have her guests return from the buffet table to elegantly or simply appointed small tables with full place settings of silver, or to the dining table itself if it is large enough for all her guests and the food has been placed on the sideboard.

- If seating is to be at the dining table or at small tables (square or round card tables are well-suited and are placed throughout the living room, library, solarium, or porch, and dining room when large enough), the tables are set with tabletop amenities to match or complement those used on the buffet table. Each small table is complete within itself, containing the necessary condiments, and, if space permits, a low centerpiece and candles. Place cards should be used to eliminate the hostess's having to direct the guests to their seats.

- A hostess may choose to have "open" seating—no place cards— if she wishes. This can be awkward, however, for a shy guest or a guest who has come alone. Open seating should, therefore, be reserved only for the most informal gathering of guests who know one another well.

- At a standing buffet or when guests are to return to sofas and chairs, ladies and gentlemen enter with whomever they are chatting with or they may enter alone. They do not all enter at once, in which case long lines would form, nor must they wait for too long a time to go in, in which case they would hold up the party. Neither do they linger at the buffet table to chat or to eat. Guests need not return to their same spot to stand or to sit—a fact that adds to the spontaneity of the buffet party!

- At a seated buffet for which place cards are used and for which the first course has not been preset, it is a nice gesture for one of the guests to gather his or her table partners so that they may pass through the buffet line together for the first course and for subsequent courses, thereby keeping their dining synchronized.
- At a seated buffet, guests are seated as soon as they have served themselves and wait until everyone at their table has been seated before beginning to eat. As she returns from the buffet table with a plate, a woman should place it on the table and seat herself, not waiting for a gentleman to assist.
- At a standing buffet, guests may begin eating once they have moved sufficiently away from the buffet table. When guests take sofa or chair seats, they should not begin eating until another guest has taken a seat beside them.
- At a seated or a standing buffet, once all of the guests have served themselves, they may return for seconds. A man may offer to get seconds for a woman or she may get them herself. When getting seconds for another, one must put the food on the plate of the person for whom it is intended, not on one's own plate with the intention of its being transferred to another's plate.

The "Family" Dinner

To be invited to a "family dinner" is an honor and one that you no doubt bestow and receive quite often. This is a lovely way to introduce your friends to your family or to be introduced to your friends' families. It is a pleasant way, too, to entertain close business acquaintances from out of town.

Although it may certainly follow the semiformal format if the hostess wishes, the family dinner usually follows the same format as the informal dinner or luncheon with the following exceptions:

- Invitations may be issued on short notice of within a few days to a week beforehand.
- The hour may be six or seven o'clock, or later, depending on the family dinner hour.

- Dress may be informal or casual as indicated by the hostess.
- There are no place cards and the hostess tells the guests where they are to sit.
- If the hostess has a servant who remains to assist with the family dinner on a regular basis (or on certain evenings), it is perfectly proper that there be one present when friends are invited. Otherwise, to engage one only when friends are invited would be pretentious.
- In some homes, it is the custom to ask one of the guests to say the blessing, an honor one graciously accepts and must be prepared to do. A short blessing that is suitable to all faiths is the most appropriate. If the family members clasp hands round the table as the blessing is said, a guest joins with them.
- Service is in the same manner as is the custom of the family's dinner, which may be any of the services described for the informal luncheon and dinner, or the dishes and platters may be placed on the table and passed round among the diners.
- When the hostess is serving without help, she may leave her seat to go into the kitchen—having organized her service in such a manner as to keep such trips to a minimum—for hot bread; to take the used plates, dishes, platters; to get the coffee or dessert. She may clear the plates herself or may have previously assigned this duty to one of the family members. A guest may offer to assist but must not insist if the hostess declines the offer.
- Coffee or tea may be served with the dinner or with and/or after dessert. When served in this manner, the teaspoon is not set to the right of the knife in the initial setting but is placed on the saucer. The cup and saucer are in place in the initial setting or may be on the sideboard if the coffee is to be served later.
- On a weeknight, guests may remain for thirty or forty-five minutes after dessert and coffee and may remain for an hour on a Friday or Saturday evening.
- Guests telephone the hostess within a day or two to thank her for her hospitality.

The "Family" Supper

Certainly the most intimate of the informal meal settings is the "family" supper—so personal, in fact, that only the closest of friends and favorite relatives are ever invited. Sunday night is usually set aside for this social occasion, and what an honor indeed to be among those invited to "supper" at a friend's house.

The family supper follows the same format as the informal luncheon with the following exceptions:

- The hour may be as early as five or six o'clock.
- Dress may be casual but should be carefully coordinated in a sophisticated "at-home" fashion.
- There is no servant present.
- There are no place cards and the hostess tells friends where they are to sit.
- All ages may be included and seated at the same table.
- The hostess may serve whatever she wishes, be it hot or cold, made anew or from leftovers. One or two courses and a dessert are sufficient.
- Food may be presented buffet-style at the sideboard from which the diners may help themselves, after which they are seated at the dining table.
- Food may be placed on the dining table and the dishes and platters passed round among the diners; everyone serves him- or herself.
- Special all-in-one dishes may be cooked or finished at the table in a chafing dish placed before the host, and the hostess may preside over the fully appointed tea tray set beside her place, offering hot tea, coffee, or hot chocolate with the meal and the dessert afterward.
- In anticipation of early Monday morning schedules, guests should leave promptly thirty or forty minutes after the dessert and coffee.
- Guests telephone the hostess within a day or two to thank her for her hospitality.

The High Tea

The term *high* tea is often misused by Americans. It does not, as it may appear, denote the refined and elegant, formal or informal afternoon tea, but rather a homespun, farmhouse supper. Served as a sit-down meal at the kitchen or dining room table, high tea approximates the "family" supper in many ways, yet it bears three distinct characteristics of its own. First, as the name implies, tea is always served. Second, meat is always served. Third, each of the courses, from savory to sweet, is placed on the table at the onset of the meal to be passed from guest to guest.

High tea features a unique menu of hearty and robust traditional foods, such as savory meat pies (often made of leftover luncheon tidbits), sausage rolls, hard- or soft-boiled eggs, cold meats and salads, homemade breads, large wedges of cheese, pots of honey, jam, and butter, relishes, and an array of oven-to-table cakes and tarts.

As a social stage, high tea adapts beautifully outside the boundaries of its origin and purpose. It serves as a lovely, informal preface to an evening at the movies, theater, ballet, concert, or a sporting event and is the perfect finale to the matinee or afternoon game.

As a budding hostess, you will want to consider the high tea as a frequent entertaining choice. Flexible, informal, comparatively easy to assemble, the meal involves foods which are simple and hearty rather than complicated, always a favorite with the masculine contingent. More casual accoutrements set the stage for an easy atmosphere during the party and an easy clean-up for the hostess afterward.

The "Late" Supper

The "late" supper is given immediately following another social occasion and includes those friends in attendance at the event that precedes the supper. Events for late suppers include: a reception following a wedding, milestone anniversary or birthday, or reception in honor of a noted person or persons; after the theater, opera, ballet, or sporting event; or a supper at a formal dance or ball.

With the exception of its beginning and ending times and depending upon the social occasion at (or after) which it is served, the late supper may follow the format of either the formal, semiformal, or informal dinner or any of the formats of the buffet. The following points are important:

- Depending upon the entertaining style a hostess chooses, she may present a supper after the theater or sporting event with the assistance of a server or two, or without help. The size of the menu depends upon whether or not the guests have been to dinner prior to the event.
- For a supper given at an evening reception (unless it is for an extremely small number of guests), a hostess may wish to engage a qualified caterer. For the supper at a dance or a ball, she may be the only hostess or she may be a member of a committee and, in

either case, usually plans the supper with a professional party planner or a caterer or a member of the private club or hotel in which it is held.

- Guests do not tarry after the late supper, for the evening is drawing to an end, if, in fact, the morning hour has not already begun.

The Breakfast and the Brunch

With the exception, of course, of the elaborate "wedding breakfast" described in the Special Occasions chapter, there are two types of breakfasts: the "morning breakfast" and the "brunch."

Taken upon awakening, the morning breakfast does just as its name implies: breaks the fast of the night. Whether the "quick-as-a-wink" weekday breakfast in the breakfast nook, the Continental breakfast rendezvous with a friend, the leisurely weekend breakfast (perhaps with houseguests) in the dining room or on the terrace, or the luxury of breakfast in bed, breakfast is always worth the waking. Brunch, on the other hand, is always worth the waiting.

The brunch, a combination of "breakfast" and "lunch," is the American version of the traditional English hunt-breakfast. Imagine, then, the scene of the hunt-breakfast: a sideboard laden with large chafing dishes and covered dishes filled with hearty breakfast foods to be eaten before the hunt. In the American style, the brunch can precede (or follow) any sporting, social, or arts event, or it may stand on its own merit.

When you elect to entertain at a brunch, keep in mind that it need not be reserved as a "guests only" occasion; it is a perfect "family only" event too, particularly after "sleeping in."

The Breakfast

Breakfast (at the table) is unique in many ways among the other seated meals in the following manner:

- Place cards and menu cards are not used.
- The table is set like the luncheon table with the addition of the coffee cup (large breakfast-size cup) or teacup and saucer (with the teaspoon in place) at the right of each plate.
- Juice may be poured and in place before the diner is seated, as may water (if it is served).
- All food may be placed on the sideboard in the buffet serve-

yourself fashion; may be on the table to be passed round among the diners; or may be prearranged on the plate and placed before the diner is seated.

- As to the manner of seating, diners may be seated all at one time, or they may come in according to their morning schedules.
- When diners are seated all at once, they wait for the hostess to begin eating before they begin, unless she asks them to go ahead; they await the hostess's dismissal of the table before taking leave. When no houseguests are present, family members may ask permission to take leave once they have finished, if that is the custom of the family.
- When diners are seated at varied times, they begin eating as soon as they have served themselves; they ask the hostess's permission before departing the table or, if the hostess is no longer at the table, they merely excuse themselves.

The Brunch

The brunch, even though it possesses a personality all its own, may follow any of the variety of formats of the buffet, bearing the following thoughts in mind:

- Depending upon whether an event is to precede or follow, the brunch may begin between ten-thirty and eleven o'clock and last until one or two.
- Guests may dress informally or casually or in the mode of any event that precedes or follows the brunch.
- Guests must be punctual when an event is to follow the brunch or arrive very shortly after an event that precedes it. When neither is the case, the arrival time follows the pattern outlined for the buffet.
- The brunch ambience should be very relaxed.
- The hostess may design her menu around any combination of breakfast and luncheon foods that complement one another. She must plan a hearty menu, bearing in mind that many of her guests may not have eaten anything beforehand and that the brunch must take the place of both breakfast and lunch.
- The table is set as for breakfast.
- Guests depart at a prescribed time when an event is to follow the brunch and follow the departure pattern outlined for the buffet

when the brunch follows an event or no event is scheduled to follow.

The Informal Afternoon Tea

The traditional taking of tea at home in the afternoon is an elegant, yet intimate and informal, occasion best shared with congenial family members and close friends. Taken in the living room, by the fire in the library, or in the garden on a summer's day, teatime can be enjoyed *à deux* or with a small group.

Anna, the seventh Duchess of Bedford, initiated the tradition in 1840 in her native England. As was the custom of the day, she ate an early and light lunch and a late and hearty dinner. To ward off her hunger pangs in the afternoon, she summoned her servants to bring her a tray of tea, thin, crustless slices of white bread spread with sweet butter, and tea cakes. In time Anna's menu grew in scope and an array of finger sandwiches, scones, and tea breads graced her tea tray as well as those of other aristocratic ladies who adopted the teatime custom of the Duchess.

In today's fast-paced lifestyle, teatime provides an exquisite return to the leisure of the past and a pleasant, petite seated meal to be shared with friends, not only at home but in plush hotel settings and charming tearooms. *L'heure de thé* at L'Ecole des Ingénues highlights each afternoon, and during our finishing tour, tea at the Ritz in London and at Angélina's, the Old-World tea salon in Paris, become fond memories.

Though one of the least expensive ways in which to entertain at home, the informal afternoon tea is one of the most theatrical manners in which a hostess can stage an intimate entertainment. As you adopt the habit of inviting friends and family to take tea with you, it is important to know that afternoon tea is known as *low* tea; the tea table accoutrements are not informal at all, but are comprised of the loveliest linens, the most gleaming silver, and the finest china; and, finally, the hostess *always* pours the tea herself. Only the hostess who acquaints herself with teatime etiquette makes teatime the effortless, elegant entertainment that it is meant to be. Etiquette tips for its success are as follows:

- The invitations may be extended and accepted face-to-face or over the telephone and as close as one day beforehand.
- The women guests wear afternoon dresses.
- The informal afternoon tea, by tradition, begins at four o'clock.
- Guests should arrive punctually at the stated time.
- The hostess greets her guests at the door, invites them into the

room where tea is to be served, and makes the necessary introductions.

- The tea table or tea cart is placed in the room where tea is to be served and is covered with a beautifully embroidered linen, lace, or organdy tea cloth.
- The hostess or a servant brings in the tea tray prior to the commencing of the tea ceremony. A servant takes leave immediately afterward and does not return until it is time to remove the tray.
- The tea tray, without a cloth, is placed on the tea table. The tray is complete with a free-standing teakettle or tea urn with an alcohol burner to keep the water hot and is placed at the center back of the tray. The teapot, its handle facing the lower right, is placed in front of the spout of the tea kettle. The tea caddy containing the loose tea leaves and the tea caddy spoon are to the left of the teakettle (if tea is to be prepared at the tea table). The tea strainer, placed on its stand, or across the waste bowl (into which any remains of tea are poured before refilling a cup or making a new pot of tea), is placed near the tea caddy. The sugar bowl, with white sugar cubes and sugar tongs, is at the immediate right of the teakettle. The cream pitcher, filled with milk (cream is not used in tea)—its handle toward the right—is positioned at the lower right of the sugar bowl. A small plate of very thin lemon slices and a lemon fork complete the tea tray.
- With the exception of the teakettle or tea urn, which must be of a heat-resistant material, the other tea-serving amenities may be of silver or china.
- The china, napkins, and silver for each guest are arranged on the tea table as follows: The small, folded tea napkin (which matches the tea cloth) is placed on the tea plate. The teacup and saucer rest atop the napkin. The teaspoon is placed on the saucer to the right of the teacup. The butter spreader or dessert knife is placed on the tea plate securely beneath the saucer and parallel with the teaspoon. Alternatively, the teacups, saucers, and teaspoons may be placed on the tea table. Tea plates, napkins, and knives may be placed separately on the tea table or on a side table (plates stacked with a napkin between and knives in a neat line).
- The tea foods may be placed on the tea table or on a side table.
- Tea foods should be designed so that they can be eaten from the fingers in one or two bites. Tea foods should never be sticky, oozy, or drippy. They comprise a mini-menu of three courses that are eaten in a prescribed sequence. Taken first are the tea

sandwiches; next, the hot tea breads (such traditional favorites as crumpets or English muffins or toast with butter and jam or marmalade, or scones to which clotted cream is added atop the butter and jam); and finally, the sweets in the form of small tea cakes, shortbreads, or slices from a large, special cake. At least one of the teatime sweets should be made by the hostess as this constitutes a special compliment to her guests!

- Seated at her place at the tea table, the hostess begins the tea ceremony. The guest of honor, seated at the hostess's right, is served first.

- Holding the teacup and saucer in her left hand, the hostess fills each guest's teacup, one at a time. She asks if the guest prefers weak or strong tea (adding hot water from the teakettle or urn to weaken it); if sugar is preferred, whether one lump or two; then, milk or lemon? After preparing the guest's tea, the hostess hands the teacup and saucer directly to the guest for whom it is intended. If the hostess cannot reach a guest, she does not rise from her seat; instead the guest rises and comes to her. The teacup and saucer are not passed from guest to guest.

- The guests help themselves to the tea foods, taking them with the fingers or with the serving piece. No more than three bite-size foods or one slice of cake may be taken at a time. Once everyone has been served, seconds may be taken.

- A small table is provided for each guest, or one to be shared by two guests, on which to place the tea plate and teacup and saucer. If a table is not within reach, a guest balances the tea plate on the lap and holds the teacup and saucer in the hand.

- When tea is finished, the hostess, or servant, removes the tea tray, tea foods, and dishes as guests continue to converse.

- The guests depart after an hour, or two at the most. Unless he or she is a houseguest, the guest of honor takes leave first.

- Guests need not telephone the hostess or write a note afterward to express their appreciation for her hospitality as a verbal expression upon departure suffices.

The Casual Style of Entertaining

If, after studying the guidelines I have set before you for the formal, semiformal, and informal styles of entertaining, there is any doubt at all in your mind about venturing out as a hostess, rest assured that there need not be, for I have saved the easiest of the entertaining styles for last.

Certainly you will feel immediately at ease and gain instant confidence as a hostess if you select the casual style of entertaining for a first-time luncheon, dinner, or supper party. The casual style is a great mixer, as well as the perfect gender-blender, for everyone pitches in and has fun in so doing.

Really, there are no rules for the casual fete—even the floor can serve as the dining table when the guest list outgrows the seating capacity. Or, you can be as fussy and formal as you like, with the setting awaiting you and your guests when you move from countertop to tabletop.

Casual entertaining allows not only that the host and hostess and the guests be involved in the service of the food, but that they also join together in the preparation—total or partial—of the food. Two or three courses are generally served. Although there may be help or waitstaff in the wings, this style of entertaining features the food preparation, presentation, and service as a part of the evening's entertainment in addition to the actual act of dining. All but the rules of good taste and appropriateness to the occasion are lifted.

I am not, then, going to provide you with an itemized format of how the casual style differs from the others, but I will say that you may take favorite bits and pieces from the informal format and incorporate them into your casual entertaining package. Surely you agree with me that the flexibility of the casual style affords the perfect entertainment stage upon which to develop and showcase *your* style!

"Firsts"

In your life you have up to now—and will in the future—experience many "firsts." Think a minute. Although you cannot remember it, there was your first step. Among those firsts you can remember might be your first bicycle ride, your first downhill ski run, your first time behind the steering wheel.

There is always the thrill of doing something for the first time even though you will do it over and over again until you do it perfectly—well, *almost* perfectly, for there is always room for improvement.

Now, why not add to your repertoire of firsts your first hostessing experience? Think not of "perfection." Think instead of "perfecting" your role as a hostess over the years to come, as you acquire the art of entertaining, that finishing touch the French call *l'art de vivre*.

CHAPTER 12

Special Occasions

As you move into adulthood, the celebration of special occasions brings happiness and meaning to others and satisfaction to you. Commemorating the various stages of maturation can introduce you to the skills that underlie the civilized life—in the most festive fashion.

Through the coming years, you, like most women, will experience these wonderful times as both the recipient and the dispenser of this special social grace. And you may find it difficult to decide which is the more agreeable: to be guest or hostess. Certainly it is enjoyable to arrive, rested and handsomely dressed, at an affair for which the planning, preparation, and stress have been assumed by another. As a guest, one has little responsibility beyond being pleasant and enjoying oneself, and since you will play the guest more often than hostess, it is well to hone those skills to perfection.

Yet the other role offers enormous satisfactions along with its considerable obligations. As the hostess, you can be creative, dynamic—the star. Yours is the prerogative of conceiving the theme, choosing the foods to be served, and compiling the guest list—that combination of personalities, which can be as important as the composition of the menu. You can set the mood of the conversation and use the occasion to enlarge and alter your circle of friends by including new acquaintances. Entertaining also begets invitations.

Full responsibility for the planning and execution of a special-occasion affair may be in the future for some readers of this book. Since, however, being a successful hostess is an acquired skill, it is never too early to begin the learning process. Your parent's home is the ideal place to start. Practice in dispensing it tends to make graciousness appear as a gift of nature rather than a carefully developed ability.

You have certainly been involved in holiday preparations for Christmas, Hanukkah, Valentine's Day, Easter, May Day, The Fourth of July, Halloween, and Thanksgiving, as well as surprises and gifts for the birthdays of your parents and siblings. You may have helped your mother with a party for your friends or passed napkins or cakes when she entertained. Such experiences are the finest background possible for the hostess-to-be.

Now you may find yourself somewhere between the tomboy who knows that she wants a skating party with pizza for her birthday, and the assured young adult who is graciously capable of planning, preparing, and serving an elegant small tea, a smart luncheon, or a romantic candlelight supper for four—or for two.

The Year-Round Hostess

Most special occasions celebrated in American and European homes have some distinctive theme—traditional, religious, patriotic, whimsical—which should be developed with as much flair as possible, and most have etiquette requirements that should be followed. Special occasions can be as simple as a dressed-up family meal (even a picnic), or as elegant and formal as a dinner dance, according to the dictates of your taste and circumstances. The important thing is to capture the spirit of the occasion through the dramatization of the theme and the incorporation of personal or family traditions.

The hostess has an array of embellishments upon which to draw. The New Year is greeted with glitter and noisemakers, Valentine's Day with hearts, flowers, and chocolates. With Easter comes the glory of renewal, from dyed eggs to bedecked bonnets. Red, white, and blue adorn patriotic holidays. Ancient legend combines apple bobbing and candy to make Halloween a merry gateway to the holiday season. Then, there is Thanksgiving with turkey and pumpkin pie. Capping the joyful sequence is Christmastime or Hanukkah, a favorite of many families.

Birthdays provide another marvelous "excuse" for celebration, uniquely suited to the development of very personal and meaningful traditions. There is much room for creativity in all these family and close-friends occasions.

Life's Landmarks

There are, however, special occasions for which celebration, in addition to good taste, demands formality and the observance of certain proprieties. These are the affairs (often once-in-a-lifetime events) that make a statement, be it religious, social, civic, educational, or cultural. These milestones, therefore, require adherence to established conventional etiquette and form on the part of the honoree, hostess, participant, and guest.

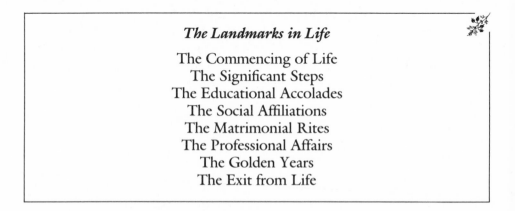

The Landmarks in Life

The Commencing of Life
The Significant Steps
The Educational Accolades
The Social Affiliations
The Matrimonial Rites
The Professional Affairs
The Golden Years
The Exit from Life

The Commencing of Life

The first of life's landmarks is birth. The arrival of a newborn is a dramatic and happy occasion for the child's parents. If not at the hospital to hear the announcement the moment it is given, family members and close friends receive the news by telephone and have the joy of spreading it through a widening circle.

If you are an immediate family member or close friend and live in the same town, your response will be a visit to the mother and child while they are in the hospital. Hospital rules dictate that you visit only during specified hours and that you view the baby through the nursery window at certain times. In addition, good manners dictate that you make each of these visits short and sweet. Remember, many others want to see the new mother and congratulate the new father. Flowers are always a lovely gift for the mother and baby; for longtime pleasure, choose small living plants brightened by bows.

Although the minimum-age ban has been lifted on the maternity floors of most hospitals, leave your little brother and sister at home when visiting. And, even though the infant may be brought to the room with guests present, leave the pleasure of holding and hugging him to his mother, father, and grandparents.

When visiting the newborn at home, proceed with great care, for the baby's days and nights are busy indeed. Telephone in advance to ask when it would be convenient for you to come—no surprise pop-ins, please. Make the visit an extremely brief and peppy one. Do not go at all if you feel the least bit under the weather. Bounce in with a smile and a little something for the baby and the mother and father, too—delectable snacks for the grown-ups, magazines, books, fresh flowers, or fruits.

Announcing the Birth

Socially, there are two written forms by which a baby's birth or adoption may be announced. Friends and relatives may be sent pretty, preprinted, in-blank birth announcements, which are filled in by the proud parents. More formally, an engraved announcement can be sent. In addition, in many communities, the news may be sent to the newspapers in the town where the parents reside and to the hometown paper of the grandparents. (Newspaper announcements are not made of adoptions, however.) Births are also an-nounced in the weekly church bulletin received by the church members.

Although you are not duty-bound to send a gift upon receipt of a baby announcement (either verbal or written), when you are a close family mem-ber or friend of the newborn's parents, you will probably want to give the baby something within a month or so. As with any gift, it must be selected within your means and be appropriate for the recipient. Consider nursery accessories, such as baby lamps, picture frames, first-time crib toys. Visit your jeweler for longer-lasting gifts in sterling or china. Baby presents should be beautifully gift-wrapped to add to the gaiety. Of course, you will expect a thank-you note from the mother.

The Ceremonies Celebrating Birth

Every major religion has a ceremony that recognizes and celebrates birth, naming, spiritual dedication, or the entrusting of the baby to the parents (with the assistance of the godparents in some faiths) for upbringing in the practiced faith until the child grows old enough to accept this responsibility on his or her own.

As with many religious ceremonies—confirmations, weddings—it is natural for close family members and friends to gather together to witness, support, and celebrate. The social gathering that follows the ceremony is determined by the time of day the religious ritual is held. It is an honor to be invited to share in both the religious and social events, and this is a lovely time to present the baby with a gift if you have not done so previously. Should you be asked to be the godmother, you will select a long-lasting gift of silver for your godchild.

As an especially invited guest you will want to take care that you dress in your best church clothes, be attentive and respectful during the ceremony, and well-mannered at the social celebration. As some religions still require that the woman's head be covered in the sanctuary, you will want to ask your hostess about the preferred custom. Although no written notes are required after attending such an event, you may certainly write the hostess if you wish, or telephone her to tell her how lovely the occasion was and that you were grateful for being asked to attend.

The Christening

Babies born to parents of the Protestant or Roman Catholic faith are baptized into their faith in the christening ceremony. In the Roman Catholic church, christenings take place within a month of the baby's birth. In the Protestant religion, although the baby is usually christened within three months, he or she is sometimes older. The christening may take place as a part of a church service, or it may be held in the parents' home.

Not unlike a wedding reception, the social celebration of a christening may be highlighted by a snow-white cake. And as in most of the celebrations of life's milestones, a champagne toast is made to the baby's health by his or her godfather. Expect this to take place after dessert at a christening luncheon or toward the end of a tea.

So tradition-bound is the christening ceremony that christening dresses are handed down generation after generation. My sons each wore an exquisite, long dress, handmade by their great-grandmother especially for them. Were you christened, no doubt you will discover a special story about your christening dress if you ask your mother. An equally lovely tradition is the sterling christening bowl. I knew someone who initiated the family christening bowl with the birth of her first grandchild. The baby girl's name and birthdate were engraved on the bowl, as will be those of the other grand-children to come. In time, the sides of the bowl will be filled with generation after generation of family babies' names and baptismal dates.

The *Brith Milah*

Baby boys born to Jewish parents are initiated into the Jewish society and given their name on the eighth day after their birth in the religious cere-mony. Performed by the *moyel,* a temple official, the *brith milah,* or *brit,* is held at the home of the infant's parents (or at the temple, if the eighth day falls on a Sabbath) and usually takes place in the morning. The circumcision is an important part of this religious ceremony.

The Naming of the Jewish Baby Girl

The baby girl born of Jewish parents is named in the synagogue or temple in a religious ceremony, which is scheduled on the Sabbath and falls within thirty days of her birth.

The *Pidyon Haben*

For the firstborn son (resulting from the first pregnancy) of Jewish parents, a special ceremony known as the *pidyon haben* is performed in the synagogue or temple in addition to the *brith milah.* In this religious rite, the Rabbi or Cohen redeems the firstborn son of his obligation to use his life in servitude to the temple (reference the story of Samuel in the Old Testament), and entrusts him to his father, who vows to raise him properly in the Jewish faith and symbolically "buys him back" (in accordance with the story in the Old Testament) for five shekels, which today equates to five silver dollars.

The Significant Steps

During your growing-up years, you take part in many ceremonies (religious, social, educational) that mark significant steps toward maturation. With each of them, you take on more responsibility for your life.

268

One of the lovely aspects of being invited to witness the religious ceremony or partake in the social celebration commemorating the maturation of
your friends is the insight it provides into the customs held dear by your
friend's faith and family. This experience broadens the scope of your understanding of religious traditions other than your own.

As a guest at a ceremonial event, you will certainly want to show utmost
respect for another's faith and cultural traditions, and dress in accordance
with the custom of their church. As there are usually several generations in
attendance, you should make it a point to acknowledge the older guests and
display the proper courtesies toward them as well as family members.

The First Communion

For the Roman Catholic child, the first of these commemorations is the
celebration of his or her First Communion. Having been taught the meaning
of this occasion by the priest, the child at age seven receives the sacrament in
a special service performed by the bishop.

A church reception for the young participants, their parents, close family
members and friends, and members of the congregation often follows. In
addition, the parents generally stage a private social salute, such as a brunch,
luncheon, or dinner (at home, in a club, or restaurant) to which close family
members and friends, and, of course, a few of the young friends of the
honoree are invited. The traditional white cake is served as dessert and
appropriate gifts are selected to have long-lasting religious meaning and
value.

The Confirmation

Among the Christian (Roman Catholic and Protestant) and Reformed
Jewish faiths, the confirmation is a landmark commemorating maturation.
As a prerequisite, the young person attends special classes to learn of the
church and the manner of living according to its doctrines. At the time of
confirmation, the student accepts the responsibility of carrying out these
teachings and incorporating them into his or her life, taking over the vows
spoken previously in the child's behalf by parents and godparents. Depending upon the faith, this initiation into religious maturity takes place when a
child is from eleven to seventeen years of age.

The joy of the religious confirmation ceremony is enhanced by a variety of
social celebrations that follow, from an intimate special family luncheon to a

small reception, brunch, or dinner (large or small). Once again, the symbolic white cake is served, and the honoree is presented with gifts of religious and lasting significance by family members and friends.

The *Bat Mitzvah* and *Bar Mitzvah*

A highlight of coming-of-age in the Jewish community is the *bat mitzvah* and *bar mitzvah* held for girls and boys respectively. This religious ceremony climaxes a study of the Jewish religion that has been in progress for years and recognizes the attainment of maturity and responsibility on the part of the thirteen-year-old boy or twelve-to-thirteen-year-old girl.

More elaborate than the social events that may follow a confirmation, the social celebration of the *bar mitzvah* or *bat mitzvah* is a major event in Jewish society. On the afternoon or evening following the Sabbath on which the religious ceremony is held, an elaborate private party is staged with dining and dancing for many friends and relatives. Gifts are lavish and often include money.

The "Coming-of-Age" Celebration

Throughout life, birthdays are important, but certain birthdays are turning points. The first of these is the sixteenth! In many states, this is the magic age at which the car keys may be turned over to a teen—a statement that maturity is all but accomplished. If you have passed sixteen, you can remember its magic. If you are approaching it, you are no doubt excited at the idea of attaining it.

A girl's favorite party, en route to the coming-of-age debut, is the social salute to her sixteenth birthday. Boys certainly celebrate this milestone, too, but not with quite the gaiety of girls. A girl's Sweet Sixteen Party can be as elaborate and formal as she wishes—perhaps a small dinner dance—or as informal as a pool party. It may star an all-girl or a girl-boy cast in accordance with the theme.

Gifts galore from friends and family are *de rigueur*, and these are more elaborate and of a longer-lasting quality than presents at other birthdays (perhaps an important piece of jewelry from parents or an heirloom piece from grandparents).

As a guest at a Sweet Sixteen Party, you will want not only your gift, but also your manners, to be special. And so, as a sophisticated young woman, you will telephone or send a note to the honoree and her mother telling them what a grand time you had and how lovely the party was.

As the "birthday girl," you will issue the invitations and select the type of party you want (under the guidelines and within the budget your parents establish). If the party is a rather formal one, you may select a special dress, and you might wear a small corsage or hold a pretty nosegay. Perhaps for the first time you will play the role of hostess, or co-hostess with your mother. You will want to make sure that your guests are presented to your parents or any other adults.

The gifts will be the center of attention when they are opened, either one at a time as they are presented (at a small gathering), or all at once for all the guests to see. Though a verbal thank you is sufficient, there is no reason not to write a thank-you note afterward if you wish. Most certainly, notes are sent to those who could not attend, but who sent a gift nonetheless.

The second, and the *crème de la crème* coming-of-age celebration, takes place at age twenty-one—that memorable year when your parents *and* the world acknowledge your attainment of full adulthood. How doubly exciting this is when it coincides with your college graduation year. As if by magic, the "kiddie champagne" of Sweet Sixteen turns to Taittinger when you reach twenty-one. Corks pop and toasts are raised to *you*—an adult at last! Parental gifts are often grand and the celebration can be a closed family affair with, of course, your man of the moment, or it can go public for family *and* friends. My favorite fete for this occasion is the formal dinner—black tie, of course— and the polished adult manners that accompany it.

The Twenty-sixth Amendment changed the age of majority to eighteen, from twenty-one, for voting, following which many states lowered the legal age. Therefore, in most states, at eighteen, a teenager is of legal age and is permitted to exercise full personal and civil rights.

Whether you elect to salute age eighteen or twenty-one (or both), attaining your majority brings privileges and responsibilities as well as celebrations—voting, serving on a jury, being bound by any contracts into which you enter, serving your country, and being introduced into society.

The Educational Accolades

Graduation from one stage of education and into another highlights growing up: nursery school to kindergarten, grammar school to junior high, high school to college, college to graduate school.

The Graduation from High School

The first milestone graduation occurs upon finishing high school. Senior year and graduation are stages in life one never forgets. For a year, the senior is the star on campus, and at the time of graduation, you are the star of your family and friends. A social whirl may engulf you: breakfasts, luncheons, teas, parties, proms. Then finally the baccalaureate service and the commencement exercises.

Should you be invited to attend the boarding school graduation of your boyfriend, you should stay in the same hotel or inn as his parents and bear the expenses of your travel, lodging, and meals (except special meals at which you are the invited guest of the parents or graduate). Should your boyfriend attend *your* graduation from boarding school, he does the same.

An elaborate agenda is often planned by the school before and after the baccalaureate service and graduation exercise. The graduate will want to advise family and guests of the social events and of the appropriate clothing they will need.

As seating is limited, a graduating senior is usually given a certain number of invitations (or sometimes tickets) for the baccalaureate service and graduation exercise. Together, the senior and his or her family decide who will receive these invitations. Of course, other friends and relatives may be invited to the other social events surrounding the graduation.

An especially nice salute to the graduate is a private reception following the graduation exercise. Given by the parents, or grandparents, this party can be staged at home, in a private club, restaurant, or hotel. In this manner, those who could not be admitted to the public events because of limited seating may share in the private commemoration of the graduate's achievement.

As with any invitation or announcement that may carry with it the obligation of a gift, a graduate or her parents should refrain from scattering graduation invitations and announcements at random. Most close family members and friends will want to be included and will want to acknowledge the milestone with a gift for the graduate. Every effort should be made to restrict the list to family and close friends and thus avoid the appearance of seeking graduation gifts galore!

Presents to the graduate may be displayed in a tasteful manner in his or her home. A skirted or draped table may be set up in the library, den, or living room, with the gifts and gift cards attractively arranged. In addition to, or in lieu of, graduation gifts, many friends and relatives send handsome congratulatory greeting cards, handwritten notes, telegrams, or even cables from abroad. These are included on the table and may stand up or be laid down. Better yet, how lovely to place these in a beautiful scrapbook as they arrive. The scrapbook is placed on the gift table. Gifts of money, always tasteful and acceptable, are displayed also—not the dollar amount, of course, but with a plain white card, placed beneath the giver's card which says "Check from Aunt Sally" or "Check from Mr. and Mrs. William Turner."

Handwritten thank-you notes (a mark of social maturity that should be second nature by the time of graduation) will be a pleasure to write. How nice that among the graduation gifts, there may well be a box or two of exquisite note papers—and even a wonderful new fountain pen. The sophisticated graduate will go the extra mile and write notes even to those she had the opportunity to thank in person.

The College Graduation

Expect less formalized fanfare in connection with the impressive ceremony at which you are awarded your college degree—and not a ripple beyond the academic circle should you later earn a master's or a doctorate.

Depending entirely upon the tradition of your college or university, festivities may be hosted in honor of the graduating class as a whole or social events may be given by the separate colleges within the university. In salute to their senior members, honorary societies and social sororities and fraternities may hold small receptions or open-house parties.

Possibly the loveliest of all graduation fetes is the intimate celebration hosted by parents in honor of their graduating son or daughter. Among loved ones (family, friends, and a fiancé- or fiancée-to-be) and away from the commencement crowd, in a serene private luncheon or dinner setting, the realization sets in that a major milestone has been reached, and, unless the pursuit of advanced degrees lies in the waiting, the real world beckons.

Gifts given at college graduation are generally lavish, but are rarely given except by intimate family members and the closest of friends.

The Social Affiliations

During each of the stages of maturation—and throughout the remainder of your life—you will experience the desire to be accepted, to belong.

And so, along with taking advantage of the educational opportunities that equip a young person to make a living, you should also be learning how to live a fulfilling life. The development of a fulfilled life is largely dependent upon one's relationships. For this reason, becoming a part of a comfortable, stimulating, sustaining, and supportive circle of friends is important. To assist each of you in accomplishing this was, in fact, my reason for writing this book. As you mature, your circle of friends widens along with your horizon and you will need to make wise choices.

Perhaps your first step toward organizational membership was joining a Brownie troop; next the Girl Scouts. With junior high and high school, the scope broadens: the music club, Latin club, Thespians, drill team, pep squad, sports teams, Candy Striper for the Women's Auxiliary of the hospital, perhaps even an honorary society or a prestigious social club.

With the college years, the spectrum grows even broader with a variety of arts, sports, academic, social, and philanthropic organizations from which to choose and be chosen. To some girls comes the bid to join a social sorority, the invitation to make their bow to society as a member of a debutante club, participation in Junior Committees, or perhaps selection for an honorary society.

After college graduation, social affiliation continues, in many instances on an alumnae basis, although new social connections arise as well. With most organizations, the goals are twofold: First, they meet the social needs of their members. Second, they meet the challenge of working toward a common interest—the community, a charity, the arts, education, or health.

Regardless of your age when you become a member of an organization, in return for the social and personal satisfaction it awards you, you must pay your dues and fulfill your commitment: a Brownie or Girl Scout sells cookies; Thespians help with the school play; Candy Stripers cheer the ill; sorority sisters work on a philanthropic endeavor; debutantes devote hours to community aid; honorary society members raise money for scholarships; Junior Leagues and similar social/service organizations work for many community, cultural, and health-related projects; the Junior Committees of museums raise money for new art acquisitions and education programs— the list goes on and on.

As a socially mature young woman, you have every right to enter into a group with whom you are comfortable and happy—to make your own social connections and social affiliations. However, as you make your selections, never lose sight of the fact that you are known by the company you keep.

274

The Social Sorority

Pi Beta Phi Fraternity, the first national secret college society of women to be modeled after the men's Greek-letter fraternities, was formed at Mammoth College in Mammoth, Illinois, in 1867. Now, as then, social societies unite college women and serve as a stage for social and service activities during the college years and beyond.

One of the closest social affiliations a young woman may experience during her college years is her sorority connection. During Rush Week the national or local Greek-letter sororities on a campus entertain prospective members and issue invitations to join.

In most instances, a young woman participates in Rush Week during her freshman year. Occasionally, however, she may decide to delay this experience—or her choice of a sorority—until her sophomore year. If her school does not have sororities or if a young woman does not elect to affiliate with one, she may seek (and will find) her sense of belonging within other organized social groups.

The decision whether or not to participate in Rush Week should be a family one. First of all, *you* must want to participate. Second, your parents should sanction your decision, for it is they (in most instances) who will be responsible for the sorority initiation fee and dues, as well as the special clothing that is required for Rush Week and the sorority pledging and initiation ceremonies.

Once a positive decision has been reached, you must complete the forms sent you by the college and National Panhellenic Conference (the national governing body of women's fraternities and sororities). Panhellenic then compiles the information for all the season's rushees and distributes it to each sorority on campus.

Prior to issuing a bid (invitation to join), a sorority relies not only upon its active members, but also on information from its alumnae. It is, therefore, helpful if you and your mother (and grandmother) canvass friends to ask if they would honor you with a recommendation to their sororities. In most instances, one official sorority recommendation form (completed and signed by an alumna in your behalf) must be on file with the sorority. In addition, personal letters of recommendation should be written for you. I suggest you aim for recommendations to as many of the sororities on campus as possible.

I counsel my ingénues and their mothers to exercise all applicable social graces in asking this favor of friends. Prepare a proper personal résumé, which can be incorporated into the text of the letters of recommendation or used as background when completing the official recommendation form. Include the name of the high school from which you graduated; the college you will be attending; scholastic record; academic, extracurricular, social, community, and church-related activities, offices, and honors; outside schooling, camps, and jobs; family background (Greek-letter fraternity and/ or sorority affiliations). In other words, include all that makes *you* special! But be honest, do not exaggerate, and do not use flowery language.

This résumé should be expertly typed and reproduced. Choose either white or ecru, 8½ x 11 inches, 100 percent cotton fiber, 32-pound paper with a vellum finish, and black ink. Include a picture of yourself along with each résumé.

If at all possible (when the alumna lives in your hometown or city), deliver the résumé in person at a prearranged time. In this way, you can meet her (she may be a friend of your mother's whom you have not met) or renew your acquaintance with someone you have not seen recently. This visit enables her to state in her note that she knows you, adding a personal impression as to your qualifications and her reasons for feeling that you would be a positive addition to her sorority.

You will certainly want to write a note to each alumna who was kind enough to prepare a recommendation letter or recommendation form on your behalf. Write it immediately, or telephone her to thank her and write to her after Rush. The advantage of waiting until after Rush Week is over to write is that you can tell her how nice it was to meet her sorority sisters on your campus and tell her which sorority you pledged. One of the letters may even say "I pledged your sorority!"

In your search for this sisterhood, it is extremely important that you enter Rush Week with an open mind. Refrain from making a premature choice or letting others talk you into setting your heart on a particular sorority before you have the opportunity to go through Rush. Throughout my sorority experience as an active and alumna member, I have known many young women to be brokenhearted because they wanted only one sorority. And I have known just as many who made a perfect sorority connection with a chapter to which they had never dreamed of belonging.

During Rush Week, open your eyes, your mind, and your heart to each sorority to which you are invited and to each active member or alumna you meet. Somehow—as though out of the blue—you will find one "just right" for you. Or you may even find that sororities are not for you and decide to seek fellowship within another type of social group.

Whatever the ultimate outcome may be, during each day of Rush Week be courteous and kind, be yourself, enjoy yourself, and think for yourself. By participating in this experience, you will make many new acquaintances and open the door to a few close friendships—even if you decide not to pledge a sorority or to delay your decision until later.

The Debut Into Society

A major turning point in a young woman's life is her entrance into adult society and her acceptance of the civic obligations and responsibilities that accompany it. This rite of passage is a metamorphosis from the ingénue to the budding sophisticate, often experienced as a formal and splendid occasion known as the debut.

As long ago as Colonial American times, socially prominent families adopted their forebears' custom of introducing their daughters to society. By the mid-18th century, "Dancing Assemblies" were introduced by fifty-nine Philadelphia families as the backdrop against which to present their daughters. Though its name has been changed to The Assemblies, its purpose and prominent position remains the same even today.

The tradition thus established was that, once the daughter of an aristocratic family reached eighteen years of age, she was "presented," "came out," was "introduced," or made her "bow." By whatever term the times deemed stylish, she made her debut into society, whether at home, at a dancing assembly, or at the contemporary mass ball.

Because of a need to broaden the scope of the older, long-established cotillions, assemblies, and clubs, the mass presentation ball, with its proceeds going to a charity, came into vogue following World War II. By coming out en masse (in a group), the cost of the ball could be shared by many families, who could each complement it with small, less elaborate parties if they wished.

In the past, the coming-out party was a formal announcement that a young woman was of marriageable age and that her parents were seeking an eligible suitor. Today, however, one who makes her bow has her mind on many goals besides immediate marriage. She will also learn to balance the "good times" of a busy debutante schedule with the added community and civic obligations that are an important part of this rite of passage. At the same time, she will be making new friends and widening her social circle.

There are many ways to make a debut, depending on the size of a young woman's hometown or city, the traditions of her family and community, and her family's social and civic prominence and means. From the most intimate of formal luncheons to the grandest of mass balls when she is presented to all in attendance, the ultimate goal is the same—the young woman is introduced into adult society and assumes the duties entailed by this step in her life.

According to an old Southern tradition (which has been widely adopted in other regions as well), a girl may be formally introduced to the friends of her mother, grandmother, and aunts at an afternoon debutante tea to which she also invites two or three of her closest friends to assist.

A deb may also come out at a *thé dansant,* a tea dance, at which her generation of young women and their escorts (plus especially invited extra young men) interact socially with her parents' generation of friends.

A small private dance—or one on a larger and more extravagant scale, a private ball—held in either a home, club, or hotel, offers a splendid setting from which a girl may make her bow. Occasionally, a few families who have been close over the years and, therefore, have many mutual friends, will join together to present their daughters. Scheduled around ten o'clock in the evening, this formal event may be preceded by one or several smaller private dinners given by various hostesses for groups of those invited to the dance. The guest list is like that of the tea dance on an expanded scale, and a live orchestra sets the tone. Guests pass through the receiving line to meet the deb and her parents and the hostess (if other than her parents). The father may stand in the receiving line or he may stand or circulate nearby to bridge the gap between the line and the other guests and dance floor. As at the tea dance, he later escorts his daughter onto the dance floor and her first dance belongs to Daddy—that is until her escort cuts in, followed by several other young men.

No doubt the most popular and prestigious debutante presentation is the mass ball, for which a young woman is selected and invited to participate. The added excitement of a coterie of sister-debs and deb-mothers and -fathers makes this kind of coming-out a favorite. At a formal ball, prefaced by several small private dinners or by one grand one, a few to a hundred or more young women may be introduced to the members of the host organization and the specially invited guests. The presentation of the debutantes is dramatic and beautiful, featuring intricate cotillion figures or a simple but elegant opening father-daughter deb waltz.

A girl's family may choose to have her come out more than once. That is, she may be invited and may accept invitations to be presented at the balls of more than one organization. Very often, a girl may make her debut in her hometown or city and also be invited to return to her mother's hometown to make her bow. She may come out where she lives and be presented again at a ball in a large metropolitan city nearby. Her parents might choose to have a daughter make her bow in several large cities and, in addition, make an international bow, at a ball held in the United States or a major city abroad. By making several bows, a deb spins a larger social web.

For a girl to be presented privately by her parents requires no outside invitation, only the family's willingness and desire. Essential to a young woman's coming out at a mass ball, however, is the invitation to do so. With some long-established social societies, clubs, and organizations, invitations are issued only to the daughters of relatives of members. With others, she may be considered upon request—letters of recommendation from a number of members of the organization who know the young woman and her family personally. The selection committee (often anonymous) sets the membership limitations and, based on the social and philanthropic involvement of her parents, as well as the girl's activities and potential as a civic and social leader, chooses the debs from among those eligible. In other instances, a young woman may be invited to make her bow at a mass presentation ball with the understanding that her parents make a contribution to the charity the event benefits.

Selections having been made, a young woman chosen to make her bow receives her invitations in the spring. Traditionally, a debutante's season lasts a year and usually begins with an opening announcement party or supper dance. In some cities, each family commits to hosting, alone or with other parents, a day or evening party for their daughter to which all debs and their escorts are invited. Friends of the family may also ask to host parties for the deb. These events, ranging from informal to formal and often with elaborate themes, are the real "mixers" of the season, at which the debs become quite close friends. In order that parties do not overlap, each is cleared and scheduled through the debutante club secretary. Every deb also supplies the secretary with a list of her escorts, from one to three, who are kept on file. The deb's family pays for all the expenses of her escort, or escorts, except for the flowers he sends on her presentation day and evening and for activities they attend after parties or the ball.

In addition to these social commitments, throughout the year the deb allots a certain amount of time to service work. Great pride is felt by the club members, when, at the end of the season, a large number of deb hours have been logged for the philanthropic endeavor.

The debutante season reaches its summit with the presentation ball. Most are staged during the school holidays in November, December, January, or in June. For this long-awaited occasion, the deb dons a long, white, demure dress, eighteen-button (over-the-elbow) glacé kid gloves, and a simple strand of real pearls. Her father and escorts wear white tie and tails and white kid or bleached chamois gloves. Her mother will wear a long, pastel ball gown and real jewelry. Flowers will arrive on "the day" from well-wishing relatives, family friends, father's business associates, and the girl's escort, or escorts. And, as with all of life's milestones, there will be treasured and long-lasting gifts from the deb's parents, adult members of her family, god-parents, and close family friends, and a scrapbook filled with photographs, invitations, and souvenirs.

The young woman who, for one reason or another, does not have the desire or does not have the opportunity to make a debut becomes no less a woman; and she has it in her power to become just as charming, outgoing, and effective as a debutante. Knowing the social proprieties, however, is as necessary and as possible in a remote village as in New York City.

The Junior Committees and Other Social Service Groups

When a young woman finishes school, she makes her entrance into a new stage of her life, for which she has been preparing for eighteen or twenty-plus years.

Her new scene will include a budding career or marriage or both. Complementing each—and vital to her happiness and development in either—is the social network she establishes. Once again, she sets out to spin a web, to seek out those with whom she wishes to socialize.

There is a natural spillover of interests from campus life that unites her with certain groups. Some of these she will want to keep. Others she may want to leave behind to make room for new and maturing interests.

Discrimination is important in establishing friendships. From the largest city to the smallest town, there is a way to carve your niche socially and civically. The problem is often that there are so many choices!

First, consider your interests. More than likely you want to maintain an active rapport with your sorority and other college connections. If so, seek out the alumnae clubs of each. Do your interests lie in the arts? Gather information on the performing, visual, and signature arts in your area and the Junior Committees that support them. Are you drawn toward the community involvement of your church? Discover groups for your age through which you can serve. Has history always fascinated you? Explore historic preservation societies and neighborhood renewal projects. Are you an animal lover? Consider the support group for the zoo or other organizations. Is medicine an interest? Research hospital auxiliaries and fund-raisers for disease study and treatment. Do you have literary leanings? Search out literary arts groups. Are your horizons worldwide? Find an international cultural affairs committee. Are you a plant lover? Join a botanical garden society. Do you feel concern for the well-being of the earth? Devote yourself to an environmental and ecological group.

If you cannot define your exact interests, you might consider affiliating with the local chapter of the Association of Junior Leagues. Founded in 1901, the Junior League reaches out to young women (early twenties through late thirties) of all races, religions, and national origins who demonstrate an interest and commitment to voluntarism.

Before joining any organization, take time out to make a personal assessment. First, list each social service organization that you feel to be of personal interest to you, including: the organization's name, statement of purpose, membership qualifications, open or closed membership, ages and sexes of the members, personality profile of members (young career, young matrons, specific professional interests), initiation dues (if any), annual or monthly dues, meeting dates and times, location of meetings, social events, fund-raising events, pledge drives (if any) held throughout the year, mandatory or suggested service hours (if any), and the beneficiary of the organization's service efforts.

Next, from your list select three favorites to form a social triangle of organizations with varied interests. Now, prepare an annual calendar on which you plot the meeting dates and times, social events, fund-raising parties and galas, and monetary and service requirements of the three chosen organizations. Tally the dollar column and weigh it against your budget. Add to these costs any special clothing requirements (a ball gown for the fund-raising gala, cocktail dresses for special parties) and, if your present wardrobe is not adequate, propose a budget to expand it. Cross-reference the meeting and social dates, the service-hour commitments. Now, budget the time the organizations require against the time your career and private commitments demand.

Further, check whether these organizations offer various levels of participation at fund-raisers. Many offer Junior Committee members entry to these affairs at a lesser donation fee. For example, at a ball, juniors may accept just the invitation to the dance and forgo the dinner, thereby offering support and having fun within a budget. In most organizations, the Junior Committees are active themselves and plan fund-raisers just for their young members.

As you consider, ask yourself: "Can my free time and my budget support my social triangle?" "Will my company support my memberships either by allotting time for participation or by paying for membership initiation fees, dues, and social event donations?" "What portion of these expenditures, if any, is tax deductible?"

In defining your interests and in choosing the social service groups to fulfill them, I suggest that you establish a broad range. Do not, however, accept every invitation you receive. By analyzing, you will not become trapped in your own social web. As you grow more mature, so will your interests. Some will remain fulfilling; others will change. Your priorities will also alter. When changes occur, rearrange your social triangle. Take time to regroup. As you replace one organization with another, send a letter asking to be placed on the inactive list (you will continue to pay dues, but are not required to participate unless you wish to do so). Or, you may resign completely, in which case a proper letter of resignation should be sent to the membership chairperson.

Social service begins with the less exciting chores. In time, though, with dedicated membership, you will rise to senior status. Leaders will seek you out to serve on their committees. You will become the co-chair, then chair of a committee yourself. You may become an officer of the organization. With each step of the way, you are taking your place in society—carving your niche.

The Matrimonial Rites

The nuptial tie is very much an affirmation of life, a symbol of continuity. Marriage is a time of great joy and hope—even in times of general despair. Marriage is also the *most* important of the landmarks in life—a solemn and serious commitment, which is intended to long outlast the celebrations, if not the memories, that surround the exchange of vows.

To surround the wedding with a religious ceremony, with minister, priest, or rabbi, and family and friends in attendance, is more meaningful and memorable than relegating it to a civil ceremony performed by the Justice of the Peace. (In some countries, both a civil and a religious ceremony are required.) To choose, therefore, an elopement in lieu of even the simplest of religious ceremonies is to cheat yourself—a shortcut no young woman and her fiancé should take without soul-searching.

The Engagement

Betrothment, as it was once called, is the act of contracting for marriage—a mutual promise to wed. Gone are the days when the betrothal was arranged by the families at the time when a boy and girl were very young, often with great amounts of money and property involved. Now, it is the young man and woman who make up their minds to become engaged.

An engagement usually lasts from three to six months. It provides a time for the prospective bride and groom to date one another exclusively. It provides for festivities in honor of the engaged couple and also ample time to plan the formal wedding and for the couple to deepen their knowledge of one another.

In our world of open communication between parents and children, the news that a son or daughter is "about to become engaged" generally comes as no surprise to the parents. Even so, once the couple has privately pledged to marry—though the "suitor" need not ask the father for his daughter's hand as he did in Victorian times—each should share the news immediately with his or her parents.

Granted, some young people become engaged with full knowledge that their parents will not approve. Nonetheless, parents should be told. To elope as an escape from disapproval may cause strife between the parents and the young couple for years to come, and no marriage should begin like this. Sometimes, open communication convinces the young man and woman that they should, for one reason or another, postpone the engagement. At other times, the parents, though they may not agree, accept the decision when the pair stands firm in their convictions.

By no means dark-age decorum, but an act of courtesy, is the "little chat" about the proposed marriage between the girl's fiancé and her father. Sometimes the bride's father will wish to discuss finances, which today means talking about how the future bride and groom will manage with blended incomes, or how the fiancé plans to provide at a later time when the two have children if the wife decides to relinquish her career for motherhood. If both—or one—are still in school, earning capabilities are small; and parents may agree, in this instance, to provide an allowance until degrees are obtained. The bride's mother and groom's parents may be brought into the discussion, since marriage truly is a merger of families.

This joining of families is instigated immediately by the groom's parents once they are told of his plans. Even though they may not have met the bride-to-be, the groom's mother (and father, also, if he wishes) writes her a warm letter expressing happiness over the forthcoming marriage. The bride answers with an equally sincere and enthusiastic letter. Further, the groom's parents (most often his mother) write the bride's parents suggesting that they meet before the wedding (if they have not already done so). The bride's parents reply immediately proposing an occasion.

After the parents are informed of the engagement, the couple should decide how to tell other family members, close friends, and godparents. If a surprise announcement party is planned, the temptation to tell must be resisted until party time! If the element of surprise is not a factor, then the mothers of the engaged couple send personal notes or telephone or telegraph. (An engraved or printed announcement of an engagement is never sent.) The engaged couple may wish to write to friends also and should do so separately—the girl using her personal writing papers with her maiden name or monogram. It is in poor taste to allow someone close to the bride or groom to hear or read about the engagement in the newspaper without having been told first.

An announcement party is a festive way to commemorate the engagement. Formerly the bride's parents hosted a grand celebratory dinner to which the groom's parents were invited. This tradition persists today, though the announcement may be made upon a variety of social stages: a large formal dinner, a small family dinner that others join at the time of the dessert course, a buffet for family and friends, a cocktail party, a reception, a tea. Most brides and grooms have another less formal party at which they celebrate their news with their contemporaries.

Given by the bride's parents or by both the bride's and groom's parents (or another relative or guardian), the invitation to the announcement party need not reveal its purpose if a true surprise is the couple's wish. For drama, the couple may wish to release a bunch of balloons inscribed with both their names, or simply await the toast given by the father of the bride during which he announces the engagement.

The proper way to announce an engagement to the public is in the newspaper, and it is the parents of the bride who make the announcement. The names of the groom and his family are a part of the announcement, as are ancestry facts, information about the bride's and groom's schools and degrees earned, social and honorary affiliations, and business position (if established at that time). The announcement is carried by both the bride's and groom's hometown newspapers. The wedding date is given if it has been set. A public press announcement is always timed to follow (preferably the day after) the announcement party.

Once you hear the news of a girlfriend's engagement, take the occasion to send the bride-elect a note expressing your excitement and send the groom-elect a congratulatory note, too, if you are friends. The prospective bride and groom should acknowledge your note separately with notes of their own, just as they will those from relatives, godparents, and adult friends. Such lovely notes are among the things that make the engagement so special, and may be kept in a scrapbook!

Close friends, family members, and godparents often give the bride an engagement gift, many times selecting one suitable for both the bride and groom, which they may use in their new home. A thank-you note from the bride-elect is in order shortly after the gift is received.

The public behavior of the bride and groom is dictated by the rules of good taste. A public show of affection beyond a greeting or farewell is not acceptable. The fiancée who is constantly cooing and courting her fiancé (or vice versa) is subjecting both of them to teasing and joking and soon becomes a bore.

Prior to marriage, some young people choose to live together openly. Although parents or friends may accept the fact, they need not condone it, and the young man and woman must abide by their parents' or friends' wishes that they reside in separate rooms when they are guests in their homes. It is in poor social taste for a young couple who have chosen to live together to announce an extended engagement—if, in fact, they announce one at all. It is in far better taste, under the circumstances, to announce the wedding as close to the date selected as possible.

Once the engagement is announced, the months preceding the wedding are laden with decisions. One of the most exciting is the selection of china, crystal, and silver, the wedding invitations, and the social paper trousseau. At this time in your life, you will want to review carefully the chapters of this book that are devoted to these subjects. You will also have the pleasure of selecting gifts for your bridesmaids, as will the groom for his ushers. And, of course, choosing the wedding dress and bridesmaids' dresses allows glamorous decisions!

When the wedding date is chosen—yet another decision—it will be important to make a personal appointment with the bridal consultant at the jewelry and department stores in your hometown or city. If you have not already made concrete decisions as to your tabletop amenities and other "wish list" items, bridal consultants can assist you. Your choices are then entered in the stores' bridal registries as are your and your fiancé's names and addresses, so that family and friends may choose a gift to suit your needs and wishes. How nice for them that they may do so in person or by telephone. From then on, all gifts purchased for you are recorded in a computerized registry to avoid duplications.

Today, the "bridal" shower may include the groom, as many couples are honored with "coed" showers. But most showers are feminine occasions: a morning coffee, a luncheon, an afternoon tea. For a coed function, a weekend brunch, a cocktail party, a cocktail buffet, or a dessert party are good choices.

The showering of gifts upon the bride should be limited to an intimate group of close friends and family members, selected by the bride in accordance with the number the hostess can entertain. The bride gives the list of names, addresses, and telephone numbers to her hostess, who issues the informal invitations. Immediate family members do not give showers for the bride, for to do so would appear to be asking for gifts for her.

A bride should take special care in preparing her guest lists that friends are not invited to more than one, or at the most two, showers, for each invitation requires a gift from the guest. Naturally, neither does she include anyone on a shower list (or any other party list) whom she is not inviting to the wedding. She does, however, include her bridesmaids and her maid of honor on all of her invitation lists, as well as her mother and the mother of her fiancé. Though the mothers of the engaged couple may enjoy giving a gift at each shower, her attendants may not be in a position to do so. The bride should ask them not to bring a gift each time. They, in turn, often join together to give her one gift at each shower. The guests who cannot attend, although they are not obligated to give a gift, will usually want to do so since it is only close friends who are invited. As pretty presents are part and parcel of the party, the guest who will be absent takes her gift to the hostess or has it sent prior to the event.

Bridal showers and other prenuptial festivities should be scheduled within the engagement period at times convenient to the bride, hostess, and guests. As the bride has so many last-minute duties to which she must attend several weeks prior to the wedding, and also has the more intimate prewedding festivities—the bridesmaid luncheon, rehearsal, rehearsal dinner, and out-of-town guests to entertain—showers and other parties should be scheduled as early as possible.

As the purpose of the shower is to "shower" the bride with gifts that will add to her household and personal trousseau, she should be consulted by the hostess as to what type of party she would like: kitchen, bath, linens, lingerie, houseplants, recipe, menu, patio, or travel accessories for the honeymoon. (Her mother can advise the hostess in confidence if a surprise shower is planned.)

The featured attraction of the party is, of course, the opening of the presents. Beautifully wrapped gifts are decoration in themselves and, except for pretty fresh flowers, none other is needed. In some communities, the lovely custom of giving a corsage to the bride and the mothers remains.

Before opening gifts, the bride should ask one of her bridesmaids or another friend to list the gifts and the givers as she opens her presents. A clever hostess provides a small, pretty journal with blank pages, on one of which she has attached the shower invitation. As the guests arrive, she asks them to sign it and include a wish for the bride. At gift-opening time, she turns the journal over to the "scribe" to enter the gifts and givers on the remaining pages. The journal is then given to the bride as a memento of the party.

No guest should linger at the end of a bridal shower. The gifts must be packed afterward and placed in the car before the bride and her mother leave. This is, therefore, one social scene when the guests depart before the guest of honor. The thoughtful hostess often invites the groom to stop by after an all-girl shower, for she knows how much fun the pair will have reviewing the gifts together.

Strictly "by the book," a bride need not write a thank-you note to the guests whom she thanks in person for their shower gift. However, how can she not want to put her enthusiasm on paper within a few days? She will, by all means, send a handwritten note of appreciation to her hostess the next day, and perhaps a small flower arrangement bearing her calling card.

The Wedding

The pomp and circumstance, the pageantry and ceremony of the wedding, complemented by the joy and jubilation of the wedding reception, culminate a young woman's coming-of-age; each celebrates the "happily ever after" of the fairy-tale princess story. But whether it be intimate or massive in scale, a storybook wedding cannot be created simply by waving a magic wand. Depending upon how elaborate the ceremony and festivities are to be, they may be months in the making.

Once the engagement is announced, the wedding plans begin to unfold. It is the bride's prerogative to decide the type, the tentative date and time, and the place for her wedding. The thoughtful bride shares her wedding dreams and wishes with her fiancé, and they make these decisions together. The bride's parents, too, are included, for, by tradition, it is they who are responsible for the financial arrangements. The proposed date and time of a church wedding must, of course, be approved by the minister in accordance with the doctrines of the church, as weddings are not performed on certain days or at certain times.

As the wedding day belongs to the bride, parents should not impose upon their daughter any arrangements with which she does not agree. A bride, on the other hand, should "hear out" any and all ideas her parents propose, for they often have greater exposure to and knowledge of the customs and rituals, which even the most modern wedding has inherited from the past. The bride, more often, has a feeling for the romantic and beautiful traditions that she has always dreamed would be part of her special day.

The bride-to-be should never outdream her parents' financial abilities. It is not in good taste for a wedding and reception to be beyond the family's means. In addition, it is pretentious for a wedding to be staged in any manner beyond the family's usual social scale. The thoughtful and considerate daughter, therefore, will keep her plans within the boundaries of her parents' limitations. In the same manner, parents who can afford—and who prefer—the most lavish wedding and reception should not impose these upon their daughter if she truly wants a small, intimate celebration.

Although social traditions change and new ones are created, for the milestone of a young woman's wedding it generally remains true that the expenses are borne by her parents, with just a few minor ones allotted to the groom and his parents. It is natural, then, that your parents act as the host and hostess of your wedding.

On occasion the groom and his parents may wish to become more involved in the wedding. Perhaps they have an extremely large family and many friends, and they wish to include on their guest list more people than the bride's parents can accommodate, or maybe the two sets of parents simply want to share in the wedding planning and expenses (either totally or partially) in order to create the lovely ambience that a large wedding affords.

When this is the case, the groom and his parents ask the bride and her parents if they might be permitted to participate, both in the planning and the paying. This request should in no way embarrass the bride and her parents. On the other hand, however, this offer should never be made solely to create a wedding beyond the means of the bride's family, for that would insinuate that they cannot afford a wedding as grand as the groom's family wishes.

Even when the groom's parents participate financially, the bride's family makes the final decisions as to the total sum to be spent, the type of breakfast or reception to be presented, and the size of the guest list. When the groom's parents contribute to a major extent, they become the co-host and co-hostess and, as such, their names are included on the wedding invitation along with those of the bride's parents.

Mutual respect and understanding between the bride, the groom, and both sets of parents, along with adherence to the religious and social customs surrounding the wedding, will ensure that the landmark event is the joyous occasion it is meant to be.

Having just touched on a few of the many details involved in a traditional wedding, we shall move on to your pleasant social duties as an invitee, a guest, or a bridal attendant at another's wedding.

The invitation to be a bridesmaid is exciting indeed and is an honor you may have many times. You may already have experienced the thrill of being invited to serve as a bridesmaid, junior bridesmaid, or a flower girl. To be asked to be the maid of honor is an even higher distinction.

The invitation to be a bridesmaid or the maid of honor is a compliment—one you should not decline, except for a very important reason. Your acceptance will, however, entail certain financial obligations. In some instances, the bride's and groom's parents, if they can afford to do so, assume the costs of the attendants' wedding attire and transportation from their hometowns to the location of the wedding.

When the time comes for you to select your wedding attendants, take special care not to ask a girlfriend who you know cannot afford to accept it. This special friend or relative could be invited instead to hostess the table at which guests sign the guest book or to pour tea or punch—there are many honors that require no expense on the part of the participant.

Upon accepting the honor of being a bridesmaid or maid of honor, offer the bride any assistance she might need before, up to, and after her wedding day. If you live in the city in which the wedding is to be held, you might offer to have out-of-town bridesmaids or guests as houseguests of your family. And there are many other tasks, such as addressing, stuffing, and stamping wedding invitations, or helping pack the gifts while the bride is on her wedding trip. The list of prewedding chores is endless and so should be your willingness to help!

As a bridal attendant, you will receive many wonderful social invitations during the prewedding period. These events require not only your presence, but your most polished social behavior before the hostess, the bride and her family, and the other guests. As co-hostess with the other bridesmaids, you may have the opportunity to hostess a special shower for the bride or to fete her with the bridesmaids' party, tea, or luncheon—her farewell party at which the bridesmaids present her with a lovely gift and she gives them each a memento of the wedding, usually of gold or silver, engraved with their initials or monogram and the date of the wedding.

The groom's counterpart to the bridesmaids' party is the bachelor party. Given by the groom, the best man, or the groomsmen, this dinner party serves to bid adieu to the groom's bachelorhood, and his ushers join him in his ceremonial toast to the bride. The groomsmen receive a gift from the groom, and present him with one.

The wedding rehearsal and rehearsal dinner are held just before the day of the wedding and reception, and as an attendant, you will be expected to participate in each. To be prompt, punctual, and attentive at the rehearsal, and properly attired for the church sanctuary or chapel, are among your social duties. It is not socially proper to "celebrate" before the rehearsal.

The rehearsal dinner, often with dancing, follows the rehearsal and is a deserved celebration of the wedding to come. It often serves as one of the first social stages upon which the merged families of the bride and groom may congregate. The presence, too, of the immediate family members of the bride and groom along with relatives and close friends who have traveled from out of town, adds greatly to the gaiety. As an attendant, you will be expected to attend, but do not ask to bring a date, for only the fiancés or husbands of the attendants are invited.

As with most social celebrations commemorating a happy milestone occasion, the rehearsal dinner features many toasts to the guests of honor—the bride and groom. Before making a toast of your own, should you be an attendant or guest, await the first toast by the host and any return toasts by the groomsmen. Certainly as a bridesmaid-guest or sister of the bride or groom, you may then propose a toast. It is also fun for the maid of honor to recite or read a poem that she and the bridesmaids have composed in the bride's honor. As with all toasts, such a verse may be clever and witty, but it must also be short and sweet without a hint of sarcasm or vulgarity.

Many brides and grooms prefer to give their wedding attendants' gifts at the rehearsal dinner. It does certainly add sparkle to the table when these small boxes, beautifully wrapped, accent the place setting of each attendant. How nice, too, for the other guests to share in the excitement of the unwrapping and viewing of these keepsakes. In the same manner, the bridesmaids may present their gift to the bride, and the groomsmen theirs to the groom, on this occasion—each with a toast from the maid of honor or best man.

When the hour of the wedding permits, the bridal party may gather on the day itself for a brunch or luncheon. Usually given by relatives or friends of the bride's family, this special gathering not only provides a lovely meal for out-of-town attendants and family members, and another opportunity for deepening the association between the two families, but it can also be a tension breaker for the bride and groom—if they are not abiding by the age-old taboo against the couple seeing each other on the day of their marriage until they meet at the altar.

The wedding day! As one of the bride's attendants, you must be scrupulous about each detail for which you are responsible: your dress, accessories, proper underpinnings, extra pantyhose, and makeup packed and ready to go; hair and makeup exactly as the bride or bridal consultant requested; yourself rested and fresh (early to bed after the rehearsal dinner!) and on time, whether another is collecting you or you are driving yourself. Arrive wearing a smile and remain unflappable (neither easily upset nor easily excited) throughout the backstage fun of dressing, the ceremony, and the reception. During the ceremony do exactly as you rehearsed, and, if you have a question beforehand, ask the bridal consultant or another bridesmaid, *not* the bride. Most importantly, just relax and enjoy yourself.

If you are the maid of honor, you will act rather as the bride's lady-in-waiting and confidante: standing near her throughout the ceremony, holding her bouquet or prayer book at the designated time, holding her fiancé's ring in safekeeping until the right moment in the ceremony, placing it in her hand (which may be trembling), lifting the blush veil from her face (unless she wants her new husband to do so) for the couple's kiss or shared smile, adjusting her train and veil after she pivots away from the altar to face the families and friends, and returning her bouquet or prayer book before she joins her husband for the recessional. Mark my word, you will experience great empathy with the bride and groom during these precious moments when you stand as witness to their solemn vows. During this time, remember my bridesmaid's pledge, "Unfailingly unflappable"—no tears, no giggles; exude only love and joy with all your heart.

Of utmost importance are the wedding photographs. When formal shots are being taken (either before or after the ceremony), be punctual; stand where you are positioned, smile nicely, and never clown; stand quietly on the sideline (do not dare to leave even for a moment); never heckle others as they are photographed; never ask the photographer to take a picture with your camera; never snap photos yourself during the session. Remember, you are not the director of this shooting; you are the model bridesmaid who does exactly as she is told. If you are the maid of honor, you may have the added responsibility of gathering the bridesmaids for the photographs and the receiving line.

If the reception is held in a location other than the site of the ceremony, arrangements are made by the bride's family for the transportation of the bridesmaids along with the other members of the wedding party. According to the bride's wishes, her bridesmaids may or may not stand in the receiving line. When they do, they stand last in the line after the maid of honor. Thus, beginning at the entrance through which the guests pass, the full wedding receiving line is as follows: the announcer (if there is one present); mother of the bride; father of the bride (if he stands in the receiving line rather than mingling with guests); mother of the groom; father of the groom (if he stands rather than mingling); bride; groom; maid of honor; bridesmaids (if they stand rather than mingle).

If you are asked to stand in the receiving line, you will exchange names with each guest and cordially share with them a welcome or a brief comment about the wedding, then introduce them to the bridesmaid next in line. The receiving line is not a place to engage in conversation. The renewal of old friendships or the beginning of new ones should be reserved for the reception.

If the bride prefers that you mingle with the guests rather than stand in the receiving line, make certain that you do so. It is not proper for the bridesmaids to huddle together. Rather, they should circulate, introducing themselves, introducing guests to each other and to the family members. In particular, seek out the older guests, who adore the attention and mannerly courtesies of young wedding party members, and the solitary guest who appears shy or does not know others—practice your "Art of Conversation!"

There are several times during the reception when the bridesmaids come together—or are beckoned by the maid of honor: for photographs; for the receiving line (if requested); to take their place at the bride's table; to participate in the toasts; when the bride tosses her bouquet; to retire with the bride and assist her in changing into her going-away attire; prior to the departure of the bride and groom.

It is also lovely to be a guest at the wedding. Once weddings begin to take place within your social circle, you will probably receive many invitations. You will attend alone or with other young guests and without your parents, as they will not receive invitations from your college or young career friends whom they do not know well.

Although you may most certainly attend a wedding together with one or more friends who have also been invited, or you may attend alone, you may *not* bring a family member, a friend, or a date who has not received an invitation.

Your first social obligation upon receipt of a wedding invitation is to send a written reply as quickly as possible. Although a mail-back reply, if enclosed with the invitation, may be used, it is more traditional to "reply in kind." Chapter 9, Invitations! will guide you in attending to this social courtesy.

Once you have responded, your next concern, and a most pleasant one, will be the selection of an appropriate gift. If you cannot attend the wedding, you are under no obligation to send a gift, but more than likely you will want to if you are a close friend of the bride and/or groom. Neither must you send a gift when you are invited just to the ceremony but not to the reception, nor when you receive an announcement of the wedding.

The gift is sent to the bride or, if *absolutely* necessary, is taken to the reception, where a table is provided especially for gifts. After the wedding, gifts are sent to the bride and groom at their new home. Nicest, of course, is to have the gift sent, or hand deliver it, to the bride's home before the wedding day so that she and her fiancé may share the fun of opening it and displaying it along with their other gifts. Early gift giving is appreciated by the bride, as she tries to write as many of her thank-you notes as possible prior to her wedding day. When gifts are sent in ample time, emergencies, such as breakage, can be handled prior to the bride's departure for her wedding trip.

As a wedding guest, you face a personal decision: "What shall I wear?" Many factors influence proper dress. The time of day, the formality of the wedding, the location, the traditions of the community, and your age determine the type of clothing you should wear. As a guest, of utmost importance is to avoid the "toos": too low-cut, too short, too bare, too transparent, too glittery, too revealing, too slinky.

The daytime wedding is one held before six o'clock in the evening, and the evening wedding takes place after six. For the ultraformal daytime wedding, select a dressy street-length afternoon dress or suit, with the dressiest of daytime fabrics reserved for the afternoon. The ultraformal evening wedding calls for a short or ballerina-length evening, dinner, or party dress—perhaps a long dress, if you are a relative or honored guest.

For the formal or semiformal daytime wedding, choose an afternoon-style dress or dressy suit. A short dinner, party, or cocktail suit or dress of a more elaborate fabric is perfect for the formal or semiformal evening wedding.

Street-length or dressy afternoon dresses are correct for the informal daytime wedding, as are short afternoon or conservative party, cocktail, or dinner dresses or suits for the informal evening wedding.

Stockings are *de rigueur;* shoes and handbags should be in keeping with the mood of the ensemble; strapless, thinly strapped, and sleeveless dresses require a coordinated jacket. Gloves are correct at all times. Although not required, it is always correct to wear a head covering to a wedding held in a church or chapel. For the morning wedding, select a small morning hat and for the afternoon, a larger afternoon hat. A special bow in the hair substitutes for a hat. Very small evening hats, cocktail veils, or dressy bows may be worn to evening weddings.

When you accept an invitation to an out-of-town wedding, you also accept the responsibility of any travel, lodging, and dining expenses incurred. You may be invited as the houseguest of friends; otherwise, make arrangements on your own.

If you are not invited to stay with friends, the bride's family will suggest a hotel, bed-and-breakfast, or inn which will be pleasant and at which other out-of-town guests will be lodged. Many times the family provides transportation to and from that location to the wedding and reception, as well as to any other social gatherings.

A wedding does not wait for a guest! Punctuality is mandatory. Therefore, arrive at the place of the wedding in time to step inside approximately twenty to thirty minutes prior to the hour stated on the invitation. Upon entering the vestibule of the church, remain there until an usher is free to escort you to a seat. He will ask if you are a guest of the bride or the groom. When there is a center aisle, the bride's family, honored guests, and friends are seated in the pews on the left, the groom's on the right. As a young woman, when you accompany your family to a wedding, you will be ushered into your seat along with your family. In this case, the usher will award precedence to your mother and you will follow behind with your father, but you do not take his arm as you would an usher's. If, however, there are many ushers, one may personally escort you and seat you with your mother and father.

When you are escorted by the usher, he offers you his right arm, which he holds in a right-angle bent position. Accept it by placing your hand on the inner side of his arm. Should you be accompanied by a male guest, he will follow after you and the usher. If there is no usher, do take particular care not to sit in the first several rows of seats as these are reserved for family members and honored guests.

At very large formal weddings, pew cards are occasionally included in the invitations of certain guests, in which case the card is presented to the usher. Or the ushers may be provided with a seating list.

When you are accompanied by a man, unlike the situation at the theater, he may enter the row first (if an aisle seat remains), so that you will be on the aisle to better see the processional, ceremony, and recessional. If you are seated in an aisle seat, you need not relinquish it, simply position your knees so that others can pass by you with ease.

The mother of the bride is the last to be seated, after which no guests may be seated and the church doors are closed. After the bride's mother takes her seat, the crescendo of the music begins and the wedding processional starts. At this time, it is permissible to turn slightly toward the aisle to witness the processional. Although you may look back at the bride as she enters, glance forward at her mother first. If she stands, all the guests should rise in deference to the bride. At the proper time, her mother sits down, and this is your cue to do the same.

Upon completion of the ceremony, the recessional takes place. Do not leave your seat until those within the ribbons have done so If you have been standing for the recessional (as is sometimes done), be seated as those in the reserved pews make their exit. When it is your turn, leave in order of convenience rather than in order of pews. The ladies are not escorted by the ushers at this time.

At the reception, if there is a receiving line, it is your responsibility to pass through it. Guests pass through the line as they arrive in no order of precedence. Should there be no one to announce your name, introduce yourself to the first in line and shake hands. As a young woman, you wait for an older woman to extend her hand first. Make a brief comment about how lovely the wedding was, or simply say "How do you do?"

When you reach the bride and groom, you may extend your best wishes to the bride, congratulate the groom, and wish them both happiness. If you are a close friend or relative, you may want to kiss the bride lightly on the cheek (best an air kiss so as not to leave lipstick or muss her hair and veil). Either before you have passed through the receiving line or after, you may be served a beverage. Do take care to set food or drink aside before going through the line, lest you spill something on someone's wedding attire.

When there is no receiving line, you must make a special effort to seek out the bride and groom and their parents and speak to them. Do not monopolize them, however, for other guests will also be vying for their time.

As the bride's parents cannot possibly introduce each of the guests to one another, it is perfectly proper to make your own introductions and converse with the other guests, much as you would if you were a bridesmaid. Make it a point to stop by the table holding the guest book. Even if you are accompanied by your parents or other family members, sign on a separate line, using your full name prefaced by the title "Miss."

There are several times during the wedding reception when you will need to refrain from talking in order to observe traditional events: the toast, the cake-cutting ceremony, the bride and groom's first dance, the tossing of the bridal bouquet and garter, and the bride and groom's departure.

At a seated reception, once the bride and groom, followed by the wedding party, take their places at the bride's table, you will settle yourself in your seat (probably indicated by a place card unless open seating is the order of the day). What more beautiful setting than this to practice perfect table manners and charming conversation!

At a very large reception, it is not necessary (or even possible) to say good-bye to your host and hostess, the bride's mother and father. If the gathering is an intimate one, however, you may certainly bid them farewell.

The exciting element of a wedding and reception is that each is different, taking on the personality of the bride and groom and their families. What I have briefly described is a *traditional* wedding and reception. You will attend both traditional and nontraditional versions as you witness the marriages of family members and friends. But as I said in the beginning, the wedding day is the bride's day. Let us wish that her dreams come true and appreciate and enjoy to the fullest her individual interpretation of this most important milestone.

The Wedding Anniversary

In this era when the divorce rate is high, wedding anniversaries have taken on a new importance. The durability of a marriage today is, in fact, a statement not only of the lasting love existing between the couple but of the existence of such important character traits as commitment, adaptability, and maturity.

Although enormously supportive and joyous, marriage is not always easy, and each additional year of "making it work" deserves commemoration. The celebration may be, and usually is in the early years, a very private affair, a momentary escape from responsibilities to recapture the romance of courtship. The event may vary from a glamorous weekend, to an elegant restaurant dinner, a late candlelight supper on an apartment balcony, or a picnic in a woodland filled with memories. A gift, ranging from a jewel to a favorite dessert, can express what some find hard to put into words.

When the couple is a happy part of an extended family, parents, brothers, and sisters may also want to mark the occasion with a less intimate gathering—a family dinner and perhaps gifts for the household.

Such family celebrations, perhaps including close friends, usually become the pattern as the years pass, especially if there are children. But most happy couples continue to find time for a special, *à deux* celebration, perhaps finally a cruise or other holiday to bring their complicated lives back to the intimate, mutual enjoyment and understanding they experienced before marriage.

Whether you wish your remembrance to be traditional or modern, certainly you will want to remember the wedding anniversaries of your parents, grandparents, married brothers and sisters, and your close friends.

Tradition recognizes four wedding anniversaries as special ones whose celebration is shared by family and friends. Referred to by their traditional names—indicating the precious metal or gemstone awarded these landmark years of marriage—these "festive, formal four" are: Silver (twenty-fifth), Ruby (fortieth), Golden (fiftieth), and Diamond (sixtieth).

Formal, splendid anniversary celebrations are rarely the rule until the Silver milestone, when the couple may wish to invite friends and children to celebrate with them. Or their children may host such a party, if they are in a position to do so. The formal commemoration of the Ruby Wedding is more prevalent in England than in the United States.

The Golden Anniversary is, of course, a gleaming occasion (almost always given by the couple's adult children) for celebrating the durable marriage. Anniversaries after the Golden Wedding are usually marked quietly by the couple, alone or with family members and/or very close friends—except, of course, for the Diamond Wedding, which certainly calls for a major celebration.

Possible celebrations for the Silver, Ruby, Golden, or Diamond Wedding are many; the longer the marriage, the grander the commemoration. The affair may be a seated dinner, a lavish cocktail buffet, a formal reception or tea—each requiring lovely engraved invitations—or a more informal gathering. At a seated dinner, the anniversary couple is seated together at the center of the head table, which is made to resemble the bride's table at their wedding. Surrounding them are any attending members of their original wedding party and their spouses as well as the couple's children and their husbands and wives and grandchildren old enough to attend.

For a formal reception, a receiving line is in order, with the hosts and the honorees (as well as the couple's children and their spouses—if not acting as hosts—who stand from oldest to youngest) lined up to greet the guests. If standing in a receiving line presents a problem for the couple, they may be seated against a pretty backdrop so that guests can pass by to extend their wishes for many more happy years.

The guest list should focus on close and longtime friends (many of whom may have attended the wedding or been a member of the wedding party), family members, and others to whom this marriage is meaningful. Details approximate the original wedding reception and feature a beautiful, white wedding cake (perhaps enhanced with silver, gold, ruby, roses, or orchids), which is cut ceremoniously by the couple; a corsage for the "bride" and a boutonniere for the "groom" and champagne toasts, begun by one of the hosting children or the best man, if he is present.

Accepting an invitation to a gala wedding anniversary celebration does require you to bring a present. Many times, however, the phrase "No gifts, please" is written on the invitation—a request that should be honored. Most couples at this stage of life are distributing, rather than accumulating, material possessions, and for this reason most gifts given are apt to be tokens, remembrances of affection, even if they are trinkets of silver or gold, as tradition decrees. Close friends or relatives might invite the couple to dinner or to the theater or send a gift certificate for flowers to be ordered at the couple's pleasure.

You may already have attended the Silver or Golden Wedding celebrations of your parents or grandparents. Your duty at such an occasion is to look and behave as charming as possible; to take your place and be cordial in the receiving line; to dine with impeccable manners and converse congenially at the head table; to assist when possible in making the celebration pleasant. A wonderful gift from you would be a small attention to the honorees, such as a personal favor requiring your time, the promise of which you could write on your pretty note paper, and the fulfillment of which you must not neglect.

The Professional Affairs

As you complete your education and begin a career, you will, perhaps early on, become involved in the social satellite affairs surrounding the climb up the ladder of success. Today's young women are often invited to attend, or even assist in arranging dinners, receptions, cocktail buffets, and other occasions honoring new members of a firm, those who earn major promotions, or retirees.

You should see your initial role as one of hostessing—introducing yourself, keeping conversations going, introducing executives with whom you may be better acquainted than they are with one another. You may even be asked to arrange and maintain a receiving line or work out dinner seating. This requires an understanding of and a respect for protocol—the ruling consideration of corporate, governmental, academic, and professional affairs.

As you learn protocol—the "pecking order," if you will—its rigid requirements may seem unfair, even heartless. But remember that modern-day business and society reward accomplishment and ability, and that these rules pave the way upward for anyone ready for the climb. Your participation, at any level, should be viewed as gracious and diplomatic.

The Golden Years

The Golden Years are a long way off for you—there is so much you want to do and enjoy in the near view. But I would like you to think about the future a little, because your consideration could help make those years brighter for others now and happier for yourself one day.

An increasing number of senior citizens are enjoying a full, healthy, prosperous retirement, filled with social and cultural activities, enjoyable travel, sports, and good family relationships. Younger family members should, however, keep in mind that elders need frequent and meaningful contacts and reliable help with physical, financial, and emotional concerns.

If you have grandparents or other older relatives and friends, you can make a difference in their lives by frequent calls and visits. It is nice, too, to arrange occasional small parties, little luncheons, or cozy afternoon teas for them and a few friends.

Time and effort thus devoted will not only make life's twilight more pleasant for them, but will shower gifts of love, wisdom, experience, and life perspective upon you. Be sure that your older family members are not left out on special occasions—birthdays, holidays, weddings, and other celebrations.

And if there is room in your life, your schedule, and your heart for others, consider volunteer work in a nursing or retirement home.

Now think a moment about your own future. Gradually begin to prepare not just with prudent financial planning, but also by protecting your health, by stretching your interests into cultural and educational areas that could become hobbies, avocations, even second careers, to fill voids now not envisioned. Predictions are that individuals of your generation might live well past their century mark. With so many decades ahead of you, your entire lifestyle could shift several times. So keep your interests varied, your friendships wide, rich, and interesting, your faith unwavering, and your approach to life flexible.

There is an old—and very true—adage that if a person does not cultivate younger friends, she will, if she lives long enough, have *no* friends. So during high school, and especially college, reach out to younger students to develop friendships and your own leadership qualities. Once you are established in the workplace, be generous in helping new employees. In volunteer work, the ability to attract, train, and enthuse new members is a wonderful asset. Your relations with your children will prosper in direct relation to your capacity to understand and accept their point of view. And when you begin to approach your own Golden Years, you will find that rapport with younger family members and friends will be your lifeline.

Make a little party, a celebration, of each meeting across the generations, and the rewards will be far greater than the effort!

The Exit from Life

Funerals are gatherings that many, especially the young, regard with a certain horror. If you find yourself filled with negative emotions and feel mystified and out of touch at a funeral, think of it (as I do) as a celebration of the life of the deceased and as a renewed dedication to life for those family members and friends who have gathered in respect and memory.

Final rites are essentially somber and sad, often excruciating for family members and others who have loved the deceased. The actual service is prescribed by the tenets and practices of the faith of the family and is an effort at comfort; it is usually brief.

During the activities and services commemorating the exit from life, decorous conduct and restraint in dress, behavior, and conversation are demanded, with few exceptions, throughout Western society.

Conversation with the bereaved is kept to a few comforting and well-chosen words (discussed in Chapter 6, p. 96). A visit to the funeral home (during prescribed hours when the family is receiving), either on the day or evening before the funeral, may be made to express your sympathy. If you are a very close friend, you may wish to call on the family at their home. Do not be disappointed, however, if the friend who answers the door advises you that the family is not receiving visitors. Simply leave your calling card upon which you write "my deepest sympathy," and do not call again. Either at the funeral home or in the vestibule of the church there will be a visitor's register, which you sign with your full name prefaced by the title "Miss."

Unless the funeral service is stated in the obituaries to be private, you will certainly make every effort to attend, for your friends are in need of the comfort of your presence. Arrive approximately thirty minutes before the stated hour of the service. You may sit on either side of the church, chapel, funeral home, or private home, and on any pew with the exception of the first several rows, which are reserved for family members and honorary pallbearers. Those who are closest to the deceased sit nearer the front and aisles. Others are kind enough to sit nearer the back and sides. Often there are ushers to assist with seating. When this is the case, you do not take the usher's arm as you do at a wedding.

There may or may not be a processional of the honorary pallbearers, the casket bearing the deceased, the widow or widower with a family member, or the parents, followed by the other family members. Often those seated stand during the processional, both as it enters and exits. You should not depart until all of the family members have exited after the processional.

When you are a very close friend, you will no doubt wish to join the family at the cemetery for the graveside service. To do so, you will join the processional by car. Do not linger after this short service. Make your departure before the actual burial, even though the bereaved and the immediate family members may remain behind.

According to the customs of the community and the wishes of the family, mourners may or may not return to the family's home after the service. It is a warm and comforting feeling, however, when the bereaved reenter their home and are met by loving and caring friends who have prepared a buffet for the comfort of all who wish to console them. By all means, return to the home if you are a close friend, but do not remain long—thirty minutes to an hour is a comfortable time, after which the family will want to be alone together.

For some, often well-known public figures, a memorial service is held several weeks after the funeral. And a family may wish to hold a private funeral followed by a public memorial service or requiem mass. Although these later services are spared the immediate emotionalism so prevalent at the time of the funeral, they are nonetheless formal occasions, and you must abide by the code of conduct set forth for the funeral itself. Following the wishes of the deceased, many of these occasions (even funeral services) are quite joyous in tone, as are the social gatherings that follow—each a celebration of life.

In addition to your respectful presence, a floral tribute (unless the family requests none) or a gift to the deceased's favorite charity, and a comforting letter of condolence (described in Chapter 7), there are many gracious things a friend can do to help: bring meals for family and out-of-town guests, answer the telephone or doorbell, and otherwise assist with the operation of the household. Close friends may invite the family to an informal meal in the days following the funeral, assist in caring for children, and make themselves available over an extended period to help solve problems and to assuage loneliness.

Within a short period of time, you will receive a handwritten note from the bereaved or a close family member thanking you for flowers or contributions to a selected charity. A handwritten acknowledgment will be sent you also in gratitude for your letter of condolence. Friends, you see, are never so dear as in a time of grief. Be certain that you are that kind of friend.

As you mature and gain life perspective, you will gradually come to an acceptable—and accepting—attitude toward death as a part of life. The fortunate, especially those with a strong religious faith, may recognize it as the final great adventure. I have spoken with enlightened older people who declare that the discoveries of modern science and our present comprehension of the endless universe give a glorious reality to former visions of heaven.

Candles Along Memory Lane

Having encapsulated life's special occasions, we see that they, alone, provide substantial reasons for a knowledge of etiquette and the social graces. What better stages—both spiritual and social—than these, then, upon which to practice all of the teachings found within the pages of *Finishing Touches*.

Special occasions and the fetes for the landmarks in life are the "bright spots" in the routine of daily living. As candles along memory lane, shedding a soft light upon happy times, they will help to keep the things you want to remember from being lost in the darkness of forgetfulness.

PART FIVE

The Elegant Touches

CHAPTER 13

The Gleam of Silver

Though many people today entertain handsomely in public places, dining reaches its ultimate perfection in the setting of an elegant, superbly accessorized home. Even the most exclusive clubs and expensive restaurants fall short of the splendor of a private dinner table. It is the setting for the most sparkling conversation and the most original and delicious menu. An invitation to dine in someone's home is a high compliment, to be treasured and appropriately reciprocated. Having and using beautiful things lift life's routine out of the "humdrum," and she who celebrates the highlights of passage with appropriate elegance becomes an artist.

As a young woman matures, she must learn to extend the aura of her personal beauty to her surroundings. Even in this era of Women's Liberation, with its wider opportunities and aspects, the developing woman treasures her femininity and visualizes herself as a charming hostess, surrounded by and using beautiful things and possessing the domestic skills necessary to create an attractive environment for family and friends, with herself in the starring role.

So enviable a position must be earned. Considerable knowledge of quality, proper usage, and tradition is required, and the learning process should begin early on. Observing and becoming involved in important celebrations at home is the natural first step. In this chapter you will learn how to acquire, appreciate—and care for—those amenities that create a gracious environment for your home entertaining. I encourage you to familiarize yourself

305

with various patterns of silver, china, crystal, and linens long before the pressures of an engagement and approaching marriage make immediate choices imperative.

The Noble Art of Setting the Table

At a well-set table, senses other than the taste buds are aroused. The grandest cuisine holds no appeal in an unattractive setting, yet a beautifully laid table can elevate the simplest of food to a festive experience.

In preparing to become an artist at setting a beautiful table, it will be necessary for you to become acquainted with the elements required: silver, china, crystal, and linen. Although creativity by no means demands that these basic elements be "the real thing," the real thing is ultimately worth the investment of both patience and money. Meanwhile, you can experiment with the elements of the table using your mother's or grandmother's accoutrements, whether they are the real thing or delightful table appointments you discover about the house and in the kitchen cupboards. Family and friends will savor the originality, charm, and style you bring to the family and company dining table.

The Sterling Story

For over 4,000 years, from its first appearance in and around the Mediterranean, silver has been used by each successive civilization as an embellishment for its homes, churches, persons, and even horses. Originally, it was not used for dining but just for adornment and ornamentation. The first silver eating implement—the silver spoon—appeared in Roman and Anglo-Saxon times. It represented tangible evidence of wealth. It soon became popular for the village housewife to take her carefully hoarded silver coins to the silversmith to be made into a few treasured teaspoons.

The word *sterling* is actually an abbreviation of "Easterling," a group of merchant traders who—for commercial purposes—moved to England during the thirteenth century. The Easterlings emigrated from the eastern part of Europe, known today as Germany. Trade with them was prized, as they paid for their goods with pieces of silver containing uniformly high, fine (pure) silver content. England began to appreciate the unvarying quality of the silver the Easterlings used and adopted their standard.

A standard regulation for sterling silver has been recognized since 1335, when King Edward III of England decreed that silver must be of uniform quality. In 1697 the English established the sterling standard and made it mandatory for the silversmith to put his trademark adjacent to the sterling mark.

Although not mandatory in America until 1907 with the passage of the National Stamping Law, many elite silver manufacturers had already adopted the .925 sterling standard before the enactment of the law. The term "sterling silver" in the United States means 92.5 percent pure (fine) silver combined with 7.5 percent copper alloy to give strength and durability. Some European silver, however, is stamped "800 Standard" indicating 80 percent pure silver and 20 percent alloy.

Silver Plating

In 1742 the first variation of solid silver—silver plating—originated in Sheffield, England. This, of course, made silver more affordable. Silver plating means that a thin coat of silver is applied over another metal. Originally, this meant sandwiching a sheet of copper or nickel between two sheets of thinly-hammered sterling silver; the metals were then heated to the point at which they fused. The original "Sheffield" silver plating was done by this method, and its makers, just as those of solid silver, had their own guild and registered trademarks. Nowadays, silver plate is not produced by the original method, and, as a result, original Sheffield plate—with its much heavier silver coating—is valued for its high silver content as well as its antique status.

Another process of applying solid silver to another metal appeared in 1840: electroplating. The piece to be plated, usually made of nickel alloy or sometimes German silver (not silver at all, but an alloy of nickel, copper, and zinc) is bathed in an electrically charged pure silver solution, which becomes attracted to it and deposited over it. The strength of the silver solution, the length of time the article remains in it, and the number of times the process is repeated determine the durability of the article. Reinforcement with silver inlays or overlays in places that will receive wear also adds to the life of the piece. (Sheffield adopted the electroplating method in 1850 and refers to it as "New Sheffield.")

In 1842, Christofle, the famous French silversmithing firm, revolutionized the industry when it purchased the patent rights to the newly discovered method of applying silver and gold onto metal by electroplating.

As an alternative to sterling silver, the best plate selected from reliable manufacturers will last virtually indefinitely, look almost as nice as silver (although, to the educated eye, it possesses a slightly gray cast as opposed to the "silver" color of sterling), and is less costly. The best of quality plate, although by no means a substitute for sterling, is desirable over poorly manufactured silver.

Vermeil

Gold has been the most treasured of the noble metals since the beginning of time and naturally made its way to the dining table.

Under the rule of the seventeenth- and eighteenth-century French kings, metalworkers began to cover more traditional silver with a thin layer of gold and created vermeil.

Unlike silver, vermeil retards tarnish indefinitely, yet it must be cleaned. The French recommend a soft cloth dampened with white wine or champagne. Because of the delicateness of gold, vermeil should never be subjected to coarse cloths or abrasive polishes.

Today gold is electroplated onto utensils made of silver plate, bronze, brass, or stainless steel, but only a layer of gold over sterling silver is rightfully called vermeil. When applied to any other metal, the process produces "gold plate." Small accents of vermeil are in far better taste than a lavish display, which may appear pretentious.

Stainless Steel

A wonderfully serviceable material grew out of armament for World War II. The product, stainless steel, quickly found its way into homes and onto the dining table as flatware. There it became symbolic of a kind of freedom—relief from silver polishing—to many postwar women.

The first stainless steel flatware was frankly boring, fashioned as it was in plain, utilitarian, unimaginative patterns, poorly balanced, finished, and sized. Its popularity, however, grew enormously because of its minimal cost when compared to sterling or plate, and because of its strength, durability, resistance to food stains, and dishwasher safety. Gradually there developed considerable aesthetic improvements, so that now many manufacturers are making stainless steel flatware with elaborate detailing and handsome finishing and polish. Even adaptations of long-admired patterns of sterling silver are now available.

Many young women today are selecting good quality stainless steel and expect to use it for the early years of their marriages and later as everyday place settings. It is appropriate for use in the breakfast nook or breakfast room, on the terrace, at a summer cottage, and it offers the continuing advantages of easy care and comparative economy, and usually the convenience of open stock replacement or additional purchases. While stainless steel is not to be equated with sterling silver, it has a place both as a temporary substitute for the real thing and as a permanent resource in certain situations.

Whatever the ultimate role of the stainless steel service, it must, like sterling, plate, or vermeil, be selected with my three Q's as a guide: *quality* of metal, *quality* of design, and *quality* of craftsmanship. There are now important guidelines for stainless steel, with a numbering system similar to that of sterling. A European alloy comprised of 18 parts chrome to 8 parts nickel reads $^{18}/_8$ as the standard for stainless steel just as $^{925}/_{75}$ is standard for sterling silver.

The manufacturers of top quality stainless steel flatware proudly stamp their symbols and names on the back, guaranteeing metal quality. Because they use no nickel, makers of cheaper sets are not allowed to use the standard stamp and rarely use their names. This absence of identifying stamp and signature should warn the purchaser to beware—the absence of nickel causes the pieces to rust if allowed to stand in water and limits design, craftsmanship, and finish.

Flatware and Hollowware

The term "flatware" or "flat silver" is applied to those personal utensils with which we eat or serve: knives, forks, spoons, ladles. You often hear a bride say she has selected her "flatware" pattern, meaning she has selected her favorite pattern in silver for eating and serving utensils.

The term "hollowware" includes articles in which food or drink is conveyed or from which it is served—bowls, trays, tea sets, goblets, pitchers—and a range of decorative pieces such as candelabra and vases. And then there are "fancy goods." As the name suggests, these are items of a more personalized or specialized nature—silver picture frames, key chains, fountain pens, pencils, mirrors, paperweights.

Silver in Our World Today

As it has been throughout the ages, sterling silver or fine plate continues today to be an heirloom of permanent value. Generation after generation, sterling silver has been the traditional gift from the bride's parents to their daughter. It is still one of the most meaningful and appropriate gifts of all—and one of the longest-lasting!

All of the decorative movements produced their own silver patterns, many of which are still available today. You will find Neoclassical motifs, for example, and Early American—the kind of strong, simple patterns created by Revolutionary War hero and silversmith Paul Revere. Designs representative of the American Colonial period exhibit the Puritan influence of restraint and austerity, as well as an appreciation of purity of form. Pieces of this period are especially elegant when graced with one's engraved family crest or monogram. Personally, I find myself drawn to the rather ornate, French-inspired Rococo and Baroque patterns. You may find you prefer Victorian, Art Deco, Art Nouveau, or Contemporary designs.

Sterling Choices

Sterling silver—known as "The Queen of Metals"—is eternal. The usual time for a young woman to think seriously about acquiring silver is when she becomes engaged to be married. In fact, choosing silver and china and crystal patterns is one of the rituals of the engagement period.

Times, however, are changing. Many young women are delaying marriage in order to launch a career. Most soon have their own quarters and well-paid positions and wish to live with a certain style throughout their "bachelorette" years. The acquisition of a basic service in sterling silver is a wise and enjoyable investment and a smart foot forward.

Even teenaged girls frequently begin collecting "hope chest" silver. Because of the high prices of silver today, a service large enough to serve guests is costly and many brides do not receive complete services. Therefore, the pieces or place settings that may have been received as gifts from family while growing up are much prized in the honeymoon household.

Because it is a major investment, and the accumulation of enough place settings for a dinner party can take a long time, I feel it is never too soon to begin. Once you decide it is time to start your silver service, master my Ten Sterling Tips before making a selection. After all, sterling silver is for a lifetime.

TEN STERLING TIPS

1. Stop to study before you select and shop. Discover the period of design you prefer, then look at, touch, and hold patterns of that period.

2. Bear in mind that the degree of ornateness should complement the china and crystal you will choose. This does not mean, however, that you must select them at the same time, for your taste will be consistent—you will naturally be attracted by designs of the same period, or complementary periods, as you begin to study china and crystal.

3. An ornate design is more difficult to clean than a simple one. However, simpler ones show scratches and wear more. If you like an ornate pattern, then by all means select it. Your fondness for it will offset the polishing time it requires.

4. Begin with a collection of demitasse spoons, each of a different pattern you like. "Live" with these awhile and before you realize it, one will become your favorite. Voilà! Your pattern is chosen.

5. If your mother's or grandmother's pattern pleases you, consider selecting it as your own. You might begin by acquiring pieces they do not have so that when you are given theirs, you will have a variety of service and eating utensils. And, should you live in the same city or town, you may borrow from one another for large parties.

6. Consider purchasing antique silver, which, according to experts, is a better investment at the time of resale. You can have the fun of shopping for it at silver shows and sales, and you may find unusual serving and eating pieces to add flair to your dinner table. The craftsmanship of old silver is rarely duplicated today.

7. Select silver from a maker or manufacturer of undisputed reputation.

8. Look for decorative design that is pleasing in its arrangement of line, form, proportion, and finish—and appropriate for its intended use. The decoration should follow the line of the piece or be placed at points that are structurally important, such as the base or the top.

9. Do not settle for less than perfection of finish—forks whose tines are smoothly polished, knives whose silver handle is

joined perfectly and smoothly to the stainless steel blade with no gap between, and so on.

10. If you decide to begin building a silver "hope chest" or sterling trousseau as a teenager or young career woman, it is wise to acquire a silver chest of ample size to accommodate a full service. Because silver oxidizes, the finish tarnishes unless stored in a properly lined case, and the silver must be polished frequently even if never used. Having all pieces together also prevents loss and provides a carrying case should you wish to place your silver and other valuables in some safer place while you vacation.

The Place Setting

"Silver" is the popular term used to describe all the utensils used at the dining table. But the term refers more precisely to the group of pieces provided each individual diner, in America called a "place setting" and in Europe called *le couvert* or the "cover."

The "basic" American flatware setting consists of five pieces: teaspoon, place fork, place knife, place spoon (which can be used for soup, dessert, cereal, or berries), and an individual butter spreader. To this, additional items are added based upon the social usage of the day and the budget of the purchaser. There may be two or three dozen different shapes included in a typical pattern today.

The main difference between the American place setting and the European "cover" is size, particularly the sizes of the dinner knife and fork. European pieces are generally somewhat larger, a discrepancy sometimes exaggerated by the American tendency to choose a "luncheon-size" knife and fork even at dinner. With the return of formality in this country, the disparity of sizes is diminishing, though a counter trend is also evident as many prestigious silver makers today offer a "place-size" pair (between the dinner- and the luncheon-size). If your budget allows only one size, the larger one should be chosen.

In addition to size, you need to decide between four-tined (pronged) or three-tined (Old English style) forks; plain or pistol-handled knives; slipper-shaped or pistol knife blades; hollow-handled or solid silver (flat) butter spreaders; and, finally, the order in which you wish to build place settings.

Once you have selected your pattern, decided between the Continental or

American dinner-, luncheon-, or place-size knife and fork, and made other choices, proceed in an organized fashion to build your sterling trousseau. In order for you to do so, I have designed The Sterling System.

The Sterling System, Part 1

Pointers for Perfecting the Place Setting

1. Begin the place setting with the following pieces: dinner (or Continental) knife and fork, salad fork (which may double as dessert fork), soup spoon (the long, oval, boat-shaped type which can also be used for dessert, berries, or cereal, called the "place" spoon by many American silver manufacturers), teaspoon, and individual butter spreader. If iced tea or iced coffee is desired, include the iced beverage spoon. This basic place setting can be enlarged as the years pass, the manner of entertaining develops, and the budget expands.

2. When possible, add the luncheon or place knife, which may be used as a salad knife. This acquisition will make it possible to design a menu with a first course of soup, the entrée, and then a salad, with all the pieces of silver flatware placed on the table when it is set. Only when it is dessert time and the table is cleared will it be necessary to wash pieces already used—the oval soup spoon and/or the salad fork—to be used as dessert implements.

3. For later additions, I suggest dessert forks rather than additional salad forks to do double duty. Then choose cream soup spoons (longer-handled, round-bowl soup spoon) to allow variety in the choice of soup and also to avoid having to use the boat-type spoon for both soup and dessert. These lovely additions bring the service up to a "full place setting" and allow for setting the table with every needed implement—from soup to dessert—prior to the meal. The dessert spoon and fork are positioned above the place plate and remain there until the dessert course is served. The hostess now can also set a lovely luncheon or breakfast table using the smaller pieces, with dainty, smaller plates and lighter menus.

4. The next additions to be considered are the fish knife and fork, which, naturally, must be added in pairs. These items can be found at estate sales or you may purchase new copies of the

pearl-handled fish sets of old. Now the fish course can be added to the menu or be served as the entrée with its proper utensils.

5. The two pieces to complete the formal place setting are the cocktail fork and the small, round bouillon spoon. Now a seafood cocktail as a "starter," an *amuse-gueule,* or an "appetizer" can begin the menu, and bouillon, too, may be served (in a one- or two-handled bouillon cup) in lieu of a cream or clear soup (in the rimmed soup plate or cream soup bowl). The oyster fork may be added or substituted for the cocktail fork, depending upon the kinds of menus you envision.

6. An extra is the dessert knife, which is positioned above the dessert spoon and fork in the formal setting. It is used to cut fruit—poached pear, or baked apple, for example. Teamed with the dessert fork, it can accompany the cheese course. It can also be used as a buffet knife to cut and spread *pâté* or cheese served as *hors d'oeuvre,* or teamed with a salad fork for other small appetizers, or to spread clotted cream and jam on teatime scones.

7. As coffee is not served at the dining table during a formal dinner (rather, in the living room in demitasse cups), demitasse spoons need not match your pattern—nor need they match one another. They can be family heirlooms, "collectibles," or travel souvenirs.

The Flat Silver Service Pieces

Sterling serving pieces—utensils other than those used by the diner for eating—are also necessary. Your plan for acquiring them should parallel that of the eating utensils so menus may be designed around the silver available. As the serving flatware need not match the diner's flatware, you might choose antique silver—indeed a pleasant shopping adventure and a good investment.

THE STERLING SYSTEM, PART 2

Pointers for Selecting Flat Silver Serving Pieces

1. There are certain basic flat silver service pieces that enable the hostess to serve a variety of menus for both family and friends. These include: one table or vegetable spoon with a solid bowl

and another with a pierced bowl for juicy foods, as well as a cold meat or buffet fork. Until the larger, more formal service fork and spoon are added, the vegetable spoon and cold meat fork can be teamed when both are required to serve from a platter or bowl. They work well, too, on the buffet table—either paired or separately. A gravy ladle will also be needed as the vegetable spoon cannot serve gravy without mishaps. Additionally, a sugar spoon (often called a sugar shell because its bowl is beautifully shaped like a shell) will be required for crystallized sugar at the table. The butter serving knife should be included in the basic serving set as it remains on the butter serving dish throughout the meal.

2. Salad can be placed on plates in the kitchen and served to each diner until a salad set, consisting of a large salad fork and spoon, is added. At that time, the large salad bowl will be added to the buffet or family table, or passed by a servant to each diner. The salad set may be carved of handsome olive wood attached to hollow sterling handles or may be made entirely of sterling. Should you select all sterling, though, care must be taken to rinse and wash the pieces immediately after use. I prefer them, however, as they can easily double as an additional serving set for a large buffet when tossed salad is not a part of the menu. Along with the salad set, add the flat server (sometimes referred to as a tomato server), an artfully pierced serving spoon available in a variety of shapes and sizes used to serve a variety of congealed salads, aspics, *pâtés,* and even cold baked chicken, tureens, and such.

3. Next, in order that condiments and garnishes may be added to the menu, I suggest adding the two-tined olive/pickle fork, which may also be used as a butter pick, and the three-tined lemon fork for serving lemon slices or wedges for beverages or garnishes. As the lemon fork will be used in the service of hot tea as well, sugar tongs are necessary at this time to serve lump sugar (the only correct sugar for teacups). The all-purpose cheese knife should be included, making it possible to serve cheese as the *hors d'oeuvre.* A jelly server will replace the teaspoon for serving jelly.

4. Although desserts can always be plated in the kitchen and served, think of the festivity of a birthday cake aflame with candles, cut and served at the table. Begin with the cake server,

which not only cuts the cake but is also large enough to slide under a piece and support it en route to the dessert plate. A cake knife, on the other hand, can successfully cut, but is not as graceful in serving. A cake breaker is the alternative for a soft, airy, sponge or angel food cake (which would be compressed by either the cake knife or cake server). The pie knife/server beautifully slices and serves fruit and cream pies, or quiches for that matter. For large tarts or large cake squares, a pastry server adds variety.

5. Important extras to be considered once the serving pieces outlined so far are in place are: a cream/sauce ladle (smaller than the gravy ladle and used for cream sauces, salad dressings, and special sauces for vegetables, meats, and desserts) and a soup ladle.

6. An investment (not only in silver, but in dining ceremony as well) is the silver roast carving set. The knife blade is made of stainless steel so that it may be sharpened for slicing, and both the knife and fork have a hone-guard to support the fingers during carving. The steak carving set is an option also, but as it is too small for roasts and fowl, the roast carving set is preferable.

7. The addition of the fish serving set allows the presentation of a whole fish at the table. The set consists of a large serving knife and fork and will allow the host to debone the fish at the table. Also, the set may be used to transfer the portioned pieces of fish to the dinner plate. These are exquisitely pierced and shaped pieces, with surfaces large enough to support the tender fish without breaking it, and the knife is designed in such a manner as to make an easy insertion, and then, along with the fork, to lift the bone from the fish.

8. Finally, there are dozens of useful, yet not always necessary, serving pieces: a punch ladle; a variety of cheese servers (a cheese knife with two prongs on the end for slicing and picking up hard cheese, pie-shaped cutter and server for medium cheese, cheese fork for soft cheese, cheese scoop for crumbly cheese); ice tongs; grape scissors for snipping small clusters of grapes from the large bunch; small mustard spoons for serving a variety of mustards from mustard "pots"; berry serving spoon equipped with a raised rim to prevent berries from rolling off during serving; condiment "scoops" (spoons) for jams, jellies,

relishes; *petits fours* tongs for small iced cakes and pastries, bonbon or nut spoon; *canapé* server; bottle opener; long-handled olive spoons and forks for retrieving olives, onions, and cherries from tall jars; and the vermeil and silver caviar ladle.

Sterling Conversation Pieces

For the antique collector, the search for the asparagus fork, asparagus server, long-handled dressing spoon, toast server, waffle server, bacon serving fork, ice cream slicer, ice cream server, or jelly cake server can lead to many serendipitous discoveries. Remember that an item of silver need not always be used as it was intended. Originality and creativity are permitted! You may also wish to add the following to your place settings over the years: sauce spoons, escargot forks, escargot tongs, lobster forks (or picks), marrow spoons, pastry forks, ice cream forks, fruit knives and forks, and vermeil and silver caviar palettes, or "gilded" egg spoons.

Caring for Silver

Silver is made to be used every day. It grows more beautiful with use, and the more service it sees the less it needs to be polished. It should, however, be used, cleaned, polished, and stored properly. The tiny, almost microscopic, scratches caused by frequent use ultimately join together to form a beautiful, soft finish called the "patina." A fine patina bespeaks loving care over the years and is often referred to as the "butler finish."

Silver does have the disadvantage of tarnishing as it reacts with the sulfur, oxygen, and pollutants in the air. It will need to be polished, but only when and where it needs it, as each polishing takes away a trace of silver.

If you are fortunate enough to have a large number of place settings, rotate the settings and frequently used serving pieces so that each piece is used and washed. In this way no piece will "outshine" the other and they will gain their patina together.

The "Silver Spoon" Heritage

The silver spoon has become all but synonymous with the good life—not implying just affluence but also a background of elegance and tradition, an environment in which beauty, comfort, and grace will be available.

318

Civilization's long evolution from the simple stone knife to the elegant shining silver knife and fork is representative of the striving of the human spirit toward beauty in all phases of life. Consider that your mother, in insisting on a well-set table, gracious mealtime manners, and pleasant conversation at the table, is continuing this civilizing effort in the face of fast food and plastic or paper plates, even when she is weary. It is to your benefit to understand and support the maintaining of the niceties of life, and it will also give you a head start to creating your own lovely home when the time comes.

Consider the many-splendored roles silver will play when choosing yours. Dream that it will someday bring ice cream to the lips of your child on his or her first birthday and that it will stir coffee in fragile porcelain cups at your parents' or grandparents' golden wedding anniversary. Properly cared for, your silver will be burnished by experience and will be as beautiful for your own golden wedding anniversary as it is today.

CHAPTER 14

The Sheen of Fine China

Although sterling flatware is likely to be the most expensive investment and the longest-lasting table accessory you will own, it is more often china that steals the scene in the drama of dining. Its color and pattern set the style for the tabletop picture and create aesthetic excitement, leading the diner gently into the pleasurable experience of dining.

Though it is usual to choose a china pattern upon becoming engaged, there is no need to wait for that occasion to begin acquiring pieces. Imagine the delight of serving tea to sorority sisters from the bone china tea set brought back from your high school graduation trip to England. Search out antique service plates and patterns to complement the family china that will be passed on to you one day. An eclectic combination of pieces begun in your teens and early twenties will express individuality and personality to your first sophisticated dinner party guests.

The Mystery of Fine China

In order for you to work excitedly, even adventurously, in combining tableware, you must know the limits of acceptability. Basic to this important understanding is a clear knowledge of the difference between porcelain (fine china) and earthenware (pottery which is simpler and, therefore, less formal). The romantic story of how exquisite plates, cups, and saucers came to be from the crude objects early men and women made of mud to hold their food and drink is fascinating. As civilization progressed, the peoples who were the most advanced in the creation of beautiful objects for use in their daily lives were also the most civilized in all other matters.

319

Ceramic objects for personal use, especially for dining, were made by the ancient Egyptians and later by the early Greeks. The Romans, too, had earthenware receptacles, some of fine quality.

Meanwhile, on the other side of the world, artisans of the artistically advanced Chinese were refining their pottery-making into a fine art form. By the ninth century A.D., they were making the glorious translucent, chip-resistant quality pieces known as porcelain. At first available only to royalty and the wealthy nobility, but gradually acquired by rich commercial families, porcelain became the rage. European artisans sought desperately to break down the formula and, as they worked, developed some attractive spin-offs, including *pâte tendre* (soft porcelain) or French porcelain.

All across Europe exciting things began happening in this new-to-the-West art form. The discovery that kaolin (a unique white clay that gives porcelain its translucence and strength) was the secret ingredient and the existence of important kaolin mines in France gave the production of porcelain on the European continent a great impetus. Great pottery-making houses, many of which are today the ultimate in china making, were founded to meet the growing demand for the finest dinnerware.

China Choices

Choosing china is one of the pleasantest duties of housekeeping—for the bride planning her new home, the young career woman creating an appropriate background for independent living, the college student adorning a first off-campus apartment, or the seasoned chatelaine finally in a position to upgrade lifestyle components. China is an extremely personal accessory, a reflection of the owner's taste, knowledgeability, and flair. The use of color, design, and the taste to arrange a setting is itself an expression of art.

One of the secrets of a successful choice is a sense of the appropriate—dining should be a comfortable, harmonious segment of everyday life. Although you may enjoy self-expression through ornate designs, you may find that elaborate china imposes bothersome restrictions on the designs of accompanying linens, even fresh flower centerpieces.

Decoration is a personal matter, of course, within the parameters of grace, harmony, and good taste. Studying fine old china is one way to develop your own taste. Another is to seriously view the patterns, shapes, and designs of major china manufacturers both in the United States and other countries.

Because many China manufacturers reproduce and re-create wonderful old patterns, it is possible to have a royal table today if you wish! Or you may turn to modern-day designers from the field of fashion who have stamped their style on contemporary china with clean, futuristic lines.

Shopping for china can be the headiest of all the shopping excursions upon which a young woman embarks: The color, the entrancing designs, the fascinating shapes are festive and alluring, provocative and tempting. But the very qualities that exhilarate you on first glance can eventually cloy, especially if, as is true for most of us, you will have but one service of fine china. Vibrant color and busy design can limit your own creativity in arranging tables. Keep in mind, a china that is attractive, even glamorous, at a one-time exposure, could be tiresome and difficult to cope with on a day-by-day, year-by-year basis. Cost must also be a consideration; china is breakable. These realities are presented not to urge you to settle for a lackluster, utilitarian pattern, but to urge you to take many things into consideration before you choose. China should be a reflection of and an inspiration for your own creativity.

Decoding the Family of Potteries

The language and terminology of the varieties of "china" from which you will ultimately select your formal and informal patterns are complex. You must develop an intelligent "eye" in order to make wise decisions as you confront this vast array.

Whether simple pottery, earthenware, stoneware, bone china or fine china, each shares the basic element—clay. The quality and longevity—and the price—of each are based on the type and quality of clay used, the additional elements and sophistication of the formula, the manner in which the pieces are fired, the method of decoration, and the complexity of the manufacturing process. The families of pottery from which you may choose fall into the following four categories:

1. Earthenware. Made of potter's clay, earthenware usually contains lime and sand, to which other ingredients are added for strength and color. It is fired at relatively low temperatures and since it is porous, it must be covered with a fine glaze to hold liquid. Earthenware in its many varieties comprises perhaps the largest group among the types of potteries. It is more durable and versatile than simple pottery and retains its color and decoration better, making it a favorite of talented craftsmen. Colorful earthenware offers the perfect escape from the formality of bone or fine china and brightens the breakfast, luncheon, and supper table. It must, however, be treated kindly to prevent chipping, and it can become crazed and discolored by high temperatures.

2. Stoneware. Stoneware is nonporous and heavy, made of a mixture of clays, including silicon clay, which, although much more refined than the clays used for earthenware, are much less refined and elegant than those used for porcelain. It is fired at high temperatures, becoming almost as hard as stone—hence its name. It is highly resistant to chipping and may be placed safely in the oven or dishwasher. It sometimes has a brownish or blue-gray hue, and although it does not require a glaze, one is often added for decorative purposes.

3. Bone China. A hard porcelain formula is used, but animal bone-ash is substituted for feldspar to create the exceptionally stark, pure white body of bone china. First fired at 1,250 degrees centigrade, it is almost as hard as hard porcelain and cannot be scratched by steel. It is the most chip-resistant of the potteries, and can be made quite thin and finely detailed without much loss of durability. It is glossy and lapidary in appearance.

4. Fine China. The crème de la crème of the family of potteries, hard porcelain (or fine china) is composed of kaolin (fine, white clay), feldspar, and quartz, which may be combined in a variety of ways with various admixtures. Its body and glaze are composed of the same substance. It is first fired at extremely high temperatures (1,300 to 1,450 degrees centigrade). It is more expensive than soft porcelain or bone china because the "biscuit" (the original paste) must be fired at a heat much more intense than is needed for other clays. Therefore, breakage is apt to be greater and colors are more difficult to apply. The body of fine china is often a dazzling bluish-white or it can be pure white or ivory-white depending on the formula. It is the hardest of all and has a glasslike sheen that is impervious to acid. When broken or chipped, it shows a smooth fracture and will not absorb dirt or food particles.

China Designs

Exploration and study will reveal your preferences of patterns and shapes. Designs fall into four general types: an allover pattern; a geometric or banded pattern encircling the rim of the plate; scenics and landscapes centered in the plate (often teamed with a banded border); and a scattered design, often of flowers, birds, butterflies.

The shapes of plates differ, too. Basically there are two: the *coupe*—a contemporary shape without a shoulder, flat in the center and rolled up slightly at the rim, simply concave with no inside ridge—and the *traditional*—a flat shape considered more formal, with a raised shoulder, or rim. These shapes are varied further by the manner in which the rim is finished or designed—perfectly round and even, gentle curves and scallops, petalled or fluted, notched systematically, or geometrically divided into four-, six-, or eight-sided shapes. Cups show particular diversity, from simple straight sides to the curvier, flat-bottomed, or slightly raised on a small rim.

To Match or Mix-and-Match

A complete set of matching china was once indispensable to a hostess and was purchased by the piece or in place settings—dinner plate, salad plate, bread-and-butter plate, a cup, and a saucer. If the bridal pattern she chose were discontinued, she would be devastated! Today, a matched set of china is considered a bore, leading only to a table of little interest. To mix-and-match is an acceptable and fashionable style by which a hostess may express her personality and individuality. By mix-and-match I do not refer to tossing together an odd lot of china remnants from various sets, but rather an artfully blended array of compatible design and color.

The cardinal rule is that all of the plates (or bowls) for any one course *must* match. Patterns may, however, differ from course to course. Of utmost importance aesthetically is that the china for each course must go well together based upon scale, color, texture, pattern, and shape.

Scale. The size of the pieces used together for any one course and throughout a meal must be harmonious.

Color. Colors must match, blend, harmonize, or complement.

Texture. Pottery and earthenware—opaque, usually thick, heavy, coarse-grained—do not mix well with porcelain and bone china—translucent, thin, light, fine-grained—because they differ too greatly in texture. Hard and soft porcelain and bone china are all basically alike in texture and weight and mix well. Stoneware—almost a cross between earthenware and porcelain—can often be combined with pottery or porcelain and bone china with pleasing results.

Pattern. Patterns can also be mixed, depending, of course, upon the character of their design. Plain china or banded patterns are most versatile and can be anything but dull when used as mixers with allover, loose or scattered, scenic or landscape patterns. Different plain patterns should not be used together, nor should different banded or allover patterns.

Shape. Perfectly round shapes mix well with the geometric shapes, and petalled and fluted bowls mix well with geometric shapes, if the number of flutes or petals equals the number of sides on the plate. Scalloped, notched, or gently curved plates mix well with round shapes, but not with the geometric or with one another. Coupe shapes should not be mixed with flat plates with shoulders.

Many manufacturers of fine dinnerware encourage mixing and matching, and their professional design boards have coordinated patterns designed to mix freely and give an individualized look.

In addition to the aesthetic qualities and the question of how it will fit in with your lifestyle and your own personality, there are some practical points the wise buyer of fine or bone china must evaluate.

First, and very important, is this pattern "open stock"—available continually for additions and replacements? Second, is it dishwasher-safe? If not, ask yourself if you will be willing to hand-wash each piece after preparing and serving each dinner party. Third, ascertain the relative strength of a particular china. Check for imperfections in structure, such as awkward cup handles, saucers in which the cup slides about because there is no socket, plate edges that feel rough or sharp to the touch and, of course, flaws in the body or imperfections in decorative work.

Most brides who have sizable weddings choose two sets of dinnerware— a fine or bone china and a less expensive second set. Although many receive only a limited number of pieces in the expensive service, it is nice to have a start.

While a second set should be much less costly and less fragile, it should be as pretty and as nice as means allow. This service should also be chosen with an eye toward versatility and simplicity so that it does not become tiresome. With such qualities, it will serve handsomely for all occasions, until the "best" china is accumulated and even afterward—especially when small children are involved.

Some brides select a third set of very inexpensive crockery for use in a breakfast nook or on the terrace. This set may well be bright and busily decorated since it will be used only in informal settings in which it will not "fight" with other table appointments or room decor. Besides, crockery chips and breaks easily and is apt to be replaced by an equally inexpensive successor before it becomes displeasing.

A Wardrobe of China

Just as a clothing wardrobe begins with the basics, so does a wardrobe of china. Patterns or combinations of patterns should be selected only after you have an idea of the period you like best, and in conjunction with your choice of a sterling pattern. Take along a piece of your silver when you go shopping for china. Crystal, which I discuss in Chapter 15, should also be a part of the total selection process. However, as I said before, if you fall in love with one before the other, you need not worry, for one always gravitates toward the same or similar periods, or toward different periods that complement one another.

Now it is time to buy! My motto is to place plates before place settings. With enough dinner plates you can always hostess a buffet—whether in your college apartment or first city flat. So study my system, The China Choices, below.

THE CHINA CHOICES

Pointers for Perfecting the Place Setting

1. I recommend that you acquire fine china not by purchasing the usual matching five-piece place setting, but instead by collecting it by course.

2. Informal entertaining often lends itself more easily to the lifestyle of a first apartment or home than does the more formal seated dinner party. The buffet dinner party allows much flexibility from casual to formal. Should you feel your lifestyle will at first center around relaxed entertaining, I suggest that you begin your china service with the place, or service, plate. Its twelve-inch size is a perfect backdrop for buffet fare, as the entrée, garniture, salad, and bread are placed on one plate. For the seated dinner, it can become a lovely oversized dinner plate for artistic, in-the-kitchen placement of the entrée and accompaniments, which is then presented to the guest. Later, it takes on its formal role as a place plate, greeting the guest upon arrival at the table, showcasing the appetizer dishes and finally the soup course before it is removed and replaced by the dinner plate.

3. If you prefer, you may start with the largest dinner plate avail-

able in your pattern—ten and one-half inches (given a quarter- to half-inch variance). Although not as large as the place plate, it, too, can be used for a buffet or seated dinner. This size is in proportion to the dinner (or Continental) knife and fork, which I have recommended. Dinner plates are the pieces upon which the entrée containing the meat course will be served. They should be flat and have a shoulder rather than the coupe shape. The shoulder can be patterned, but the center is best plain or of a monochrome pattern, as the food creates its own unique design. Colors that are too vivid distract from food, as does heavy, embossed gilding.

4. To serve a meal of four courses—appetizer, entrée, salad, dessert—the flat, shouldered salad plate is the next addition. Should you decide to serve salad as a separate course before or after the entrée as I do rather than with the entrée, select the large seven- to eight-inch plate. This size is large enough to look nice alone, centered before the diner, and it can also be used for dessert, the appetizer, or breakfast plate. Selected in a pattern other than the dinner plate, it provides interesting variety. If, however, the salad is to be served along with the entrée, the plate must be the smaller, seven-inch size, so that it fits nicely to the upper left of the dinner plate. In this case it should match the dinner plate. The crescent-shaped salad plate, which nestles against the curve of the dinner plate, is handsome and space saving, although it is often difficult to obtain in all but the oldest European or English patterns. It, too, should match the dinner plate exactly or be a well-thought-out complement. Glass plates, either round or crescent, are also an alternative, and are contemporary rather than traditional. The final possibility, and one to which I strongly object, is to place the salad directly on the dinner plate along with the entrée. Hot and cold do not go well on the same plate, and I find that serving salad as a separate course gives a relaxed pace to a formal or special meal.

5. The classic rimmed soup plate (seven to eight inches in diameter) and its underplate should be added to the china wardrobe next. Now a fifth course may be added to the menu or a simple soup supper may be served. The underplate is about three fourths of an inch or as much as an inch and a half larger in diameter than the soup plate, so that about a half inch to one

inch of the plate shows. An underplate is not properly proportioned if it is the same diameter or smaller than the soup plate. Traditionally, the two were a matched pair. Fashion and taste now permit that they be mixed. Remember, only the border of the underplate shows so you need not be concerned with the rest of the pattern. The design of the soup plate should be determined by the type of soup being served. At the most formal dinners clear soups are served and a pattern around the rim or shoulder *only* is the rule. On the other hand, almost any pattern is fine beneath a thick soup, as it is not seen until the soup is finished.

6. Although I am listing the bread-and-butter plate last, many would consider it a must along with the dinner plate. I am basing my decision on the fact that, traditionally, the bread-and-butter plate was properly placed on the luncheon table only, *never* on the formal dinner table. This rule is fading, and bread-and-butter plates on the dinner table are gathering wide acceptance at any but the most rigidly formal dinners. Butter plates must match one another. As they are on the table when the guests are seated, they must also go well with all the plates, except the dessert plates. Why? Because the bread-and-butter plate remains on the table with each of these courses. That is another reason why I prefer its purchase last. In all but the "matched set," it is a difficult plate to select. The effort will pay off handsomely, though; for this classic, flat-shouldered, four- to six-inch plate can serve so many purposes. It can be used alone to serve a small "starter," an *amuse-guele,* or an "appetizer" in the living room, or it can be placed on the place plate at dinner for the same purpose. It is a handsome *hors d'oeuvre* plate for stand-up parties and a fine tea plate.

7. When just the perfect set captures your eye, the addition of dessert plates is a delight. Classic dessert plates are eight or nine inches in diameter. They, too, can serve dual purposes— appetizer, salad, cheese, dessert, or fruit; for this reason I prefer the larger size. Selected solely as dessert plates, they need not go with any of the pieces for courses that preceded them. If selected to use for other courses, they must coordinate with all the pieces with which they are used. They can be bold, gilded, and elaborate, but must be flat, without the shallow bowl you find in some of the older china patterns.

8. As coffee is not served at the dining table during a formal dinner (rather afterward in demitasse cups in the living room), the demitasse cups need not match your pattern, nor need they match one another. They can be family heirlooms, "collectibles," or purchases made during travel. However, when serving breakfast, brunch, lunch, supper, or tea, the cups and saucers are placed on the table and must, therefore, match any other plates that they accompany, and they must match each other. Depending upon the meals for which you wish to use your bone china or porcelain, demitasse, expresso, or tea cups—or larger breakfast cups and saucers for café au lait or hot chocolate—may be added accordingly and in a quantity equal in number to the other pieces of the place setting with which they will be coordinated.

9. As your menus and entertaining styles become more sophisticated, you may wish to add two-handled cream soup bowls (cups) and their accompanying saucers. Although somewhat difficult to find, the one- or two-handled bouillon (or consommé) cups—some of which are designed with accompanying lids—and saucers are a lovely addition, too. Although these bowls or cups and saucers must be designed to go together, they may match or harmonize with the place plate upon which they are positioned. The tiny pots without handles and with matching lids used to serve *petits pots de crème* (custard) are a plus for dessert service. Egg cups, too, are a charming addition for breakfast and brunch.

Caring for China

"Doing the dishes" can be fun when you consider it an art appreciation endeavor. Consider yourself the curator in a museum—your personal museum in which your cache, large or small, is an expression of your love of beauty and desire to share it with others. Your prized collectibles and treasured possessions will, in trade for their tender beauty, require lots of T.L.C. (Tender Loving Care).

Check with the store where your china is sold or with the manufacturer to see if the fine china or porcelain you are considering is dishwasher-safe. Generally speaking, plain china or china decorated by the underglaze or inglaze technique can be washed in the dishwasher. However, china with overglaze patterns or trims is not dishwasher-safe.

You and the China Connection

The personality of the china has a subtle effect on any meal—easing it toward formality, gaiety, coziness (perennial romantics and young women are especially sensitive to this influence). For this reason, a woman's china, with which she will create pleasures over a lifetime, should strike a responsive chord in her spirit.

The pretty parties ahead of you can be an opportunity to learn and discover what your own taste is, for that is something you must find out for yourself.

CHAPTER 15

The Sparkle of Crystal

The moment has arrived. After all the planning and preparations, the hostess is composing her dinner party table. Linens are in place, as is the centerpiece of flowers, fruit, art objects, or whatever is appropriate to the occasion. Silver place settings shine and the finest china glistens. Now she adds, with special care, the stemware—that exquisite, fragile final touch—knowing that when the tapers are lighted or the crystal chandelier (discreetly dimmed) is turned on, the light will refract the glow, pouring magic upon the setting. The slim, elegant glasses, rising above their companions on the festive table, will become the dominant influence and take sparkling command.

Crystal's Sparkling Past

Glass was discovered during the Bronze Age (approximately 2500 B.C.). As was the Chinese porcelain formula, the early secrets of crystal making were so guarded that the artisans of the thirteenth-century Venetian glassmaker's guild were moved to the isolated island of Murano. And, so precious were their secrets that escaping the island was punishable by death! In the sixteenth century, some of the artists given permission to travel outside Murano never returned and settled instead in other countries. They later became the founders of glassmaking concerns in Bohemia (Czechoslovakia), France, Germany, and England.

Crystal's most sparkling secret of secrets is attributed to the English glassmaker's guild whose research revealed that by mixing oxide of lead with the other ingredients needed to make glass, a clearer, heavier kind of glass was produced which not only added the long-sought-after clarity, but achieved strength and thickness so that these "lead glass" pieces could be deeply cut in delicate patterns, imparting a vivacious sparkle to the glass. After further intensive research and experimentation, the lead glass attained both the purity and the brilliance of rock crystal and, in 1676, "crystal" as we know it today was created. The basic methods for its creation and decoration have not changed for almost four centuries.

We find two dominant trends in the more recent history of glass and crystal—the colored and the brilliant. Toward the end of the nineteenth century, with movements such as Art Nouveau and Impressionism in the field of painting, colored glass was in demand on both sides of the Atlantic. Colorful, innovative glass creations by Emile Galle, Eugène Rousseau, Dawn Frères, and other artisans in Europe, and the sublime Favrile glass of Louis Comfort Tiffany in America, created quite a stir.

In 1918, a clear crystal star appeared in America—Steuben Glass, owned by Corning. Steuben became regarded internationally as *the* American glass and rivaled Europe's best—Baccarat, Saint Louis, Lalique of France, Orrefors and Kosta of Sweden. Steuben, like its competitors abroad, designed exquisite table services exclusively for individual customers, combining specially designed patterns with the family coat of arms, crest, or personal monogram.

Some American glassmakers produce marvelous hand-blown, handcrafted crystal stemware; others sell under their own name stemware made in the historic European centers for glassmaking. Steuben concentrates on decorative or useful artistic pieces, which have, in a tradition begun by President Truman, become the choice of gifts by American presidents to heads of state and other notables on appropriate occasions.

Reflections

Aside from glass's optical qualities (think of a world with no magnification; some could not read; no one could study the stars), crystal has always commanded our aesthetic attention. The artist shapes the light-filled substance, then cuts, engraves, etches its surface into patterns that bring out all its brilliance.

Glass is unique in the same way that fire is unique. There is nothing else like it, for it is not so much a substance as a moment in chemical change. The glassmaker performs magic in capturing this moment of change.

What makes glass magic to you? What reminiscences do your early encounters with crystal hold? One of my fondest childhood memories is of teatime with my mother on a hot Louisiana afternoon. Mother, my brother, and I would each sit in our favorite wicker rockers on the porch, fanning ourselves with a palm fan and, of course, sipping iced-tea. Mother prided herself on her iced tea, presweetened with sugar while still hot, in the Southern tradition, and with a sprig of fresh mint from the herb garden rising proudly from the ice, a full circle of lemon slice resting artistically on the rim of the crystal iced-tea glass. The sterling silver iced-tea spoon always felt so cold as I pushed the lemon and the mint through the ice cubes to the bottom of the glass. Mother also brought out water-starched linen tea napkins, but the glasses always "sweated" as the icy-cold contents met the heat and humidity, so my napkin was never fresh for long.

My brother and I were cautioned to be very careful with Mother's prized glasses, and to this day we have never told her that when she stepped inside for more cucumber sandwiches, we would wet the rims of our glasses and run our fingers around and around until we caused the shrill exciting ring real crystal makes. Nor did we tell her that we would tilt our glasses, sometimes spilling our tea, to catch the afternoon sun in just the right position to capture its rays in the deeply cut design and throw the colors of the rainbow across the brilliant white of the linen tea-table cloth.

Crystal Clear Terminology

As with all things of value, with greater understanding comes a deeper appreciation. The basic recipe for glass, be it Mother's iced-tea glass or a soda bottle, begins with silica (found in nature as flint, quartz, or sand). To make common glass, known as "lime glass," only soda, lime, and potash need be added. For quality "crystal," lead oxide is substituted for the soda and potash and a minimum content of 24 percent lead oxide is required by law. Hence the term "lead crystal." To create "full lead crystal," 30 percent lead must be used.

One need not be a chemist to tell crystal from glass. Lead gives crystal its starlike qualities. You can tell crystal by its weight, remarkable clarity, and metallic sheen, by the sparkle and brilliance that catch the light in a way other glass cannot match. Glass is dull and has a blue or greenish cast, whereas crystal is free of color. Heavier than glass, crystal rings with a lingering metallic note when tapped, while glass emits a rather flat one. Crystal is far more expensive than ordinary glass, but also tougher and less liable to chip.

The Selection Process

Crystal stemware adds the final side to the tabletop triangle—sterling, china, and crystal. Choosing stemware is like icing the cake; it is the last ingredient to be added. Now that you are aware of periods of design, line, shape, form, proportion, balance, and color, your standards for aesthetic judgment have become stimulated if not formulated. This same knowledge will serve you well in your crystal choices.

In choosing crystal, I wish you could begin at 31 bis, rue de Paradis in an out-of-the-way, tranquil neighborhood of Paris, in the fascinating Baccarat museum and showroom of antiques and one-of-a-kind pieces. There you would see goblet patterns chosen for present-day monarchs as well as for kings and emperors of long ago; and there, also, are goblets that could be yours for the choosing. Most impressive, as though a monument to the magic of crystal, there stand two candelabra, adorned with ninety lights. As the story goes, these were the last of six, commissioned by the last czar of Russia but never delivered because the revolution intervened.

Perhaps more practical than wishing for a crystal shopping spree in Paris, begin the pleasant and creative journey toward choosing this final element of your tabletop triangle by paying close attention to the various types of stemware set before you in different places and situations. Note to yourself the pieces that light your own spirit, as well as other components of the service. Consider the effects of their being filled with fluids—water, iced tea, or perhaps wine; is the glass enhanced or diminished? Consider the fact that crystal must be touched—handled, washed, stored—and begin arriving at a decision as to the characteristics that best suit your personality and the lifestyle you visualize for yourself. And bear in mind my Crystal C's, some practical considerations.

The Crystal C's

Complement. As the final major selection for your tabletop triangle, crystal is the catalyst, the spark that brings everything together. It completes and perfects. Stemware, therefore, must be chosen specifically to harmonize and enliven the other components. It must be congenial in mood, aesthetically appropriate, flattering in hue (if a colored crystal is chosen), and comparable in quality.

Counterpoint. Think of sterling and china as an existing melody. To be successful, crystal must counterpoint that melody. When successfully teamed, sterling, china, and crystal become three melodic lines, which harmonize, yet retain their individuality.

Contrast. Without going to extremes, your crystal may have a striking dissimilarity to its companions. Opposing elements of line or period placed side by side become dramatic when artfully teamed.

Create. Perhaps the greatest joy of all is to create, and this you can do as you complete the tabletop triangle.

Concentrating upon my Crystal C's (Complement, Counterpoint, Contrast, Create), consider the many avenues available for the acquisition of your crystal stemware. Patterns from estate sales and auctions, from grandmother and mother, may be placed alongside new patterns, chosen to work together as a tabletop team.

It may take many hours of treasure-hunting to locate the perfect blend of stemware patterns, but the prize is a setting unlike any other, one that is never dull or boring. On the other hand, it can be heartbreaking when a treasured goblet shatters and cannot be replaced.

The creative alternative, however, is to select stemware *en suite* (in a matching set) so that every piece when grouped together on the formal table matches one another. This formal approach need never be boring—quite the contrary. A sparkling and unadorned crystal can cast its glow over the more outspoken patterns of sterling and china. It is then that the liquids themselves are showcased, which was the original intent of classically plain crystal stemware.

As you move toward finalizing your selection, do so with my Ten Crystal Clues in mind.

Ten Crystal Clues

1. Choose crystal last, after sterling and china patterns have been determined.
2. Decide what type you like best: multifaceted cut, solidly sculptured, delicately or deeply engraved, intricately etched, classically plain.
3. Apply the Crystal C's as you begin to finalize the tabletop triangle.
4. Insist upon quality and open stock replacement or replacement by special order (which only the top crystal makers will guarantee).

5. Hold the piece of crystal in your hands; it must feel "right." Look at it; it must look "right." This is to say it must be balanced—the foot, stem, and bowl are in scale and harmony with one another. The foot (base) must be heavy enough to balance the bowl, both visually when it is empty and actually when it is filled with liquid. Long-stemmed goblets, in particular, tend to look top-heavy when a harmonious balance or symmetry has not been achieved.

6. Carefully run your fingers along the foot, stem, and bowl as well as the edges to check for smoothness, making certain there are no irregularities.

7. The contour and structure of a piece of crystal stemware should be suited to its purpose—to hold liquid—and pleasing to the touch of both the fingers and lips.

8. If decorated crystal is your preference, make certain it is not overly ornate, but that ornamentation has been added as a subtle enhancement, placed for accent along the stem or around the bowl, ending well below where the lips will touch. Any pattern should be evenly spaced and perfectly finished.

9. Examine a piece of stemware against one of another manufacturer. This is the only way to compare brilliance, clarity, luster, and absolute absence of color. Dullness, cloudiness, and hints of color quickly show up in this comparative test, disqualifying the less-than-perfect piece.

10. Last, but not least, apply the tone test by flicking the bowl of the goblet with your fingernail as you hold it by its foot. Listen for the beautiful crystal chime.

A Crystal Wardrobe

Thanks to your new knowledge, you may begin immediately to enjoy any crystal with which you come into contact. Before you set forth to select crystal of your own, carefully box a dinner plate (if your china has been chosen) and a full place setting of your silver if you have one (a piece or two will serve if you are just starting), and take those with you so that you can test the interplay. Reread any notes you may have made on patterns you have liked.

When the time comes, however, start with the basics and follow my system, The Crystal Choices.

THE CRYSTAL CHOICES

Pointers for Perfecting the Place Setting

1. As with china, I recommend that lead crystal stemware not be acquired by purchasing the usual matching five-piece place setting, but instead by assembling it by course. Start with the water goblet. This becomes the centerpiece of the stemware place setting and, as it is the largest and the most important, it also becomes the standard for the scale and design of additional pieces. As you first begin to build a crystal wardrobe, a handsomely designed goblet can be used for everything: water, iced tea, wine, fruit, berries, ice cream.

2. If you adopt my mix-and-match system rather than buying *en suite,* one rule applies: The stemware for each separate beverage served throughout the courses of a meal must match. Patterns may, however, differ as the beverage changes with the courses. The variety of patterns selected for each course may (unlike china) be placed together on the table.

3. The goal in building a stemware collection should be to acquire the same number of glasses for a specific course as there are china and silver flatware settings. Thus china, sterling, and crystal grow together, progressively, enabling additional courses to be added when entertaining. It is foolish to have a glass for a particular use at the table if you do not have the china or flatware required for that course and vice versa.

4. The various courses of a festive or formal luncheon or dinner can quite properly be served accompanied with water throughout, in which case the handsome water goblet stands alone. You must decide whether you prefer the American water goblet or the smaller Continental version. (Some manufacturers refer to the American water goblet as No. 1, the Continental as No. 2.) Why two sizes? Americans have traditionally drunk larger quantities of water with meals than Europeans—Europeans preferring a variety of wines. For that reason, a size is made for each need. Some crystal makers simply call the American an "oversized" goblet. I personally prefer it as it gives a hostess more flexibility (as I shall explain below). If you like both sizes, make certain you select a pattern from a maker who offers both American and European.

5. When you choose to serve wine as an accompaniment and complement to the various courses comprising a special meal, it is time to add wine glasses. Traditionally, there are five different ones that accompany a dinner. In the order in which they are served, they are: sherry, white wine, claret, red wine (or red Burgundy), champagne.

6. After you have collected the number of water goblets you need, move on to the glass for the beverage that accompanies the entrée. As you begin to entertain, you will no doubt serve only one beverage with a meal in addition to water, and you may offer guests a selection of iced tea, a red, or a white wine. So you would not include at each place setting a glass assigned specifically for each, but would instead choose a handsome all-purpose piece of crystal stemware that is compatible with the water goblet. Many crystal makers offer an oversized wine glass to suit all these needs. As it is balloon-shaped, it serves as a nice companion to the water goblet and may be used for juice or milk at breakfast and lunch. A similar piece, with a long graceful stem and a smaller (most often round although not always) bowl is the "hock" glass. Originally designed for Rhine (white) wine, this is a nice alternative to the all-purpose glass and is a delightful piece to hold. Wine connoisseurs permit only the hock glass to have a colored bowl, usually of cased (cameo) glass. Lovely though the colors may be, however, if this is to be used as an all-purpose glass, it should be purchased in clear crystal so that the color and clarity of the wine rather than of the crystal can be appreciated.

7. Should one of your goals in entertaining be to become fluent in the understanding and serving of wines, I suggest that you begin to fashion your stemware accordingly. The red wine (or red Burgundy) glass should be the first addition. To accompany the American, or oversized, water goblet, select the Continental water goblet in which to serve red wine, and if that option is not available, the red wine (red Burgundy) glass.

This piece will handsomely hold red, claret, or white wine, fruit, and even certain desserts, freeing the water goblet for water alone. It serves better as an all-purpose glass than the oversized balloon. Why? It mixes better with the water goblet, and as your stemware wardrobe grows, it steps into the role for which it was designed: to enhance red wine and add its individual rhythm to the trio, quartet, quintet, or sextet of crystal stemware, which will ultimately adorn your formal table.

8. As champagne is considered quite festive and special on many occasions, I advise the champagne flute (an elongated tulip shape) be added next. It is preferred by connoisseurs for genuine champagne and sparkling wines, as the effervescence of the bubbles remains through the last sip. It can be used before dinner, throughout the entire meal, and/or during the dessert course. The tabletop stemware trio is now comprised of the water goblet, all-purpose glass (or hock glass, Continental water goblet, or red wine glass, if you prefer), and champagne flute. As a hostess, you are now prepared to offer water, a choice of red or white wine, and champagne with dessert—a splendid idea for special events when a toast is to climax the meal! The flute can also be used as a parfait glass to showcase a colorful layered dessert.

9. As you begin to serve specific wines with specific courses, you may add a white wine glass. It can be used also for claret or red Bordeaux as well as for after-dinner port (although there is a special glass for port in some patterns). Now you can set a table with a glistening quartet of stemware: water goblet, white wine, red wine, and champagne glass at each place, and you can plan a menu to follow suit.

10. To be truly traditional, you would serve a glass of sherry as an accompaniment to the soup course. Although this is not done as often as in years past, it is certainly an added touch. The choice in sherry glasses is between the standard one whose V-shaped bowl ends in a point or the Spanish sherry glass with a straight-sided bowl gently curving into a rounded bottom. With this addition, you have arrived at the stemware quintet with which you can serve five courses.

11. Next, consider the classic champagne saucer (often referred to as the American champagne sherbet), which gives the hostess an array of serving possibilities. This glass dates back to the reign of Louis XV, a time when sweet champagne was popular and so was dipping a piece of Madeira cake into the filled glass. It is now used for any sweet, sparkling wine, and is also an appropriate stemware piece for an opening fruit compote or cold seafood cocktail, an intermezzo sorbet course, and many desserts. To have both the champagne saucer and flute is neither a necessity nor a luxury, but rather a nicety.

12. A short, wide-stemmed dessert dish with a wide base is available from some crystal makers. I find this to be a rather awkward piece, poorly proportioned. In lieu of it, I suggest the china dessert plate or the American champagne sherbet.

13. The finger bowl, with or without its matching underplate, goes in and out of fashion. But think not of trends, but of needs. If you want to serve any of the finger foods that can properly be offered at a company table, your guests will need to "wash up" afterward. What could be lovelier than to do so in a crystal finger bowl? When the menu does not require it, an amazing number of additional uses will be found, from cold soups, to nuts, fruits, and puddings.

14. As a charming last, but not least, accessory to a crystal wardrobe, consider a delicate glass for serving a special dessert wine such as sauterne. To be absolutely proper, this piece should be somewhat smaller than the claret or white wine—a nice antique collectible. As a substitute, a round-bottomed, tulip-shaped sherry glass may be used, or the claret glass itself.

15. After the festive or formal dinner, guests are offered after-dinner coffee in the living room. Should you wish to do so, you may also offer a *digestif* (after-dinner drink). Suitable stemware falls into two broad categories: glasses for cordials and liqueurs and glasses for brandy and cognac. The former are tiny, one to one-and-a-half ounce in capacity, and usually have a long delicate stem (although some are short-stemmed). The glass for brandy or cognac, called the brandy snifter, brandy balloon, or brandy warmer, is from four to twelve ounces in capacity, yet only an ounce is served in it. Its large round bowl rests atop a very short stem and the bowl is held in the palm of the hand to warm the brandy or cognac. I agree with connoisseurs that the huge snifter is pretentious, and I suggest you select the smaller size. Crystal stemware designed especially for *digestifs* is delightful to collect. Patterns and stem heights can be mixed, as can the old with the new.

Caring for Crystal

Crystal is heavier than ordinary glassware because of its lead content, and its weight may give a false appearance of strength. However, though crystal is more resistant to breaking than one might imagine, great care needs to be

340

taken in handling, washing, and storing it. Given the proper care, its beauty and brilliance can be maintained for a lifetime.

Crystal—A Lovely Dream

Because crystal is so fragile, so formal, and so subject to accidents, it is by no means an everyday resource. But it is the only proper choice for a formal dinner (silver goblets are correct and very elegant for luncheon). Use your crystal when the occasion dictates, but handle it as you would a lovely dream that will vanish if you move too suddenly.

The Luxury of Linen

Scarlett O'Hara pulled down the velvet drapes and turned them into a ball gown. In the same way, many of the gorgeous white dresses you and my ingénues wear might have been made from table-linen trousseau treasures pulled from grandmothers' trunks. In fact, influenced by these white linen-and-lace dresses, I raided, not my grandmother's trunk, but an antique store, where I discovered a bin of old linen and lace napkins and tablecloths of all descriptions, many in mint condition. Putting aside a few to adorn special-occasion tables, I took the rest to my dressmaker. The result is a now-treasured dress of the softest fine linen and lace with a beautiful patina and polish that only happens to these fibers after years of loving hand-care.

Perhaps such a dress is more a novelty nowadays than a necessity, but it captures the niceties of bygone days just like the traditional and elegant linen tablecloth. And there are times when the formal white cloth is a necessity, when it must make its regal appearance at the table. It sets and states tradition. It makes a glamorous statement at family festivities and holidays, and special occasions like christenings, coming-of-age celebrations, debutante and bridal teas, bridesmaids' luncheons, parents' twenty-fifth and grandparents' fiftieth wedding anniversaries.

Linen—Past and Present

The covered table has for centuries been a symbol of hospitality. As early as the fifteenth century "to share the cloth" with one's host was an indication of equality and acceptance.

The tablecloth not only provided protection for the table, but in chilly, damp castles and homes, it also provided protection for the diners by keeping the cold draft from their knees. And, if you can imagine, until the napkin appeared during the seventeenth century, the tablecloth was used to wipe the mouth as well.

Linen (the cloth made from the long fibers of the flax plant) was one of the first fabrics made. Linen reached its peak of popularity in certain parts of England, in northern Ireland, in Scotland, Russia, Austria, Germany, Holland, and Belgium; and through most of the eighteenth century linen-making was one of Europe's most widely dispersed and extensive domestic industries.

Even today we look to these countries for the finest examples of table linen, and for the exquisite handwork that often embellishes it. During one of L'Ecole des Ingénues' finishing tours, we saw a very old woman in the Belgian city of Bruges wearing her bonnet of handmade lace as she sat upon a small stool, her lap laden with her bobbins and lace and luminous linen yarn, all resting upon a pillow as her hands moved the shuttle to and fro, making the delicate lace. This sight added immeasurably to our purchase of Belgian lace-trimmed linens. Go a step off the beaten path when you travel abroad and you will capture such charm, adding to your postcards and souvenirs the linens and laces of the countries you visit. Even the smallest doily for a bread basket, a dainty guest towel, or a baby pillow cover will be enough to whet your appetite and create the determination to someday have a fine linen cloth despite the care it might demand.

The beauty of linen lies in the fact that it is made of flax. The finish of linen is lustrous and resilient, and its glow grows with use and proper care. For that reason, it becomes prettier with age—a fine reason to use it for life's everyday pleasures as well as for special occasions.

Of course, with the pluses come some minuses. The first, its initial expense, is easily justified, as you need only one truly formal cloth and set of napkins because of their durability. The second drawback is one today's homemaker will not always accept: the tender loving care linen demands in hand-laundering and ironing. There are times, however, when the desire for a formal table covering and matching napkins overcomes the awareness of the care required.

From the roughest of "low" brown heavy sails to the most delicate fine handkerchief, linen knows no equal. But the use of the word *linen* to denote all household linens is as misleading as using "silver" to denote all cutlery, or "crystal" to denote all glassware. To be called linen, material must be made of 95 percent or more flax.

To Bare or Not to Bare

Lovely table linens, even if limited to one formal set, are to the table as icing is to the cake. Like a cake, which may be elaborately iced or served beautifully plain, so may a table be embellished by linens and laces or dare to be bare to exhibit its perfectly polished wood or gleaming glass top. It is not necessary to cover a tabletop. Today's new finishes, even on the finest or rarest of woods, can be mar-proof, heat-proof, scratch-proof. For some occasions, the table alone offers beauty enough as a background for the finest china, gleaming sterling, and sparkling crystal. For other events, this is far too bare, and still others demand something in between.

A tablecloth unifies, tying all of the elements of the table together. Further, it provides an elegant backdrop. Light from candelabra-held candles and crystal chandeliers is softly reflected from the pure white, pale ecru white, or muted pastels of the tablecloth, and cast upward onto the diners' faces in a most flattering fashion. For these reasons, a tablecloth is the nicest for a large table set with many places and accessories and circled by a number of guests.

For the less staged, yet equally elegant, gathering of friends, handsome "formal" placemats of fabrics considered appropriate for the full tablecloth are the perfect in-between solution. Placemats cause a visual breakup of space and allow the prized surface of the table to star as well. They provide a nice way to make a large table—which can sometimes appear cold with an intimate grouping of guests or a romantic twosome—come together.

The Perfect Backdrop

The most traditional of the formal tablecloths is the richly woven damask linen cloth. The designs of damask are woven into the material, with real Irish damask considered the best. The patterns have been passed down through the generations and are traditionally floral or scenic, always the same color of the cloth itself, white being the choice for formal occasions and cream acceptable otherwise. Although lovely, I do not consider the delicate pastel damasks acceptable for formal occasions. In addition to the patterned damask, cloth woven with simple bands of light-reflecting satin damask is an extremely sophisticated formal table adornment.

Damask is suitable to any setting, but the pattern of the damask should be selected to harmonize with the degree of formality of the furnishings and place settings. Damask with no pattern or with simple patterns of ferns or roses is the least formal and goes well with provincial and Early American or English country decor. Heavier, Middle-European furnishings call for the classic, exquisite, elaborate scenic damask cloths. Many German damasks present landscapes complete with figures or hunting scenes. What a wonderful, theme-setting backdrop upon which to add tabletop accessories in keeping with the story told in damask! On the other hand, modern, contemporary furnishings with sleek lines and streamlined tabletop appointments are made even more sophisticated and clean-cut when topped with a smooth damask cloth or one with shiny, satinlike woven borders and bands.

The sturdier formal linens are handsomely embroidered in a heavier, yet hand-done, fashion, and are often of a pale ecru-white tone. These are most often Czechoslovakian- and Italian-made, and provide a nice backdrop for the heavier sterling, china, and crystal place settings and warm provincial furnishings.

Although beautiful over a white silencer (a pad beneath the tablecloth), cloths with lace inserts or delicate embroidery look spectacular over a dark tabletop. The contrast of the wood showing through highlights the handwork in the linen. However, if slippage or damage from dampness, heat, or cold is a concern—as it is for certain wood finishes—a brown silencer may be used. For this reason it is wise to invest in a silencer that reverses from white to brown.

Needless to say, lace cloths are at their greatest beauty when placed over the natural darkness of a tabletop. They are quite interesting also when they overlay an exposed refectory table of glass. Some hostesses find it pleasing to place a lining of color under the lace cloth, though this is more a "fun" idea than a "formal" treatment, since the colorful underlay causes a distraction once the place settings are in position. In a formal situation, consider the lace and wood as a team.

Lace inserts and trims must, like other decorations, be in keeping with the overall scheme and period of other appointments. For example, heavier laces such as *point de Milan* or the Battenberg laces of Belgium are different from the more delicate *point de Paris* and *point de Binche*. For that reason you will find the more delicate embellishments placed on the lighter-weight linen backgrounds and the heavier ones on the thicker linen cloths. When this is not the case, the cloth is poorly designed and you should pass it by.

The Embellishing of Linen

As lovely as they are without embellishment, table linens are often enhanced by a variety of handwrought decorations, from the heavy embroidery of peasantlike designs, so perfect for the informal table with earthenware settings, to the delicate drawnwork on the sheerest of formal linens.

In assessing linens with adornment, you must always insist on work that has been done by hand for your treasured formal cloth or placemats. To accept machine-made embroideries, appliqués, drawn, open, and cutwork, hemstitching, or laces is not in keeping with the quality you seek in your sterling, china, and crystal. For everyday use, you may feel free to pick and choose as you wish from the colorful array of easy-care fabrics, without which we cannot live in today's fast-moving world.

Creating the Table

Though it is the first item to be placed on the formal table, linen is often the last to be considered, as the sterling, china, and crystal capture the limelight. It is, however, like the backdrop in any theatrical *mise en scène* (staging), necessary for the success of the total production.

As the set director for your tabletop, you will design and create the atmosphere by your choice of backdrops—a beautiful, bare table on which the giant damask napkin makes a bold statement, individual dining vignettes created by exquisitely adorned placemats, or the timeless serenity of the formal linen or lace cloth. You will find occasions for each. In addition, you will design some lighter productions with handsome informal backdrops of easy-to-care-for fabrics and synthetics.

Linen Choices

As the "easy-care" *faux* linen placemats, napkins, and cloths are less expensive and are replaced often, I will limit my discussion to the formal "real" linens, which are inimitable, permanent, and comparatively expensive.

THE DOZEN LEAD-INS TO LINEN

1. Table linens should be selected after silver, china, and crystal patterns have been chosen.
2. The Crystal C's (Complement, Counterpoint, Contrast, and

Create) apply equally to the selection of fine linens; review page 333 through 334.

3. As you will require just a few formal pieces, invest only in real linen or real linen damask. All embroidery, appliqué, drawn, open, and cutwork, and lace inserts should be hand-done, as should hems. Limit the amount of embellishment to the size of the budget, remembering to purchase quality rather than quantity of adornment. Laces must be exquisite ones, even if that means you can afford only a touch of fine lace.

4. Do not invest initially in linens that are too fussy and feminine, as men are not as comfortable with them. Wait until you have the basics for a mixed-company dinner (quite as nice for an all-girl affair) before adding delicate pieces.

5. As linen possesses a strong resistance to dye, colored linens should be marked "vat-dyed" or guaranteed colorfast.

6. Napkins come in a variety of sizes and are square: dinner napkins, twenty-four inches; luncheon napkins, no less than fifteen inches (can double for breakfast); tea napkins, twelve inches. Cocktail napkins, four by six inches, are rectangular in shape or they may be five or six inches square. Before purchasing, find out if the size of the piece as quoted is before or after hemming.

7. Napkins should match the tablecloth if it is damask. To accompany cloths of lighter weight, and delicate linens with embroidery, lace, or drawnwork, napkins should be of the same fabric and simple, with just an accent of matching embellishment. Cloths made entirely of lace may have lace-trimmed or plain linen napkins. Remember that the napkin must have enough plain fabric to wipe one's mouth.

8. Placemats vary in size and shape from small round ones of twelve to fourteen inches in diameter (which just peek from beneath the dinner or service plate) to grand twenty-four-inch ones (which hang gracefully over the table's edge). A round table looks best with round or crescent-shaped mats, while a rectangular table looks best with square or oblong ones. Placemats other than plate-size round ones should be large enough to hold the entire place setting, otherwise the table looks spotty and without unity. Individual placemats should not touch or overlay one another.

9. Table runners are sometimes sold to coordinate with individ-

ual placemats. They are nice when a table is wide and long enough to allow space between the runner and mats. On a narrow table, long runners can be interesting used down both sides of the table with place settings positioned along the way leaving the ends empty. Likewise, runners can be used across the table to mark places. In any event, they must be long enough to allow the proper overhang.

10. Formal tablecloths must fit the table properly. To ascertain the correct size, the table size must be known and the cloth must be large enough to allow an equal overhang on all four sides of the table as follows: buffet, twenty inches; formal dinner, eighteen to twenty inches; formal luncheon or tea, twelve to fifteen inches; informal luncheon or breakfast, eight to twelve inches.

11. Explore antique stores and garage sales. If, after close examination, the linens are free from tears and stains, you may have found some fine examples of handwork rare and expensive in today's market.

12. Seek out linen shops when you travel. Many exquisite varieties (damask, lace, embroidered, appliqué, drawn, and cutwork) can be purchased duty-free during a visit to the country or a possession of the country in which they are made.

A Linen Trousseau

It is difficult to predict the size of a future dining table at the time you are selecting formal table linens. It is also impossible to know the size of your future living quarters and the style and scale of the entertaining you will do. Still, you will want to make some initial choices. Follow my Linen Trousseau Tips for assistance.

LINEN TROUSSEAU TIPS

Pointers for Perfecting the Linen Trousseau

1. Start with the basics for a beautiful buffet by investing in a dozen fine, full-sized formal dinner napkins. Their ample twenty-four-inch size opens to cover a lap and underlie the

buffet or dinner plate. I suggest sturdy damask napkins as these will be used often. A satin-banded damask would fit nicely in any situation.

2. A buffet ideally requires the use of two napkins per guest: one beneath the plate and another for wiping the fingers and mouth. You can either divide your basic dozen in half and serve six diners or add another dozen and double your guest list. I suggest adding a dozen matching damask luncheon napkins, either the large eighteen-inch or the smaller fourteen- to sixteen-inch size.

3. With your double dozen damask napkins you can also hostess a seated dinner party at the dining table, depending, of course, on whether or not you yet have one, and, if you do, it is one you dare to bare!

4. Before a dining table comes along, I recommend staging sit-down dinner parties on sturdy card tables. Depending upon space, one, two, or three look beautiful when covered with fine linens and topped with your tabletop trio of silver, china, and crystal. Purchase matching cloths for the tables (mismatched would look too cluttered). The cloths will probably come with matching napkins. If not, purchase them. Make certain that the cloths are large enough to allow a ten- to twelve-inch overhang on all sides of the table. Place a silencer of white cotton flannel beneath.

5. Once you have a dining table, the time has come to add the pleasant dining alternative of placemats. Choose one lovely set of twelve with matching napkins and a center runner (if a matching one is available). Truly elegant placemats have met acceptance for formal dining in our world today.

6. Last come your first (or only) formal cloth and napkins. By this time, your linen preferences will have been established, and the time will have arrived for you to express yourself fully.

7. At any time you may search for specialty pieces to enhance your table. A wonderful remembrance of travels can be small pieces such as cocktail napkins, bread tray doilies (necessary for all dry finger foods), *petits fours* doilies. I fondly recall one ingénue's delight when discovering and purchasing six Belgian linen fingertip towels with Battenberg lace inserts. Why such pleasure? Three were pastel pink and three were pale mint green—the colors of Sweet Briar, her college!

Linens—a Luxury Worth the Care

Needless to say, linen must be kept immaculately clean. The finest of damask, the daintiest of embroideries, is not attractive with any spots regardless of its beauty or cost. A linen cloth with any crease other than a perfectly straight one down the middle should not be placed on the table. A napkin with a lipstick stain will take away anyone's appetite.

With proper care, the lustrous finish, so much the beauty of linens, will grow even more beautiful with age. Just as is the case with a treasured linen-and-lace dress, the maintenance of table linens is time-consuming if done by hand at home and expensive when done professionally by a hand laundry. But sad to say, when both the treasured dress and the cloth have been neglected and covered with stains, scorches, and spots, they will find refuge only in a garage sale.

Luxury Linens

Linens are the most demanding of dining appointments and caring for a sizable collection can be quite a formidable responsibility. For this reason I urge you not to be greedy; select only an assortment to provide ensembles for the situations you expect to face. Save space in your linen chest and a reserve in your budget. Keep your linen stock (like your figure) trim enough to allow you to look forward to the next meal.

CHAPTER 17

Monogramming Your Treasures

Perhaps you will be fortunate enough to have treasured pieces of silver, china, crystal, and linen—each bearing the markings of the original owners—passed down to you from previous generations. If not, you may wish to think of beginning this lovely custom yourself.

Just as the manufacturer's unobtrusive hallmark, signature, or other significant marking is a very old practice, so is personal marking of silver, china, crystal, and table linen. Some families even hand down exquisite place plates that bear the family crest on the rim or in the center. If you are to inherit marked tabletop pieces, you will want to mark yours in the same general style, but if you are beginning such a tradition anew, thought should be given to make sure that markings are in the best of taste, proportion, and design.

Markings, whether engraved, etched, or embroidered, should be hand-done. This process is expensive, but to try to economize by having them done in any other manner is a mistake. It is better not to mark silver, crystal, and linen at all, or to delay marking them until the budget permits the proper techniques.

There are many ways to mark silver, china, crystal, and linen. The cipher is a design combining or interweaving initials and is most attractive when using three letters. Two or four do not produce a pretty cipher, and a separate single initial is not in the best of taste as it is not sufficiently personal. An acceptable monogram can only be formed by the intertwinement of two or more letters. The designs for ciphers and monograms are limitless but choice should be governed by the rules of proportion and good taste.

In days past when a girl started a hope chest at a young age, the items of her trousseau were marked with her maiden initials. Although a young woman may follow this custom today, it has become more the fashion to delay marking these items until she is engaged to be married. As you begin to acquire items of your trousseau, you need to be aware of correct ways to mark them—now or later.

When a young woman marks her silver and other trousseau items after she is married, she may combine her initials with those of her husband in two ways. The oldest custom is to use the initials of her first and second baptismal names—her first and "middle" names—and her husband's surname. The more modern usage is to employ the initials of her first baptismal name, her maiden, or family surname, and her husband's surname. The husband's surname, in either case, is the largest and center letter in a monogram.

A third design is to create a monogram of both the woman's and man's baptismal names combined with his surname. The first initial of the husband's baptismal name is placed on the left, hers on the right, and the initial of his surname is centered atop the two to create a triangle. The older alternative would be an inverted triangle made up of her two maiden initials atop his surname initial. A fourth option, if available, is the use of the husband's crest on the flatware, crystal, or china or his full coat of arms on large hollowware pieces. A final possibility, but one that I offer with reservation, is the use of the single initial of the husband's surname in a simple design or embellished to give the appearance of a monogram.

Silver Markings

A personal marking reinforces the fact that silver is steeped in sentiment and tradition and personalizes it permanently for the pleasure of the family. Markings should be selected to be appropriate and should be in proportion to the pattern of the silver flatware or hollowware, enabling it to blend attractively into the design. If the design of the flatware does not allow space to place the marking on the front, it may be placed on the back as is the English custom.

Crystal Markings

Extreme care must be taken with the marking of crystal. The last effect one would desire would be that of inexpensively marked glasses sold by the dozen! Markings must be in quiet overtones to complement the overall design and embellishment of the stemware. Monograms must be perfectly hand-etched. Remember that the markings will be viewed en masse, in large numbers, as from one to six pieces of stemware will be placed before each diner, so simple elegance must be the guideline.

China Markings

China, too, can be personally marked. The decision to do so must be made, however, prior to the manufacturing process, as it is during this time that the marking is applied. Depending upon the decoration of the china, the marking may be in one of the colors, or a combination of the colors, found in the design or it may be done in gold or platinum. Additional time, usually from four to nine months, must be budgeted, of course, as must the additional cost.

Linen Markings

Placement of markings on table linens is determined by the piece to be marked and the patterns or hand embellishment that the piece already contains. Monograms should be in the same mood as any other trim and should always be hand-embroidered. Markings that are square in shape are prettiest when placed in line with the table edge, and irregular ones look best positioned at the corner when the tablecloth is on the table.

White markings are used on white linens, while a matching or slightly darker color is used on colored linens. A colored linen with white appliqué and embroidery is marked in white also.

A large dinner tablecloth may be marked in the middle, about five inches nearer the center of the table than where the hostess's place plate will be positioned. The marking may also be placed near the hostess to the side of the center, midway between the center and corner of the table. Care should be taken that a marking is not positioned so that it will fall under the hostess's or another diner's stemware, causing the stemware to tilt. A marking may also be placed near the corner of the cloth, on the portion which overhangs the table.

Smaller dinner or card table cloths are marked on one corner midway between the center of the table and the corner or the side edge. As elaborately decorated tea cloths often do not have space for marking, they are left unmarked and only the napkins are marked.

The size of the markings is in proportion to the piece. Tablecloth monograms are from three and one half to five inches in size. The marking on the large twenty-four-inch dinner napkin is from two to three inches and is placed in the center so that it will show when the napkin is folded twice into thirds.

To decide where the marking will be placed on napkins of other sizes, fold the napkin exactly as it will be folded for placement on the table and put a pin in the center of the folded napkin to indicate the position. This will usually be on one corner of the napkin, placed across the corner or straight depending upon the fold. Smaller luncheon and tea napkins are marked on the corners in this manner with a one-and-one-half- to two-inch monogram.

The marking of tabletop treasures is aesthetically difficult, and, in addition, expensive. Do consider the manner in which you will mark sterling, crystal, china, and linen as a whole. You are in essence designing a "logo" for your prized possessions; and just as a family crest, if selected, would be the same on each, so must initials, ciphers, or monograms be alike in design. Select a simple, gently curved, or beautifully blocked, elegantly designed cipher or monogram. Markings are so personal a matter that you will want to share the responsibility of decision-making, as well as the pleasure your choices will bestow, with your fiancé.

In addition to the sentimental value of having your treasures marked, there is also the advantage of identification should they be stolen. Along with marking, you should carefully inventory your lovely possessions and, of course, see that they are adequately insured.

Life's Finer Things

The most important reason to learn about lovely things, to seek and absorb beauty everywhere—from nature, from human-made objects, from people themselves—is that searching for and enjoying loveliness will lift your life to a higher plane. So I urge you to love beautiful things and also to sincerely appreciate them.

As a bride or a young career woman establishing independent living arrangements, you will need—and will deserve to own—enough of the lovely things I have described for you to serve inviting meals and to entertain, thus taking your proper place in the circles in which you will move.

I have mentioned that teenaged, even preteen-aged, girls often begin collecting hope chest items as gifts from relatives and as mementos of their own travels. This is a delightful and rewarding custom, but I submit that such a hobby should be regarded more as an exercise in developing taste and as a sentimental pursuit—not as a dowry builder. Preferences change drastically during growing-up years, and, furthermore, the circumstances of a young bride some years hence may be vastly different from those of a young girl in her parents' home.

The trick is to "acquire" all the things you see in a spiritual sense simply by enjoying them and to *actually* acquire just the right items to meet your needs, to satisfy your aesthetic yearnings, and to care for without physical or financial stress.

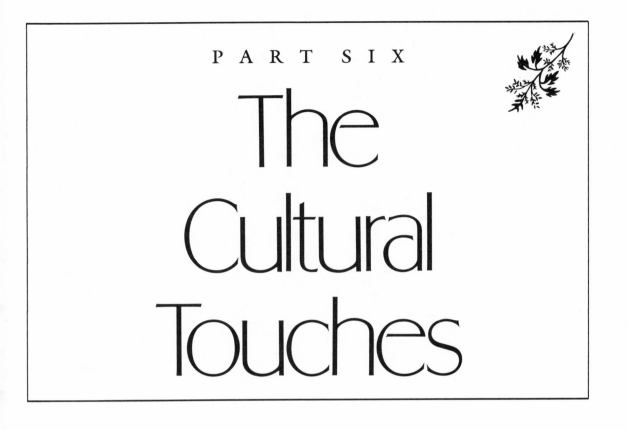

PART SIX

The Cultural Touches

CHAPTER 18

Etiquette for the Arts

Perhaps the greatest fear that young women have is of appearing ridiculous or ignorant. Unfortunately, this agonizing insecurity sometimes causes that very impression. Anxiety is especially prevalent when you venture into the cultural world, where the rest of the audience may appear so sophisticated, so sure of itself.

Do not give in to the "cold feet syndrome." The arts not only provide respite from a fast-paced daily life, but they are now an integral part of modern society, and an ambitious young woman must be comfortable with the arts in order to ascend to the top. An accident of birth is no longer the key to social acceptance or to professional success. In all major cities and most sizable towns in this country, social life centers around the enjoyment and support of aesthetic pursuits.

One has only to read the newspapers and magazines to understand that the balls, galas, festive luncheons, lecture/demonstrations, auctions, tours, and expositions that make the spotlight are benefits for symphony orchestras, museums, libraries, theater and dance groups. The bright, motivated young woman can find a happy and rewarding place in this stimulating world if her interest is sincere, she is willing to give of her time and talents, and she knows how to behave at affairs and performances in an appropriate manner.

The following pages will prepare you to deport yourself with proper, inconspicuous decorum even in a crowd of seasoned connoisseurs.

357

358 Your Role in the Performing Arts

From her early teens, a young woman begins her involvement with the arts. At first she may participate in clubs or be asked to sell tickets for a concert or school play; but starting with high school or college, and especially after she starts a career or is married, her social life will revolve around cultural activities, and she will need to move comfortably in this world. You will find the rules relatively simple and completely reasonable, and soon they will fit as comfortably as your favorite shoes.

Because of the nature of the performing arts, and the intensity and immediacy of the interaction between artist and audience, a somewhat formalized etiquette has developed. Its purpose is to minimize the possibility of one individual in a large crowd disturbing or annoying fellow members of the audience or interfering with the concentration or the mood of the performer. Regardless of the size or intimacy of the occasion, the rules always apply.

Obvious disinterest, whispering, or restless movements send a negative signal to the performer. Even sitting still with a bored expression can be wounding to a sensitive spirit. Your interest and appreciation are the fuel that drives an artist to achieve full potential and can be the spark that sends him or her on to greatness.

When you applaud at the next performance you attend, think of my Ten-Finger Exercise for becoming a spectacular accessory for the arts you enjoy.

TEN-FINGER EXERCISE

1. Go with someone whose company is special. Together you build up a little history of events you have enjoyed together. Let your aunt or your grandmother know you would be proud to attend the opera with her. Invite the girlfriend with whom you often spend Saturday afternoon to see an exhibition at the museum. The someone special may be a date; it is very civilized to invite a young man to a cultural event with you, with the tickets your treat. If perhaps, the tickets were given to you by a relative or passed on by someone who could not use them, here is an occasion when your treat would be a gentle way of not intimidating or obligating your date to pay back.

2. While we are on the subject of romance, keep pleasantly in the back of your mind that the arts constitute a lovely and natural

forum to meet desirable friends of the opposite sex. At private parties after the theater, from fancy benefits for the arts to less elaborate fund-raisers, students or young careerists meet and mix.

3. Few young women realize they, too, can be patrons of the arts. On the boards and committees of dance and theater companies are a range of people—some with the means to make financial contributions, but also volunteer workers who give tirelessly of themselves.

4. Volunteer *now*. Being young, pretty, and energetic is an asset. You might dress attractively and give out programs. This is your chance, for example, to see more opera or ballet, hear more classical music, and see more plays than you might otherwise!

5. You are like a pebble in a pool, spreading out rings of effect, when you toss in your support. Investigate community groups and Junior Committee-sponsored performances where you can be of service.

6. Skim broadly. The cultural interest you choose later as your preferred one will place demands on your free time. You have, no matter who you are, only so much time and money to give. Mrs. Astor, for instance, one of the great patrons of the cultural life of New York City, concentrates on the New York Public Library and the zoo. You, too, will develop your allegiances.

7. Refer to your experience in the past when you enjoy a new performance. This will hold it in your memory and give you a deeper understanding. Childhood memories of the *Messiah* or the *Nutcracker* are part of your history if you have experienced them at a church or local ballet (or even on television).

8. Listen to what others like and dislike when they discuss performances. Is your experience like theirs at the same event? Let your sense of what is most exciting grow.

9. Broaden yourself by experimenting, dabbling, if you will, by attending plays and shows that are avant-garde and different. This is as important as developing your repertoire of the classics.

10. Give tickets to friends or take a date at your expense only if you can buy at least fairly good tickets. Do not share the cheapest seats—despite good intentions, that makes you look cheap,

360

too. If you are going "dutch," of course, even stand-up matinee space can be a lark.

Dressing for the Occasion

When faced with any new social situation the very first question to enter your mind is probably, "What do I wear?" We know that every social situation carries with it a dress code, and again "good taste" and "appropriate" are the words to keep in mind. Among all theater-goers, balletomanes, opera buffs, and classical music lovers we find certain ways of dressing.

While the theater-goer certainly has no need to one-up the leading lady, dressing presents an opportunity for a woman to make an attractive appearance, appropriate to the sophisticated company, and to give pleasure to her companions. Contemporary custom allows for the individual to dress as she likes so long as general rules of neatness are followed.

Practical considerations and the prevailing attitude regarding formality and informality in your region should dictate wardrobe choice. Should you be arriving directly from school, the workplace, or another daytime appointment, street clothes are acceptable. If, on the other hand, you are a member of a theater party and the evening includes a meal or other refreshments before or immediately following the event, a slightly dressier costume is festive and nice.

An elaborate long gown for you and black-tie regalia for your escort are called for only for opening nights or benefit galas that include receptions prior to curtain time or following the performance. On other special evenings, short, covered cocktail or dinner dresses and theater suits are lovely for young women, and dark suits are appropriate for their escorts.

Smart evening hats come and go with the cycles of fashion, but understand that the theater, or cocktail, hat is but a wisp of whimsy, which, by virtue of its close-to-the-head design, obstructs no one's view. If you choose a larger, inappropriate hat, you will find your hat in your hand more often than on your head—at the irate request of the person seated behind you. Also beware of bows and beaus. Broad hairbows can block someone's view, as can two heads nestled together. So save shoulder-to-shoulder hairbows and cheek-to-cheek chatting for later.

At the opera, people tend to dress more formally than at the theater. Clothes that are quite dressy are worn to New York City's fashionable Monday night performances. Those with a box at the opera or dress circle at the theater, concert, or ballet also dress more formally (gentlemen in black or white tie and ladies in short or long gowns). The balcony, by contrast, is a dress "down" section, for those with a serious interest in the artistry and little or no concern about "being seen," although you will on occasion see an elegantly dressed couple who simply prefer the view from the balcony.

Perhaps because of its appeal to a younger, more avant-garde audience, dress for the ballet is often less formal than for the other performing arts. Personally, I am not in favor of dressing as if you were in a dance rehearsal when you attend the ballet, though warm-up apparel is often seen in the audience.

I do not condone a sloppy, come-as-you-are dress code—jeans, warm-ups, tennis shoes—for young women attending any aesthetic event. Hose, neat pumps or flats, a pretty dress or a nicely tailored suit, even a blazer, skirt, and a blouse are appropriate, but trousers are not. Dressy boots are allowed for severely cold weather, as are whatever outer garments are needed. Proper dressing shows savoir faire and also respect for the performers and for other members of the audience who have made the effort to be attractive. As a model, I always gave a better performance on the stage when a chic, well-groomed audience was present. Proper attire also allows you to go directly from an afternoon matinee to dinner, or from an evening performance to supper or out dancing. You will see eccentrics in concert, theater, ballet, even opera crowds, but you should avoid being one of them.

"Artsy" Evenings

One of the most delightful aspects of "artsy" evenings is the socializing before and after the performance itself. Preperformance exchange over a light bite to eat eliminates any temptation to idle chatter at a time when you should be scanning the Playbill. Postperformance conversation over a yummy dessert eliminates the need to discuss the performance while it is going on—a social no-no!

Never allow your socializing to make you late. If you suspect that service in the restaurant you plan to patronize is slow or if you or your friends have a tendency to dawdle, plan accordingly and refuse to make a "dramatic" entrance.

In large cities, restaurants often offer a pretheater dinner seating, which, with its shorter menu and expedient service, promises that you can enjoy a lovely dinner and be on time too. If you have the good fortune to attend the theater in London, choose one of the restaurants that presents a starter and entrée pretheater, then *après*-theater dessert and coffee—all at a fixed price. Or, you may nibble on finger sandwiches before the curtain rises or during intermission and even enjoy a light supper served in your box, should you arrange it in advance, at The Royal Opera House.

In addition to allowing adequate time for preperformance activities, remember to include the necessary time for travel to and from the theater. Traffic jams can be terrible in popular theater districts. If your schedule is tight, plan your preperformance rendezvous within walking distance of the theater.

Showtime

The rising of the curtain is magic, an instant that no real play-goer wishes to miss. Even if you are willing to cheat yourself of the moment, do not intrude on the opening scenes by a careless, late arrival. Latecomers unsettle the performers and distract the audience.

Late arrivals are usually asked to wait for a suitable break before being seated. If this request is not made and you must decide for yourself, remain quietly in the back until the conclusion of the first scene, musical number, or dance routine.

The pluses of arriving early are many: There is time to people-watch, locate your seat and settle comfortably, read the program, and chat.

Let me caution you that the acoustics in an entertainment hall are superlative and that voices carry. So while you are waiting for the performance to begin, be very careful that you do not let your excitement and anticipation raise the level of your speaking voice so that you attract attention to yourself. Keep any conversation private, moderate your laughter, and be certain any comments you make concerning the production or the actors do not reach anyone beyond your companion. As curtain time draws near, quiet yourself and slip into the mood of the occasion.

Coats and Cameras

In America a theater-goer has the choice of keeping or checking any coats, hats, and parcels. In England and Europe, however, it is often mandatory to check them. You are always required to check cameras because the flash distracts and annoys artists and members of the audience alike. To expedite the retrieving process, keep the claim check handy and have a small tip ready for the coat attendant when abroad (the theater coat attendant is seldom tipped in America but there is sometimes a charge).

Given the option, should you choose not to check your coat, you must deal with it once seated with as much ease as possible. If you are alone, you may accept the assistance of a seated neighbor. If accompanied by an escort, your escort will assist you and will place the shoulders of the coat over the back of the seat. Feel free to return the courteous favor and assist him if he needs it. You have the alternative choice of removing your coat, rolling it into a ball and placing it under your seat, or, if you fear it could become soiled, you may hold it in your lap. Any method of storage is fine as long as it does not interfere with your neighbors.

The Libretto, Playbill, and Program

Programs are both enjoyable and educational. Your first encounter with the array of printed material is in the lobby as you are offered a program or libretto. Libretto is an Italian word meaning "little book," and that is exactly what it is. It contains a synopsis of the story and scenes of an opera, a copy of the sung or spoken text, and is a delightful souvenir item. Sometimes there is a charge but generally a fairly modest one. The purchase of the libretto, however, does not entitle you to read it nor flip through its pages during the performance. At an opera hall, study your libretto *prior* to performance time. The symphony concert hall, however, differs from the opera house in that house lights remain relatively high throughout the performance, enabling you to follow the program text, if you take care never to ruffle pages during the performance.

At the theater you will be handed the Playbill. (In the United States and Europe there is no charge, but there often is in Great Britain.) The Playbill tells you about the performers and the play, including a brief synopsis of acts, scenes, and intermissions.

Collecting Playbills, librettos, and programs is like keeping a diary of your aesthetic experience and can lead to a delightful and informative scrapbook. A lovely idea is to keep such items in leather or vinyl covers especially designed for them. This binder also has pages on which to write your comments about the performance, friends with whom you attended, and other memories. Occasionally you may have your Playbill or souvenir program autographed and that will make it a treasure in later years.

Entrances and Exits

At the theater, not only the performers make entrances and exits—it is also important for you to be familiar with your cues.

More than likely, the tickets will have been purchased ahead of time. Should the event be your treat, hand them to your escort at an inconspicuous time, as it is he who takes the lead from that point on. Should you be hostessing an all-girl party, then you will be the leader and the others will follow.

If tickets have been reserved and are held at the box office, your escort (you, if you are the hostess) will get in line. If the line is long and you want to chat with your escort, feel free to do so if space allows. It is a courteous gesture, however, to step aside once his turn has come so that he may take care of payment or settle any discrepancies privately and singlehandedly. This also eliminates any apparent curiosity on your part as to the cost of the tickets.

Once tickets are in hand and coats are checked (if desired or required), if there is time you may have refreshments or purchase souvenir programs. Resist the temptation, however, if it is too close to curtain time. And be forewarned that the usher will ask you to discard even a full glass before you are seated. Unlike many movie houses, theaters rarely permit food or drink in the auditorium.

You now advance to the ticket-taker. Your escort will step back to allow you to move past, then the two of you will proceed together to the head of the aisle to which you have been directed. Should you encounter an usher there, your escort will hand over the ticket stubs and the three of you will proceed down the aisle in this order: usher leads, you follow, escort last. Often the usher is found partway down the aisle, in which case your escort leads and you follow. When you reach the usher and your escort hands over the ticket stubs, he then steps back so that you may precede. If your party is large, pair up in the order in which you will be sitting and follow the leader, be it the usher, an escort, or the hostess of an all-girl party.

Once you have reached the proper row, you enter first. Your escort will follow you and, of the two seats assigned to you, will take the one that is nearer the aisle.

Exercise grace and gentleness as you find your seat. Take particular care that you stomp no toes nor hit any heads with your handbag. It is polite for the strangers you pass to stand and fold back their seats to allow you to pass, and I urge you to do this when others pass you. In any case, even if they only move their knees to the side, "think thin" and pass as unobtrusively as possible. As you go by, you should say "Excuse me, please," adding "Thank you" after you have passed.

When the time comes to leave your seats, you will exit in reverse order and your escort will reach the aisle first, then step aside and wait for you to join him. If room permits, you may walk side by side, but if not, you walk up the aisle first and your escort follows. Should there be a real crush in the aisle, your escort will move ahead of you to make way and you will follow closely behind. In a theater party, each of the boy-girl pairs acts individually as described, and in all-girl parties, the hostess takes the leading role.

What, you may be thinking, if my escort does not know these ins and outs? Do not worry, simply position yourself in the correct place and say, "I'll move ahead a bit," "I'll wait for you over there," "After you," "Will you lead the way," "I'll follow you," or "I'll follow the usher." All of these gentle phrases will give him the cues he needs to think he knows his way around!

Foreign Friends

As travel and educational exchange is an everyday part of our world, you will find that friends from other countries follow social customs that differ from ours. In particular you will note that as they enter the row, Europeans pass face-to-face with their neighbors. This is indeed convenient as you can personally excuse yourself as you look people in the eye and you can also be extra careful not to step on any toes.

When escorted by a European, you will find that he makes sure to seat you on his right. To put you in the "place of honor," he may invite you to precede him into the row and then pass in front of you to sit at your left. He may place you on his left, however, if seats are placed so that you would otherwise be on the aisle—considered a second-choice seat because passers-by often brush the person in the aisle seat.

On the other hand, do not be offended if an escort from one of the Scandinavian countries seats you on his left. It is his custom to award the place of honor to the person on his left—his heart's side!

When two couples are seated together, you may arrange the seating as you like. I have found it compatible to allow one of the men to enter the row first, followed by his date, then the other woman followed by her escort. In this manner the women are cushioned by their escorts from the unknown neighbors. But never allow this seating arrangement to lead to a session of girl talk. Keep both escorts involved when conversing.

366

Tipping Tips

In America, members of the audience are not expected to tip ushers. Attendants are paid by the performing agency or they are volunteers.

Abroad, however, you will encounter the word *pourboire,* generally accompanied by the usher's outstretched open palm. Unless you respond, you may be embarrassed by a lecture.

On the European continent (with the exception of Germany and Switzerland), and in Asia and Latin America, those attending theater, ballet, operatic and musical events are expected to tip ushers or usherettes with a middle value coin (about a quarter). Too large a tip is considered gauche and showy; too small, miserly and insulting. Even attendants at movie theaters in some foreign countries must be tipped. In England the usher is not tipped, but if there is a program, expect a charge for it.

Intermission Encounters

Intermission is the "half-time" of the performing arts. Whether you choose to stay seated or elect to wander about is up to you. Be prepared, however, to be ever so polite and patient if you remain while your neighbors elect to stretch.

Remember, even in the most formal setting, any activities in which you engage must fit within the time frame allotted. In England, intermission can be a lovely affair thanks to the tradition of placing an order and paying for a beverage, finger sandwiches, or sweets, *before* the performance itself. How delightful to walk up to the appointed spot or table and find that your order awaits you.

Do respect any restrictions assigning certain refreshment areas to particular ticket-holders. Do not be a "gate-crasher."

Applause Means *Merci*

Applause is a thank-you from the audience to the performers for the gift of their effort and talent. It should be enthusiastic and even lengthy in response to outstanding accomplishment, but should never break the rhythm of the performance itself or cause the artists to lose concentration.

At opera, ballet, concert, and musical theater performances, the first applause occurs when the concertmaster (the first violinist) walks onto the stage after the other members of the orchestra have been seated. The conductor makes an entrance last, shakes hands with the concertmaster, steps up onto the podium, faces the audience, and takes a bow, at which time the audience applauds. At concerts, the guest soloist or soloists are also applauded when they walk onto the stage. This routine is repeated each time either the concertmaster, conductor, or soloist makes an appearance throughout the program. You will find that this respectful round of applause is quite brief and stops abruptly the moment the concertmaster or soloist finishes a bow or the conductor turns to face the orchestra.

At the theater applause is appropriate at the rising of the curtain and at the first entrance of any prominent actors. Entrances and exits should not be applauded on the ballet or opera stage, although sometimes enthusiastic audience members do not refrain.

Whereas applause is never appropriate after a song or instrumental solo (except at a jazz performance), or between movements of a composition performed in concert, an ovation is proper at the ballet after a magnificent dance solo or *pas de deux,* at the opera following a difficult or well-sung aria, or at the theater following a marvelous dramatic episode. Applause must be withheld, however, until the final musical note has cleared the air, the dancer has relaxed his or her breathtaking position, or the singer or actor has completed the crucial scene. Appreciation at this moment, although quite complimentary to the artist, must be very brief so as not to render the performer unable to hear the music or to interfere with the rhythm or continuity of the performance itself. The singer or dancer often responds with a bow, or, if that would cause chaos, continues with the action.

As operas are sometimes quite lengthy, curtain calls are frequently made between acts. The same is true at the ballet, and applause is given at the end of each act or at the end of a scene.

Lavish applause at the conclusion of a performance is natural and enjoyable to the audience as well as the performers. The truly enraptured audience may even rise while clapping—a standing ovation. Whether seated or standing, the audience applauds each time the conductor or stars come from the wings to take a bow, and when solo artists or supporting cast members are acknowledged by the stars or conductor. Also, usually the conductor of the orchestra comes up from the orchestra pit onto the stage to formally take a bow following an opera, ballet, or musical theater performance.

Depending upon the enthusiasm of the audience, and the popularity of the artist, a series of curtain calls may honor the cast and musicians. Often, particularly during musical concerts, an encore is presented, at which point the audience quickly sits down and quiets for the final piece.

To Boo Is Taboo

Few performances are perfect. An outward demonstration of disapproval is more common in European countries, while the American custom is to remain more reserved. To shout "Boo!" is not polite. Simply award a brief but sincere clapping of your hands in respect of the efforts of the performers and make your departure—but only at the polite and proper time: intermission, at the conclusion of an act, or at the end of the performance, never during the performance.

To begin gathering your possessions toward the end of the last movement—or act—is extremely rude. Granted, there are taxis and trains to catch, *après*-theater supper reservations to meet, crowds and curfews to accommodate. But it is rude to spoil the pleasure of the rest of the audience.

If you *must* leave before the final curtain, plot your exit quickly and quietly between movements or acts. And arrange to have aisle seats so that you will not disrupt your neighbors or those behind you.

When a performance has ended, you may leave, having applauded, even if others are still clapping. And if there is an encore, you may decline it as you would an after-dinner mint.

Should your schedule—or your interest, for that matter—necessitate your leaving before the encore, take care to act quickly during the first rush of applause. Once the encore begins and the audience reseats itself, a hush falls, and you are trapped.

Bestowing Bouquets

Being a star may bring not only applause but also bouquets. An appreciative audience member can make prior arrangements to have a bouquet brought in from the wings and presented to the artist as the final bow is made.

Most exciting and personal of all is to make prior arrangements to present your bouquet in person, should the artist be receiving in the dressing room after the performance. Otherwise, you may ask that flowers be delivered to the dressing room by the florist. Always remember to enclose your calling card!

No, No, Nannette

Any breach of civilized behavior in public, especially when attending an artistic performance, is unthinkable. Register my lucky thirteen restraints for the performing arts so that your performance will be star-worthy.

1. No vulgar, revealing, or trashy clothes.
2. No view-blocking headgear.
3. No jingle-jangle jewelry.
4. No gum-chewing anywhere.
5. No eating or drinking at your seat (except a coughdrop).
6. No talking or whispering during the performance.
7. No telling the ending.
8. No primping in public.
9. No humming, singing, or tapping.
10. No napping.
11. No love scenes with your escort.
12. No clapping until everyone else does.
13. No exits until intermission or finale.

Culturally Conversant

Although discussing any performance while it is taking place is bad form, talking about it later with close friends is one of the wonderful bonuses of attending. But you must have some knowledge to back up your conversation.

Just as you should know Monet from Manet, you should know a *pointe* from a *pas,* a bass from a baritone, a trumpet from a trombone, *andante* from *allegro.* You must strive to enliven your vocabulary in order to become culturally conversant.

Movie Manners

The movies, although not always as artistically elevated as the performing arts, are nonetheless an art form of our times. The movie house is also a fine rehearsal stage for learning the rules required at more socially demanding events.

Once you have mastered your manners for the performing arts, I hope you will also become much more polite at the movies. No doubt you will agree with me that viewers' manners at the movies are not always at their best. Perhaps the more relaxed at-home atmosphere of television has spilled over into the movie theater. Why not take it upon yourself to become a quiet leader among your friends by taking your company manners along the next time you go to a movie.

Begin your campaign by upgrading your mode of dress, moderating the volume of your voice, taking your fair turn in line, choosing a seat and sticking with it, ceasing conversation the minute the screen comes alive (from opening music to the final credits), and controlling your reactions and emotions.

Although you are often free to eat and drink in the movies, remember that the rattling of wrappers is disturbing to others and dropped food fragments are repulsive and damaging to furnishings and to clothing. Of course, do not chew gum in the movie or in any social situation. Gum-chewing is an ugly, often noisy habit and is a social taboo.

Athletic Event Etiquette

On the sports scene, good manners are as imperative as fair play. Whether you are a spectator or a participant, the rules of the game must be followed.

Socially speaking, the spectator has the opportunity to let her hair down a bit—to root her team toward victory, to thrash about somewhat, to belt out fight songs, to "munch," and to converse congenially throughout the event (except, of course, during the invocation, national anthem, or alma mater).

Just remember that common courtesy holds center court in any social arena, and pack your public politeness along with your pennant to assure a social victory, whether your team wins or loses.

Aesthetically Beautiful

For better or worse, you are coming to maturity in a time when being beautiful will not guarantee your success. As you attend concerts, opera, theater, and dance performances with thoughtful appreciation and acquaint yourself with paintings, sculpture, and architecture, the beauty and even something of the creativity they represent will become part of you. This will make a difference, not only in your personality and your character, but in your actual appearance. You are beautiful today because of the freshness and vigor that belong to youth. If you are beautiful fifty years from now it will be because you have done something right. Proper living, noble thoughts, and intense, beautiful feelings will work outward and show in your face. Remember that you are actually beginning to paint your portrait as a mature woman by what you think and do today.

Many of the rewards for concentrating your time and energies on the aesthetics are immediately visible. Personal enjoyment of the arts is expanded by the kind of associations it brings. The arts develop rich friendships that cross the lines of sex and age. The arts have become a major socializing force in modern life, as almost all glamorous social events are interwoven with the enjoyment and support of various cultural endeavors. Attach yourself to a favorite. Your input of time, energy, and appreciation can earn you a position that even a rich inheritance could not buy.

Museum Manners

Enjoyment of the arts falls into two rather distinct categories. For the performing arts, as you have seen, the viewer/listener has an important responsibility to contribute to the creative effort through enthusiasm and empathy and especially by refraining from any activity that might interrupt the fragile process.

The other category of artwork—painting, sculpture, architecture, literature—we will call, for want of a better term, the "signature arts," because the artist has completed the work before the audience sees it, and therefore audience reaction has no direct impact on the work at all.

The enjoyment of the signature arts is usually a much more private experience than that of the public performance. Although there are exceptions, art lovers go to museums, monuments, gardens, and architectural sites, alone or with one or two congenial companions. (Often, however, one wisely elects to join a tour, in which case common courtesy and manners are sufficient guides to behavior.)

Reading is almost exclusively a solitary experience, which may be pursued curled up on your bed or in a favorite garden spot. Literary groups do have formalized readings, however, and here the rules for the performing arts apply.

That so many beautiful and moving things have miraculously been preserved through the ages to inspire us is a priceless part of our heritage. One cannot thank or encourage long-dead artists (though you can support and encourage the living), but always take scrupulous care that you in no way damage or endanger an artwork. And consider joining a group that assists in the care, preservation, and public presentation of these objects.

The Museum

A museum offers entertainment—but only for the culturally sophisticated. People with no love and no knowledge of art rarely enter. For the sensitive, however, a museum, with its store of treasures, is a superb place in which to spend a day. When you travel, allot some time in each important city for a visit to a museum for a better understanding of the area's culture and take continuing advantage of such facilities in your home city.

Museums are either free or moderately priced and offer an extravagant opportunity for enjoyment at your own pace when you have a bit of time on your hands. Do not allow yourself to be bored—ever. Find something to enjoy, and the higher the level of enjoyment, the more stimulated you will be.

Dressing "Up" and Dressing "Down"

Museums, like parks, are for people! You dress "up" for the opening of an exhibition as for an opening at the theater, but otherwise you dress "down." Your clothes are casual yet fashionable—never, I caution, dress down to the point of appearing to be a vagrant, an antifashion freak. Be sure to wear comfortable shoes, as your visit is mostly standing.

If the museum has no coatroom, carry with you as little as possible. Also, keep in mind that museums, for the most part—especially on a busy Saturday or Sunday—are warm.

Special openings and galas staged to benefit the museum will range in dress from black tie to business suits for men, and long gowns to short cocktail or dinner dresses to dressy business clothing for women. The formality or informality of the affair, however, will be properly noted on your invitation, and you should dress accordingly.

Fee Facts

Both in this country and abroad, a nominal entrance fee is charged for those who are not members of the museum. This fee is but a token toward the upkeep and should be paid with a smile. On certain days and/or evenings, museums waive the fee. Do, however, expect large crowds and longer lines at these times.

Students are granted a lower entrance fee and a student I.D. must be shown for this privilege. Savings can be obtained during foreign travel by obtaining a special student I.D. for museums and historic landmarks, a must for a journey budgeted in time and money.

Interestingly, many museums post a "suggested" fee or donation for entry. If you are not a member, pay at least the recommended amount. If a donation is an option, never slip by, for to do so is to be a "freeloader." Even if you *are* a member, you will feel right and good to deposit what you can afford into the donation box. This is important patronage of the arts.

Expect to pay an additional fee for special exhibitions that are not a part of the museum's permanent collection. These shows are on loan and travel from one museum to another, hence the mounting, crating, and shipping costs are substantial. We are fortunate in America that large corporations underwrite the majority of these handsome exhibitions, as there is no way we as individuals or the museums alone could absorb the costs.

As you plan your travels at home and abroad, research traveling exhibitions that will be on display in the cities on your itinerary. Just as you order theater tickets, so should you order tickets to these special showings in advance. This is certainly a safeguard when you are traveling long distances in hope of viewing a popular exhibition. It also saves standing in the long ticket line, though you will not be exempt from the entrance line to the gallery itself.

Coats and Cameras

As you enter the museum you often encounter a sign requesting that coats, cameras, and parcels be checked. This is a reasonable regulation for a number of reasons.

I remember how saddened and disappointed the ingénues and I were on one finishing tour to see Rembrandt's *Night Watch* at the Rijksmuseum in Amsterdam. It had been slashed with knives and was enveloped with scaffolding as restorers attempted to save it.

Fortunately, there are few such art criminals. Yet the regulations established by museums and other public institutions are protective measures for safety, and they provide for our comfort as well. Laden with wraps and bags, you will not have the physical stamina to enjoy a museum. Also, accidents do happen, and paintings and sculptures can be scratched and objects broken unintentionally by swinging coats, cameras, and bags. In addition, camera flashes can destroy colors and are absolutely *not* allowed in museums or anywhere there are preserved treasures. If you do want *your* own photograph, learn to use a camera with a long exposure and slow-speed film. Most museums permit this, but always ask first.

I recall a time when the selfishness of just one person caused many to suffer. As the ingénues and I stood with many other visitors in front of the Mona Lisa in the Louvre, there was a flash. The guard quickly drew the curtain over the painting and we all departed with a real disappointment. Each of us had traveled so far to enjoy this famous painting only to have just a glance.

The Paced Tour

If you are serious in your study of the arts, the paced tour directed by a knowledgeable guide can increase the value of a museum visit enormously. Guides and docents have been specially schooled and have spent a good deal of time familiarizing themselves with the various collections and their creators. They are usually sensitive to the reactions of the group and seek to make the experience meaningful. Some talks are conducted in a lecture hall, which is a good break from standing in the galleries.

There is no charge for guided tours in most museums in the United States, as their costs are included in the entrance fee. In Europe, however, tickets are often sold for tours. Unless you are quite conversant in a foreign language, be certain to find an English-speaking guide.

One of the most pleasant tours I recall was one of the Louvre in Paris. I had written ahead to engage an English-speaking guide for an "ingénues-only" tour. The guide took us through the famed museum with a flair and enthusiasm that was catching and provided us a store of wonderful memories.

A taped tour is an excellent alternative, especially if you are visiting alone, but it can hamper the nice exchange when you go with friends. There is, of course, a rental charge for the tape, but for the information it reveals, the dollars are well spent.

Touring by instinct can also be rewarding. Sometimes it is better simply to wander and stop to study only things that appeal to you. Think of it this way: When you look out to sea and lose yourself in its beauty, you are not measuring the speed with which clouds pass or the precise blueness of the water, you may not even be remarking on the fine view—you are taking it *inside.* And so, even if you forget where you are and to what century or artist the artwork belongs, in your visual pleasure you have shared the artist's vision and effortlessly increased your aesthetic awareness. So decide whether you are in a mood to learn or simply to feel.

Tipping Tips

Tipping is not allowed in the museums of America. The majority of the guides are volunteers who are donating their time and accrued knowledge for the benefit of the museum. On the other hand, guides in museums abroad are paid employees, and although it is not mandatory to present the guide with a small gratuity at the end of the tour, it is acceptable to do so, particularly if the guide goes out of his or her way to add a spark. Should a guide ever refuse a tip, do not become embarrassed. Simply say, "Thank you for the tremendous tour! I'm adding this to my donation in honor of your enthusiasm!"

The Hand Sheet and Labels

By availing yourself of the printed material offered, you can also learn a great deal about pieces in a museum's permanent collection and special exhibitions. Most museums provide free handouts or hand sheets, with information on both permanent and temporary exhibitions. Your visit will be more meaningful if you read these before you tour, but you may also read as you approach a particular piece. In the National Gallery in Washington, the appropriate handout is available in every room, an especially convenient procedure.

Paintings and other art items are also labeled. Fortunately, the trend among museum curators today is to give a great deal of technical, historical, and biographical information on the labels, especially on temporarily mounted works.

The Museum Shop

Posters of different works, inscribed with the name and location of the museum and the exhibition dates, adorn my office walls and provide instant recalls of pleasant viewings. I urge that you visit the museum shop, too, and begin to collect during your museum visits, even if only art postcards or note cards which take up no luggage space at all.

The Mannerly Viewer

In addition to dressing in quiet good taste, keeping the voice low, not blocking the view of the work, not littering, not endangering or touching valuable pieces (all common courtesy basics), the mannerly museum viewer refrains from passing in front of a person who is engrossed in the study of a work. When your turn comes to admire a painting, piece of sculpture, or decorative art, do be aware of others who await the experience and do not "hog" it by taking longer than your turn. Return, if necessary, for an additional viewing.

In a museum certain areas are roped off or distances are established to let you know how close to a work you may stand. Never overstep these boundaries, even if you think no one is looking. Remember, rules are rules, and minding your manners means that you obey them.

Most museums prohibit eating or drinking in galleries, so do not nibble or, of course, chew gum.

My last advice is to be sure to leave the museum before you and your companion become weary. Better to return another time. You want to emerge from a museum refreshed and full of pleasure at the sights you have just taken in.

Refreshing Interludes

Museum trekking can develop your appetite!

Fortunately, most large museums offer a restaurant or cafeteria in which to relax and have lunch or a snack. How nice, too, to plan a Saturday or Sunday museum spree with a friend, be it young man or woman, and a leisurely lunch together as well. The ingénues on our finishing tour always enjoy our lovely luncheon break at the Tate Museum, as fashionable a dining spot as any in London.

Museum Membership

As public institutions, museums open their doors to everyone and thereby serve an important educational and aesthetic purpose. For those who have more than a one-time or casual interest, a museum membership is a wonderful step. It also allows you to make a contribution of time to the arts.

378

Student memberships are ordinarily very low-cost and often are matched by public or private grants, which further benefit the institution. You may already be covered by a family membership; if that is the case, take full advantage of the privilege.

Members receive special treatment that can make joining doubly worthwhile. Membership opens the door to a members' room provided by most museums, where you may relax and where frequent "members-only" events are held. Other perquisites of membership (depending upon the classification, governed by the amount of the fee) include free admission, discounts at the gift shop and/or bookshop, invitations to previews and openings, notices of exhibitions, free catalogues, and a newsletter, which in the case of large institutions such as the Smithsonian in Washington, D.C., the Art Institute in Chicago, and the Metropolitan Museum of Art in New York, takes the form of a full-fledged magazine.

The Art Gallery

The gallery differs from the museum mainly in that it is a private enterprise rather than a public institution. The gallery is understandably smaller and it often limits its collections to a particular type, period, or other classification of art, which is usually for sale.

I sincerely wish that I could introduce you to gallery-going—or reintroduce you—by taking you to the Fenn Galleries in Santa Fe, *the* favorite gallery haunt of the girls who summer with L'Ecole des Ingénues. Why? Inviting little signs placed beside the sculptures, ceramics, baskets, and beads read "please touch." Our hospitable Southwestern hosts and hostesses encouraged us to rub the cold bronzes, stroke the pottery, and cradle the beads in our hands. Naturally, touching the paintings was not allowed, but we were able to stand as close as we wished.

Most large cities in this country and abroad have numerous galleries that make a valuable contribution by offering the works of contemporary and regional artists, arranging shows of the works of young and less well-known artists from around the world, and providing a sophisticated resource for those seeking to collect beautiful things, at prices they can afford. Of course, a few prestigious galleries have works of the masters and of already renowned contemporaries at less affordable prices.

Galleries stage special exhibits and often hold gala or informal receptions similar to museum events; etiquette codes for these affairs are identical. You may enjoy browsing in galleries when you have free time. By picking up exhibition handbills or complimentary catalogues you may learn a surprising amount about rising artists and could possibly find inexpensive works that appeal to you. Unlike the museum, the gallery offers the added excitement that you may purchase that which you peruse.

So that you may become a part of the special evenings or afternoons a gallery provides, sign the guest book or ask that your name be placed on the mailing list. In this way you will receive special notices of showings and invitations to social events, which last only a half hour or so but are wonderful "starters" for a festive evening.

The Library

Can you imagine throwing a glamorous party in the public library? One of the most prestigious social galas in New York City is staged against the backdrop of the magnificent New York Public Library.

Do consider yourself a "friend" of the library. Realize that half of knowledge is knowing where to find it. In America's many and well-stocked libraries repose the wealth from the greatest minds of the ages. Books are yours to use without charge (unless you lose them or forget to return them).

It was the free libraries that gave immigrants the opportunity to educate themselves and become a part of mainstream America. Not only education, but also practical information and tools needed to earn your daily bread, are offered in the millions of books housed in these great and important structures; uplifting thoughts and sheer pleasure are there, too.

But you must respect the needs of others when using a library, and take care that you never damage a volume, folio, or other item, and that you return borrowed books on schedule, especially if there is a waiting list for popular new works. Your grade school rules regarding books hold true and will never fail you, whether the books are your own or borrowed from the library or a friend: Never write on the pages, fold them down, press them open to the point of breaking the spine, dent the corners, or soil them with food or makeup. Be courteous and appreciative when library staff members assist you.

Literary groups are not necessarily earmarked "for bookworms only." You can find friends among devotees of mystery books, historical novels, bestsellers, poetry—any topic that captivates you. Join with them for study and discussion, or plan to go together to meet an author or to booksigning events. It is indeed special to hear an author read his or her own words. Before attending a bookclub meeting, do your homework by reading the work to be discussed or reviewed so that you can make your contributions to the group.

The Architectural Tour

Tours of various kinds are among the most pleasant and rewarding of cultural experiences. One can get the "feel" of past eras on tours of historical sites in this country and abroad, especially if an enthusiastic and knowledgeable guide is in charge. Old and quaint buildings that contain fine architectural elements and furnishings can carry one back decades or even centuries and put you in a time-out-of-mind mood.

Churches, especially in Europe—Saint Peter's of Rome, Notre Dame of Paris, London's Saint Paul's and Westminster, and dozens of other enormous Gothic cathedrals—are regularly open for tours. Some historic American churches, too, offer splendid opportunities for architectural study. These tours teach a great deal about the life of the people who worshiped there; nicest of all is to do your viewing at the time of the service, so that you experience the grandeur to its fullest as you sit among the congregation.

While touring churches the visitor is expected to respect the spirituality of the building by circumspect behavior and to comply with requests for quiet. When services are in progress, visiting is sometimes prohibited or restricted to certain areas. The same rules apply for cameras as in a museum. A donation box for gifts to defray the expense of having the building open and perhaps to support charities is usually placed near the doorway, and a contribution is definitely in order.

Castles throughout the world open their doors in an organized, businesslike manner. A fee is charged and a guide is provided, usually one conversant in a variety of languages. The usual rules often apply as to checking cameras, coats, and parcels. Strange as it may seem, even shoes may be checked or left at entrance doorways and woolly slippers worn instead. This, of course, provides the needed protection for the pathways trod by millions of tourists upon centuries-old floors. The spirited guide adds spark and can most certainly be tipped if you wish.

Historic houses in this country and homes in Europe from cottages to mansions give the traveler a marvelous insight into the daily life of the people who lived in them. It is a treat indeed to be able to enter modern palaces in such places as Newport, Rhode Island, see where the wealthy and influential lived and to enjoy their priceless furnishings and art treasures.

Tours of private homes in this country are usually limited to fund-raising projects for the various performing and signature arts. The owners, often at great personal inconvenience, allow their houses to be invaded by throngs of strangers. Pre-Christmas tours, especially, are popular, and there are a number of famous holiday tours in large, art-conscious cities.

As a visitor you have a responsibility to in no way damage the property by such thoughtless acts as walking on carpets with muddy shoes, touching fragile objects, or dropping trash. You should not linger past visiting or tour hours, intrude into restricted areas or beyond ropes, or purloin so much as a book of matches. Sadly enough, the generosity of homeowners has been abused and valuable items have been taken.

Socially Benefitting and Befitting

Support groups for museums, libraries, historic sites, and other culturally valuable endeavors function similarly to those for the performing arts. Fund-raising galas, balls, and preview exhibitions are delightful social occasions at which the sensitive young person makes friends with kindred spirits of both sexes. The beneficiary is both you and the arts.

Volunteering your services in the gift or bookshop of a museum, historic locale, or other institution, or serving as a hostess for a house tour, is a worthwhile endeavor. Belonging to special guilds or support groups may entail a small membership fee. And for some groups you must be sponsored by another member. The fee offsets the cost of mailings, handbooks, and other operating expenses.

Your participation in support groups for the arts can take many different forms. Whether you lend your pretty handwriting and free hours to the addressing of invitations, or add your outgoing personality as hostess at the *hors d'oeuvre* table at parties, your rewards are manifold: social poise, new friends, community involvement, and personal fulfillment. Once you are out of college, these groups are the bridge between the comfort of the college campus life and the "real" world, and can make that world less cold and lonely. You will find a fraternal ambience among those of your age and artistic interests.

The benefits of involvement are not just the arts' alone. You, too, will become the beneficiary. You will develop your skills as a future leader and make stimulating contacts that may become lifelong on both the social and business scenes.

I hope that in your efforts to add my "finishing touches" to your life, you will become aesthetically aware, enhancing your social countenance through a lifelong contact with the literary arts, the performing arts, and the visual arts. Begin today to become the philanthropist of tomorrow by exchanging your talent and time for cultural gains. Remember, many can give money, but all are short on time—the most precious gift of all!

On Your Way

Women can take great pride in their contributions to the artistic and cultural heritage to which the modern world is heir. Restrained in the past, our sex has not (with many notable exceptions) authored the most famous literature, music, drama, artwork, or architecture. Social and cultural forces have served to hinder female genius in most civilizations. Yet we have nonetheless been the inspiration, the nurturers, and the protectors of great art, and the creators of much of the beauty and refinement of the civilized life.

Contributions by women to the fields of business, science, and the professions have also been limited up to now by unequal levels of education and personal freedom. The years of childbearing and child-rearing also have had an effect. Yet this most fulfilling form of creativity brings its own rewards and has given women a singular sensitivity and inner power, which promises superlative achievement in the future.

As a young woman today, you have choices your grandmothers and even your mothers could scarcely have imagined. You face questions about priorities and potential. Your identification of personal goals early on and your ability to pursue them with unflagging dedication will, in large measure, determine not only your success but, more important, your happiness and that of those whom your life will touch. Such decisions are among the most crucial you and your generation will be called upon to make.

First, I should like to charge you to make the most of your young womanhood. Do not wish away this pleasant and important time, carefully guarded by most parents to allow their daughters to mature physically, intellectually, and spiritually without undue stress. Your body continues growing and changing well into your third decade, preparing itself for accomplishment and the possibility of childbirth. Damage to both an immature body and a sensitive spirit can result from experimentation with sex apart from real love and the commitment of marriage, and such experiences also pose the dangers of disease.

Other health considerations—a wholesome diet free of damaging substances, exercise, adequate rest—should be given high priority. Throughout your life, whatever career direction you choose, health and vigor will be essential to your capacity to work, live, and love.

Availing yourself of the marvelous educational opportunities now open to you is also a necessity during this time. If you have dreams of a dazzling career, you must certainly obtain the academic or technical background required. Even a somewhat routine office position demands a command of grammar and mathematics. And the demanding roles of wife, mother, and community leader also require well-rounded knowledge. Finally, you, as a person, will be more complete and fulfilled if you possess an education. More individualistic pursuits such as writer, artist, actress, designer, or interior decorator demand no less an understanding of history, literature, and mathematics. Seek schooling while you are young, so that your education becomes a natural component of your personality. True, older women have earned college degrees and made dramatic achievements, but the effort is more difficult later.

Once you are grown and have the finest education you can absorb, it is a good idea to test yourself in the workplace. Before making long-term decisions, try a field that seems greenest to you and give yourself an opportunity to find out if the appeal is real. Learn to live on your own, if your circumstances allow it, and learn to handle money. A first real job is a post-teenage course of singular value to everyone from the homemaker to the bank president.

Learn to work intelligently and gain satisfaction from it, because work you certainly will. There is nothing new about women working; only the locale of the effort and the matter of remuneration have changed. Throughout history women have needed, or been forced, to work, sometimes alongside men, sometimes in more sheltered circumstances, as in the home.

There is almost complete acceptance today of women in the workplace, in the professions, and in the arts. Talents that in earlier times would not have been allowed to develop now enrich life for all and provide fulfillment to those who possess them. Yet, as with most changes, the opening of previously closed doors has created certain pressures for the female population suddenly confronted with the need to make the choice between the traditional world of "vine-covered cottages," marriage, and children and the inviting pursuit of self-fulfillment, fame, and fortune. How does a young woman choose wisely or learn to blend the two?

A significant percentage of competent, highly successful career women often experience an emptiness as the years pass unless their emotional and physical needs are met as well. Some regret, quite publicly, the fact that marriage and motherhood had been passed by on the way to the top. Few of you are apt to arrive at so sad an impasse. Your education and your social experience will have brought you to intelligent decision-making and the avoidance of extremes. I encourage you during these years of limitless choices to focus on your goals and dreams and to return regularly to the Four R's I gave you in Chapter 1. The Four R's will help you monitor your life's direction as well as make certain that you are moving toward reasonable goals without undue stress, while still having the time and inclination to fully enjoy an unexpected, unplanned, happy moment—without any guilt.

We have looked into your mirror and seen your fresh beauty, your developing potential. Now, look into your mind's eye to find how you see yourself a decade in the future. Will you be racing toward the excitement of achievement, attracting respect, power, wealth? It is absolutely right that you have the choice of what you do with your life, but I counsel you to understand that such a single-minded drive may not be completely fulfilling for all women.

I submit that a glorious pattern for a woman's life can include love, children, *and* personal accomplishment. Once she is mature, educated, socially adjusted, and the possessor of some experience in the workplace, a young woman should be receptive to love, should accept the great truth that human emotions, as plants, bloom more gloriously in season. Marriage, built upon dreams and optimism, is still the safest anchor for a woman today. A carefree "honeymoon" time during which to build mutual understanding and a partnership, as well as the bank balance and the household inventory, is a fine prelude to a long and satisfying marriage.

When children arrive, you may wish to consider an extended career break. You may find, as many women do, that you are more fulfilled if you are on hand for the first tooth, the first word, the first step. You may feel it is important that you be there to ease social adjustments and tend skinned knees; and, by any criteria, an educated, loving mother is the best person to pass on to a child family standards, traditions, values, and gentle manners.

Confining and demanding as housekeeping and child-rearing is, it is yet more flexible than most regular employment. A creative woman can manage her schedule not only to allow joyous time with her child but time for herself and the pursuit of her creative interests.

As the children grow and enlarge their own worlds, mothers can arrange more extended time to volunteer their service to community, charitable, or cultural projects. Such activities are not only important contributions and personally fulfilling experiences, but acceptable résumé entries for later employment as well. Part-time jobs are feasible career steps as children grow, and such positions can be parlayed into interesting and remunerative pursuits. Usually by her early forties—depending upon her children's ages and individual needs—a woman is free to return to a part- or full-time career, if she so desires.

Your great-grandmothers were old women at forty. But at forty today's woman is just reaching her physical and intellectual prime. And, with a life expectancy of at least another forty years, any career that appeals is within her reach. Some employers prefer women of this age group, finding them more dependable, less inclined to absenteeism, more assured.

So, you see, you can have it all—education, career, marriage, and motherhood! You must, however, prepare yourself to make some important decisions: whether you satisfy your yearnings by concentrating on them one at a time, or whether you juggle them all at the same time.

Although the beautifully paced sequential approach to education, career, marriage, and motherhood may be desirable for some, it is not the answer for all women. For financial or for temperamental reasons, it could be wrong for some to attempt motherhood on a full-time basis.

However, for many modern young women, motherhood on a full-time basis is the answer. Evening classes, with husband babysitting, can be a delightful and inexpensive way to detonate the shock a young woman can feel after withdrawing from the exciting career scene with only baby for company—whose conversation is charming but rarely stimulating. Advanced or continued education will be a welcome intellectual challenge and could well be a plus when returning to a career or extensive social or civic service as the nest empties.

Already you are seeing that life has rhythms. Your childhood has been a series of stages: baby to tomboy (or perhaps budding "femme fatale"), uncertain teenager to increasingly charming, assured young woman. The stages will continue to flow, joyously, I hope, through career, marriage, motherhood, rich and productive maturity, reflective latter years, each filled with interest rather than regret. The life of a woman, as woman herself, can be a thing of beauty—proportioned, graceful, changing as it flowers, yet linked by strong roots to a firm and sustaining world.

This is an exciting time for a bright, creative, caring woman to take her place in contemporary society. The study of *Finishing Touches,* and accep-

386

tance of the philosophy behind it, will enable you to become poised, polished, and beautifully prepared for an exciting life ahead. A growing self-confidence will let you forget yourself so that you can concentrate on those about you and on making the world around you a better place. Fulfillment and joy will be your rewards.

Glossary

Flatware Finesse

The ABC's of the American and Continental Styles of Eating

A. *"Cutting" Position:* When cutting food, the knife is held in the right hand. The end of the handle is positioned in the center of the palm and the forefinger is placed at the end of the knife handle on the narrow side, not onto the blade (cutting edge facing the plate). The thumb rests on the wide side of the handle, and the fingers are gently curved around the handle to secure it. At no time should any portion of the handle extend beyond the palm, nor should the handle be grasped in the fist.

B. *"Spearing" Position:* When spearing food to cut with the knife, the fork is held in the left hand with the prongs, or tines, pointed down. It is held as the knife, except that the forefinger rests on the flat back side of the handle and the thumb rests on the slender edge.

C. *"Cutting" Action:* The food is cut with the knife close to the fork tines securing it. Cut and eat only one piece at a time. The elbows extend from the sides no more than four inches during any dining action.

The American "Zigzag" Style of Eating

1. *"Fork Alone" Position:* After cutting, place the knife in the "rest" position and assume the "fork alone" position by transferring the fork (tines up) to the right hand. (This transferring from hand to hand has caused the American style to be called

"zig-zag.") The fork is held near the end of the handle allowing no more than one-half inch of the handle to extend over the top of the hand. The handle rests on the side of the first joint of the middle finger and is secured gently with the pads of forefinger and thumb (thumb on the top and forefinger on the side). The two remaining outer fingers are gently curved and support the middle finger. With the food securely on the fork tines during the transfer from the left to the right hand, move on to the "conveying" action in Step three.

2. *"Adhering" Action:* The fork remains in the right hand in the "fork alone" position. Meat, vegetables, and starches are eaten with the fork held in the right hand in the "fork alone" position. Slip the fork tines beneath the food and lift it on the tines. Some foods may be successfully lifted by inserting the fork tines into them at an angle (never "stab" the food). Held in the left hand, a small piece of bread may be used, if absolutely necessary, to gracefully push food onto the end of the fork. After its use as a pusher, the bread is eaten with the fork. If no bread is served, the knife may be used for this purpose, although this is an awkward procedure at best and may be used only when all other strategies fail. To do this, pick the knife up with the right hand and transfer it to the left. Hold it in the "cutting" position behind the vegetable or starch and, keeping the knife stationary, slip the fork tines beneath or through the food and push against the knife tip. The knife remains in the left hand as the food is conveyed to the mouth on the fork after which the fork is placed in the "rest" position. Then transfer the knife to the right hand and place it in the "rest" position.

3. *"Conveying" Action:* With the fork in the right hand (tines still facing up), slightly twist the wrist (palm up) and convey the food to the mouth on the top of the fork tines.

4. *"Rest" Position:* Place the knife at a diagonal across the top fourth of the plate. The knife handle extends beyond the right side of the plate rim no more than an inch or the tip one-half inch beyond the top center. The fork (tines up) rests below and parallel with the knife (cutting edge facing the fork). The knife tip faces twelve on the clock and the handle faces three.

5. *"Finished" Position:* Place the knife and fork parallel and side-by-side in the center of the plate. The handles extend beyond the right side of the plate rim no more than an inch. The knife (cutting edge facing the fork) rests above the fork (tines *up*). The tips of each are inside the plate and face eleven on the clock while the handles face five.

The Continental Style of Eating

1. *"Adhering" Action:* The fork remains in the left hand in the "spearing" position. With the meat, vegetable, or starch still on the fork tines, push the fork against the lower end of the knife (held stationary against the plate) and slip the knife blade beneath the meat to secure it to the fork. Along with the meat, a *small* bite of vegetable and starch may be speared with the tines of the fork by pushing the fork against the knife, or they may be lifted with the knife and placed on the back of the fork behind the meat. Sauce may be lifted over the meat with the knife. Throughout this entire style, the elbows extend from the sides no more than four inches.

2. *"Conveying" Action:* With the fork remaining in the left hand (tines still facing down), slightly twist the wrist and lift the forearm to convey the food to the mouth on the back of the tines of the fork. The knife remains in the right hand with the right wrist on the table's edge—never over two or three inches above the plate—or place it in the "rest" position.

3. *"Rest" Position:* The fork (tines down) crosses, or rests, over the knife (cutting edge toward the table's edge). The knife handle extends to the right and the fork handle extends to the left over the lower outside rim of the plate. The fork tines face two and the handle faces eight on the clock; the knife tip faces ten and the handle faces four. Each handle extends an inch or an inch and a half over the rim of the plate.

4. *"Finished" Position:* Place the knife and fork parallel and side-by-side in the center of the plate. The handles extend beyond the right side of the plate rim no more than an inch. The knife

Glossary

390

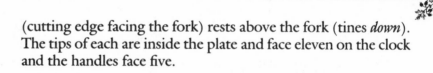

(cutting edge facing the fork) rests above the fork (tines *down*). The tips of each are inside the plate and face eleven on the clock and the handles face five.

The Solitary Fork

1. When the fork is positioned without a companion piece at the place setting, it is meant to be used alone. Special forks which fall into this category are: the cocktail fork, oyster fork, escargot fork, lobster fork, pastry fork, ramekin fork, ice cream fork, and berry fork. In the American and English place settings, when a knife is not placed for salad, the salad fork also falls into this category.

2. Although a course for which the dinner, luncheon, fish, salad, or ramekin fork is to be used may not require a knife to cut it, the correct knife *may* be positioned in the place setting for use by the diner should he or she need it or wish to follow The Continental Style of Eating. Among such foods are: meatballs, chopped steak, boneless fish, soufflés, casseroles, lasagna, firm *pâté,* green salad, chicken or seafood salad. If the knife is not used, it is left on the table.

3. *"Solitary Fork" Position:* The "solitary fork" position is assumed in the right hand in the same manner as the "fork alone" position described in The American "Zigzag" Style of Eating. Once the knife has been engaged, however, the fork must be used in the left hand (tines down) or may be "zigzagged" from the left to the right hand (tines up) if the American style is used.

4. *"Cutting" Position:* Should food require cutting with the solitary fork, the fork is used in the same manner as the knife with the side of the tines becoming the blade.

5. *"Cutting" Action:* The solitary fork cuts with the side of the tines held in the "cutting" position. The side of the fork is placed perpendicular to the plate. Some forks designed to be used alone have one tine which is wider and notched, such as the salad or pastry fork.

6. *"Adhering" Action:* When the solitary fork is used, the food is adhered to the fork by positioning the food on the bed of the tines or gently inserting them into the food as in The American "Zigzag" Style of Eating.

7. *"Conveying" Action:* As in The American "Zigzag" Style of Eating, the food is brought to the mouth on top of the fork tines.

8. *"Rest" and "Finished" Positions:* As in The American "Zigzag" Style of Eating, the solitary fork is placed tines up facing eleven o'clock and the handle at five. The cocktail, oyster, ramekin, ice cream, or berry fork assume the "rest" and "finished" positions *on* the lining plate and *behind* the stem of the glass or base of the ramekin.

The Solitary Spoon

1. Among the spoons that are used alone as "solitary" spoons are: the cream soup spoon, round-bowl soup spoon, oval soup spoon, bouillon spoon, dessert spoon (when not accompanied by the dessert fork), fruit spoon, ice cream spoon, chocolate spoon, iced beverage spoon, teaspoon, five o'clock teaspoon, after-dinner teaspoon, coffee spoon, demitasse spoon, and salt spoon.

2. *"Solitary Spoon" Position:* The spoon is held (bowl up) in the right hand in the same manner as the "fork alone" position.

3. *"Cutting" Position:* Should food require cutting with the solitary spoon, the spoon is held in the "cutting" position described in The ABC's of the American *and* Continental Styles of Eating. The forefinger does not extend beyond the handle.

4. *"Cutting" Action:* Foods are cut with the side of the spoon held in the "cutting" position.

5. *"Adhering" Position:* The spoon is held in the "solitary spoon" position and slipped beneath the food. Beverages are not, however, placed in a spoon nor sipped from a spoon.

6. *"Conveying" Action:* When conveying food to the mouth, use the "conveying" action outlined in The American "Zigzag"

Style of Eating. Liquids are sipped from the side of the spoon. Solids are eaten from the end of the spoon, which is placed about halfway into the mouth and removed between closed lips.

"Rest" and "Finished" Positions

7. *Iced Beverage Spoon, Teaspoon, Five O'Clock Teaspoon, After-Dinner Teaspoon, Coffee Spoon, Demitasse Spoon:* Although iced tea and coffee or hot tea and coffee are not served at the table at formal dinners, they are served at formal and informal luncheons, brunches, and breakfasts. After the spoon is used to stir the beverage, the "rest" and "finished" positions are alike. It is placed on the coaster or lining plate behind the foot of the stemmed glass or base of a tumbler or on the saucer and behind the teacup or coffee cup. In all of these placements, the handle faces three on the clock and extends over the rim of the plate or saucer an inch. The bowl faces up and is pointing to eleven. When a stemmed glass or a tumbler is placed on the table without a coaster or lining plate, the spoon may be left in the glass and held against the back of the rim with the forefinger while drinking. As an alternative, the spoon may be placed on the bread-and-butter plate or, if there is none, the dinner plate. On either plate it is positioned on the rim with the bowl facing down. The handle extends onto the table.

8. *Dessert Spoon, Fruit Spoon, Ice Cream Spoon, Chocolate Spoon:* During informal occasions, the dessert spoon may be used alone. At a formal dinner, however, it is never used without the dessert fork. When sorbet is served as an intermezzo, a solitary spoon is appropriate. When eating fruit, ice cream, sorbet, or pudding from a stemmed compote, champagne saucer, small raised-sided bowl, ramekin, or *petits pots,* the proper spoon is placed on the lining plate or saucer in the same "rest" and "finished" position as the iced beverage or teaspoon. When ice cream, sorbet, pudding, or fruit is placed directly in the dessert or fruit plate, or in a wide, shallow bowl, the spoon assumes the

"rest" and "finished" positions on the plate or in the bowl. The bowl of the spoon faces up and points to eleven and the handle extends an inch beyond the rim and faces five on the clock.

9. *Cream Soup Spoon, Round-Bowl Soup Spoon, Oval Soup Spoon, Bouillon Spoon:*

   a. *"Filling" Action:* Each of these spoons is held in the "solitary spoon" position, parallel with the tabletop, and skimmed away from the diner allowing it to fill as it passes through the soup. The spoon may be tipped away from the diner slightly in order to fill it. It is filled four-fifths full.

   b. *"Conveying" Action:* Upon reaching the back of the bowl, the spoon is held parallel to the tabletop and raised from the soup. The base of the spoon may be barely touched to the soup one time as the spoon passes over the bowl during the return trip to ensure that a drop will not fall as the soup is conveyed to the lips.

   c. *"Tipping" and "Sipping" Actions:* "Tipping" the soup plate is permissible, as is "sipping" from the bouillon cup and the cream soup bowl. The soup plate is tipped away from the table's edge in order that the diner may fill the spoon with the last sips of soup. The handles of the cream soup bowl are held between the pads of the thumb and forefinger (other fingers gently curved and palm down) of each hand and the bowl is lifted to the lips. The bouillon cup is held in the same manner, using the right hand alone if it has just one handle. Any soup garniture is eaten with the spoon either before or after sipping or between sips. Needless to say, sipping is silent.

   d. *"Rest" and "Finished" Positions:* Each of the soup spoons assumes the previously described "rest" and "finished" positions. It remains *in* the rimmed soup plate and *out* of the two-handled cream soup bowl or bouillon cup *on* the saucer beneath. The handle extends to the right one inch over the rim of the soup plate or saucer. The handle faces five on the clock and the bowl (up) faces eleven.

The Fish Knife and Fish Fork

1. *"Spearing" Position:* The fish fork is held in the left hand in the same manner as a fork used for spearing meat, except that the thumb, forefinger, and middle finger are *not* extended all the way into the straight position. This is *somewhat* different from the way the dinner fork is held because tender fish does not require as firm a grip as does meat.

2. *"Cutting" Position:* The fish knife is held in the right hand in the "fork alone" position described in The American "Zigzag" Style of Eating, except that the thumb, forefinger, and middle finger are extended to an *almost* straight position. This is notably different from the way the meat knife is held because tender fish does not require as much leverage for cutting as does meat.

3. *"Cutting" Action:* The fish fork remains in the left hand in the "spearing" position as the fork tines are gently inserted into the fish. With the fish knife held in the "cutting" position, a bite of fish is cut from the fillet or from the bone. To separate a bite of fish from the bone, the notched end of the fish knife is slipped beneath the fish and above the bone using a backward movement (pushing away from the table's edge). The notch may also be used in the same manner to lift the skin of the fish from the flesh.

4. *"Adhering" Action:* When using The Continental Style of Eating, a bite of fish is easily lifted with the broad blade of the fish knife and placed on the back of the fish fork, or it may be speared with the fork tines and adhered to the fork with the assistance of the fish knife. In the American style, the bite of fish is scooped up into the bowl-like surface of the fish fork or pierced with the tines. In either style, the flat tines hold the fish more easily; the outside broad notched tine aids in flaking the fish and the notch assists in securing the fish.

5. *"Deboning" and "Filleting" Action:* Fish served at formal or semiformal meals is filleted at least partially so that the diner may easily complete the procedure by interlocking the notch of the fish fork with the notch of the fish knife beneath the backbone and lifting it from the fish.

6. *"Conveying" Action:* The fish fork is conveyed to the mouth in the manner of the style of eating adopted.

7. *"Rest" and "Finished" Positions:* The fish knife and fish fork assume their "rest" and "finished" positions in the manner of the style of eating adopted.

The Dessert Spoon and Dessert Fork

The Dessert Knife

1. The dessert spoon and the dessert fork are used together, with the dessert spoon assuming the role of both a spoon and knife. The dessert fork serves only as a pusher. The food is cut with the dessert spoon rather than a knife and is eaten with the spoon rather than the fork. Occasionally a dessert knife accompanies the dessert spoon and fork and is used in lieu of the spoon for cutting as described in Step 3.

2. *"Spearing" Position:* When spearing a portion so that it may be cut with the dessert spoon, the dessert fork is held in the spearing position described in The ABC's of the American *and* Continental Styles of Eating.

3. *"Cutting" Position and Action:* When used for cutting, the dessert spoon is held in the "cutting" position and the food is cut as described in The Solitary Spoon. The spoon is furthermore inserted into the dessert and against the tines of the fork. For desserts requiring the use of the dessert knife, it is held in the "cutting" position and the dessert is cut in the manner outlined for each procedure in The ABC's of the American *and* Continental Styles of Eating.

4. *"Adhering" Action:* When using the dessert spoon and dessert fork together, once a bite of dessert is cut with the side of the spoon, the spoon is transferred to the "solitary spoon" position. The bite is then pushed into the bowl of the spoon with the tines of the fork. If the dessert knife is used for cutting, it is

placed in the "rest" position after use and the diner picks up the dessert spoon with which to eat.

5. *"Conveying" Action:* When conveying a bite of dessert to the mouth with the dessert spoon, do so as described in The Solitary Spoon.

6. *"Rest" and "Finished" Positions:* The dessert spoon and dessert fork assume the same "rest" and "finished" positions for both the American and Continental styles of eating. The spoon (bowl up) replaces the knife, and the dessert fork (tines down) replaces the dinner fork in both positions. When the dessert knife is also used, it is placed parallel with and above the dessert spoon in both positions.

7. Both the dessert spoon and the dessert fork are used together when dining formally; however, they may be used alone when dining informally. For example, if cake or pie is eaten with the dessert fork only or custard or ice cream is eaten with the dessert spoon only, each is used in the same manner as described in the steps outlined in The Solitary Fork and The Solitary Spoon, respectively. When only one piece of dessert silver is used, the unused piece is left on the table.

Index